LOKI

MISTRESS OF MISCHIEF

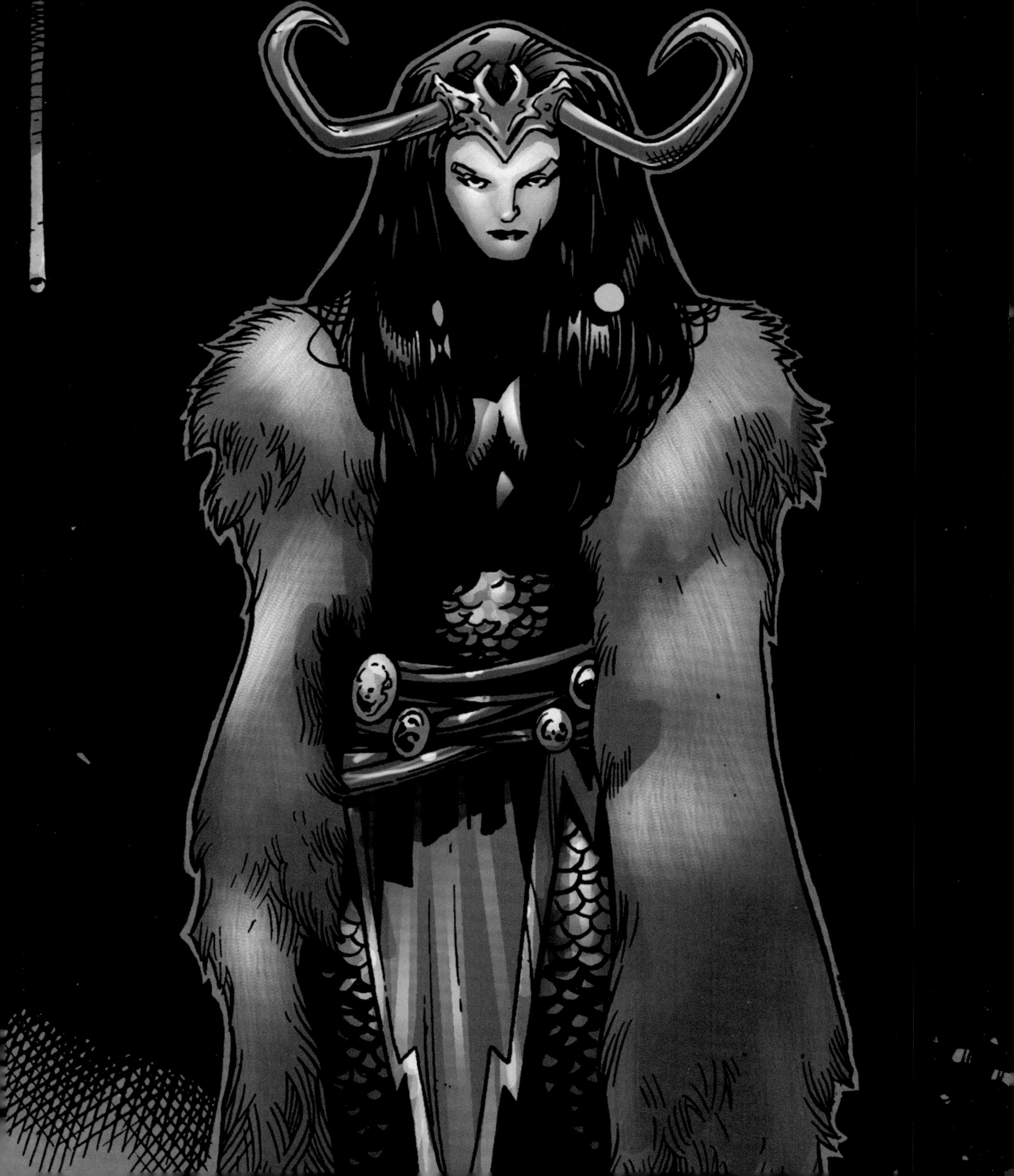

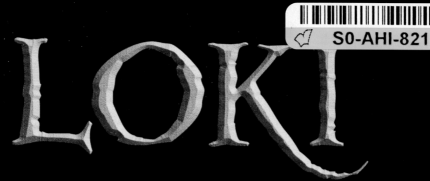

LOKI

MISTRESS of MISCHIEF

THOR #5, #9-10 & #12

J. Michael Straczynski
WRITER

Olivier Coipel
PENCILER

Mark Morales with
Danny Miki & **John Dell** (#9) and
Crimelab Studios' Allen Martinez
& **Victor Olazaba** (#10)
INKERS

Laura Martin with **Paul Mounts** (#5)
COLORISTS

Chris Eliopoulos
LETTERER

Olivier Coipel, Mark Morales & **Laura Martin**
COVER ART

THOR #600

J. Michael Straczynski
WRITER

Olivier Coipel with **Marko Djurdjević**
PENCILERS

Mark Morales with **Marko Djurdjević**
INKERS

Laura Martin
with **Paul Mounts** & **Christina Strain**
COLORISTS

Chris Eliopoulos
LETTERER

Olivier Coipel, Mark Morales & **Laura Martin**
COVER ART

DARK REIGN: THE CABAL

Peter Milligan
WRITER

Tonci Zonjić
ARTIST

Jose Villarrubia
COLORIST

Blambot's Nate Piekos
LETTERER

Daniel Acuña
COVER ART

Tom Brevoort
EXECUTIVE EDITOR

THOR #601-602

J. Michael Straczynski
WRITER

Marko Djurdjević
PENCILER

Danny Miki with **Mark Morales** (#602)
INKERS

Paul Mounts
COLORIST

Chris Eliopoulos
LETTERER

Marko Djurdjević
COVER ART

Greg Land & **Justin Ponsor**
FRONT COVER ART

Alejandro Arbona
ASSISTANT EDITOR

Warren Simons
EDITOR

LOKI created by
Stan Lee, Larry Lieber
& **Jack Kirby**

LOKI: MISTRESS OF MISCHIEF. Contains material originally published in magazine form as THOR (2007) #5, #9-10, #12 and #600-602; and DARK REIGN: THE CABAL ONE-SHOT (2009). First printing 2021. ISBN 978-1-302-93280-0. Published by MARVEL WORLDWIDE, INC., a subsidiary of MARVEL ENTERTAINMENT, LLC. OFFICE OF PUBLICATION: 1290 Avenue of the Americas, New York, NY 10104. © 2021 MARVEL No similarity between any of the names, characters, persons, and/or institutions in this magazine with those of any living or dead person or institution is intended, and any such similarity which may exist is purely coincidental. **Printed in Canada.** KEVIN FEIGE, Chief Creative Officer; DAN BUCKLEY, President, Marvel Entertainment; JOE QUESADA, EVP & Creative Director; DAVID BOGART, Associate Publisher & SVP of Talent Affairs; TOM BREVOORT, VP, Executive Editor; NICK LOWE, Executive Editor, VP of Content, Digital Publishing; DAVID GABRIEL, VP of Print & Digital Publishing; JEFF YOUNGQUIST, VP of Production & Special Projects; ALEX MORALES, Director of Publishing Operations; DAN EDINGTON, Managing Editor; RICKEY PURDIN, Director of Talent Relations; JENNIFER GRÜNWALD, Senior Editor, Special Projects; SUSAN CRESPI, Production Manager; STAN LEE, Chairman Emeritus. For information regarding advertising in Marvel Comics or on Marvel. com, please contact Vit DeBellis, Custom Solutions & Integrated Advertising Manager, at vdebellis@marvel.com. For Marvel subscription inquiries, please call 888-511-5480. Manufactured between 5/31/2021 and 6/22/2021 by

PREVIOUSLY...

After centuries of searching, Loki finally found the long-hidden mold in which Thor's great hammer, Mjolnir, was created. Enlisting Surtur to use the mold to forge new weapons with which to equip his mighty army, Loki rained destruction down on the Nine Realms, triggering Ragnarok — the endless sequence of death and rebirth in which the Asgardians have been trapped for eons.

After watching those he loved fall one by one, Thor summoned up the awesome power necessary to not just defeat Loki's schemes — but also to finally shatter the cycle of Ragnarok once and for all. With Asgard destroyed and his fellow Asgardians dead, Thor slept the slumber of the gods, finding peace at last in a true end.

After many months, Thor's rest was disturbed by a strangely familiar voice — that of Dr. Donald Blake, his old human form created long ago by Odin. Persuaded by Blake that the mortal world needed its protector, Thor willed himself back into existence — returning to a Midgard very different to the one he left behind.

In Broxton, Oklahoma, Thor found a home — raising a glorious new Asgard from the ground, and into the skies immediately above the town. Now, once again dividing his time between living as Thor or Donald Blake, he travels the world in search of the mortal forms in which his fellow Asgardians' spirits live on. They need to be found, and awakened, before it is too late.

So far in his quest, Thor has returned the all-seeing Heimdall and the intrepid Warriors Three — Hogun, Fandral and Volstagg — to Asgard's halls. Many more allies are out there, yet to be discovered — and none that Thor longs to locate more than his beloved Lady Sif. But the hidden souls that only Heimdall can perceive are gradually disappearing from view...and of those that remain, there are certain Asgardians that Thor would rather never see again...

COLLECTION EDITOR **Jennifer Grünwald**
ASSISTANT EDITOR **Daniel Kirchhoffer**
ASSISTANT MANAGING EDITOR **Maia Loy**
ASSISTANT MANAGING EDITOR **Lisa Montalbano**
ASSOCIATE MANAGER, DIGITAL ASSETS **Joe Hochstein**

VP PRODUCTION & SPECIAL PROJECTS **Jeff Youngquist**
RESEARCH **Jess Harrold**
BOOK DESIGNER **Jay Bowen**
SVP PRINT, SALES & MARKETING **David Gabriel**
EDITOR IN CHIEF **C.B. Cebulski**

SPECIAL THANKS TO **Cathy Leamy**

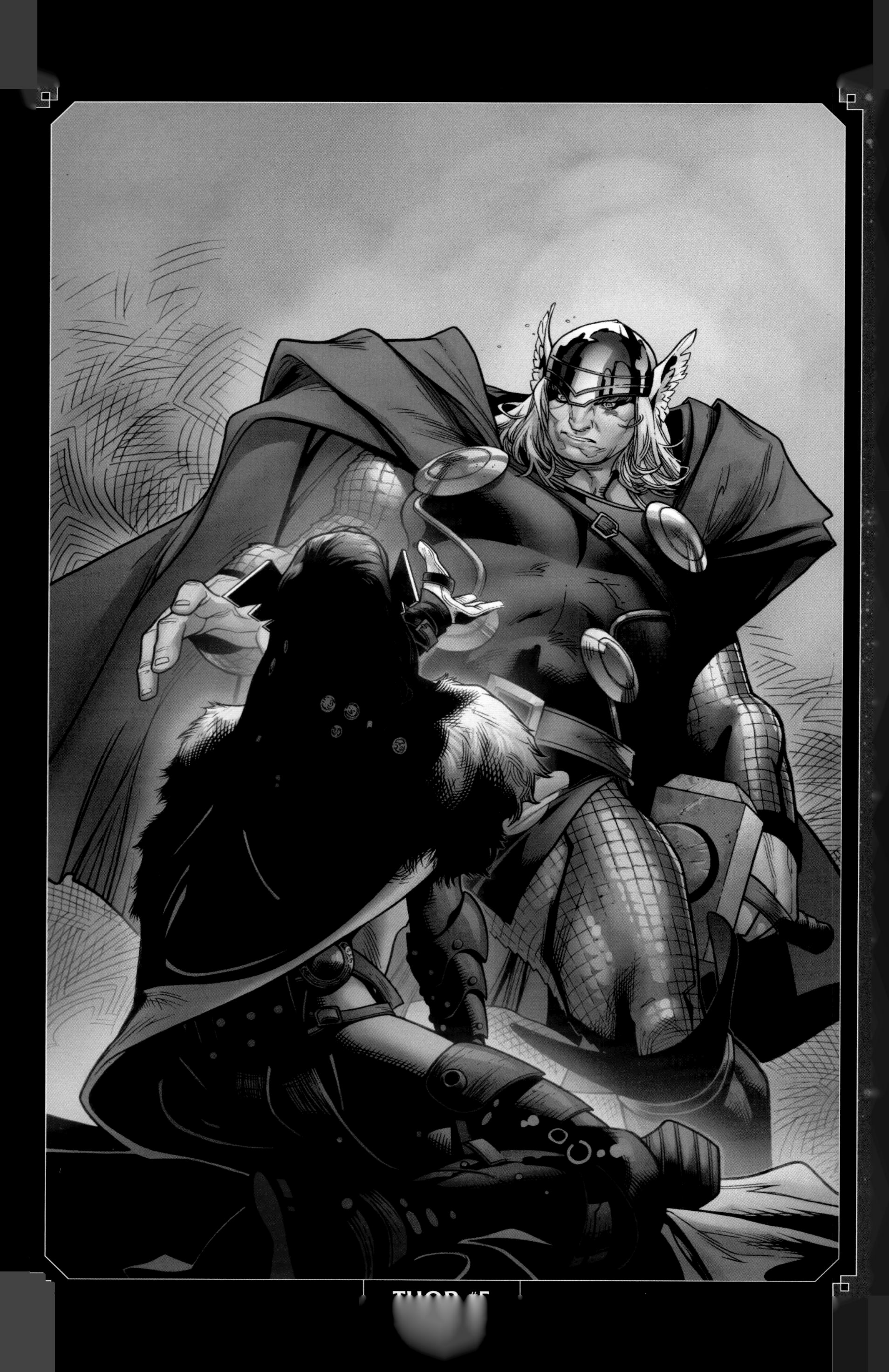

THOR #5

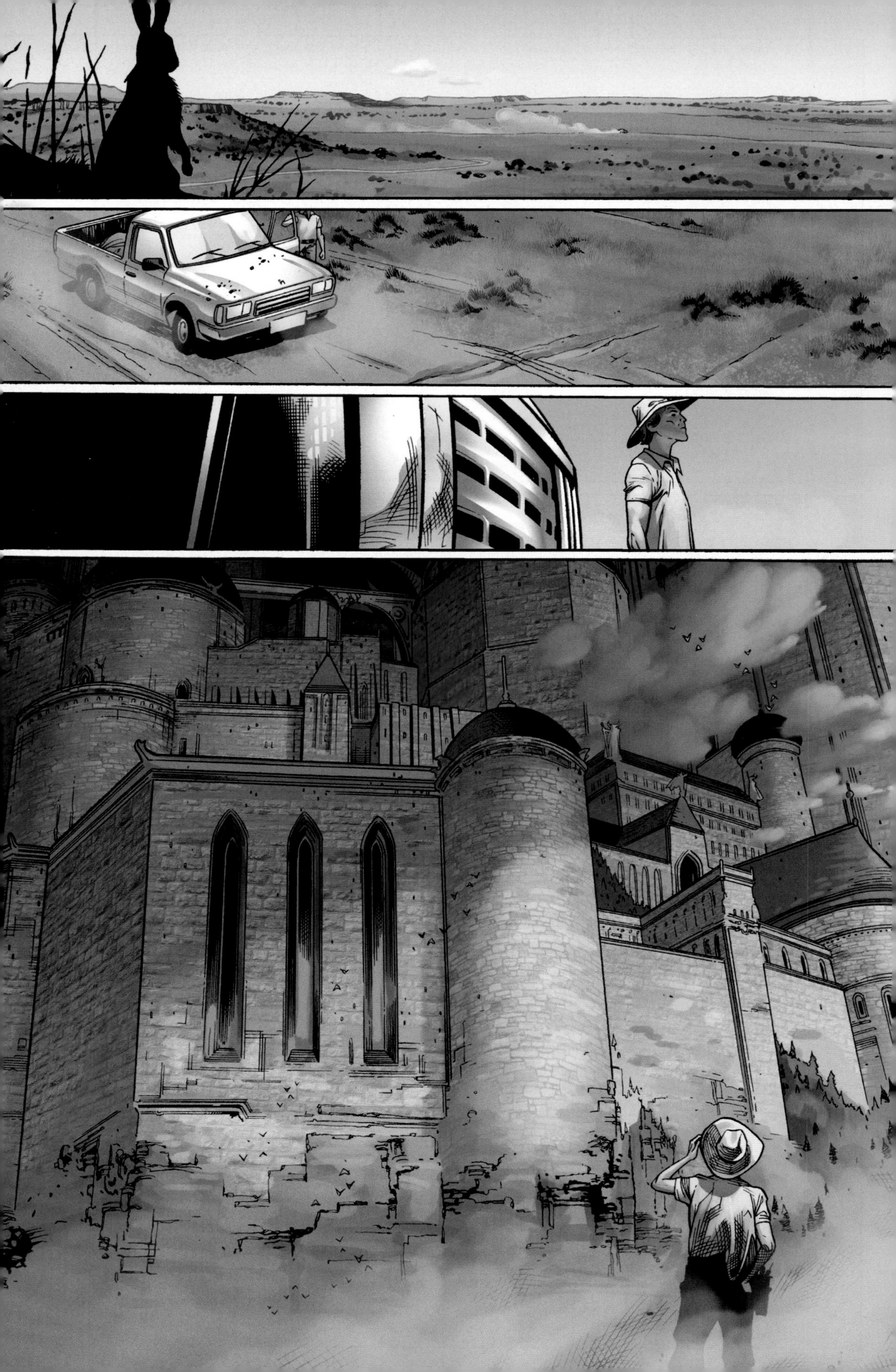

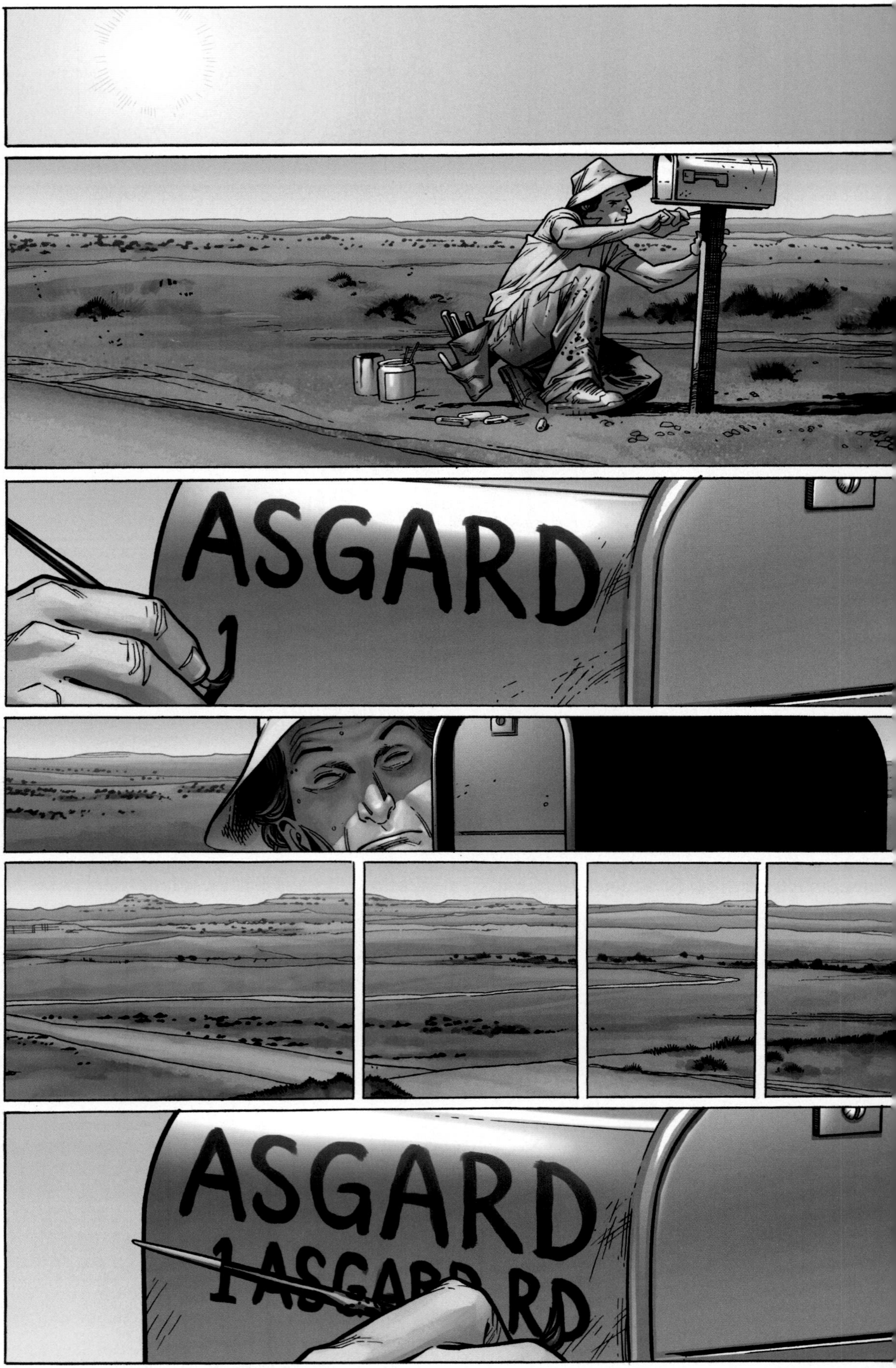
ASGARD
ASGARD
1 ASGARD RD

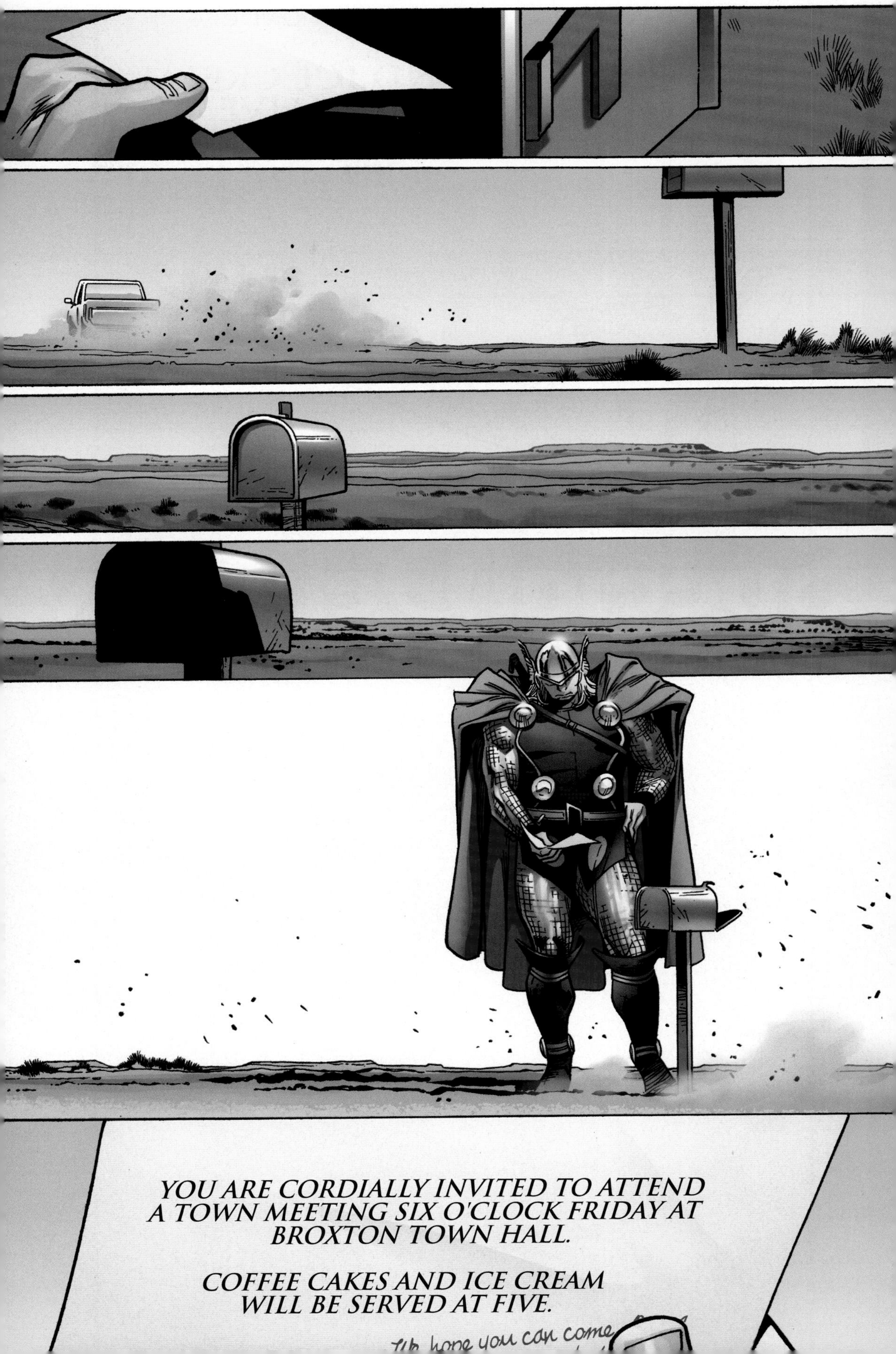

YOU ARE CORDIALLY INVITED TO ATTEND
A TOWN MEETING SIX O'CLOCK FRIDAY AT
BROXTON TOWN HALL.
COFFEE CAKES AND ICE CREAM
WILL BE SERVED AT FIVE.
hope you can come

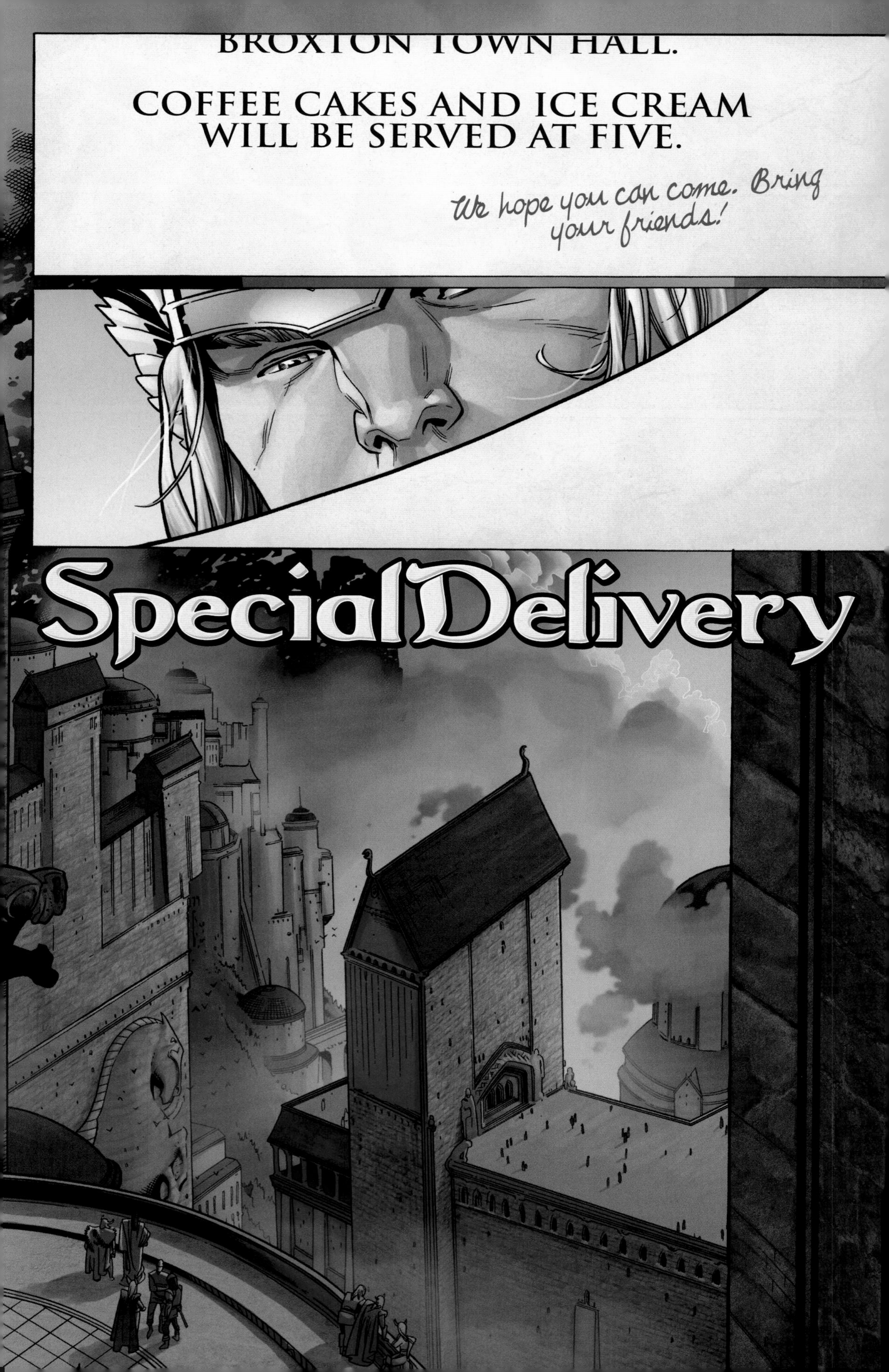
BROXTON TOWN HALL.
COFFEE CAKES AND ICE CREAM WILL BE SERVED AT FIVE.
We hope you can come. Bring your friends!
Special Delivery

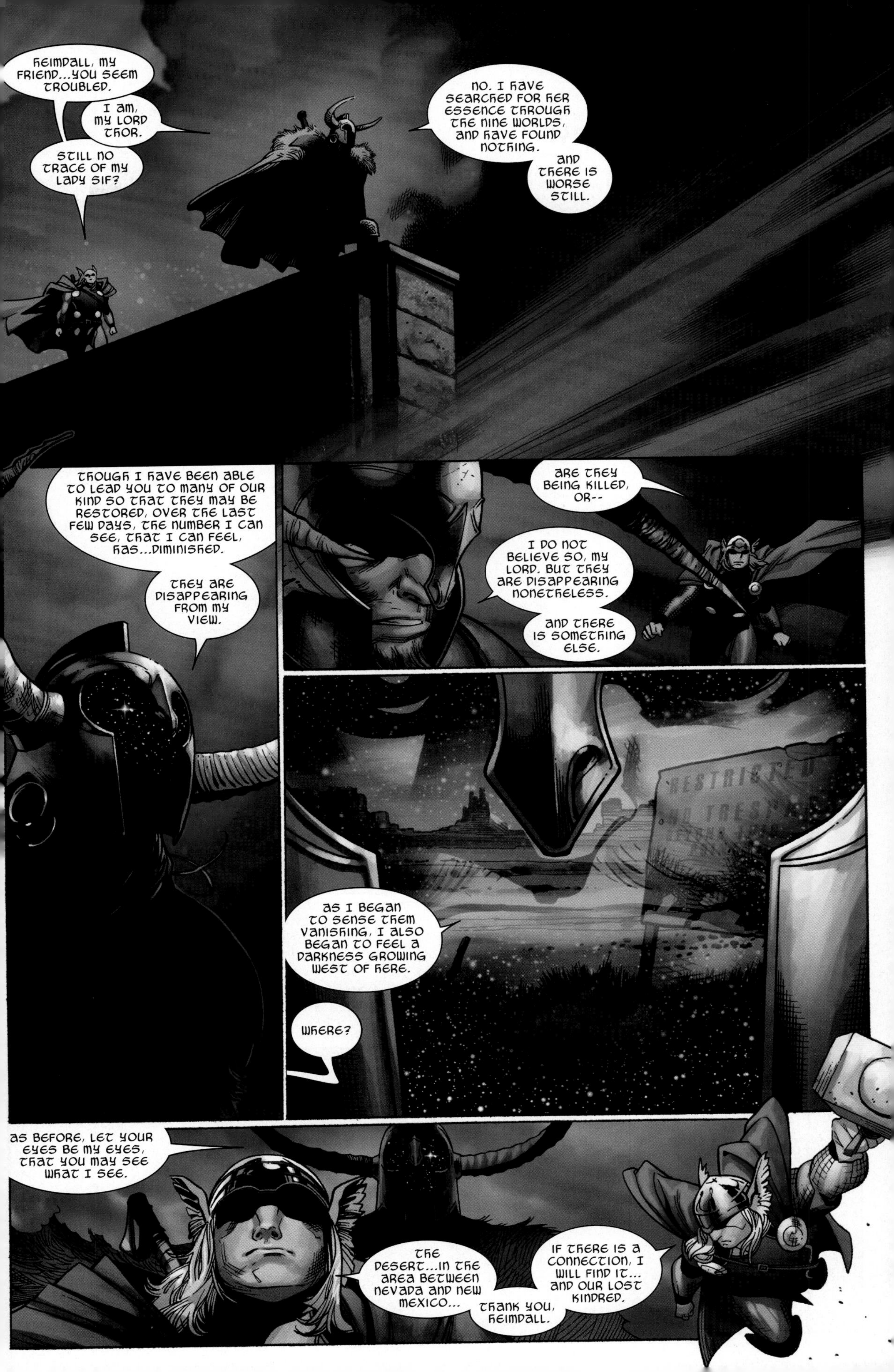
HEIMDALL, MY FRIEND...YOU SEEM TROUBLED.
I AM, MY LORD THOR.
STILL NO TRACE OF MY LADY SIF?
NO. I HAVE SEARCHED FOR HER ESSENCE THROUGH THE NINE WORLDS, AND HAVE FOUND NOTHING.
AND THERE IS WORSE STILL.
THOUGH I HAVE BEEN ABLE TO LEAD YOU TO MANY OF OUR KIND SO THAT THEY MAY BE RESTORED, OVER THE LAST FEW DAYS, THE NUMBER I CAN SEE, THAT I CAN FEEL, HAS...DIMINISHED.
THEY ARE DISAPPEARING FROM MY VIEW.
ARE THEY BEING KILLED, OR--
I DO NOT BELIEVE SO, MY LORD. BUT THEY ARE DISAPPEARING NONETHELESS.
AND THERE IS SOMETHING ELSE.
AS I BEGAN TO SENSE THEM VANISHING, I ALSO BEGAN TO FEEL A DARKNESS GROWING WEST OF HERE.
WHERE?
AS BEFORE, LET YOUR EYES BE MY EYES, THAT YOU MAY SEE WHAT I SEE.
THE DESERT...IN THE AREA BETWEEN NEVADA AND NEW MEXICO...
THANK YOU, HEIMDALL.
IF THERE IS A CONNECTION, I WILL FIND IT... AND OUR LOST KINDRED.

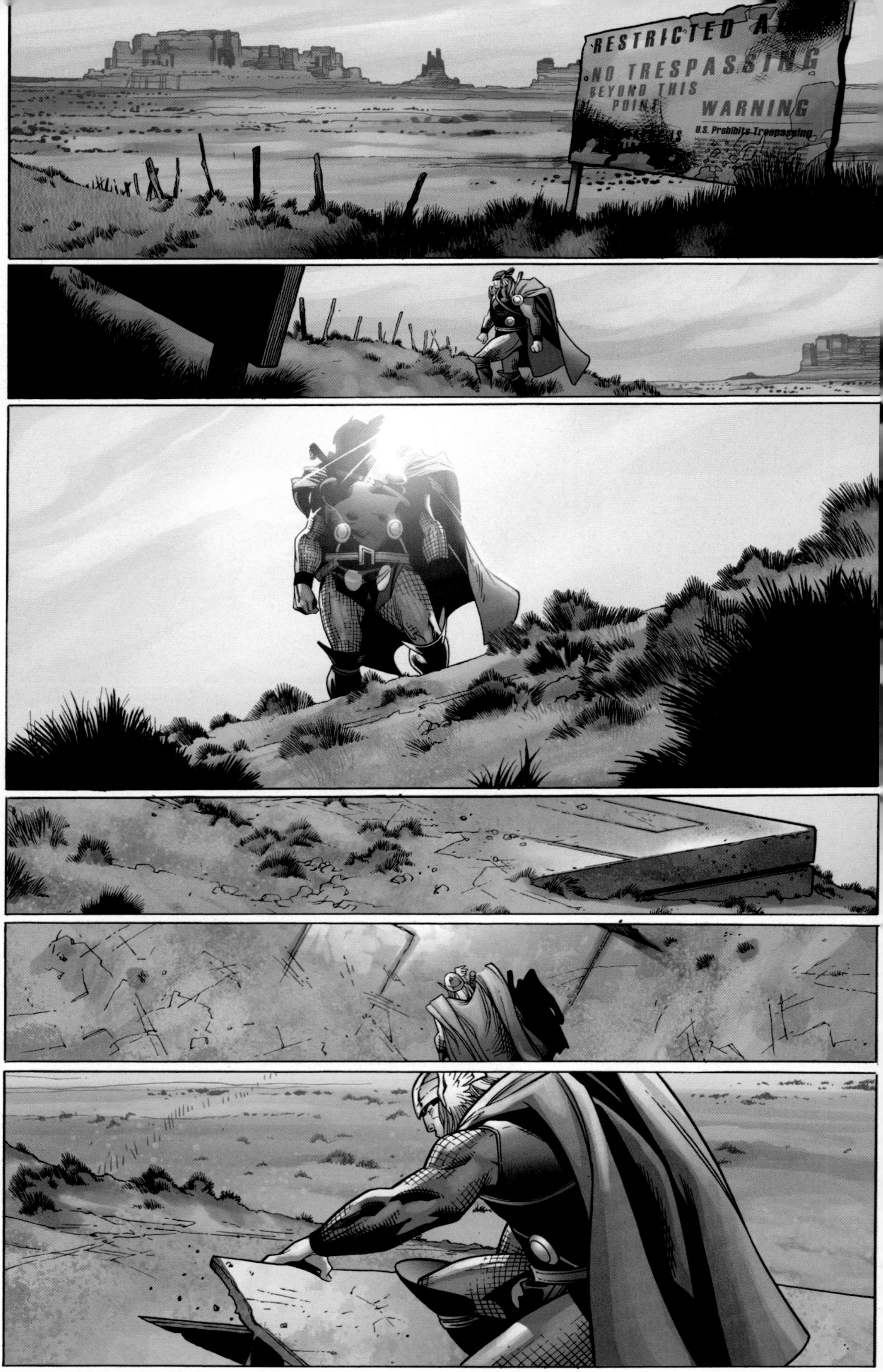
RESTRICTED
NO TRESPASSING
BEYOND THIS
WARNING
U.S. Prohibits Trespassing

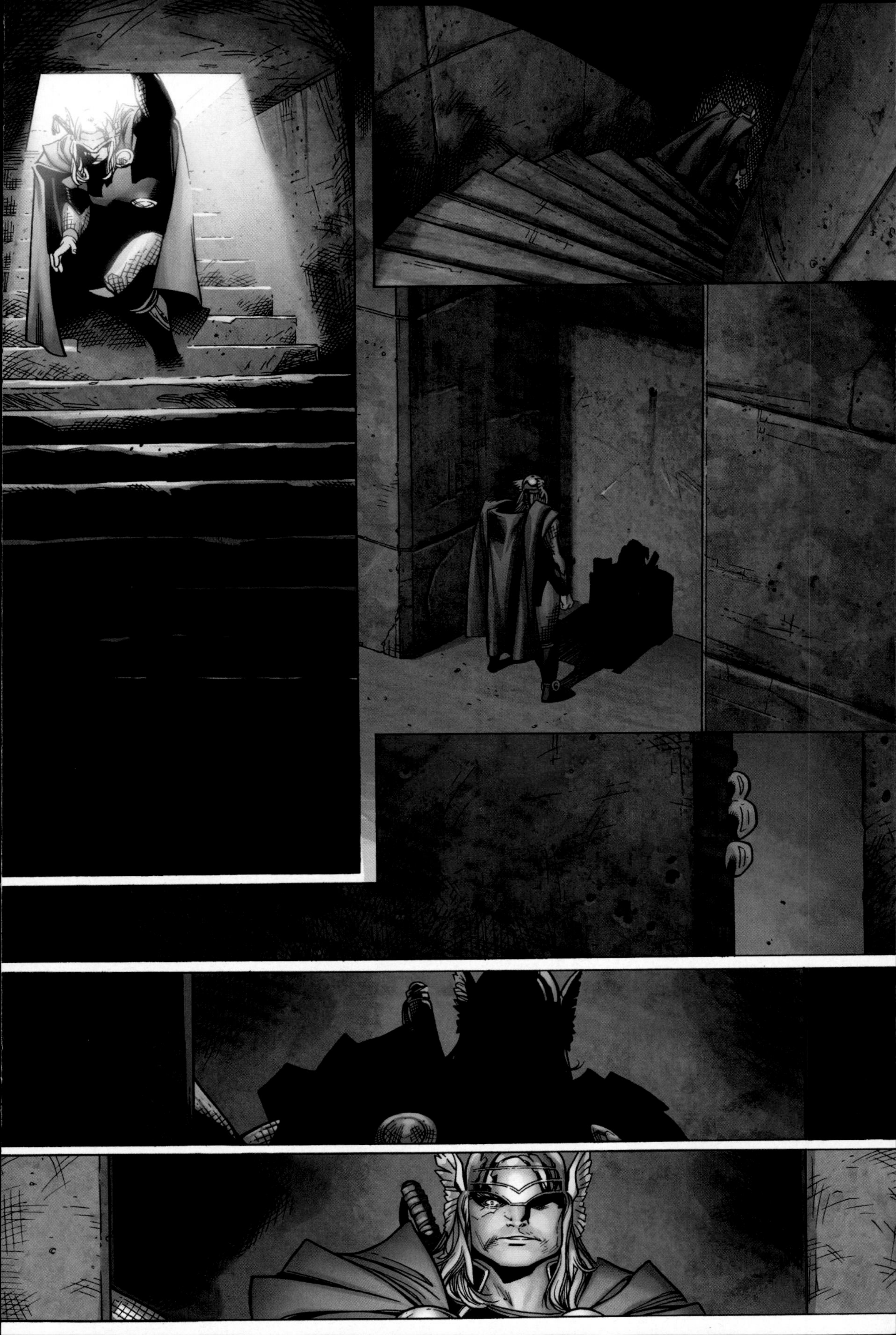

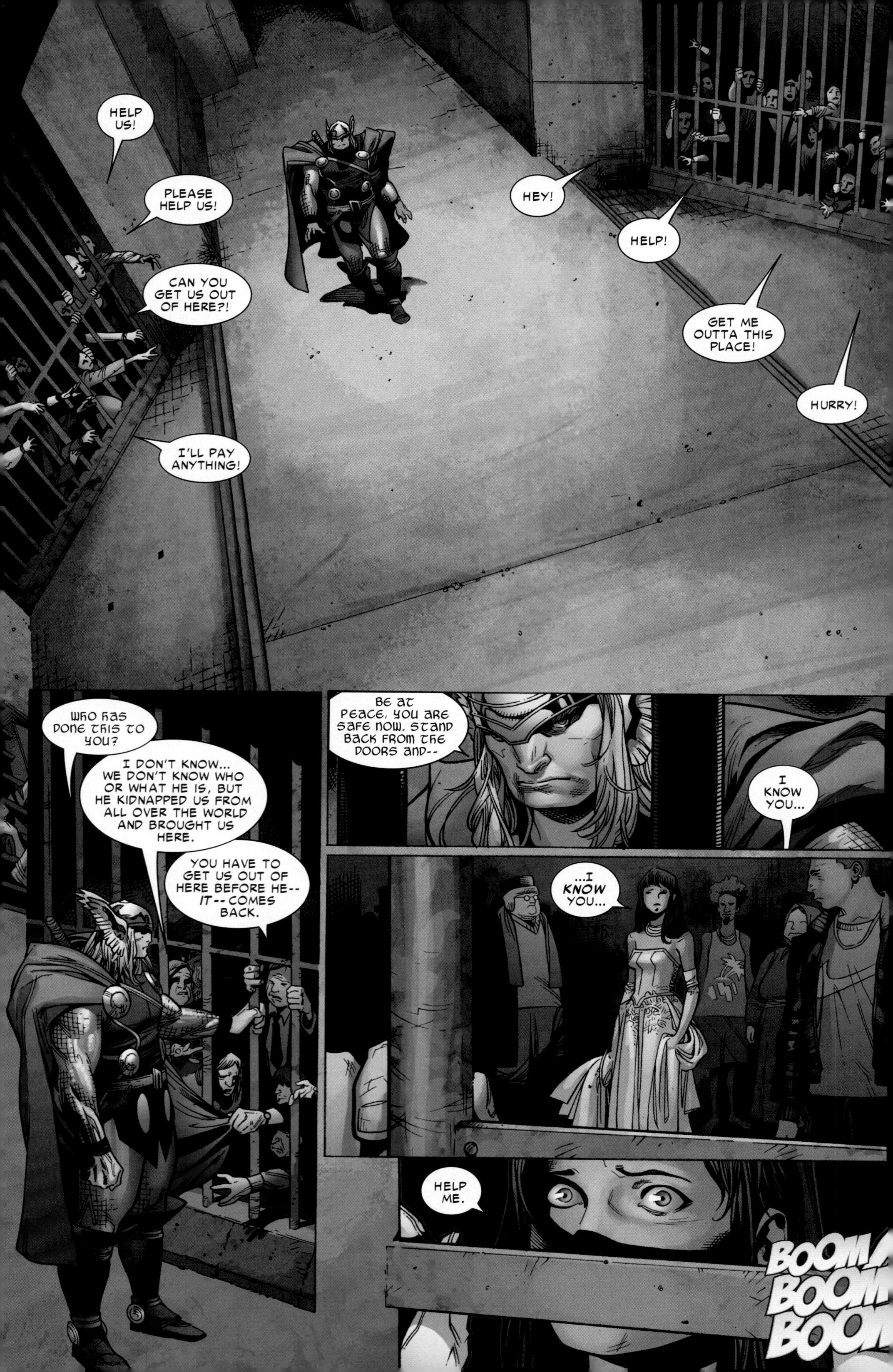

HELP US!
PLEASE HELP US!
CAN YOU GET US OUT OF HERE?!
I'LL PAY ANYTHING!
HEY!
HELP!
GET ME OUTTA THIS PLACE!
HURRY!
WHO HAS DONE THIS TO YOU?
I DON'T KNOW... WE DON'T KNOW WHO OR WHAT HE IS, BUT HE KIDNAPPED US FROM ALL OVER THE WORLD AND BROUGHT US HERE.
YOU HAVE TO GET US OUT OF HERE BEFORE HE-- IT-- COMES BACK.
BE AT PEACE, YOU ARE SAFE NOW. STAND BACK FROM THE DOORS AND--
I KNOW YOU...
...I KNOW YOU...
HELP ME.
BOOM BOOM BOOM

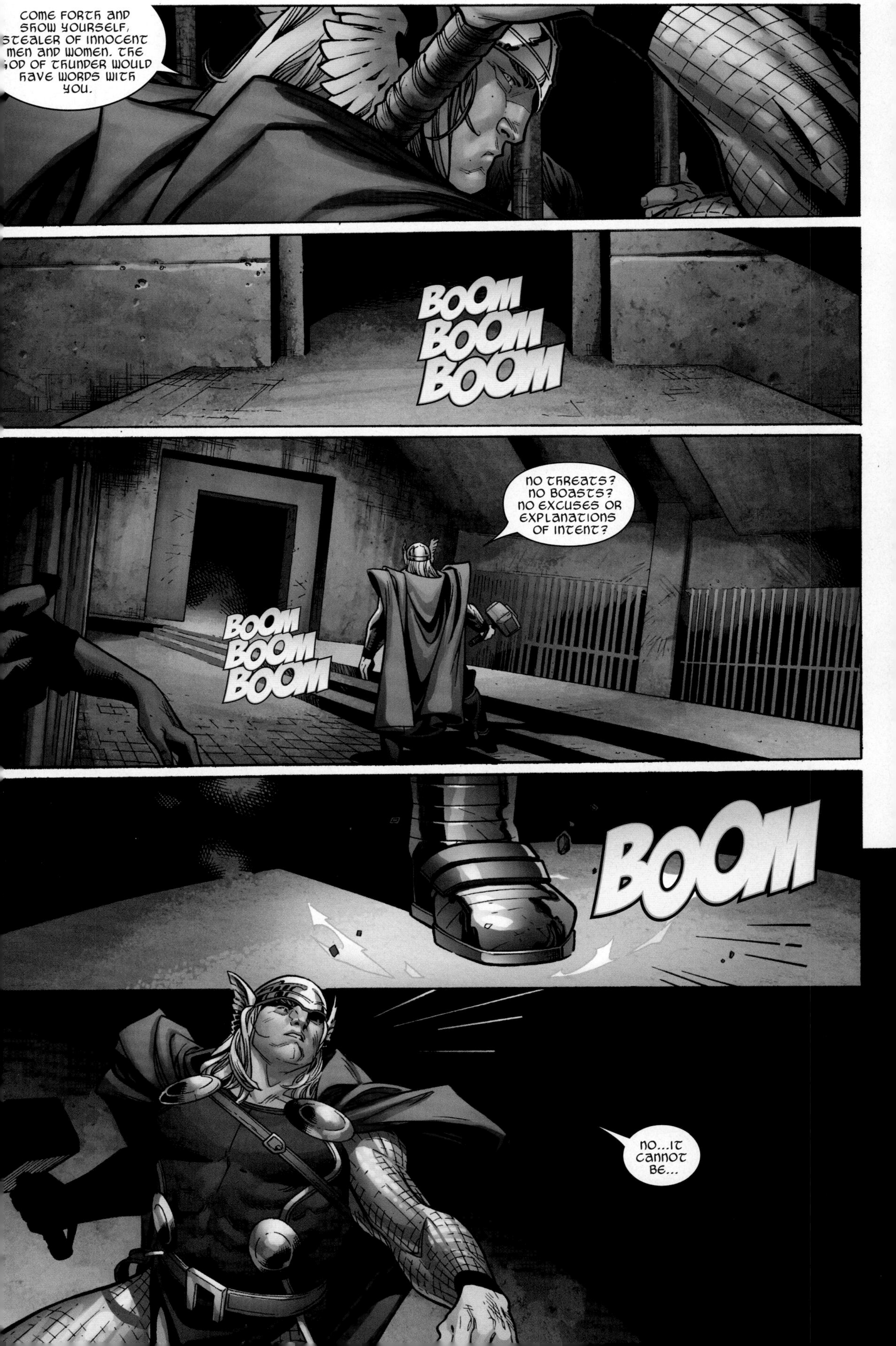
COME FORTH AND SHOW YOURSELF, STEALER OF INNOCENT MEN AND WOMEN. THE GOD OF THUNDER WOULD HAVE WORDS WITH YOU.
BOOM BOOM BOOM
NO THREATS? NO BOASTS? NO EXCUSES OR EXPLANATIONS OF INTENT?
BOOM BOOM BOOM
BOOM
NO...IT CANNOT BE...

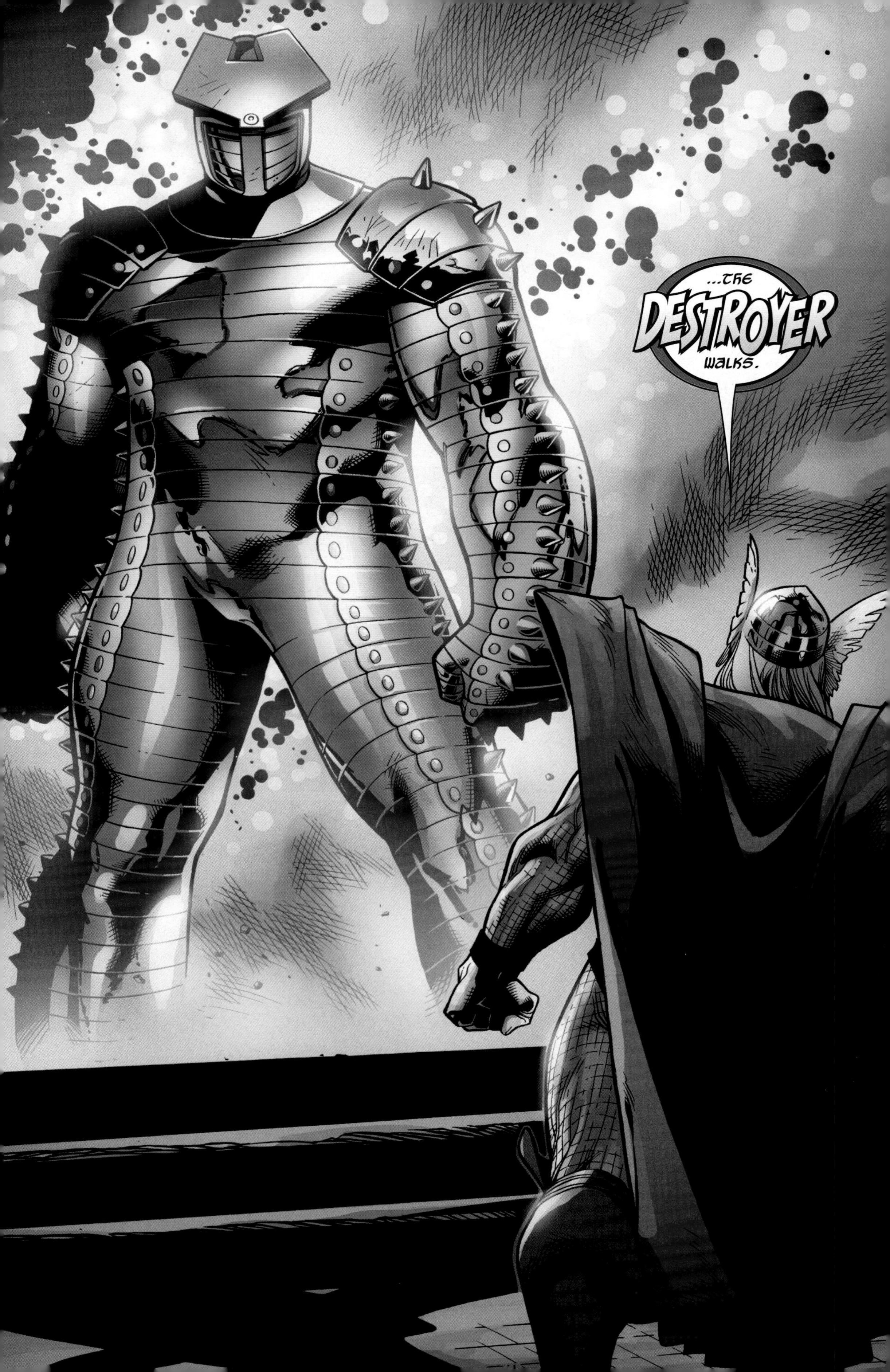
...THE DESTROYER WALKS.

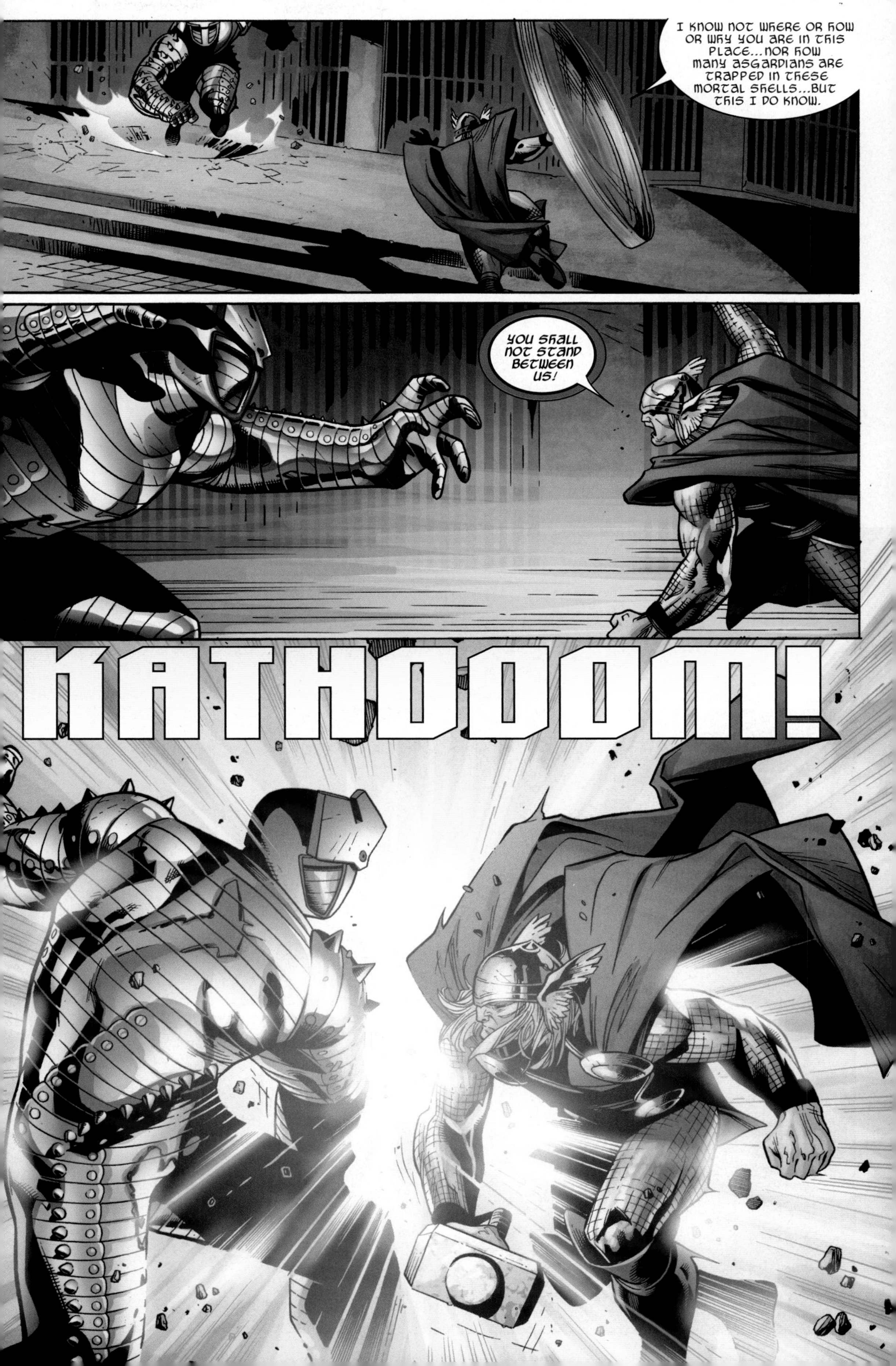
I KNOW NOT WHERE OR HOW OR WHY YOU ARE IN THIS PLACE... NOR HOW MANY ASGARDIANS ARE TRAPPED IN THESE MORTAL SHELLS... BUT THIS I DO KNOW.
YOU SHALL NOT STAND BETWEEN US!
KATHOOOM!

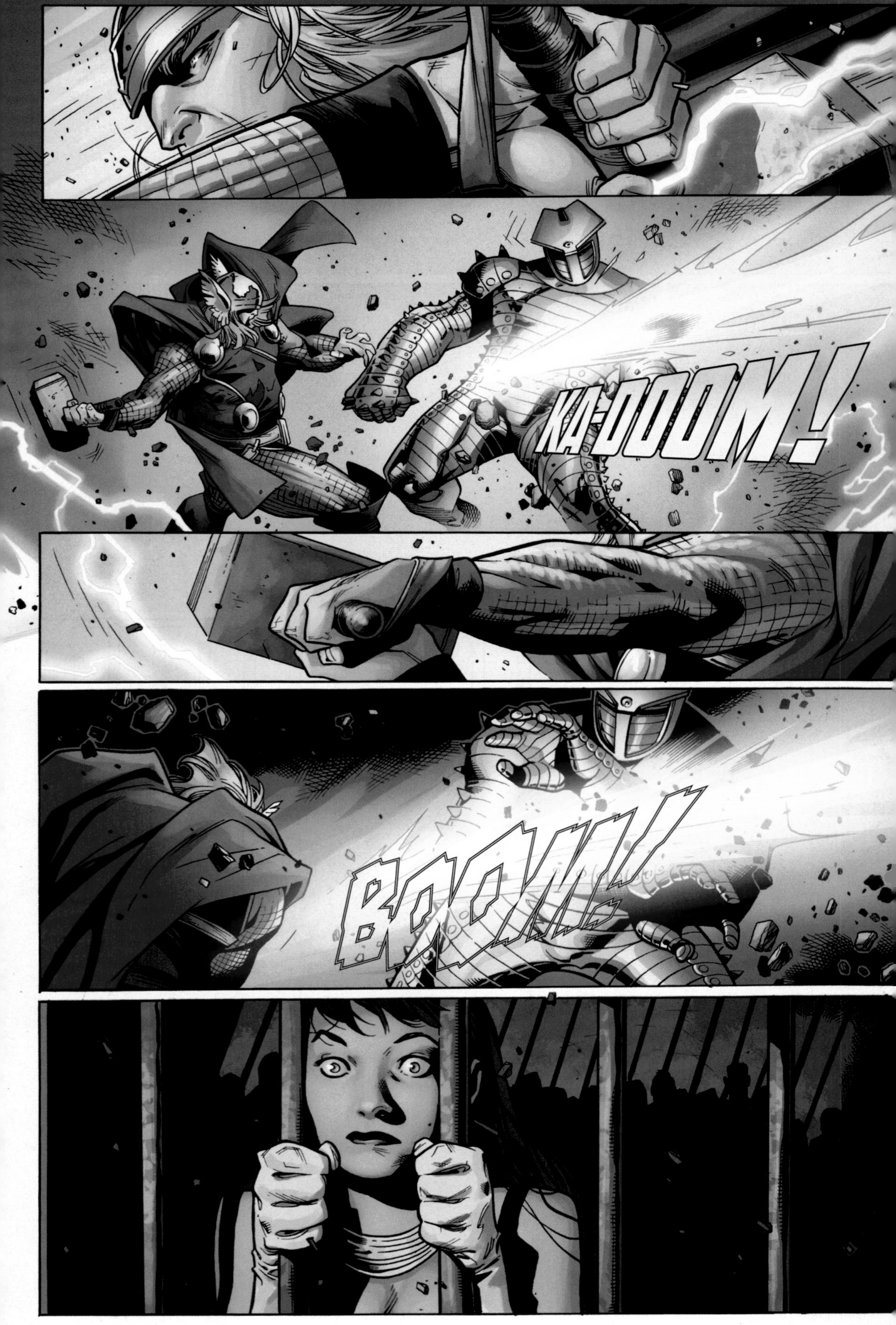
KA-DOOM!
BOOM!

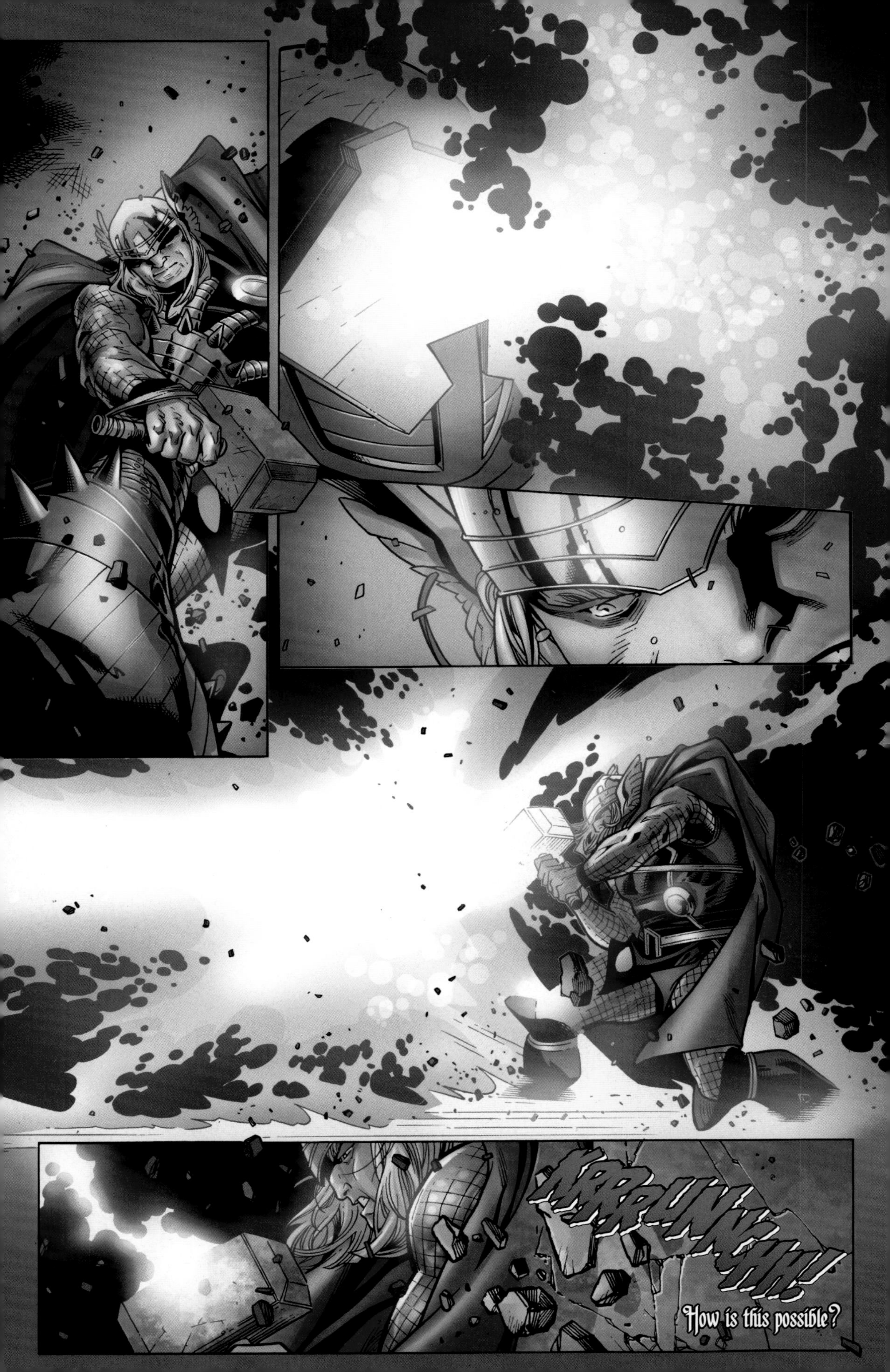
KRRRUNNCHH!
How is this possible?

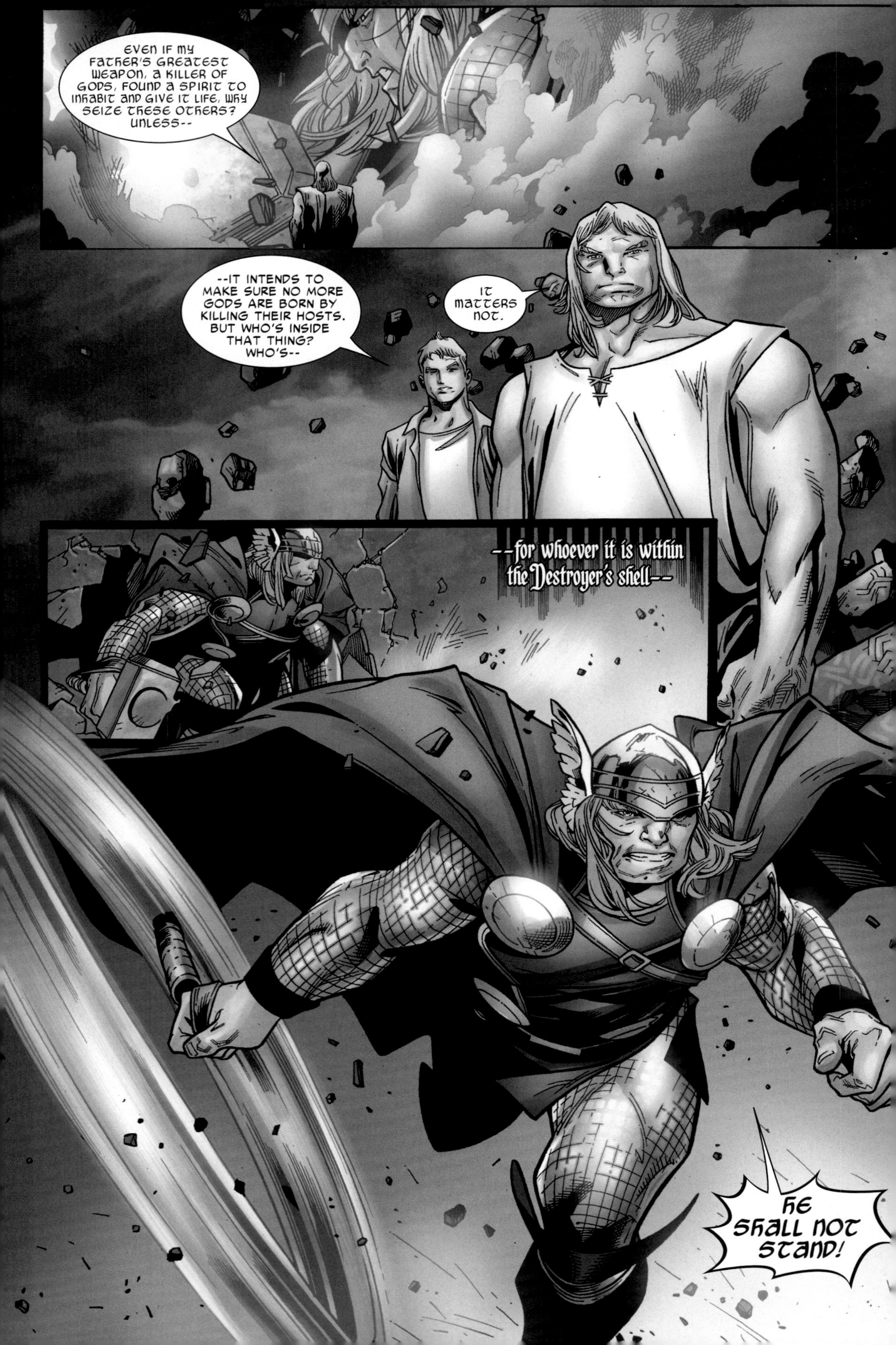
EVEN IF MY FATHER'S GREATEST WEAPON, A KILLER OF GODS, FOUND A SPIRIT TO INHABIT AND GIVE IT LIFE, WHY SEIZE THESE OTHERS? UNLESS--
--IT INTENDS TO MAKE SURE NO MORE GODS ARE BORN BY KILLING THEIR HOSTS. BUT WHO'S INSIDE THAT THING? WHO'S--
IT MATTERS NOT.
--for whoever it is within the Destroyer's shell--
HE SHALL NOT STAND!

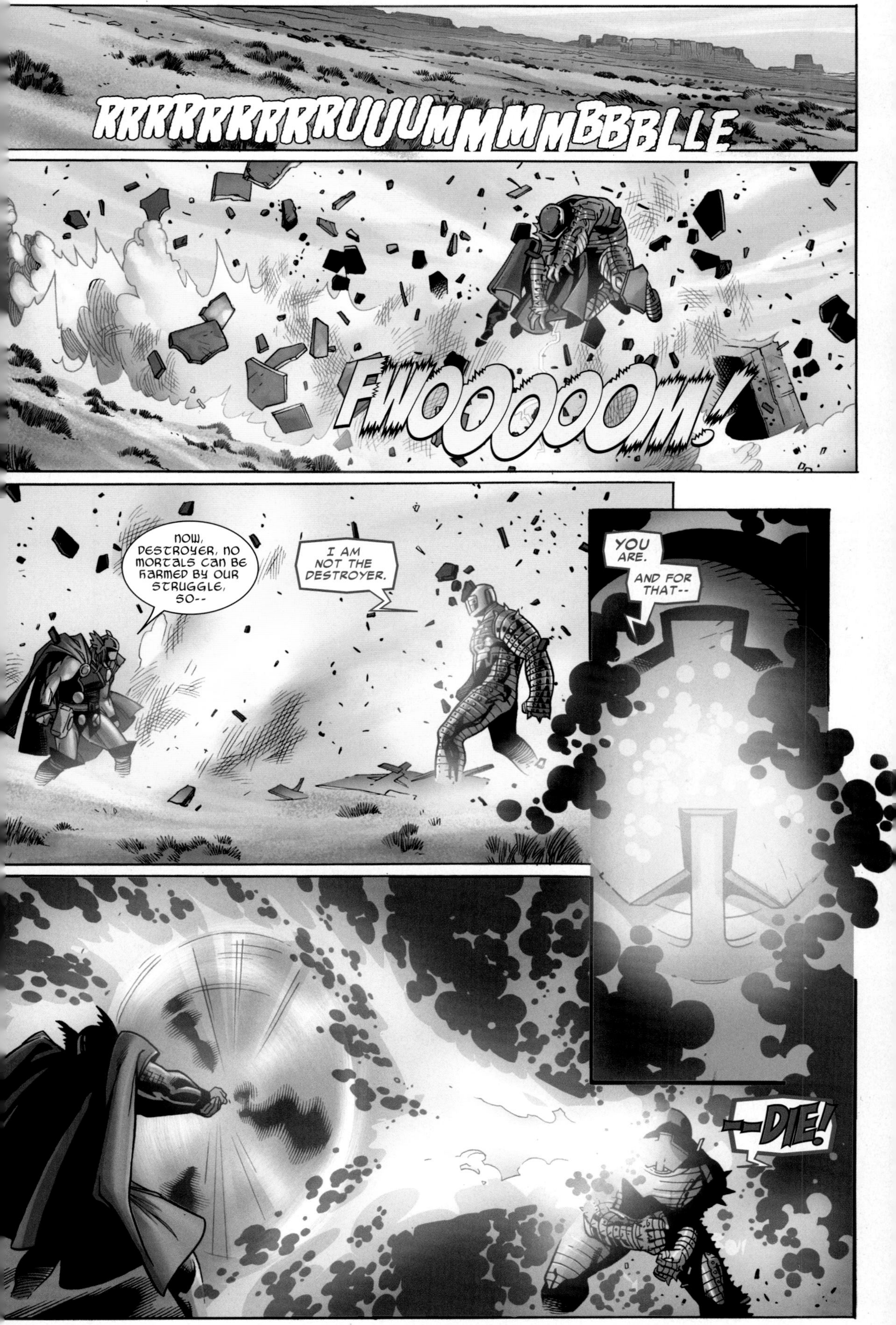
RRRRRRRRRRRUUUUMMMMMBBBLLE
FWOOOOOOM!
NOW, DESTROYER, NO MORTALS CAN BE HARMED BY OUR STRUGGLE, SO--
I AM NOT THE DESTROYER.
YOU ARE.
AND FOR THAT--
--DIE!

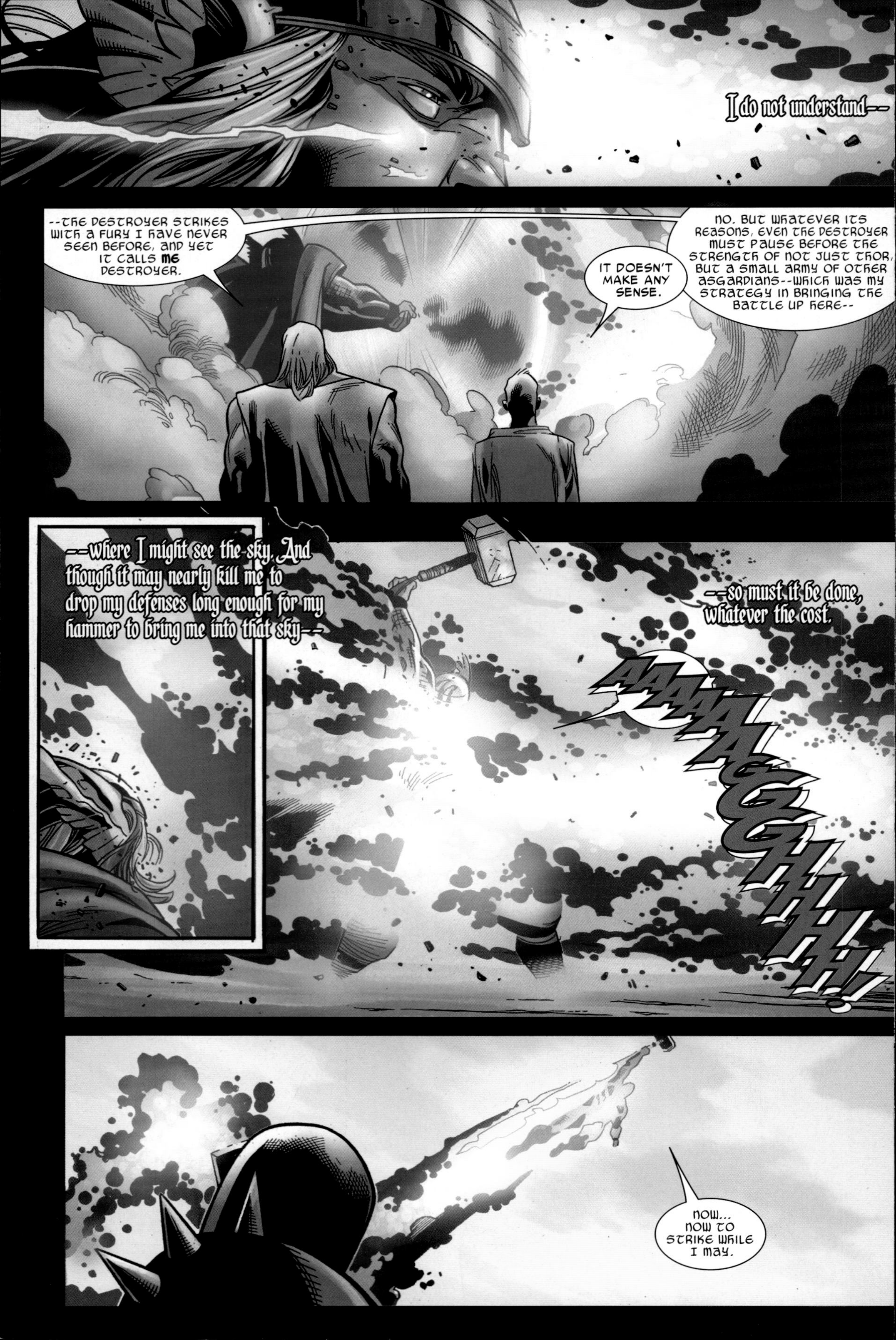
I do not understand--
--THE DESTROYER STRIKES WITH A FURY I HAVE NEVER SEEN BEFORE, AND YET IT CALLS ME DESTROYER.
IT DOESN'T MAKE ANY SENSE.
NO. BUT WHATEVER ITS REASONS, EVEN THE DESTROYER MUST PAUSE BEFORE THE STRENGTH OF NOT JUST THOR, BUT A SMALL ARMY OF OTHER ASGARDIANS--WHICH WAS MY STRATEGY IN BRINGING THE BATTLE UP HERE--
--where I might see the sky. And though it may nearly kill me to drop my defenses long enough for my hammer to bring me into that sky--
--so must it be done, whatever the cost.
AAAAAAGGHHHH!!
NOW... NOW TO STRIKE WHILE I MAY.

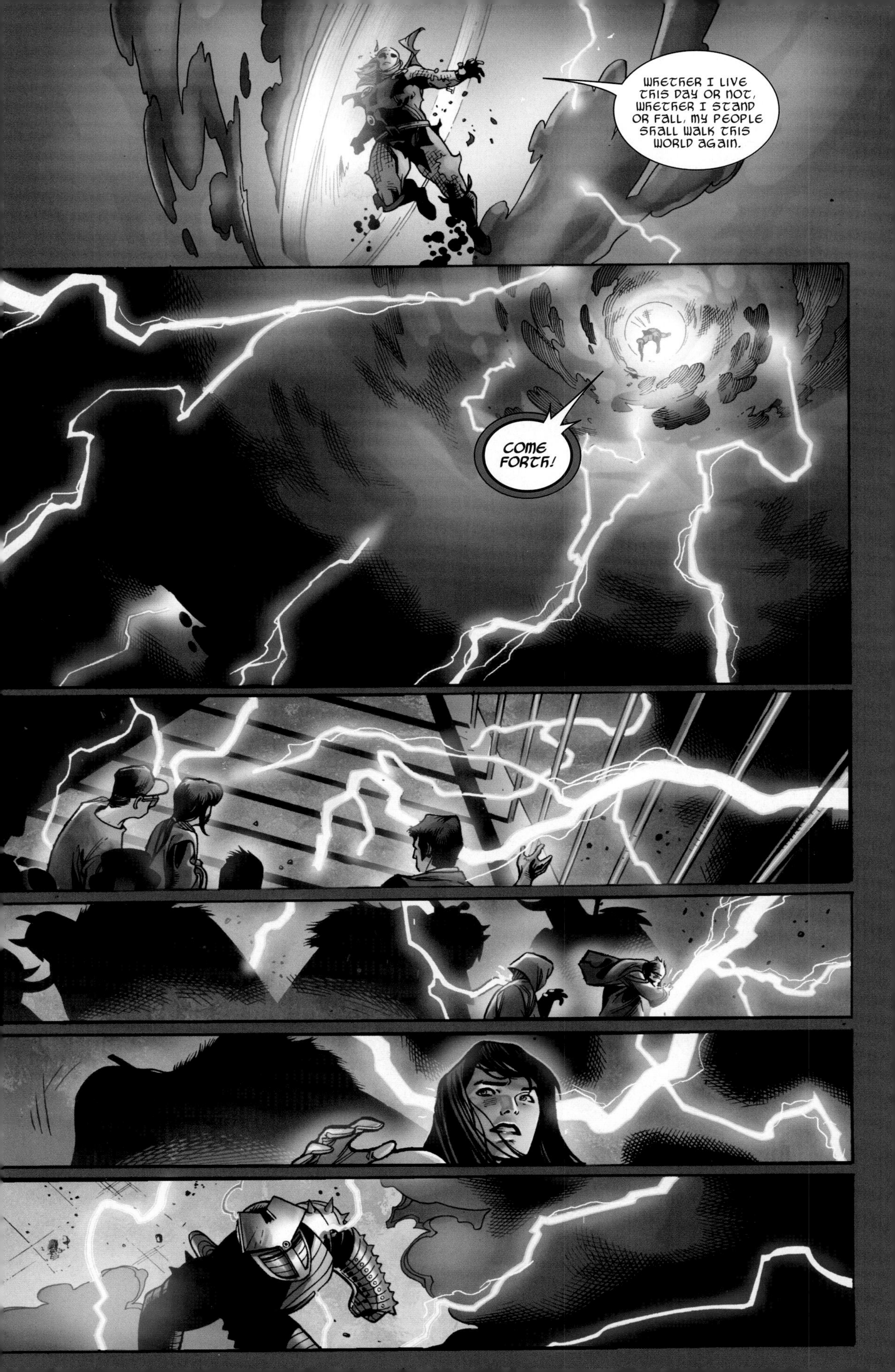
WHETHER I LIVE THIS DAY OR NOT, WHETHER I STAND OR FALL, MY PEOPLE SHALL WALK THIS WORLD AGAIN.
COME FORTH!

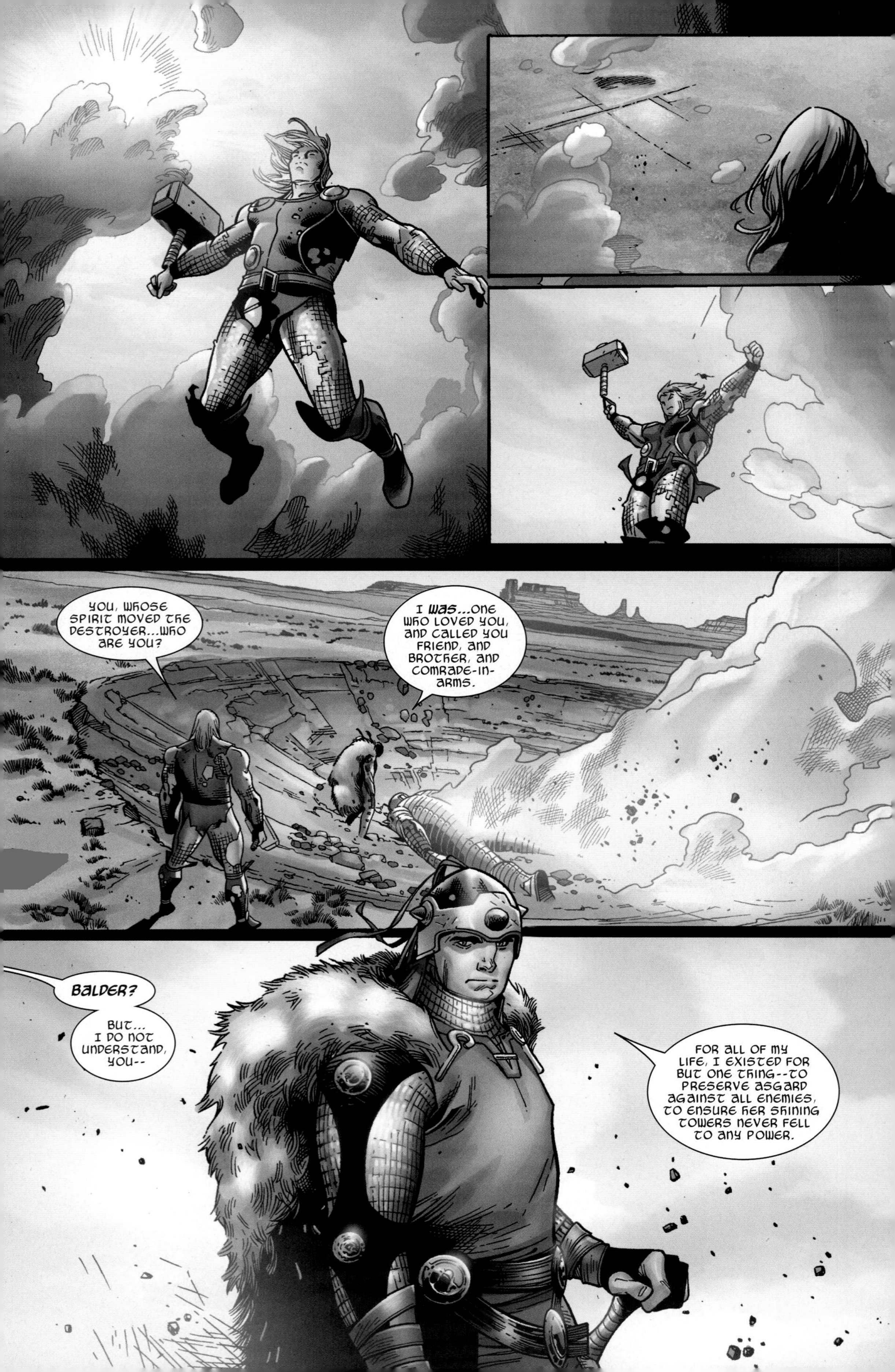

YOU, WHOSE SPIRIT MOVED THE DESTROYER...WHO ARE YOU?
I WAS...ONE WHO LOVED YOU, AND CALLED YOU FRIEND, AND BROTHER, AND COMRADE-IN-ARMS.
BALDER?
BUT... I DO NOT UNDERSTAND, YOU--
FOR ALL OF MY LIFE, I EXISTED FOR BUT ONE THING--TO PRESERVE ASGARD AGAINST ALL ENEMIES, TO ENSURE HER SHINING TOWERS NEVER FELL TO ANY POWER.

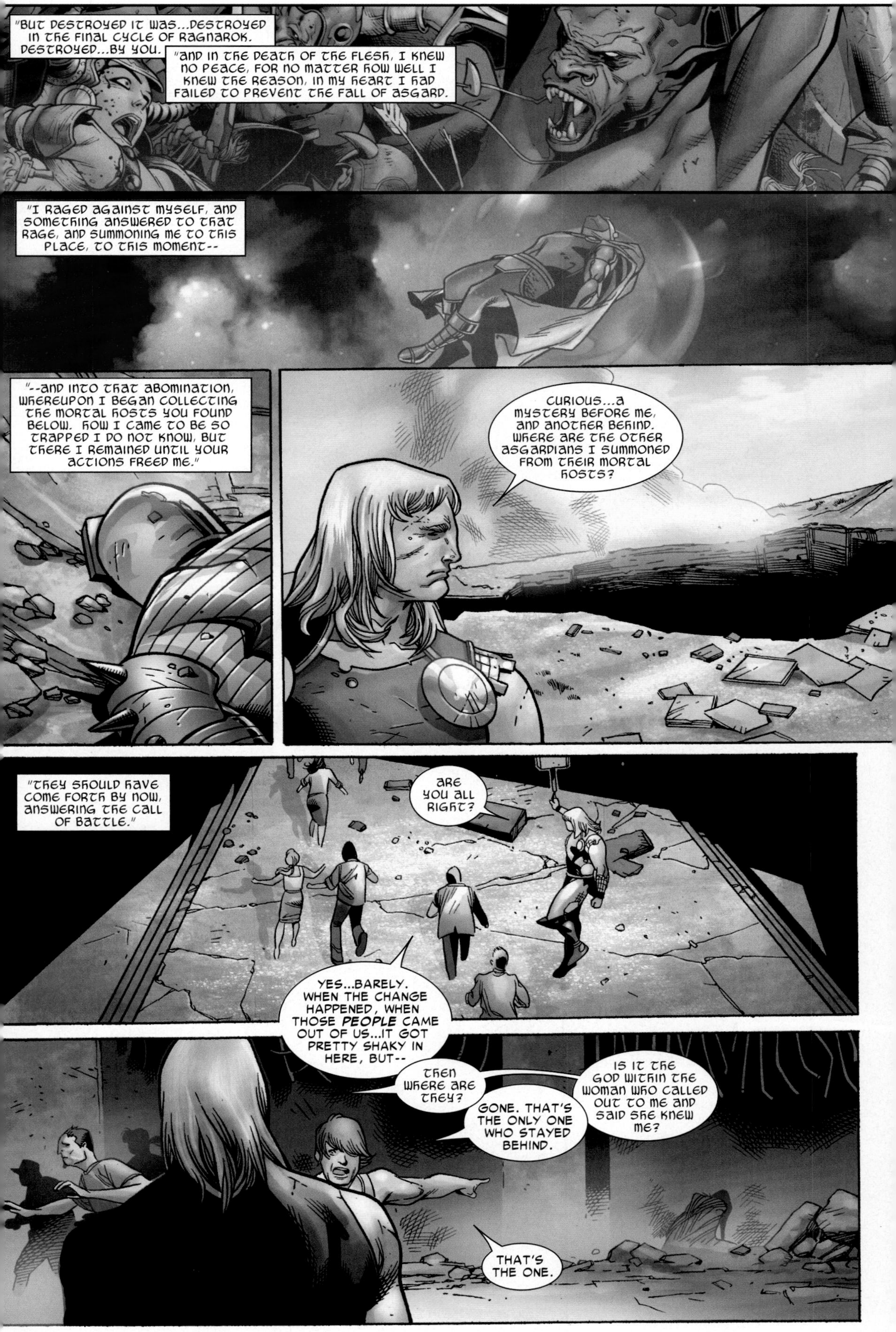
"BUT DESTROYED IT WAS...DESTROYED IN THE FINAL CYCLE OF RAGNAROK. DESTROYED...BY YOU.
"AND IN THE DEATH OF THE FLESH, I KNEW NO PEACE, FOR NO MATTER HOW WELL I KNEW THE REASON, IN MY HEART I HAD FAILED TO PREVENT THE FALL OF ASGARD.
"I RAGED AGAINST MYSELF, AND SOMETHING ANSWERED TO THAT RAGE, AND SUMMONING ME TO THIS PLACE, TO THIS MOMENT--
"--AND INTO THAT ABOMINATION, WHEREUPON I BEGAN COLLECTING THE MORTAL HOSTS YOU FOUND BELOW. HOW I CAME TO BE SO TRAPPED I DO NOT KNOW, BUT THERE I REMAINED UNTIL YOUR ACTIONS FREED ME."
CURIOUS...A MYSTERY BEFORE ME, AND ANOTHER BEHIND. WHERE ARE THE OTHER ASGARDIANS I SUMMONED FROM THEIR MORTAL HOSTS?
"THEY SHOULD HAVE COME FORTH BY NOW, ANSWERING THE CALL OF BATTLE."
ARE YOU ALL RIGHT?
YES...BARELY. WHEN THE CHANGE HAPPENED, WHEN THOSE *PEOPLE* CAME OUT OF US...IT GOT PRETTY SHAKY IN HERE, BUT--
THEN WHERE ARE THEY?
GONE. THAT'S THE ONLY ONE WHO STAYED BEHIND.
IS IT THE GOD WITHIN THE WOMAN WHO CALLED OUT TO ME AND SAID SHE KNEW ME?
THAT'S THE ONE.

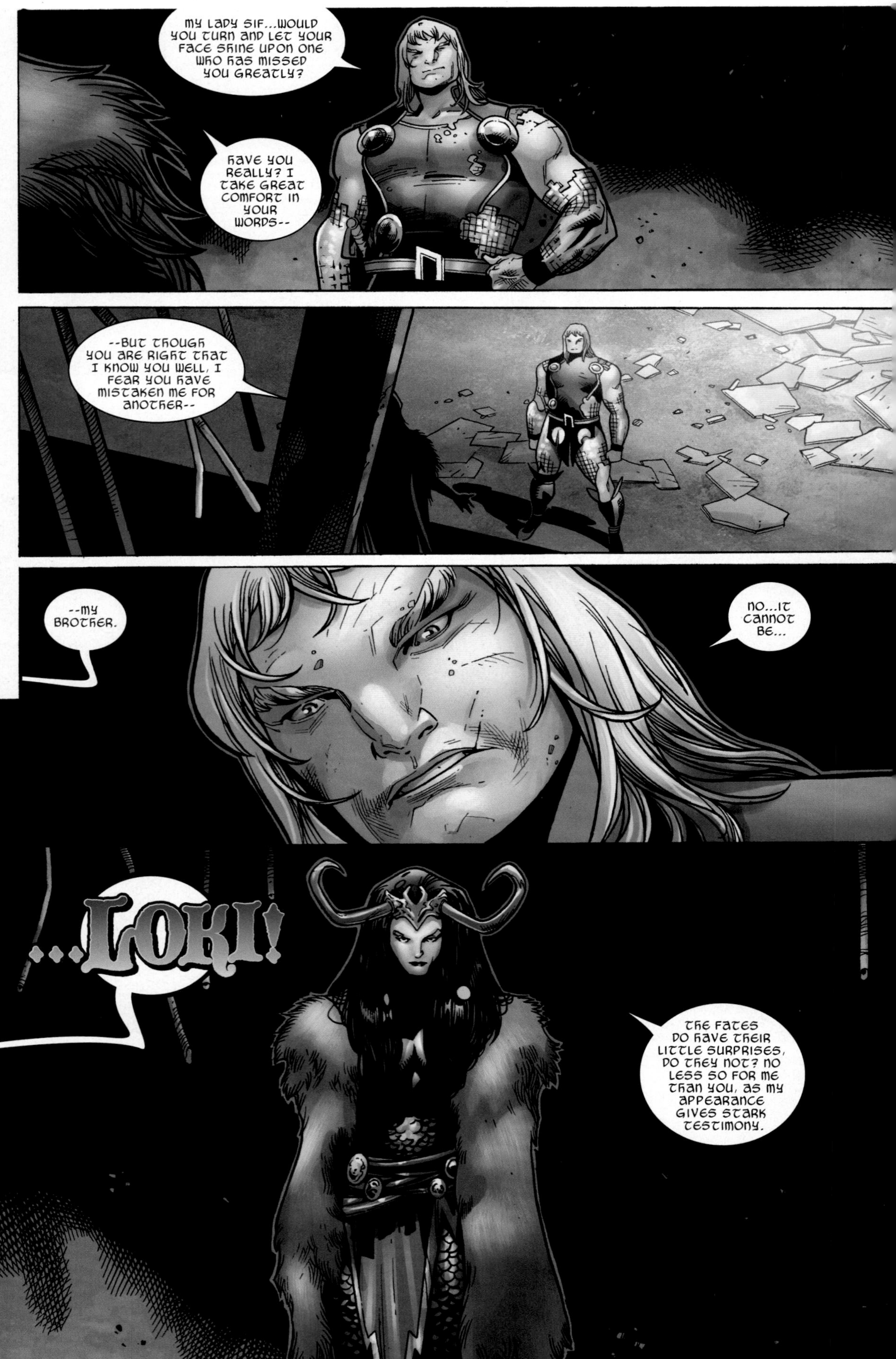
MY LADY SIF...WOULD YOU TURN AND LET YOUR FACE SHINE UPON ONE WHO HAS MISSED YOU GREATLY?
HAVE YOU REALLY? I TAKE GREAT COMFORT IN YOUR WORDS--
--BUT THOUGH YOU ARE RIGHT THAT I KNOW YOU WELL, I FEAR YOU HAVE MISTAKEN ME FOR ANOTHER--
--MY BROTHER.
NO...IT CANNOT BE...
...LOKI!
THE FATES DO HAVE THEIR LITTLE SURPRISES, DO THEY NOT? NO LESS SO FOR ME THAN YOU, AS MY APPEARANCE GIVES STARK TESTIMONY.

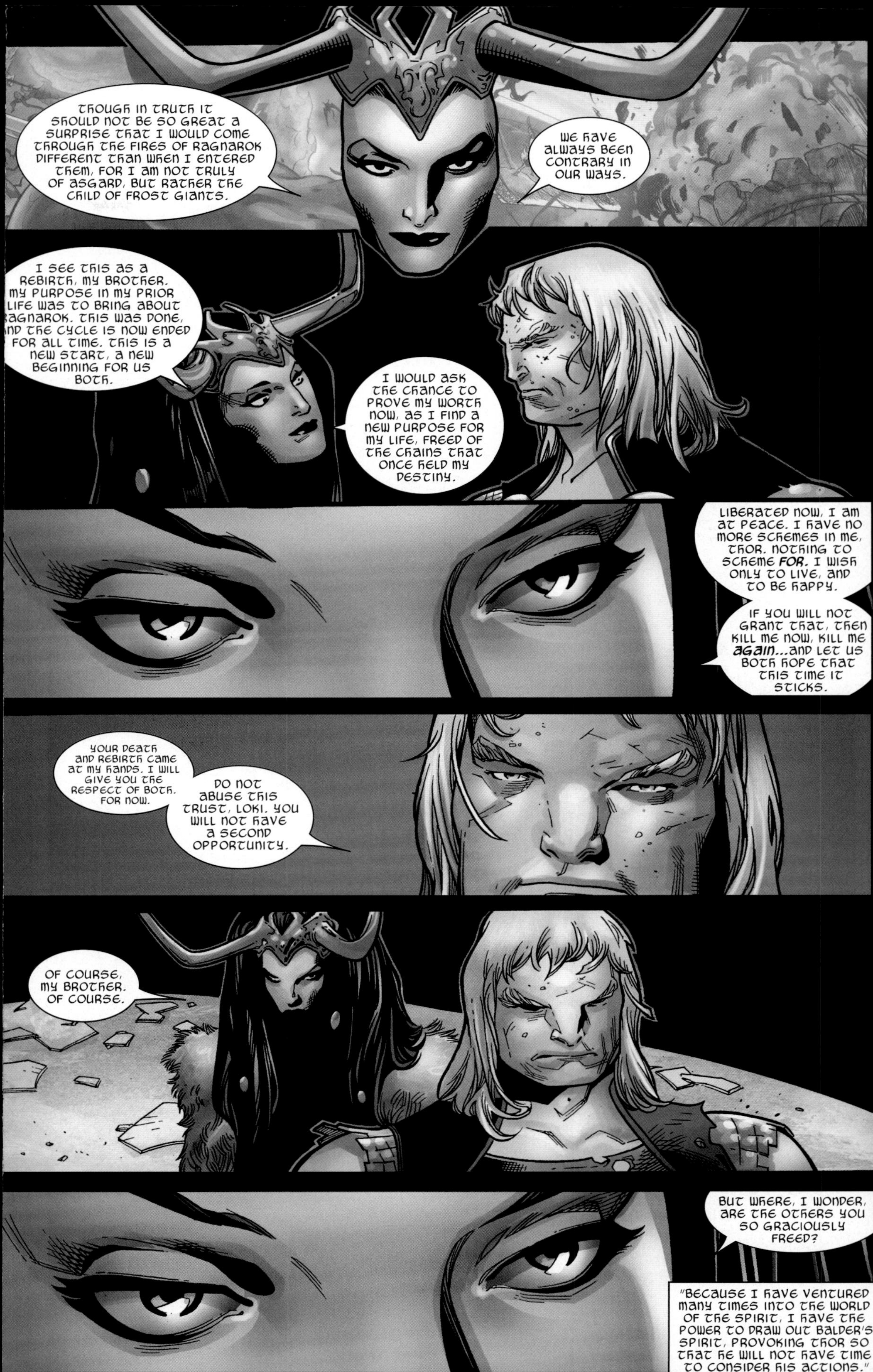
THOUGH IN TRUTH IT SHOULD NOT BE SO GREAT A SURPRISE THAT I WOULD COME THROUGH THE FIRES OF RAGNAROK DIFFERENT THAN WHEN I ENTERED THEM, FOR I AM NOT TRULY OF ASGARD, BUT RATHER THE CHILD OF FROST GIANTS.
WE HAVE ALWAYS BEEN CONTRARY IN OUR WAYS.
I SEE THIS AS A REBIRTH, MY BROTHER. MY PURPOSE IN MY PRIOR LIFE WAS TO BRING ABOUT RAGNAROK. THIS WAS DONE, AND THE CYCLE IS NOW ENDED FOR ALL TIME. THIS IS A NEW START, A NEW BEGINNING FOR US BOTH.
I WOULD ASK THE CHANCE TO PROVE MY WORTH NOW, AS I FIND A NEW PURPOSE FOR MY LIFE, FREED OF THE CHAINS THAT ONCE HELD MY DESTINY.
LIBERATED NOW, I AM AT PEACE. I HAVE NO MORE SCHEMES IN ME, THOR. NOTHING TO SCHEME FOR. I WISH ONLY TO LIVE, AND TO BE HAPPY.
IF YOU WILL NOT GRANT THAT, THEN KILL ME NOW, KILL ME AGAIN...AND LET US BOTH HOPE THAT THIS TIME IT STICKS.
YOUR DEATH AND REBIRTH CAME AT MY HANDS. I WILL GIVE YOU THE RESPECT OF BOTH. FOR NOW.
DO NOT ABUSE THIS TRUST, LOKI. YOU WILL NOT HAVE A SECOND OPPORTUNITY.
OF COURSE, MY BROTHER. OF COURSE.
BUT WHERE, I WONDER, ARE THE OTHERS YOU SO GRACIOUSLY FREED?
"BECAUSE I HAVE VENTURED MANY TIMES INTO THE WORLD OF THE SPIRIT, I HAVE THE POWER TO DRAW OUT BALDER'S SPIRIT, PROVOKING THOR SO THAT HE WILL NOT HAVE TIME TO CONSIDER HIS ACTIONS."

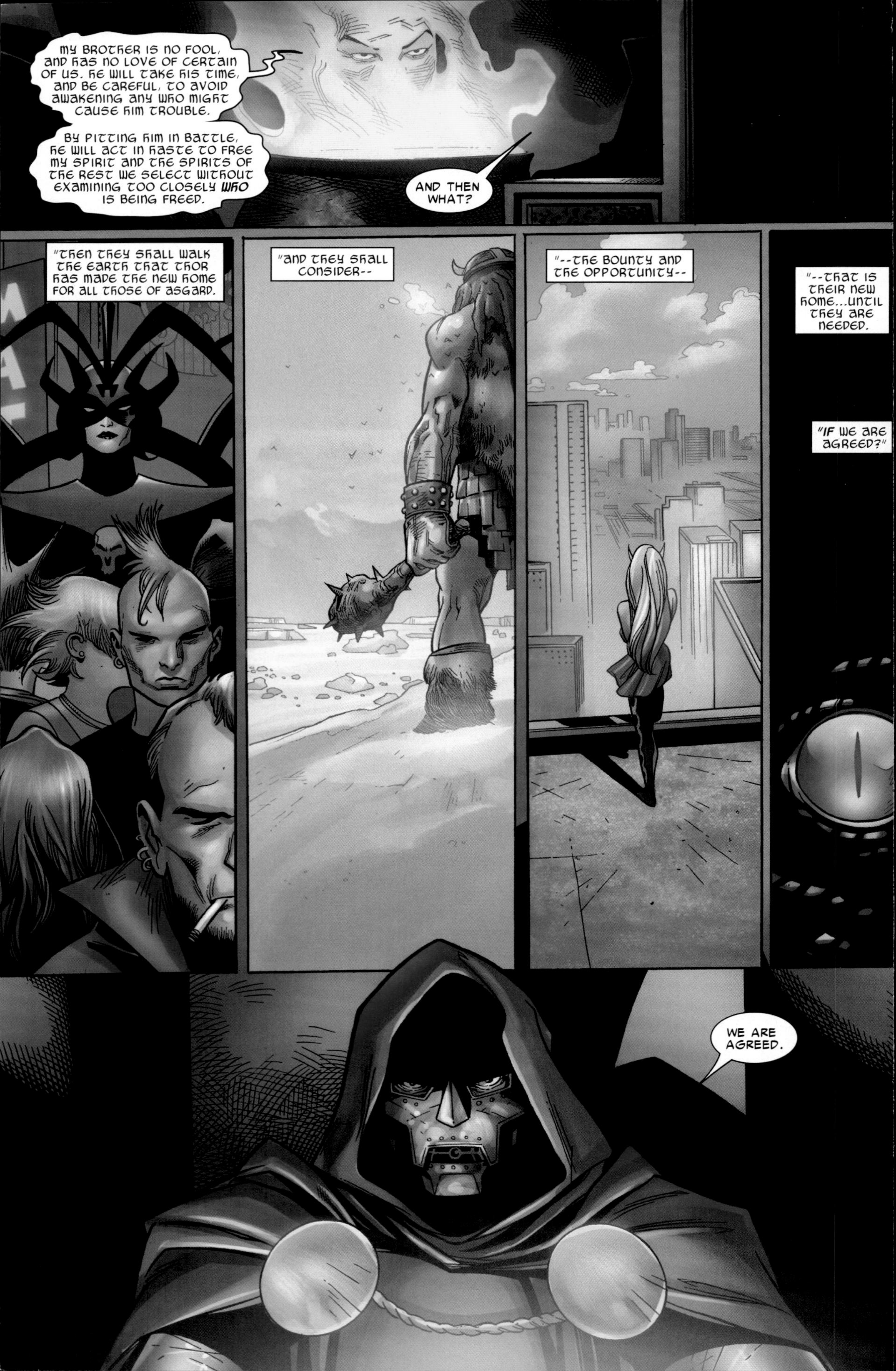
MY BROTHER IS NO FOOL, AND HAS NO LOVE OF CERTAIN OF US. HE WILL TAKE HIS TIME, AND BE CAREFUL, TO AVOID AWAKENING ANY WHO MIGHT CAUSE HIM TROUBLE.
BY PITTING HIM IN BATTLE, HE WILL ACT IN HASTE TO FREE MY SPIRIT AND THE SPIRITS OF THE REST WE SELECT WITHOUT EXAMINING TOO CLOSELY *WHO* IS BEING FREED.
AND THEN WHAT?
"THEN THEY SHALL WALK THE EARTH THAT THOR HAS MADE THE NEW HOME FOR ALL THOSE OF ASGARD.
"AND THEY SHALL CONSIDER--
"--THE BOUNTY AND THE OPPORTUNITY--
"--THAT IS THEIR NEW HOME...UNTIL THEY ARE NEEDED.
"*IF* WE ARE AGREED?"
WE ARE AGREED.

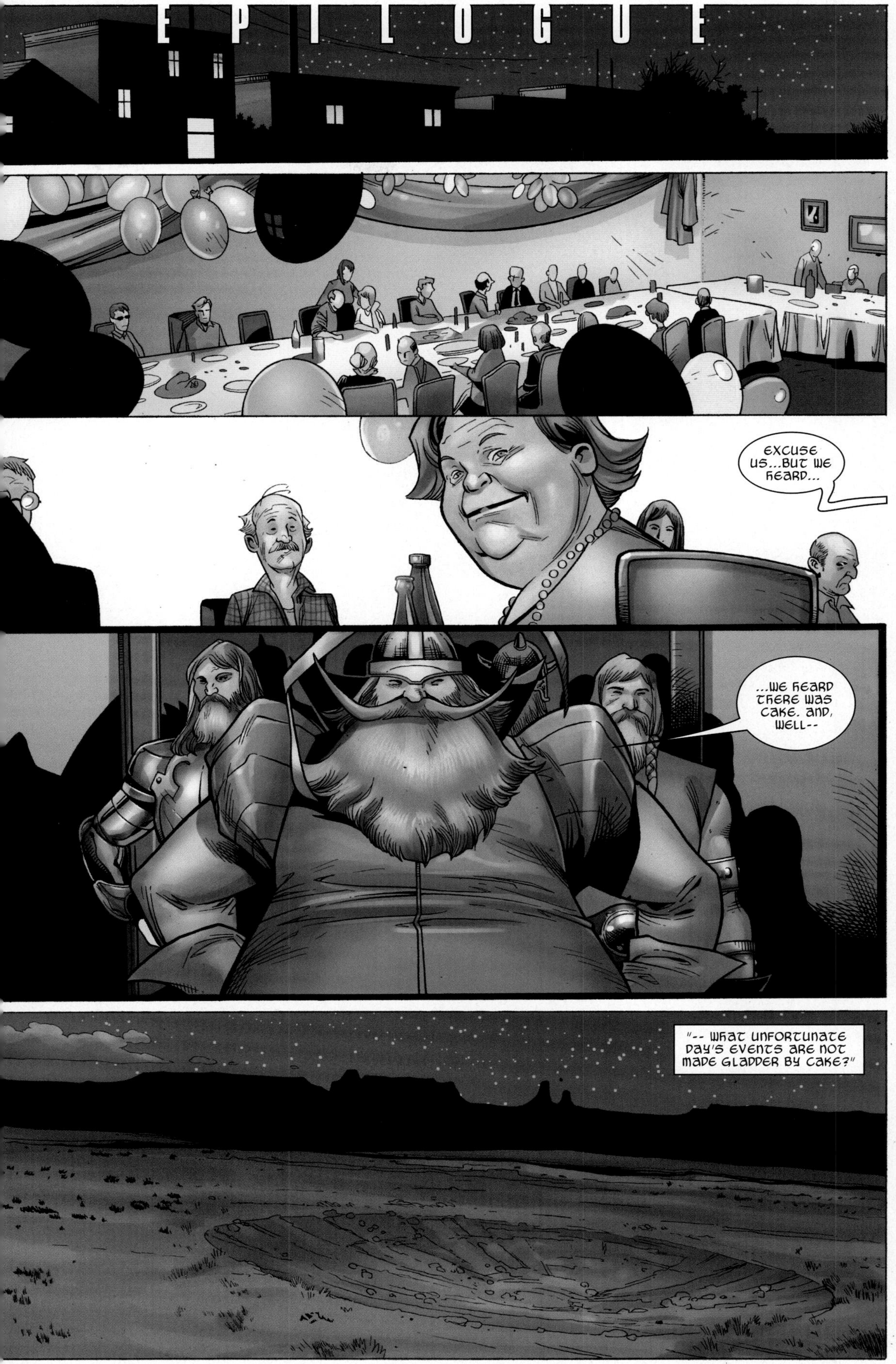
EPILOGUE
EXCUSE US...BUT WE HEARD...
...WE HEARD THERE WAS CAKE. AND, WELL--
"-- WHAT UNFORTUNATE DAY'S EVENTS ARE NOT MADE GLADDER BY CAKE?"

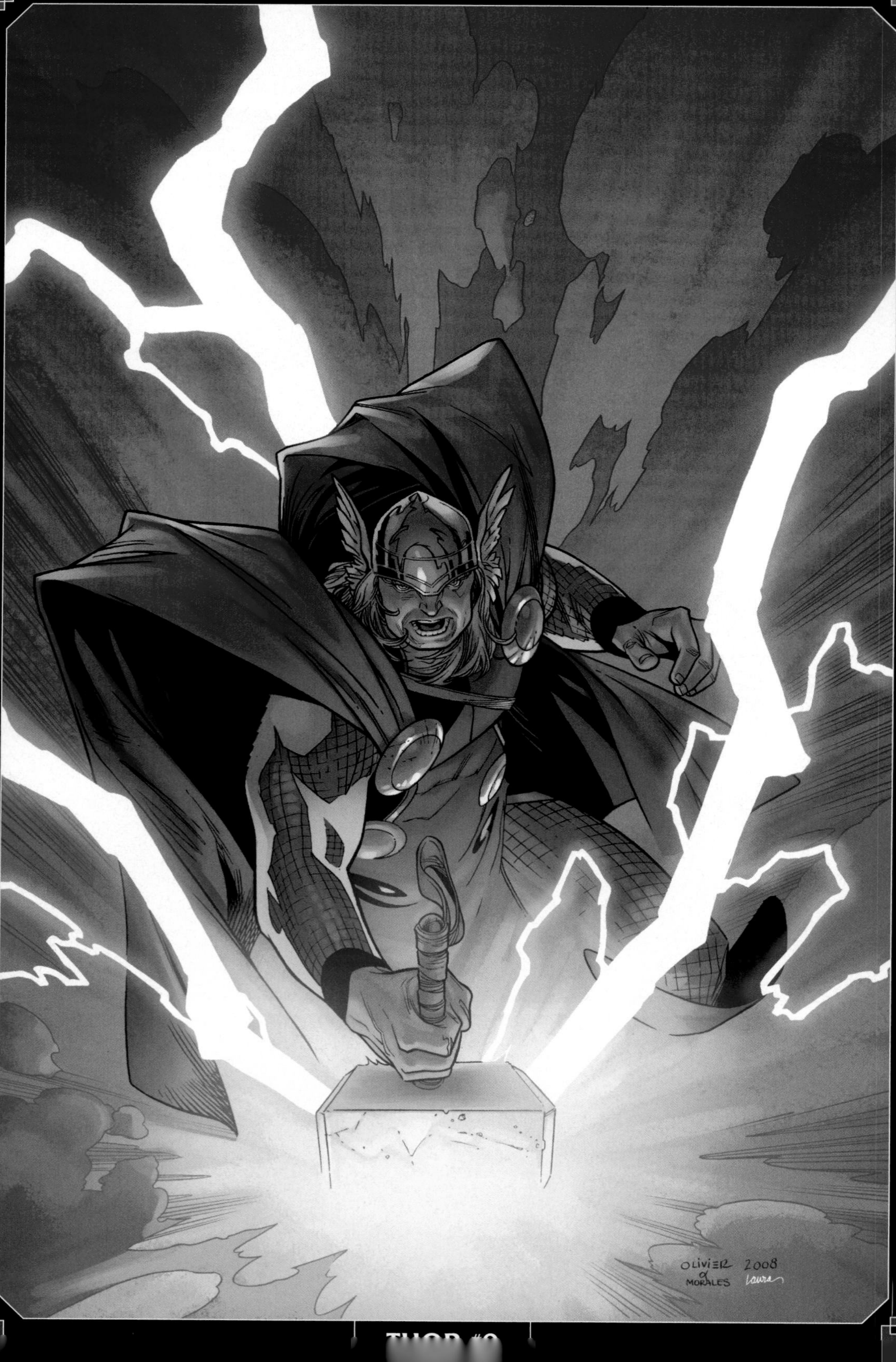
OLIVIER 2008
MORALES
Laura

THOR #0

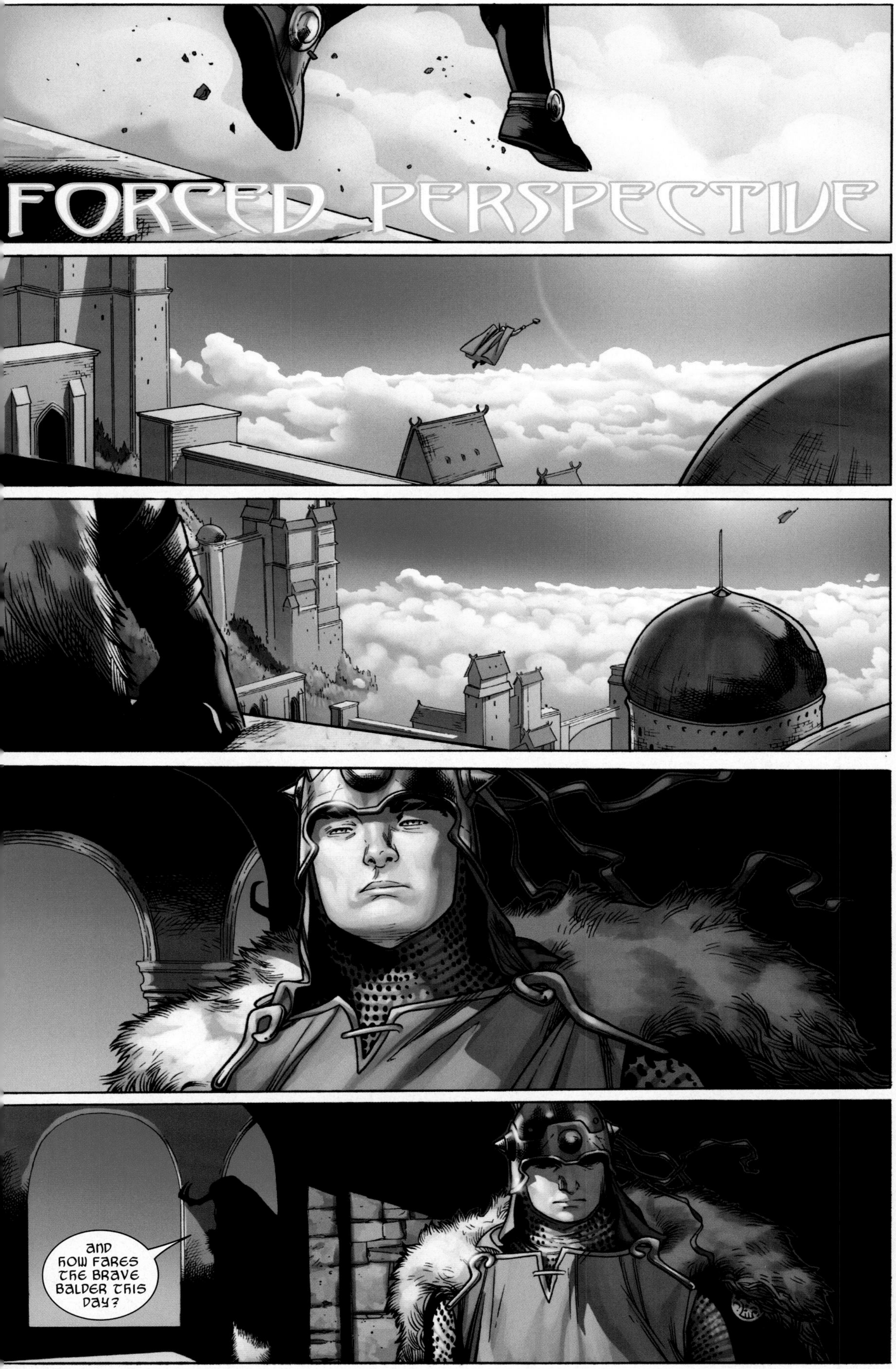
FORCED PERSPECTIVE
AND HOW FARES THE BRAVE BALDER THIS DAY?

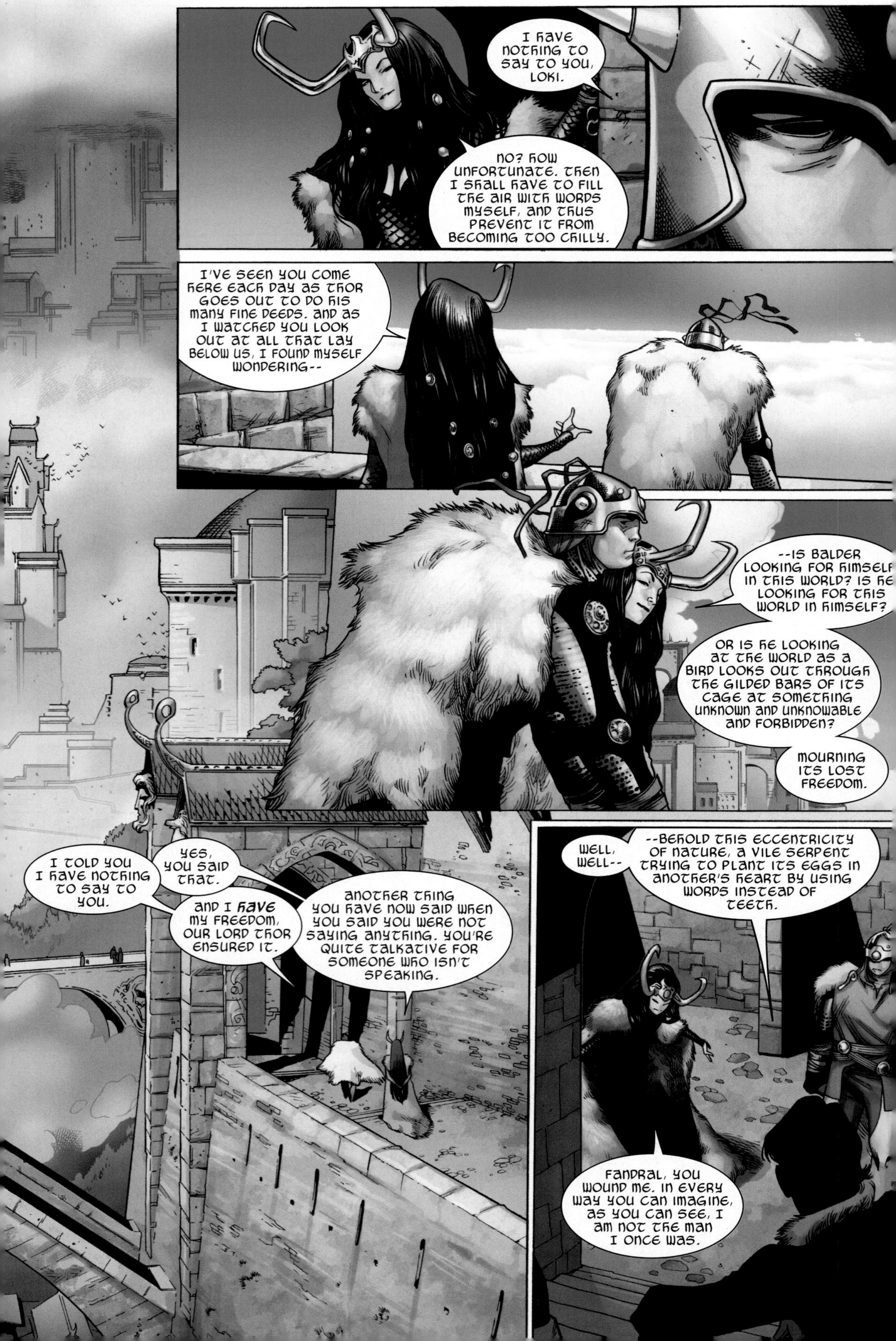
I HAVE NOTHING TO SAY TO YOU, LOKI.
NO? HOW UNFORTUNATE. THEN I SHALL HAVE TO FILL THE AIR WITH WORDS MYSELF, AND THUS PREVENT IT FROM BECOMING TOO CHILLY.
I'VE SEEN YOU COME HERE EACH DAY AS THOR GOES OUT TO DO HIS MANY FINE DEEDS. AND AS I WATCHED YOU LOOK OUT AT ALL THAT LAY BELOW US, I FOUND MYSELF WONDERING--
--IS BALDER LOOKING FOR HIMSELF IN THIS WORLD? IS HE LOOKING FOR THIS WORLD IN HIMSELF?
OR IS HE LOOKING AT THE WORLD AS A BIRD LOOKS OUT THROUGH THE GILDED BARS OF ITS CAGE AT SOMETHING UNKNOWN AND UNKNOWABLE AND FORBIDDEN?
MOURNING ITS LOST FREEDOM.
I TOLD YOU I HAVE NOTHING TO SAY TO YOU.
YES, YOU SAID THAT.
AND I *HAVE* MY FREEDOM, OUR LORD THOR ENSURED IT.
ANOTHER THING YOU HAVE NOW SAID WHEN YOU SAID YOU WERE NOT SAYING ANYTHING. YOU'RE QUITE TALKATIVE FOR SOMEONE WHO ISN'T SPEAKING.
WELL, WELL--
--BEHOLD THIS ECCENTRICITY OF NATURE, A VILE SERPENT TRYING TO PLANT ITS EGGS IN ANOTHER'S HEART BY USING WORDS INSTEAD OF TEETH.
FANDRAL, YOU WOUND ME. IN EVERY WAY YOU CAN IMAGINE, AS YOU CAN SEE, I AM NOT THE MAN I ONCE WAS.

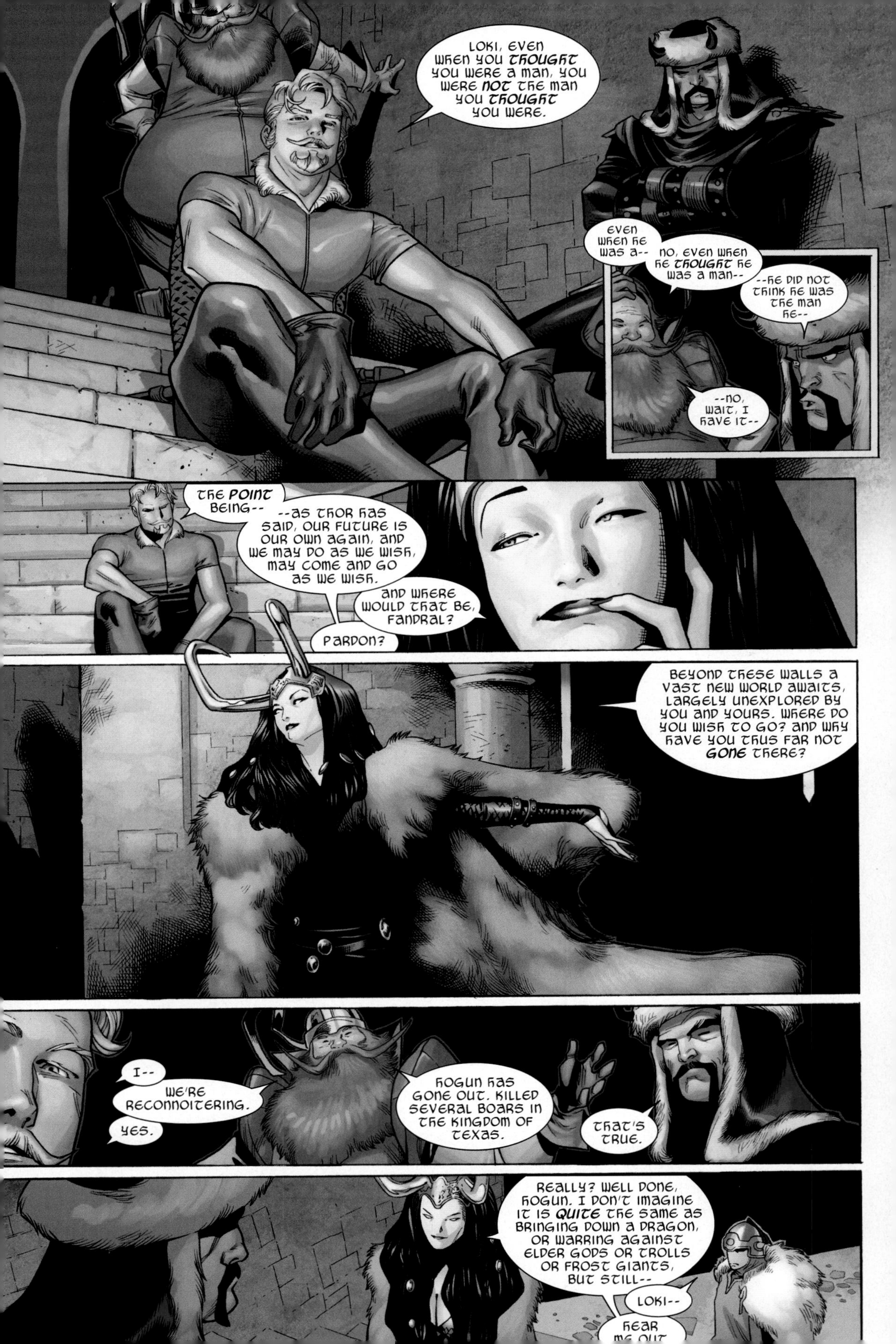
LOKI, EVEN WHEN YOU THOUGHT YOU WERE A MAN, YOU WERE NOT THE MAN YOU THOUGHT YOU WERE.
EVEN WHEN HE WAS A--
NO, EVEN WHEN HE THOUGHT HE WAS A MAN--
--HE DID NOT THINK HE WAS THE MAN HE--
--NO, WAIT, I HAVE IT--
THE POINT BEING--
--AS THOR HAS SAID, OUR FUTURE IS OUR OWN AGAIN, AND WE MAY DO AS WE WISH, MAY COME AND GO AS WE WISH.
AND WHERE WOULD THAT BE, FANDRAL?
PARDON?
BEYOND THESE WALLS A VAST NEW WORLD AWAITS, LARGELY UNEXPLORED BY YOU AND YOURS. WHERE DO YOU WISH TO GO? AND WHY HAVE YOU THUS FAR NOT GONE THERE?
I--
WE'RE RECONNOITERING.
YES.
HOGUN HAS GONE OUT. KILLED SEVERAL BOARS IN THE KINGDOM OF TEXAS.
THAT'S TRUE.
REALLY? WELL DONE, HOGUN. I DON'T IMAGINE IT IS QUITE THE SAME AS BRINGING DOWN A DRAGON, OR WARRING AGAINST ELDER GODS OR TROLLS OR FROST GIANTS, BUT STILL--
LOKI--

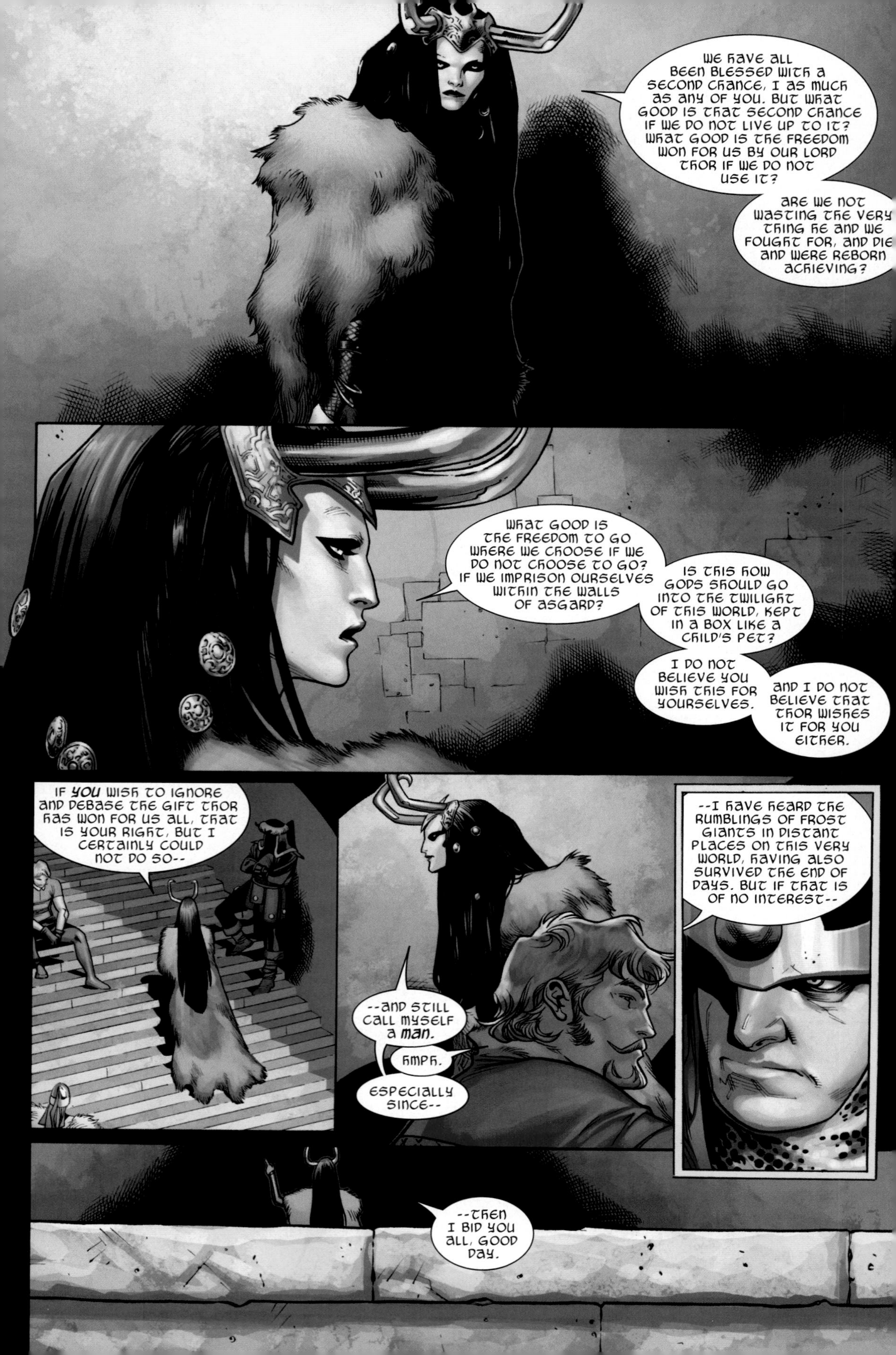
WE HAVE ALL BEEN BLESSED WITH A SECOND CHANCE, I AS MUCH AS ANY OF YOU. BUT WHAT GOOD IS THAT SECOND CHANCE IF WE DO NOT LIVE UP TO IT? WHAT GOOD IS THE FREEDOM WON FOR US BY OUR LORD THOR IF WE DO NOT USE IT?
ARE WE NOT WASTING THE VERY THING HE AND WE FOUGHT FOR, AND DIE AND WERE REBORN ACHIEVING?
WHAT GOOD IS THE FREEDOM TO GO WHERE WE CHOOSE IF WE DO NOT CHOOSE TO GO? IF WE IMPRISON OURSELVES WITHIN THE WALLS OF ASGARD?
IS THIS HOW GODS SHOULD GO INTO THE TWILIGHT OF THIS WORLD, KEPT IN A BOX LIKE A CHILD'S PET?
I DO NOT BELIEVE YOU WISH THIS FOR YOURSELVES.
AND I DO NOT BELIEVE THAT THOR WISHES IT FOR YOU EITHER.
IF YOU WISH TO IGNORE AND DEBASE THE GIFT THOR HAS WON FOR US ALL, THAT IS YOUR RIGHT, BUT I CERTAINLY COULD NOT DO SO--
--AND STILL CALL MYSELF A MAN.
HMPH.
ESPECIALLY SINCE--
--I HAVE HEARD THE RUMBLINGS OF FROST GIANTS IN DISTANT PLACES ON THIS VERY WORLD, HAVING ALSO SURVIVED THE END OF DAYS. BUT IF THAT IS OF NO INTEREST--
--THEN I BID YOU ALL, GOOD DAY.

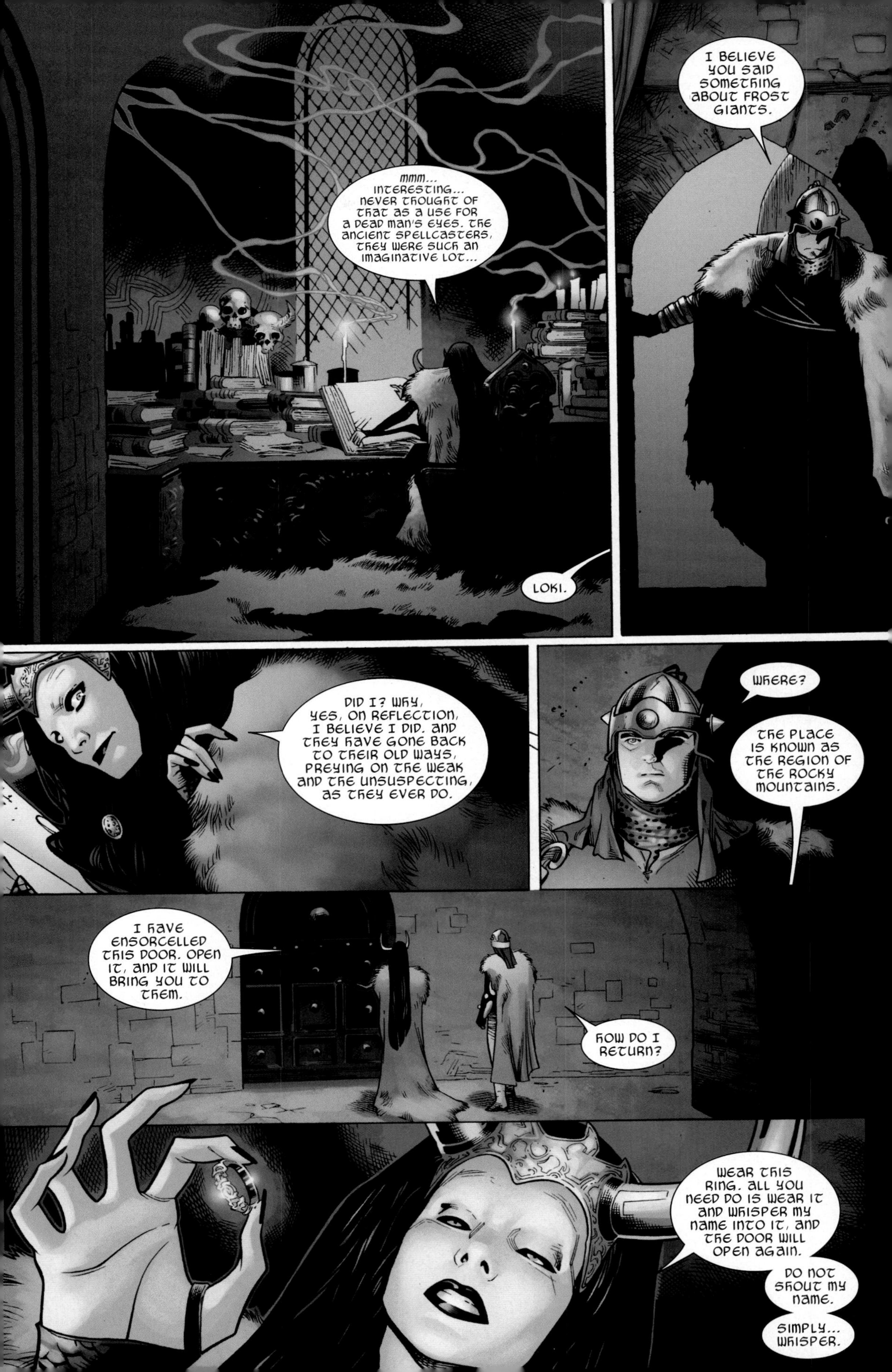
MMM... INTERESTING... NEVER THOUGHT OF THAT AS A USE FOR A DEAD MAN'S EYES. THE ANCIENT SPELLCASTERS, THEY WERE SUCH AN IMAGINATIVE LOT...
LOKI.
I BELIEVE YOU SAID SOMETHING ABOUT FROST GIANTS.
DID I? WHY, YES, ON REFLECTION, I BELIEVE I DID. AND THEY HAVE GONE BACK TO THEIR OLD WAYS, PREYING ON THE WEAK AND THE UNSUSPECTING, AS THEY EVER DO.
WHERE?
THE PLACE IS KNOWN AS THE REGION OF THE ROCKY MOUNTAINS.
I HAVE ENSORCELLED THIS DOOR. OPEN IT, AND IT WILL BRING YOU TO THEM.
HOW DO I RETURN?
WEAR THIS RING. ALL YOU NEED DO IS WEAR IT AND WHISPER MY NAME INTO IT, AND THE DOOR WILL OPEN AGAIN.
DO NOT SHOUT MY NAME.
SIMPLY... WHISPER.

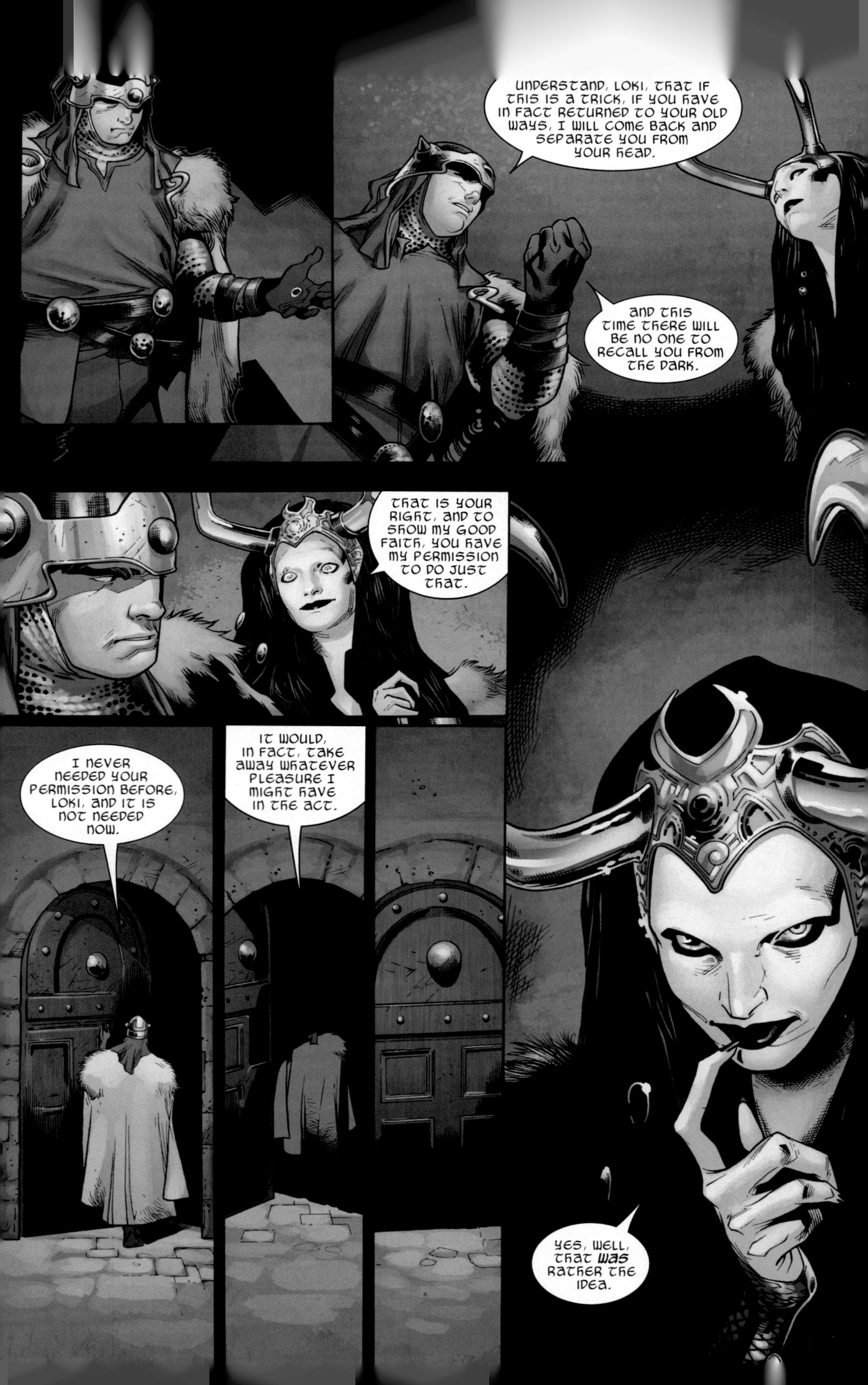
UNDERSTAND, LOKI, THAT IF THIS IS A TRICK, IF YOU HAVE IN FACT RETURNED TO YOUR OLD WAYS, I WILL COME BACK AND SEPARATE YOU FROM YOUR HEAD.
AND THIS TIME THERE WILL BE NO ONE TO RECALL YOU FROM THE DARK.
THAT IS YOUR RIGHT, AND TO SHOW MY GOOD FAITH, YOU HAVE MY PERMISSION TO DO JUST THAT.
I NEVER NEEDED YOUR PERMISSION BEFORE, LOKI, AND IT IS NOT NEEDED NOW.
IT WOULD, IN FACT, TAKE AWAY WHATEVER PLEASURE I MIGHT HAVE IN THE ACT.
YES, WELL, THAT *WAS* RATHER THE IDEA.

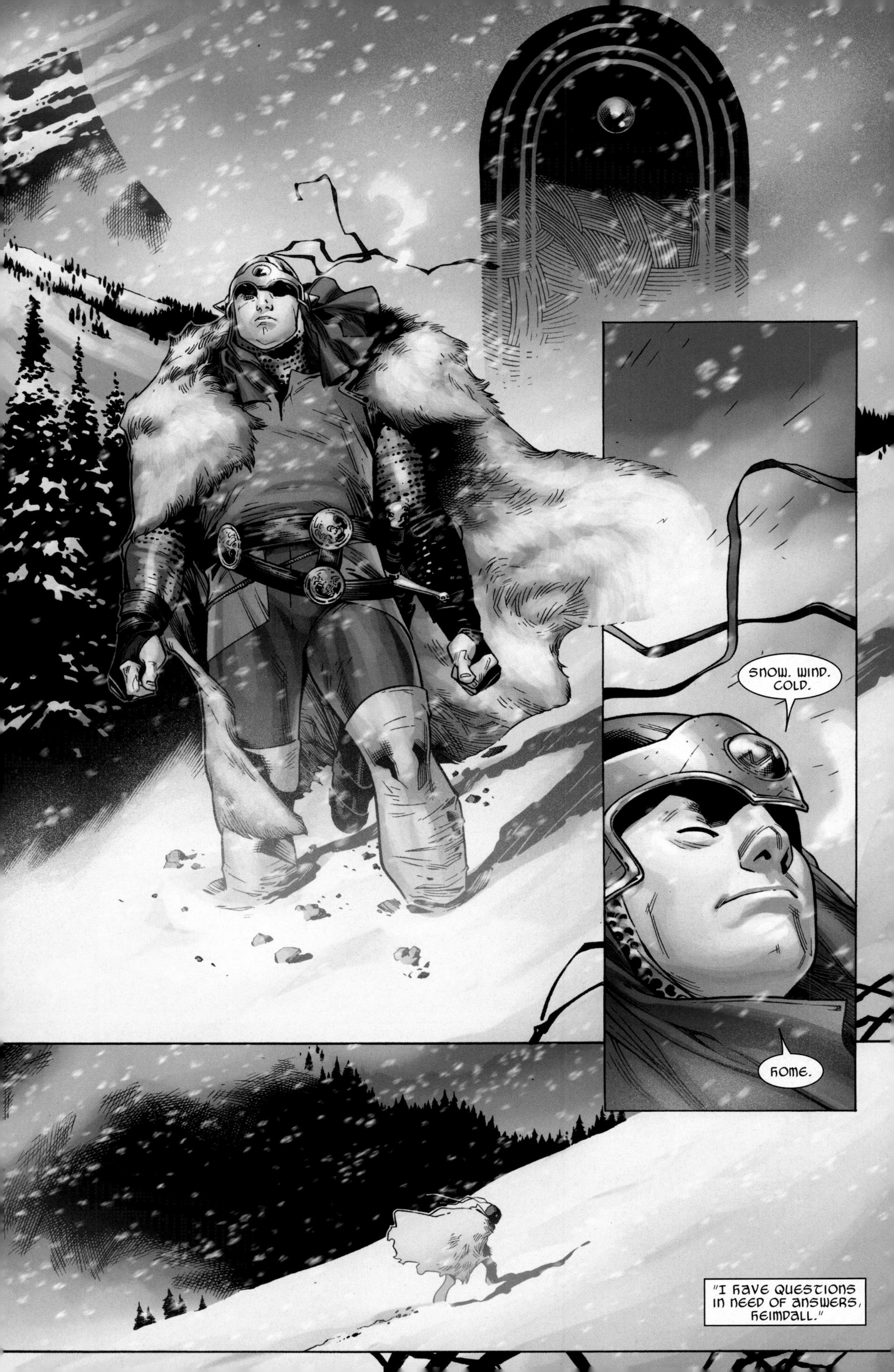
SNOW. WIND. COLD.
HOME.
"I HAVE QUESTIONS IN NEED OF ANSWERS, HEIMDALL."

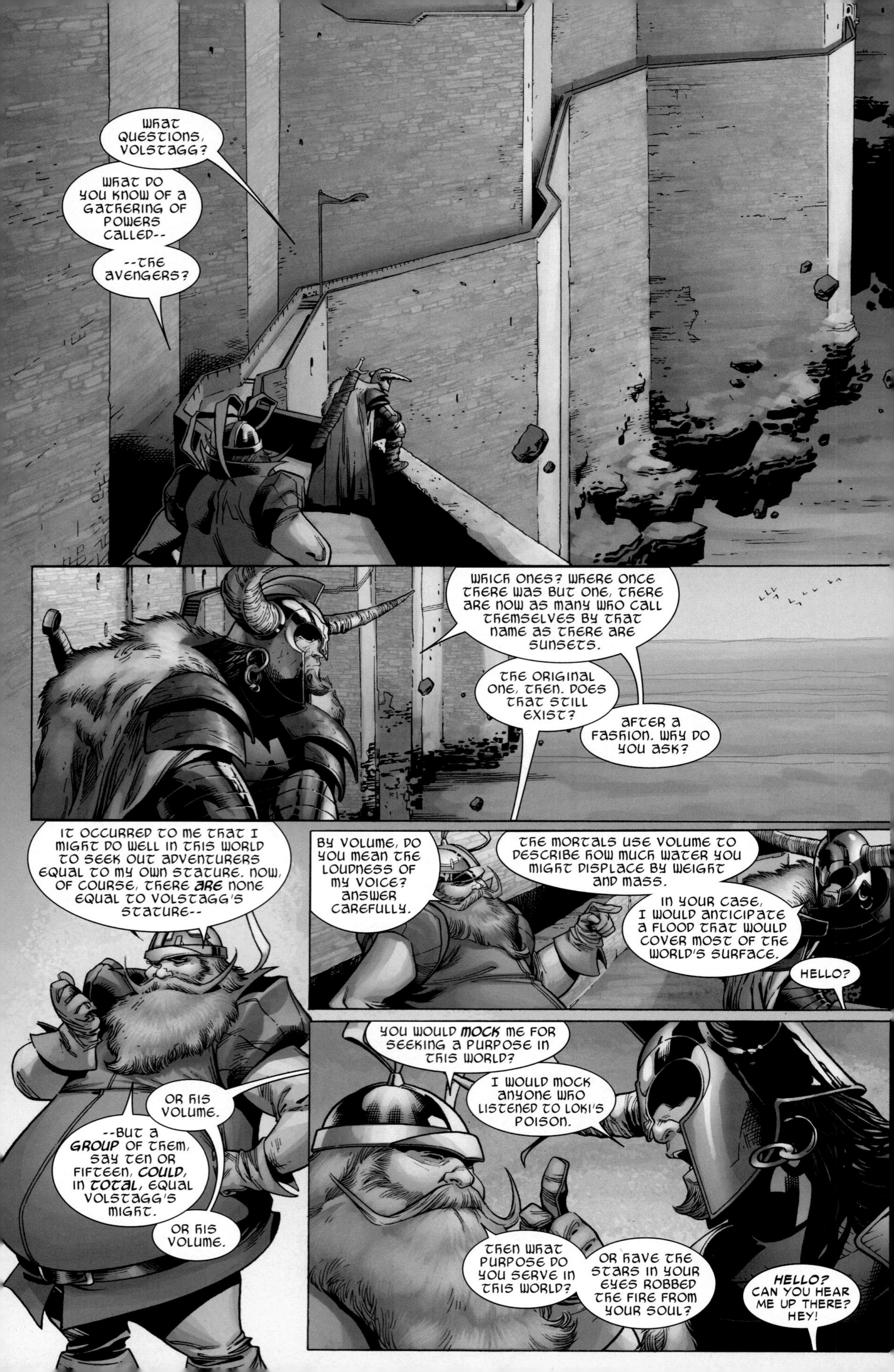

WHAT QUESTIONS, VOLSTAGG?
WHAT DO YOU KNOW OF A GATHERING OF POWERS CALLED--
--THE AVENGERS?
WHICH ONES? WHERE ONCE THERE WAS BUT ONE, THERE ARE NOW AS MANY WHO CALL THEMSELVES BY THAT NAME AS THERE ARE SUNSETS.
THE ORIGINAL ONE, THEN. DOES THAT STILL EXIST?
AFTER A FASHION. WHY DO YOU ASK?
IT OCCURRED TO ME THAT I MIGHT DO WELL IN THIS WORLD TO SEEK OUT ADVENTURERS EQUAL TO MY OWN STATURE. NOW, OF COURSE, THERE ARE NONE EQUAL TO VOLSTAGG'S STATURE--
OR HIS VOLUME.
--BUT A GROUP OF THEM, SAY TEN OR FIFTEEN, COULD, IN TOTAL, EQUAL VOLSTAGG'S MIGHT.
OR HIS VOLUME.
BY VOLUME, DO YOU MEAN THE LOUDNESS OF MY VOICE? ANSWER CAREFULLY.
THE MORTALS USE VOLUME TO DESCRIBE HOW MUCH WATER YOU MIGHT DISPLACE BY WEIGHT AND MASS.
IN YOUR CASE, I WOULD ANTICIPATE A FLOOD THAT WOULD COVER MOST OF THE WORLD'S SURFACE.
HELLO?
YOU WOULD MOCK ME FOR SEEKING A PURPOSE IN THIS WORLD?
I WOULD MOCK ANYONE WHO LISTENED TO LOKI'S POISON.
THEN WHAT PURPOSE DO YOU SERVE IN THIS WORLD?
OR HAVE THE STARS IN YOUR EYES ROBBED THE FIRE FROM YOUR SOUL?
HELLO? CAN YOU HEAR ME UP THERE? HEY!

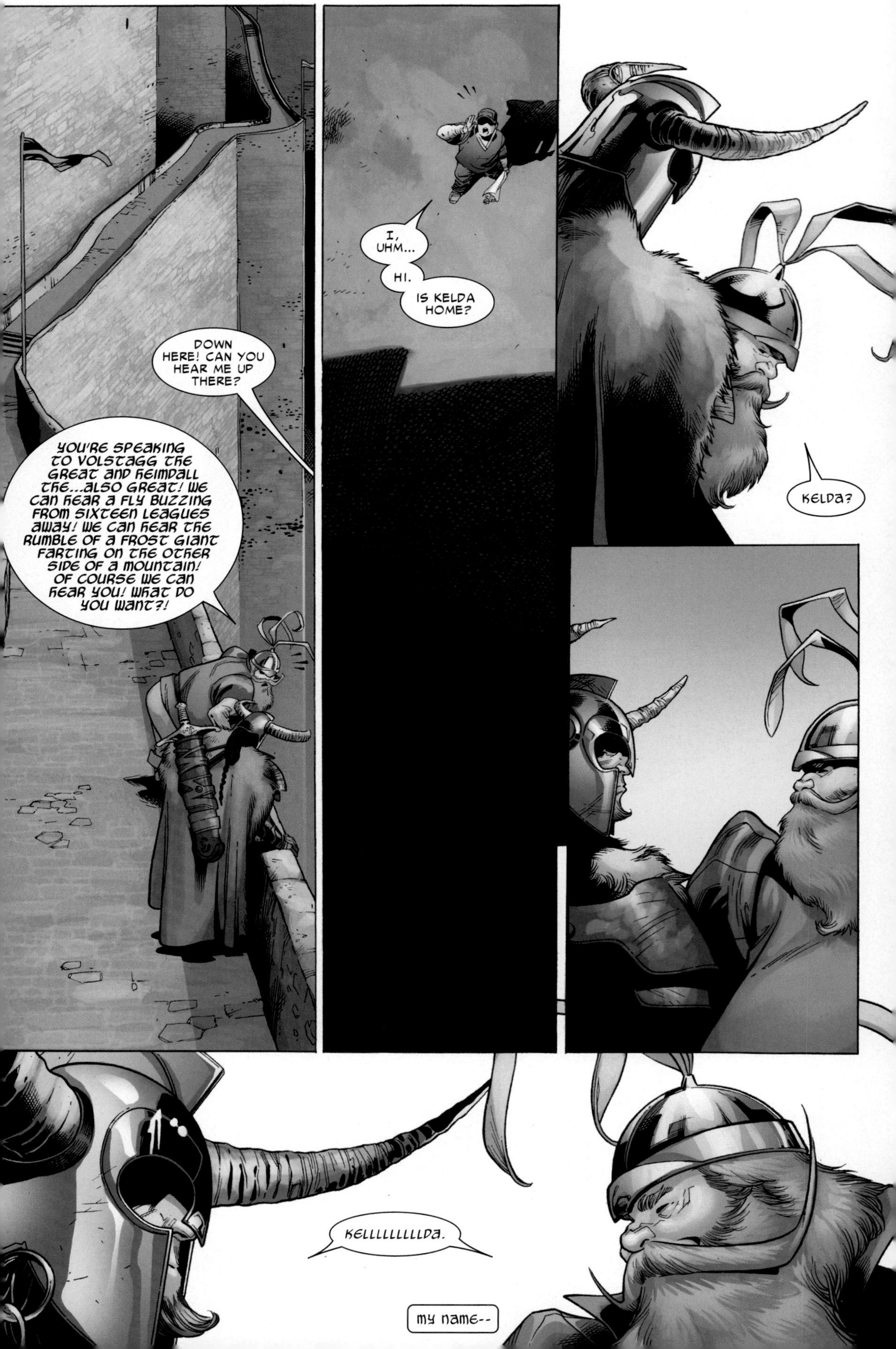
DOWN HERE! CAN YOU HEAR ME UP THERE?
YOU'RE SPEAKING TO VOLSTAGG THE GREAT AND HEIMDALL THE...ALSO GREAT! WE CAN HEAR A FLY BUZZING FROM SIXTEEN LEAGUES AWAY! WE CAN HEAR THE RUMBLE OF A FROST GIANT FARTING ON THE OTHER SIDE OF A MOUNTAIN! OF COURSE WE CAN HEAR YOU! WHAT DO YOU WANT?!
I, UHM...
HI.
IS KELDA HOME?
KELDA?
KELLLLLLLLLLDA.
MY NAME--

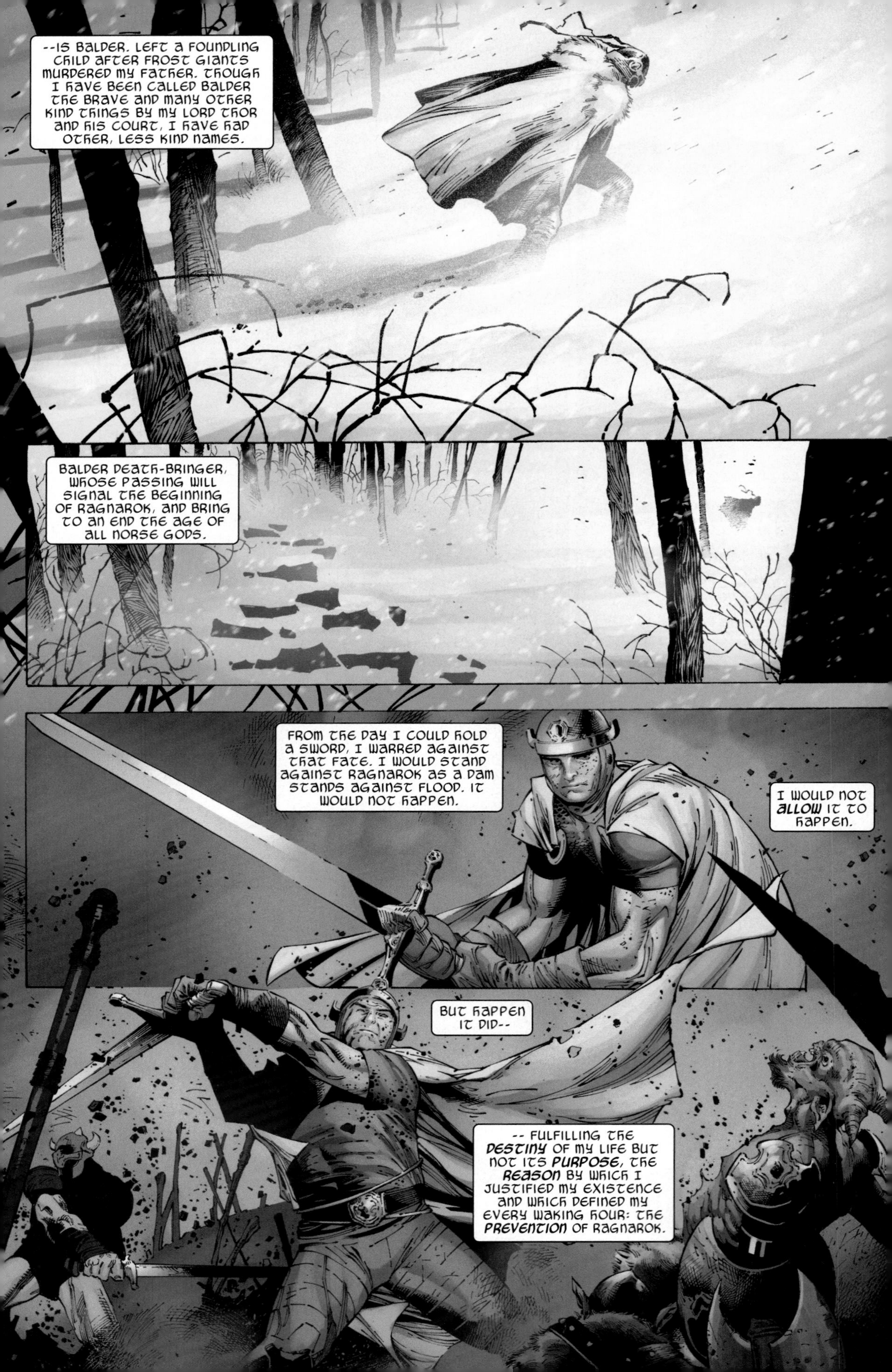
--IS BALDER. LEFT A FOUNDLING CHILD AFTER FROST GIANTS MURDERED MY FATHER. THOUGH I HAVE BEEN CALLED BALDER THE BRAVE AND MANY OTHER KIND THINGS BY MY LORD THOR AND HIS COURT, I HAVE HAD OTHER, LESS KIND NAMES.
BALDER DEATH-BRINGER, WHOSE PASSING WILL SIGNAL THE BEGINNING OF RAGNAROK, AND BRING TO AN END THE AGE OF ALL NORSE GODS.
FROM THE DAY I COULD HOLD A SWORD, I WARRED AGAINST THAT FATE. I WOULD STAND AGAINST RAGNAROK AS A DAM STANDS AGAINST FLOOD. IT WOULD NOT HAPPEN.
I WOULD NOT ALLOW IT TO HAPPEN.
BUT HAPPEN IT DID--
-- FULFILLING THE DESTINY OF MY LIFE BUT NOT ITS PURPOSE, THE REASON BY WHICH I JUSTIFIED MY EXISTENCE AND WHICH DEFINED MY EVERY WAKING HOUR: THE PREVENTION OF RAGNAROK.

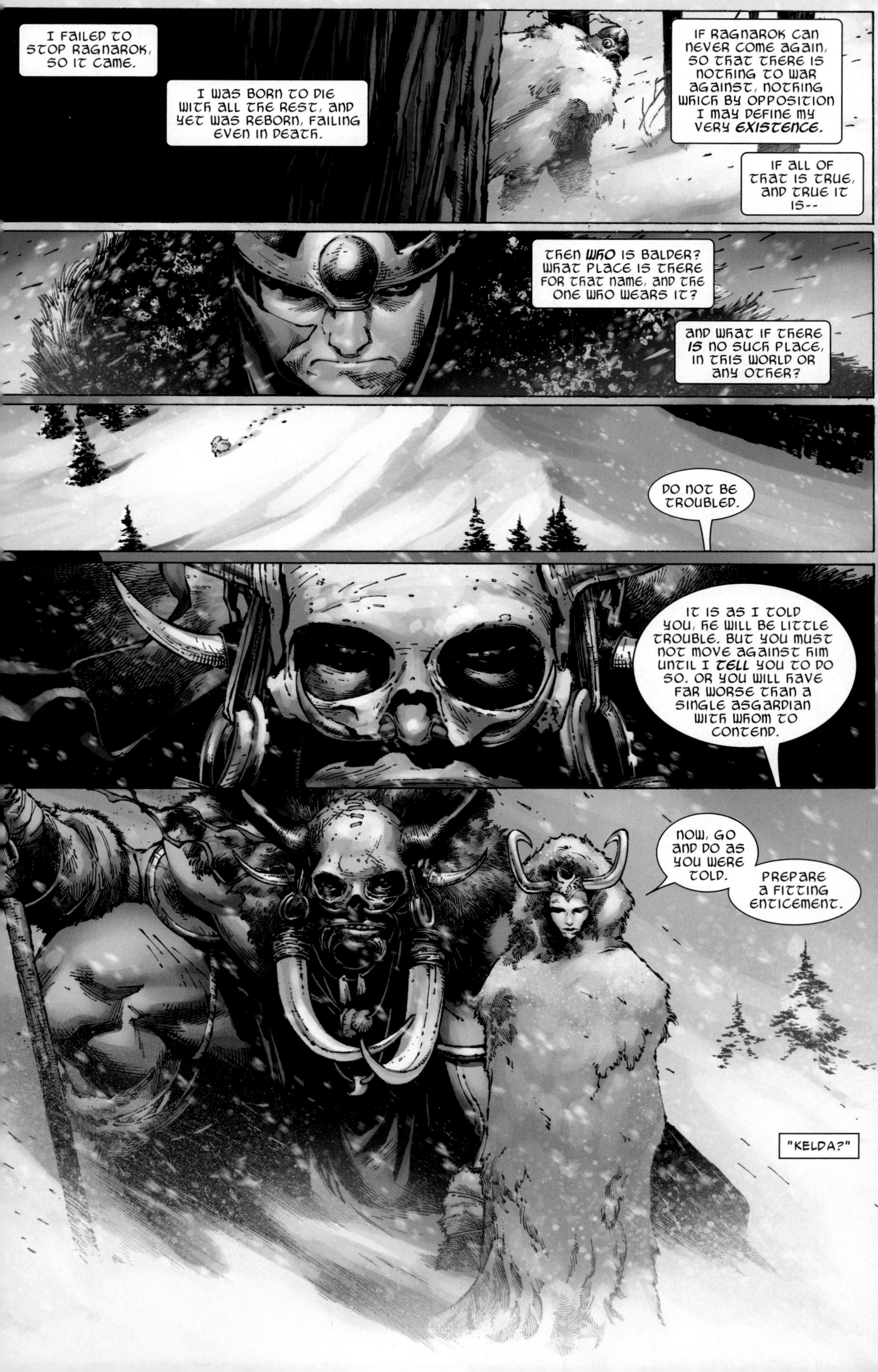
I FAILED TO STOP RAGNAROK, SO IT CAME.
I WAS BORN TO DIE WITH ALL THE REST, AND YET WAS REBORN, FAILING EVEN IN DEATH.
IF RAGNAROK CAN NEVER COME AGAIN, SO THAT THERE IS NOTHING TO WAR AGAINST, NOTHING WHICH BY OPPOSITION I MAY DEFINE MY VERY EXISTENCE.
IF ALL OF THAT IS TRUE, AND TRUE IT IS--
THEN WHO IS BALDER? WHAT PLACE IS THERE FOR THAT NAME, AND THE ONE WHO WEARS IT?
AND WHAT IF THERE IS NO SUCH PLACE, IN THIS WORLD OR ANY OTHER?
DO NOT BE TROUBLED.
IT IS AS I TOLD YOU, HE WILL BE LITTLE TROUBLE. BUT YOU MUST NOT MOVE AGAINST HIM UNTIL I TELL YOU TO DO SO. OR YOU WILL HAVE FAR WORSE THAN A SINGLE ASGARDIAN WITH WHOM TO CONTEND.
NOW, GO AND DO AS YOU WERE TOLD.
PREPARE A FITTING ENTICEMENT.
"KELDA?"

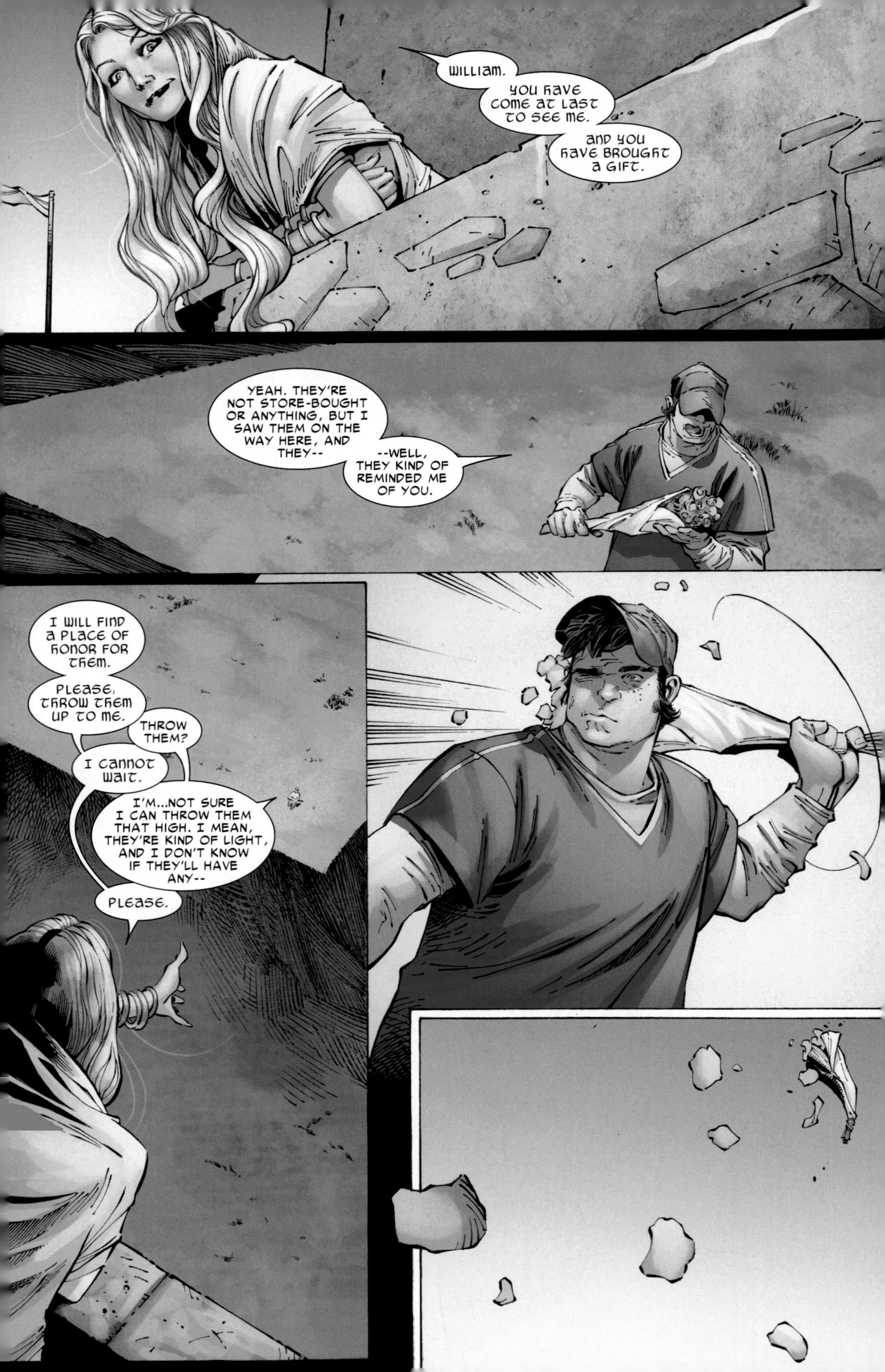

WILLIAM.
YOU HAVE COME AT LAST TO SEE ME.
AND YOU HAVE BROUGHT A GIFT.
YEAH. THEY'RE NOT STORE-BOUGHT OR ANYTHING, BUT I SAW THEM ON THE WAY HERE, AND THEY--
--WELL, THEY KIND OF REMINDED ME OF YOU.
I WILL FIND A PLACE OF HONOR FOR THEM.
PLEASE, THROW THEM UP TO ME.
THROW THEM?
I CANNOT WAIT.
I'M...NOT SURE I CAN THROW THEM THAT HIGH. I MEAN, THEY'RE KIND OF LIGHT, AND I DON'T KNOW IF THEY'LL HAVE ANY--
PLEASE.

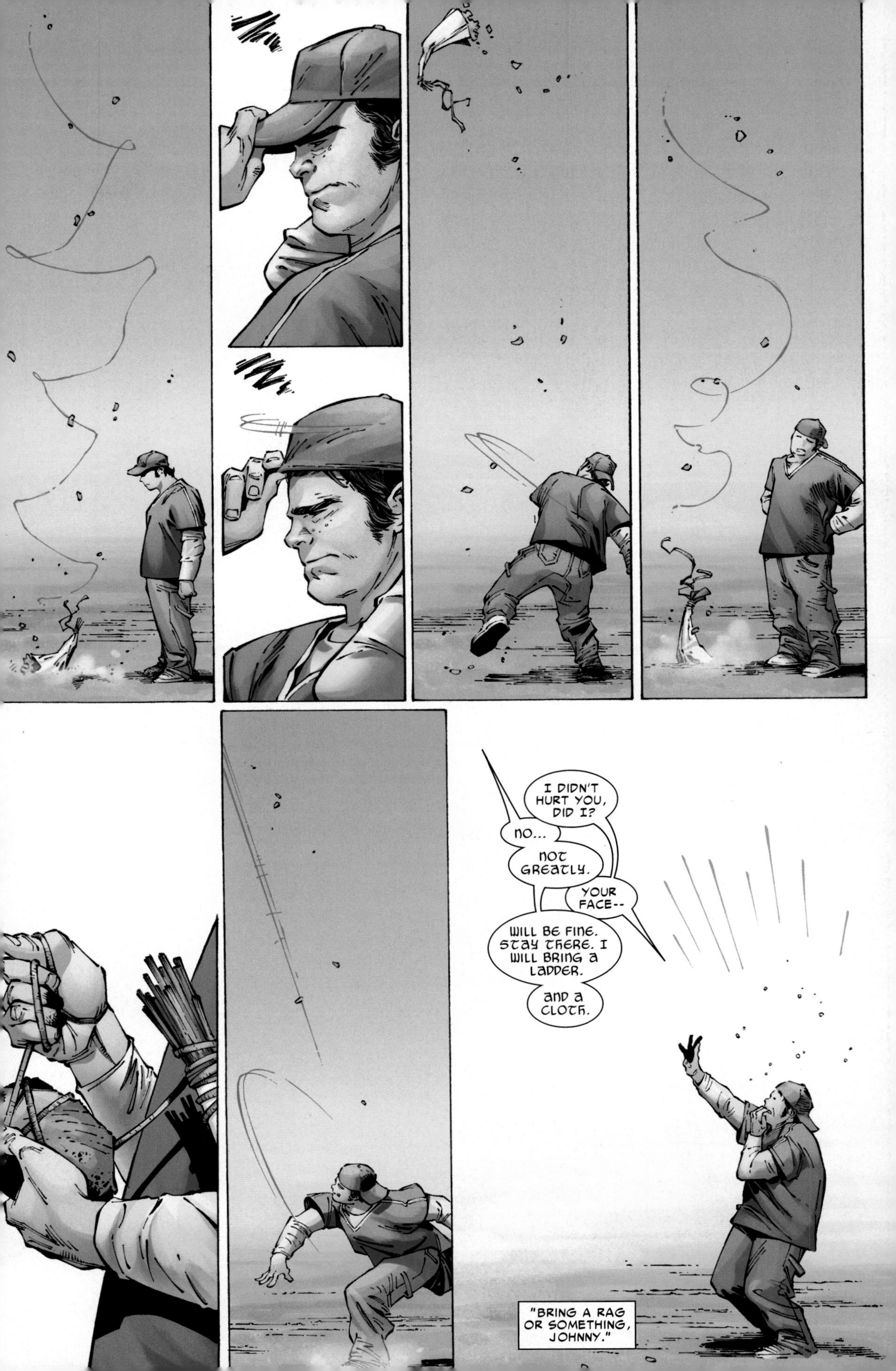
I DIDN'T HURT YOU, DID I?
NO...
NOT GREATLY.
YOUR FACE--
WILL BE FINE. STAY THERE. I WILL BRING A LADDER.
AND A CLOTH.
"BRING A RAG OR SOMETHING, JOHNNY."

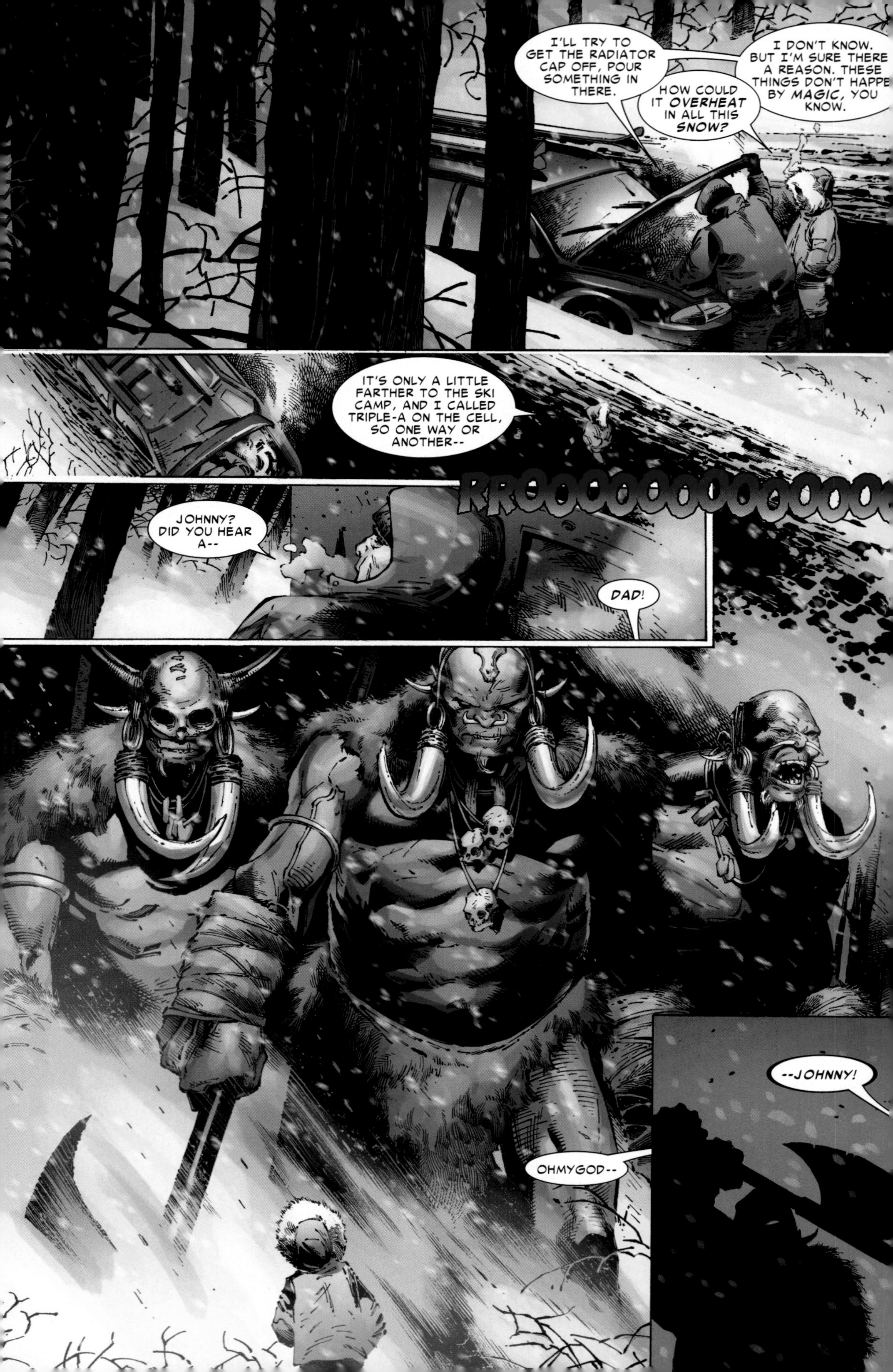

I'LL TRY TO GET THE RADIATOR CAP OFF, POUR SOMETHING IN THERE.
HOW COULD IT OVERHEAT IN ALL THIS SNOW?
I DON'T KNOW. BUT I'M SURE THERE A REASON. THESE THINGS DON'T HAPPE BY MAGIC, YOU KNOW.
IT'S ONLY A LITTLE FARTHER TO THE SKI CAMP, AND I CALLED TRIPLE-A ON THE CELL, SO ONE WAY OR ANOTHER--
RROOOOOOOOOOOOOO
JOHNNY? DID YOU HEAR A--
DAD!
--JOHNNY!
OHMYGOD--

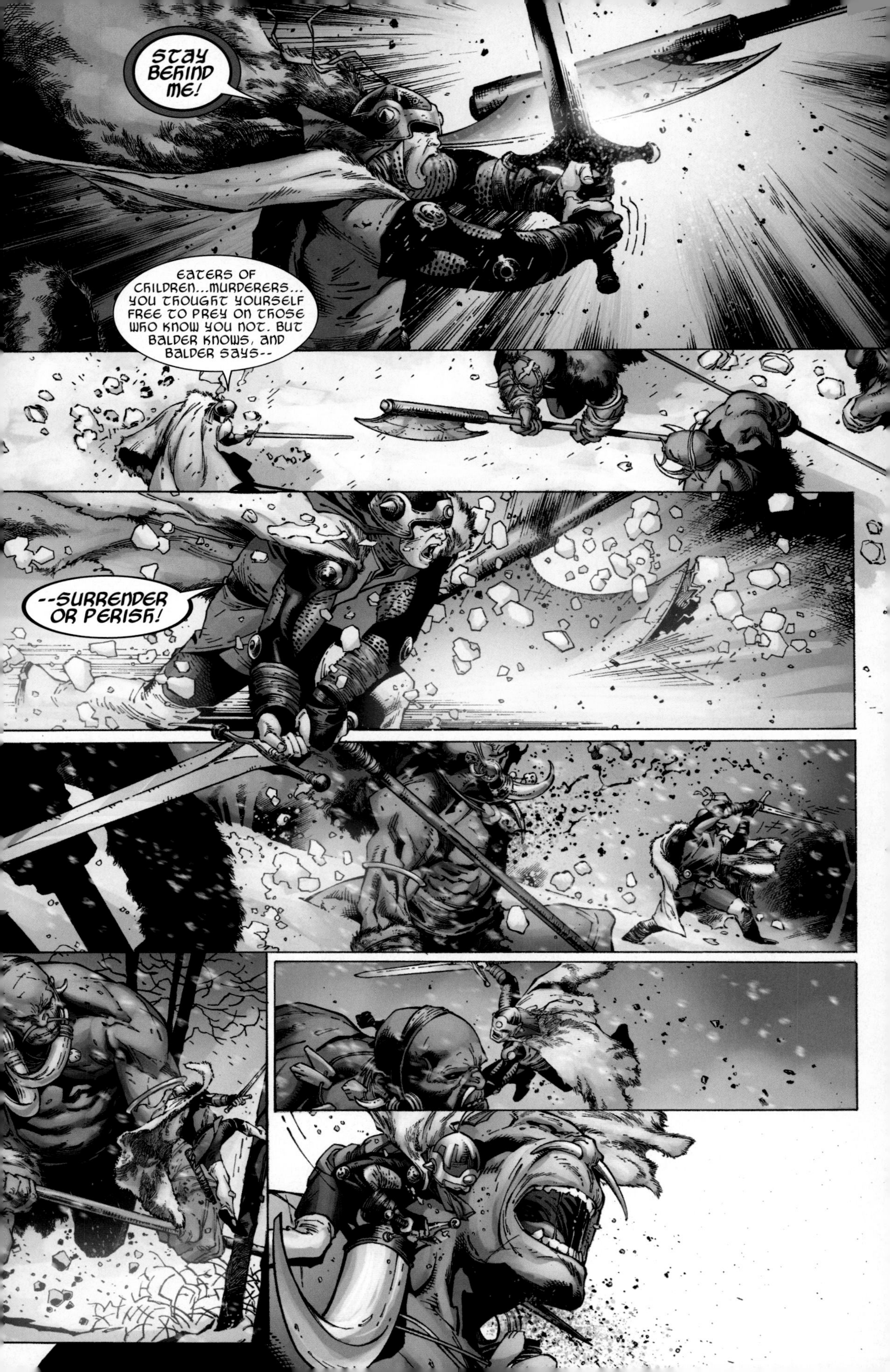
STAY BEHIND ME!
EATERS OF CHILDREN...MURDERERS... YOU THOUGHT YOURSELF FREE TO PREY ON THOSE WHO KNOW YOU NOT. BUT BALDER KNOWS, AND BALDER SAYS--
--SURRENDER OR PERISH!

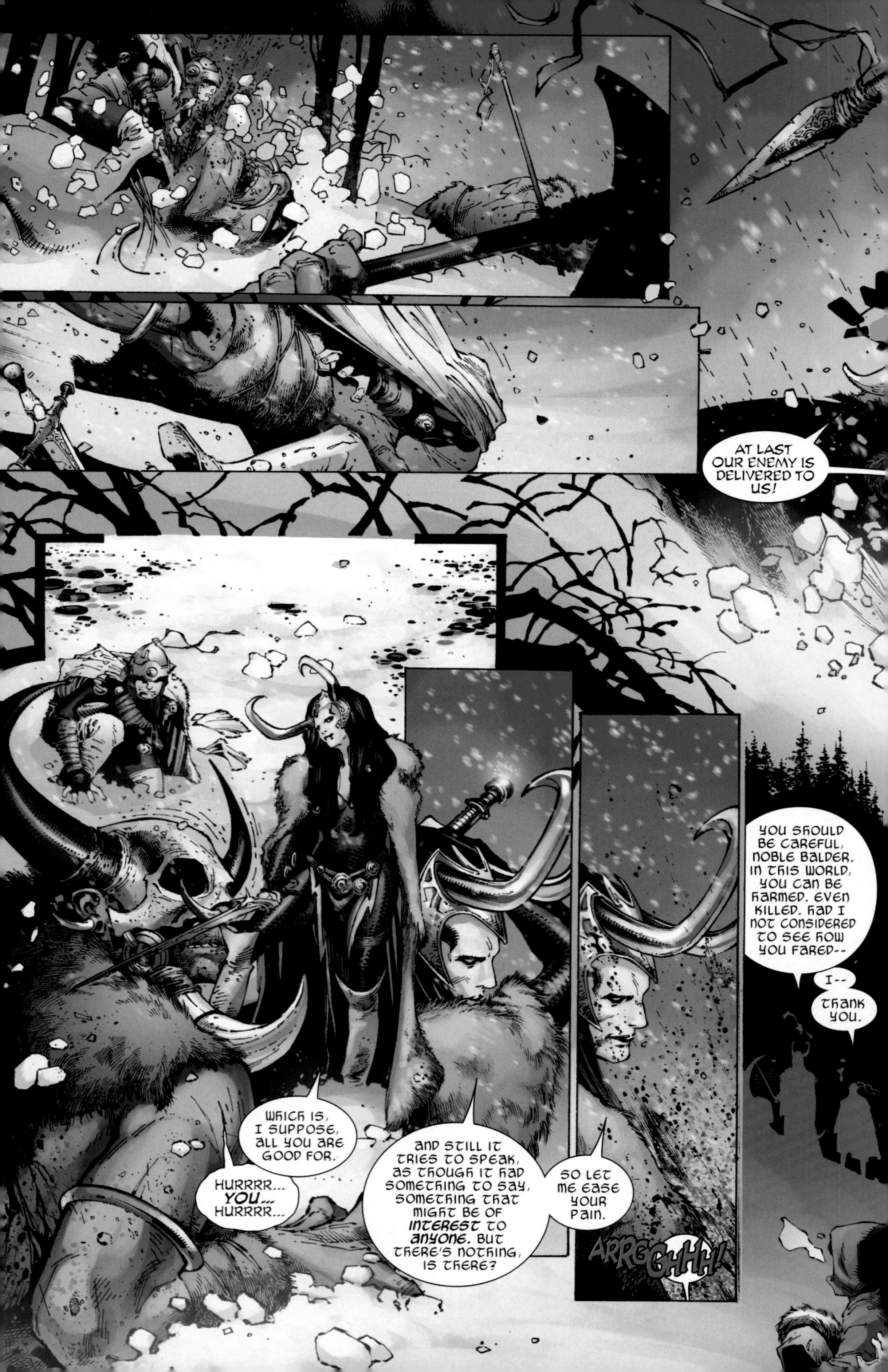
AT LAST OUR ENEMY IS DELIVERED TO US!
YOU SHOULD BE CAREFUL, NOBLE BALDER. IN THIS WORLD, YOU CAN BE HARMED. EVEN KILLED. HAD I NOT CONSIDERED TO SEE HOW YOU FARED--
I--
THANK YOU.
WHICH IS, I SUPPOSE, ALL YOU ARE GOOD FOR.
HURRRR... YOU... HURRRR...
AND STILL IT TRIES TO SPEAK, AS THOUGH IT HAD SOMETHING TO SAY, SOMETHING THAT MIGHT BE OF INTEREST TO ANYONE. BUT THERE'S NOTHING, IS THERE?
SO LET ME EASE YOUR PAIN.
ARRGGHHH!

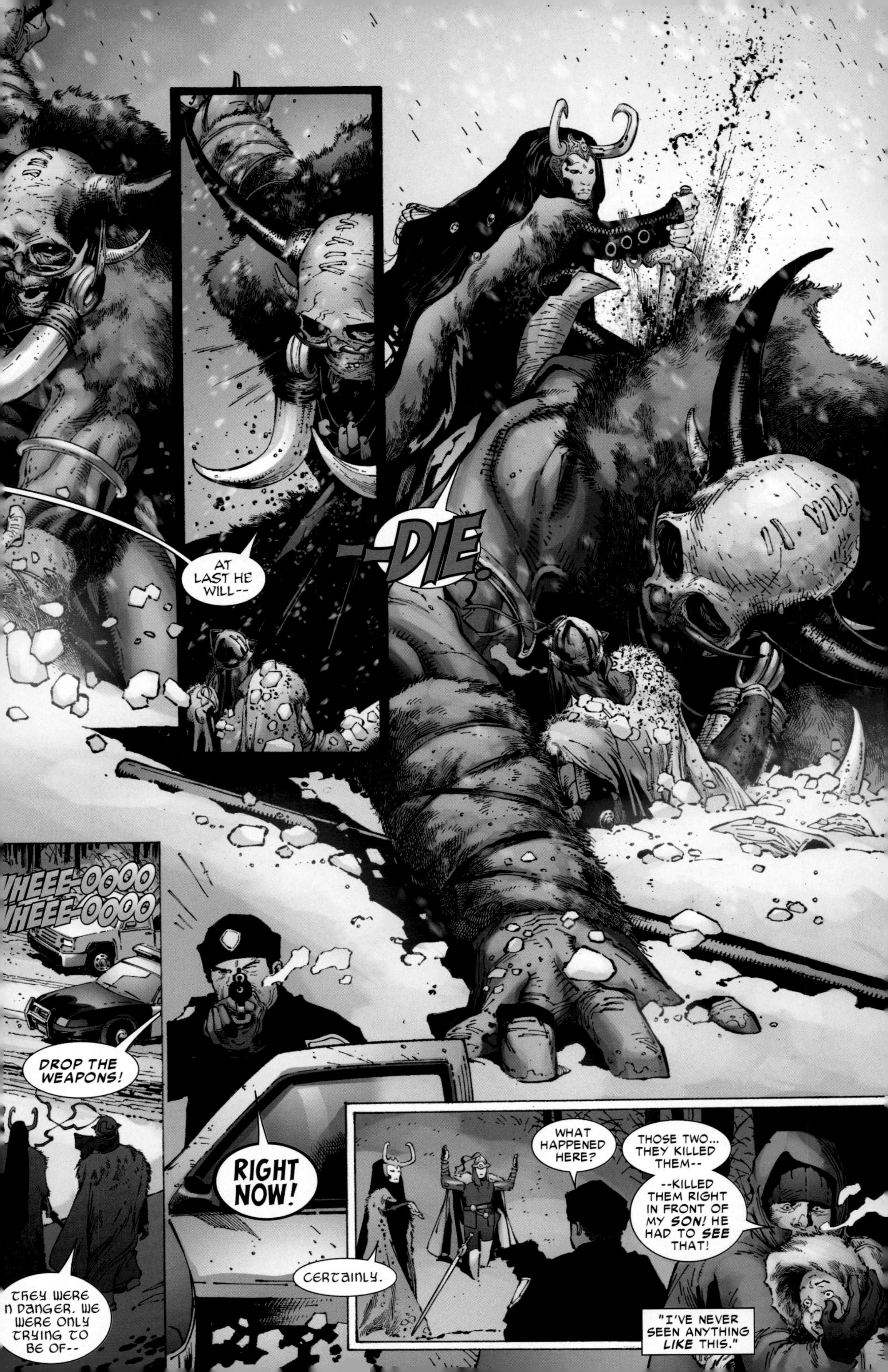
AT LAST HE WILL--
--DIE
WHEEE-OOOO WHEEE-OOOO
DROP THE WEAPONS!
RIGHT NOW!
THEY WERE N DANGER. WE WERE ONLY TRYING TO BE OF--
CERTAINLY.
WHAT HAPPENED HERE?
THOSE TWO... THEY KILLED THEM--
--KILLED THEM RIGHT IN FRONT OF MY SON! HE HAD TO SEE THAT!
"I'VE NEVER SEEN ANYTHING LIKE THIS."

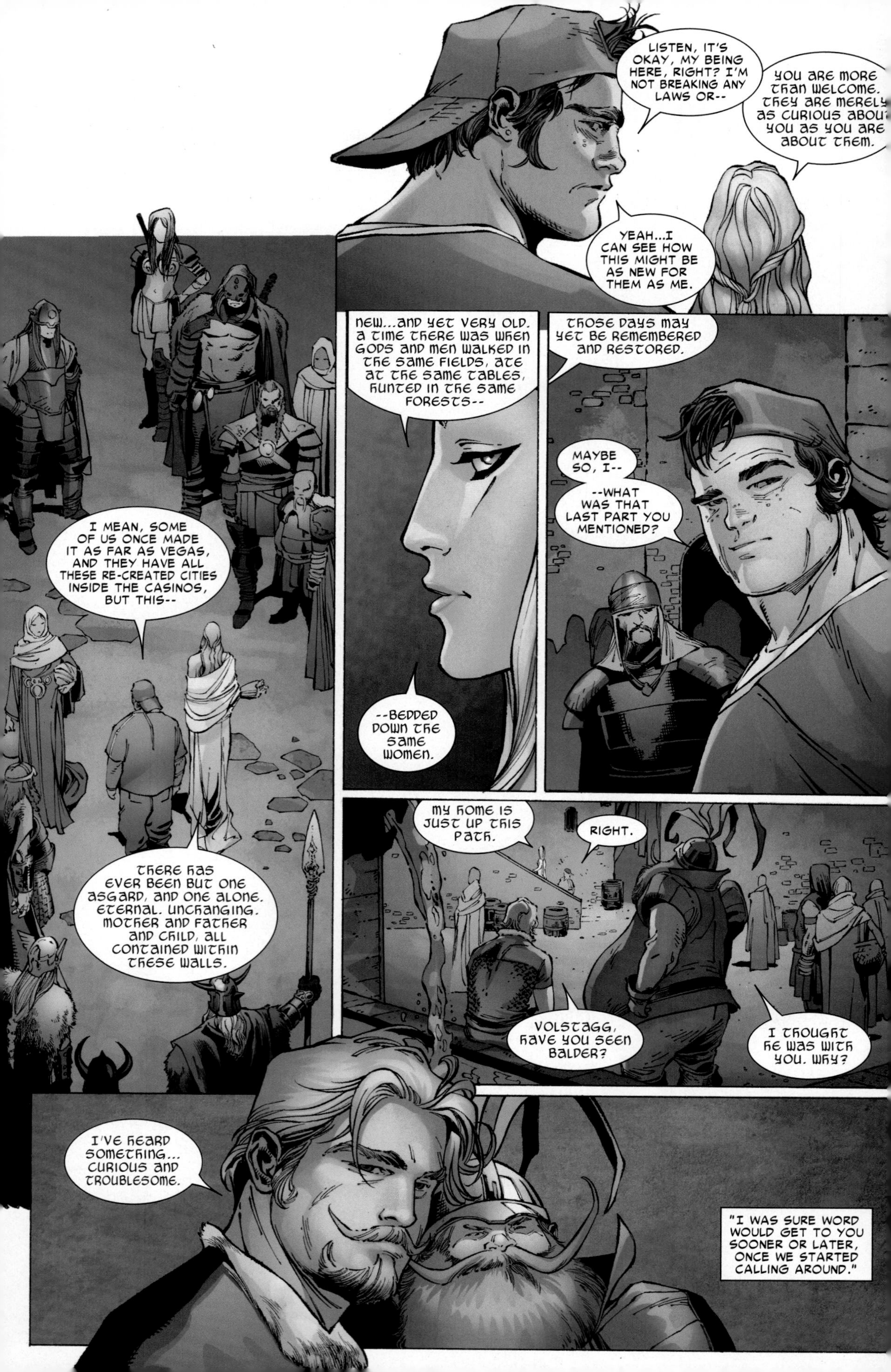

LISTEN, IT'S OKAY, MY BEING HERE, RIGHT? I'M NOT BREAKING ANY LAWS OR--
YOU ARE MORE THAN WELCOME. THEY ARE MERELY AS CURIOUS ABOUT YOU AS YOU ARE ABOUT THEM.
YEAH...I CAN SEE HOW THIS MIGHT BE AS NEW FOR THEM AS ME.
I MEAN, SOME OF US ONCE MADE IT AS FAR AS VEGAS, AND THEY HAVE ALL THESE RE-CREATED CITIES INSIDE THE CASINOS, BUT THIS--
THERE HAS EVER BEEN BUT ONE ASGARD, AND ONE ALONE. ETERNAL. UNCHANGING. MOTHER AND FATHER AND CHILD, ALL CONTAINED WITHIN THESE WALLS.
NEW...AND YET VERY OLD. A TIME THERE WAS WHEN GODS AND MEN WALKED IN THE SAME FIELDS, ATE AT THE SAME TABLES, HUNTED IN THE SAME FORESTS--
--BEDDED DOWN THE SAME WOMEN.
THOSE DAYS MAY YET BE REMEMBERED AND RESTORED.
MAYBE SO, I--
--WHAT WAS THAT LAST PART YOU MENTIONED?
MY HOME IS JUST UP THIS PATH.
RIGHT.
VOLSTAGG, HAVE YOU SEEN BALDER?
I THOUGHT HE WAS WITH YOU. WHY?
I'VE HEARD SOMETHING... CURIOUS AND TROUBLESOME.
"I WAS SURE WORD WOULD GET TO YOU SOONER OR LATER, ONCE WE STARTED CALLING AROUND."

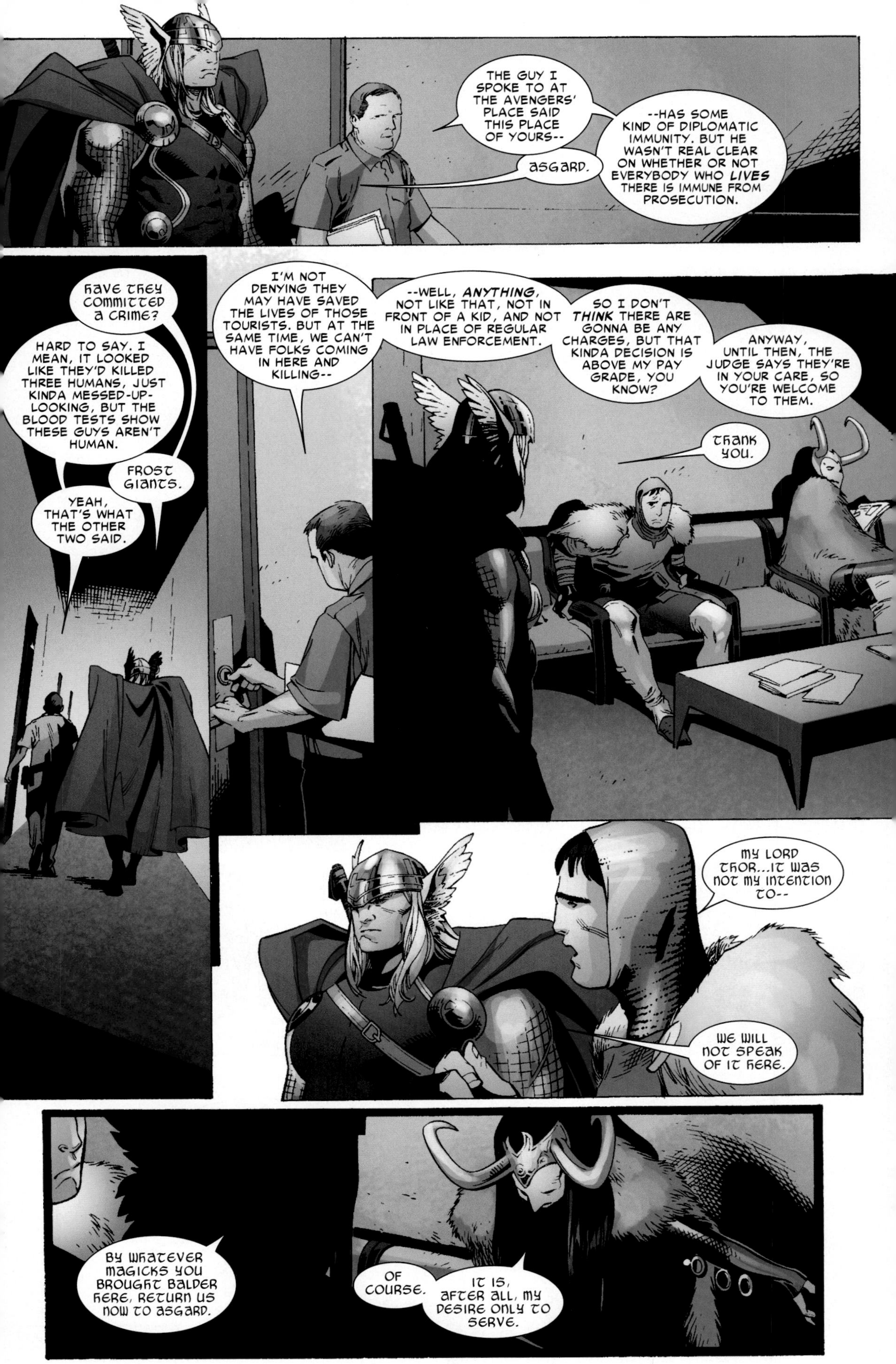
THE GUY I SPOKE TO AT THE AVENGERS' PLACE SAID THIS PLACE OF YOURS--
ASGARD.
--HAS SOME KIND OF DIPLOMATIC IMMUNITY. BUT HE WASN'T REAL CLEAR ON WHETHER OR NOT EVERYBODY WHO LIVES THERE IS IMMUNE FROM PROSECUTION.
HAVE THEY COMMITTED A CRIME?
HARD TO SAY. I MEAN, IT LOOKED LIKE THEY'D KILLED THREE HUMANS, JUST KINDA MESSED-UP-LOOKING, BUT THE BLOOD TESTS SHOW THESE GUYS AREN'T HUMAN.
FROST GIANTS.
YEAH, THAT'S WHAT THE OTHER TWO SAID.
I'M NOT DENYING THEY MAY HAVE SAVED THE LIVES OF THOSE TOURISTS. BUT AT THE SAME TIME, WE CAN'T HAVE FOLKS COMING IN HERE AND KILLING--
--WELL, ANYTHING, NOT LIKE THAT, NOT IN FRONT OF A KID, AND NOT IN PLACE OF REGULAR LAW ENFORCEMENT.
SO I DON'T THINK THERE ARE GONNA BE ANY CHARGES, BUT THAT KINDA DECISION IS ABOVE MY PAY GRADE, YOU KNOW?
ANYWAY, UNTIL THEN, THE JUDGE SAYS THEY'RE IN YOUR CARE, SO YOU'RE WELCOME TO THEM.
THANK YOU.
MY LORD THOR...IT WAS NOT MY INTENTION TO--
WE WILL NOT SPEAK OF IT HERE.
BY WHATEVER MAGICKS YOU BROUGHT BALDER HERE, RETURN US NOW TO ASGARD.
OF COURSE.
IT IS, AFTER ALL, MY DESIRE ONLY TO SERVE.

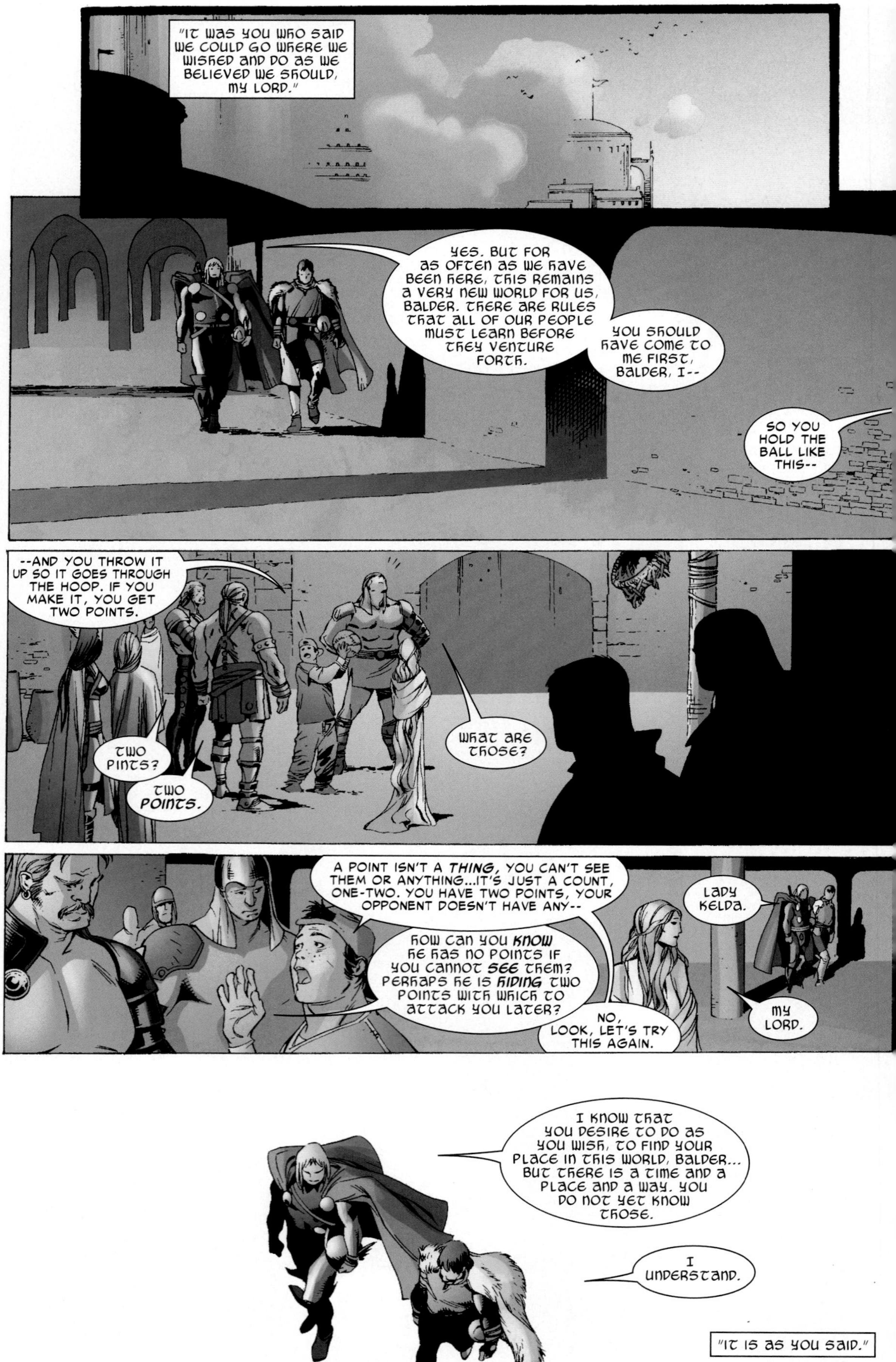
"IT WAS YOU WHO SAID WE COULD GO WHERE WE WISHED AND DO AS WE BELIEVED WE SHOULD, MY LORD."
YES. BUT FOR AS OFTEN AS WE HAVE BEEN HERE, THIS REMAINS A VERY NEW WORLD FOR US, BALDER. THERE ARE RULES THAT ALL OF OUR PEOPLE MUST LEARN BEFORE THEY VENTURE FORTH.
YOU SHOULD HAVE COME TO ME FIRST, BALDER, I--
SO YOU HOLD THE BALL LIKE THIS--
--AND YOU THROW IT UP SO IT GOES THROUGH THE HOOP. IF YOU MAKE IT, YOU GET TWO POINTS.
TWO PINTS?
TWO POINTS.
WHAT ARE THOSE?
A POINT ISN'T A THING, YOU CAN'T SEE THEM OR ANYTHING...IT'S JUST A COUNT, ONE-TWO. YOU HAVE TWO POINTS, YOUR OPPONENT DOESN'T HAVE ANY--
HOW CAN YOU KNOW HE HAS NO POINTS IF YOU CANNOT SEE THEM? PERHAPS HE IS HIDING TWO POINTS WITH WHICH TO ATTACK YOU LATER?
NO, LOOK, LET'S TRY THIS AGAIN.
LADY KELDA.
MY LORD.
I KNOW THAT YOU DESIRE TO DO AS YOU WISH, TO FIND YOUR PLACE IN THIS WORLD, BALDER... BUT THERE IS A TIME AND A PLACE AND A WAY. YOU DO NOT YET KNOW THOSE.
I UNDERSTAND.
"IT IS AS YOU SAID."

HE SAYS WE ARE FREE TO CREATE OUR OWN FUTURES, TO FIND OUR OWN WAYS, BUT HE WANTS US TO DO THEM IN *HIS* WAY, AS HE TELLS US, AND--

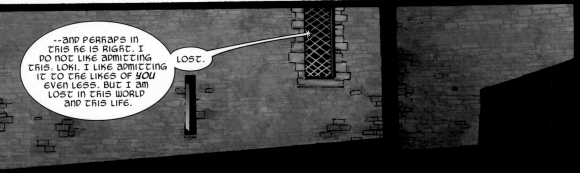

--AND PERHAPS IN THIS HE IS RIGHT. I DO NOT LIKE ADMITTING THIS, LOKI. I LIKE ADMITTING IT TO THE LIKES OF *YOU* EVEN LESS. BUT I AM LOST IN THIS WORLD AND THIS LIFE.

LOST.

YES. BUT YOU HAVE *EVER* BEEN LOST, HAVE YOU NOT, NOBLE BALDER?

WHAT ARE YOU--

YOUR FATHER, KILLED BY FROST GIANTS, YOUR ROLE, YOUR *PLACE* DETERMINED BY OTHERS THAN YOURSELF. ALWAYS HAS BALDER BEEN AT THE SERVICE OF FORCES BEYOND HIMSELF--

--FOR BALDER HAS NEVER KNOWN, IN HIS HEART, WHO *HE* WAS.

I KNOW WHO I AM.

I AM BALDER.

I SERVE MY LORD THOR IN ALL THAT HE DOES.

AND WHY DO YOU SERVE HIM?

BECAUSE HE IS MY FRIEND. BUT GREATER STILL, THOR IS THE SON OF ODIN, A PRINCE OF THE REALM, AND RIGHTWISE KING OF ASGARD.

SO YOU MAKE *ALLEGIANCE* TO THOR BECAUSE HE IS YOUR *FRIEND,* BUT HE HAS YOUR *LOYALTY* BECAUSE HE IS ODIN'S SON, AND THUS IS *ENTITLED* TO THE CROWN AND *ENTITLED* TO YOUR LOYALTY.

YES.

BUT DEAR, NOBLE BALDER, WHAT IF I WERE TO SAY TO YOU THAT YOUR FATHER WAS *NOT* KILLED BY FROST GIANTS?

WHAT IF I WERE TO SAY TO YOU--

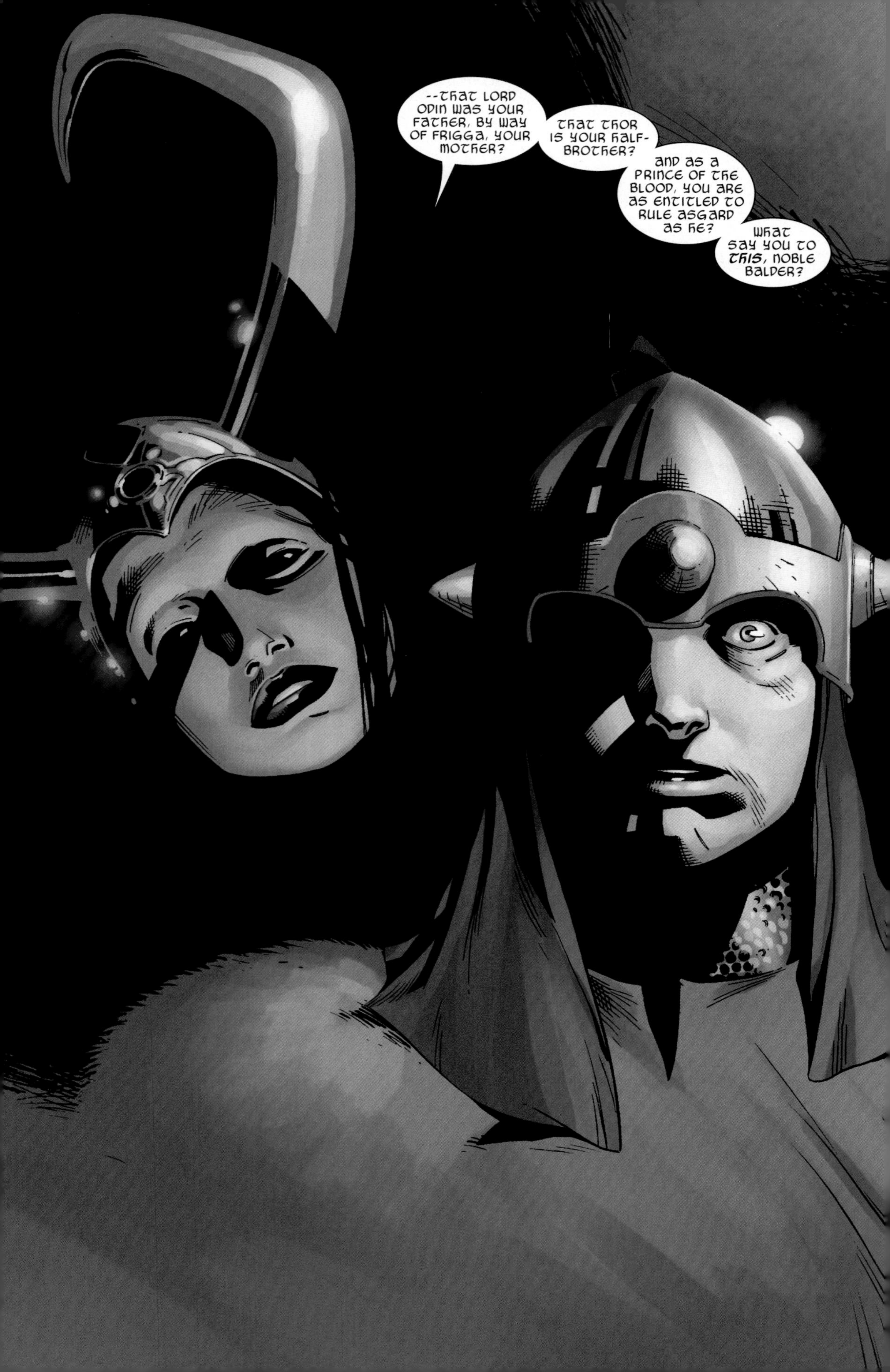
--THAT LORD ODIN WAS YOUR FATHER, BY WAY OF FRIGGA, YOUR MOTHER?
THAT THOR IS YOUR HALF-BROTHER?
AND AS A PRINCE OF THE BLOOD, YOU ARE AS ENTITLED TO RULE ASGARD AS HE?
WHAT SAY YOU TO *THIS*, NOBLE BALDER?

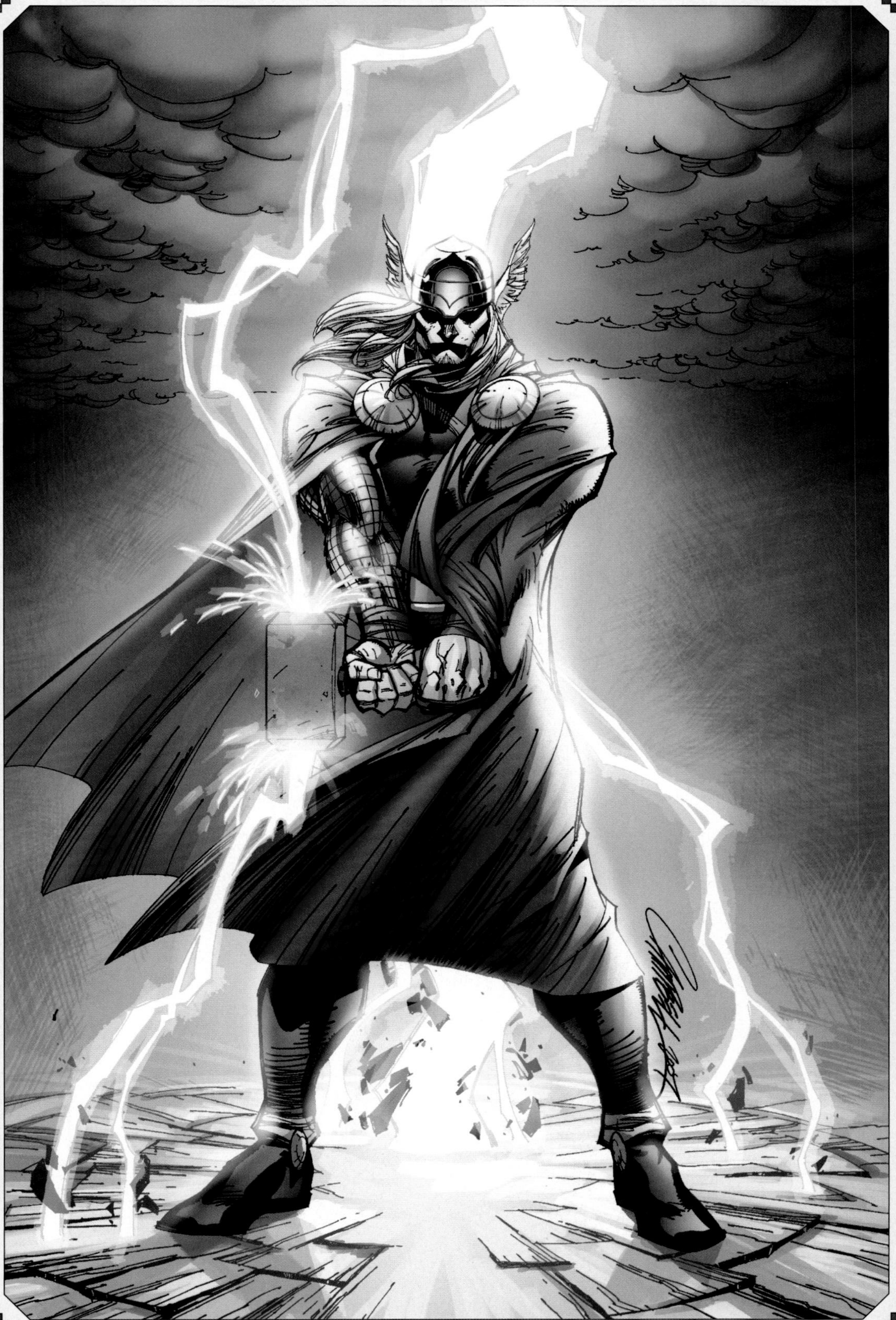

Thor #5 variant by J. Scott Campbell & Laura Martin

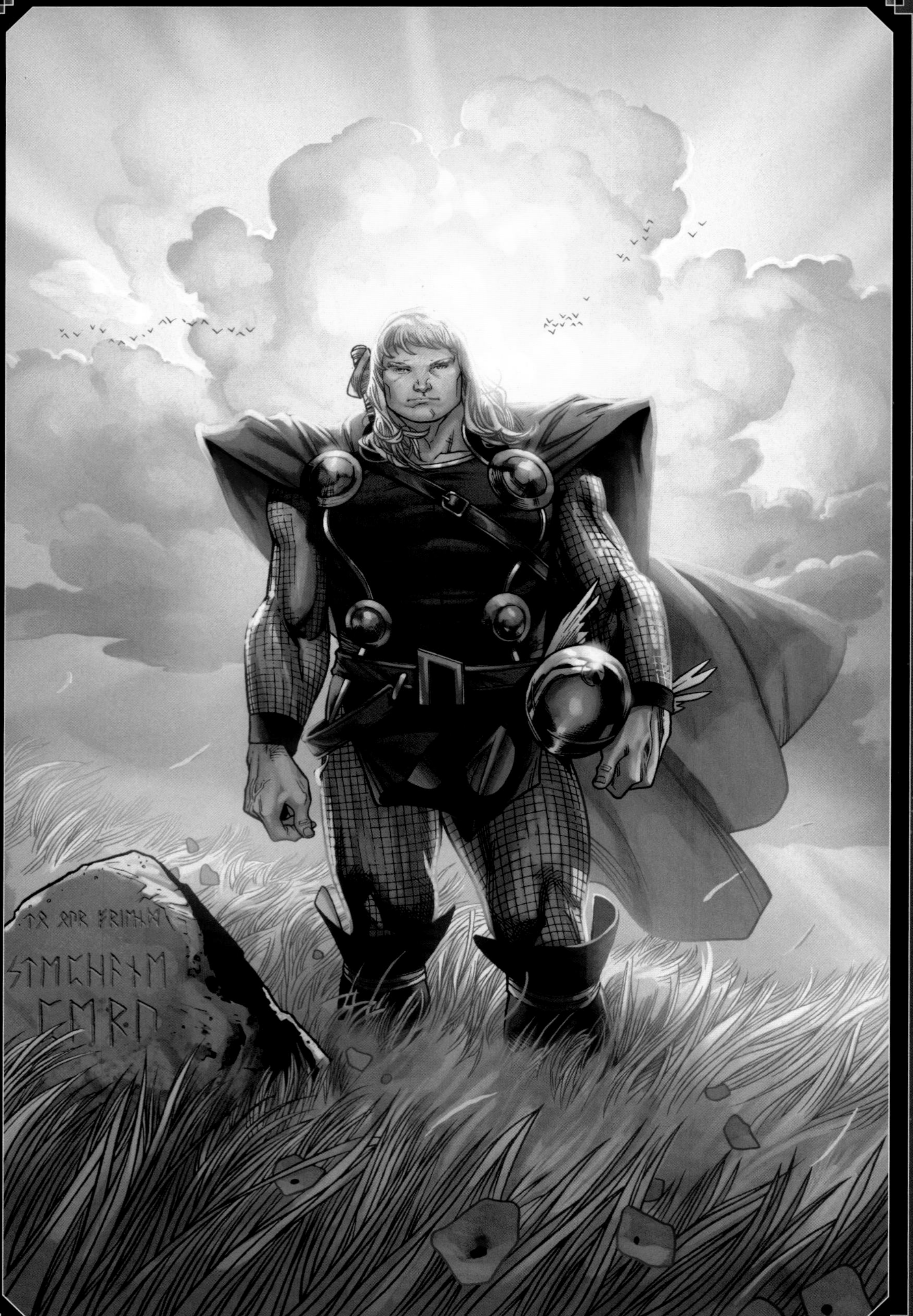

THOR #10

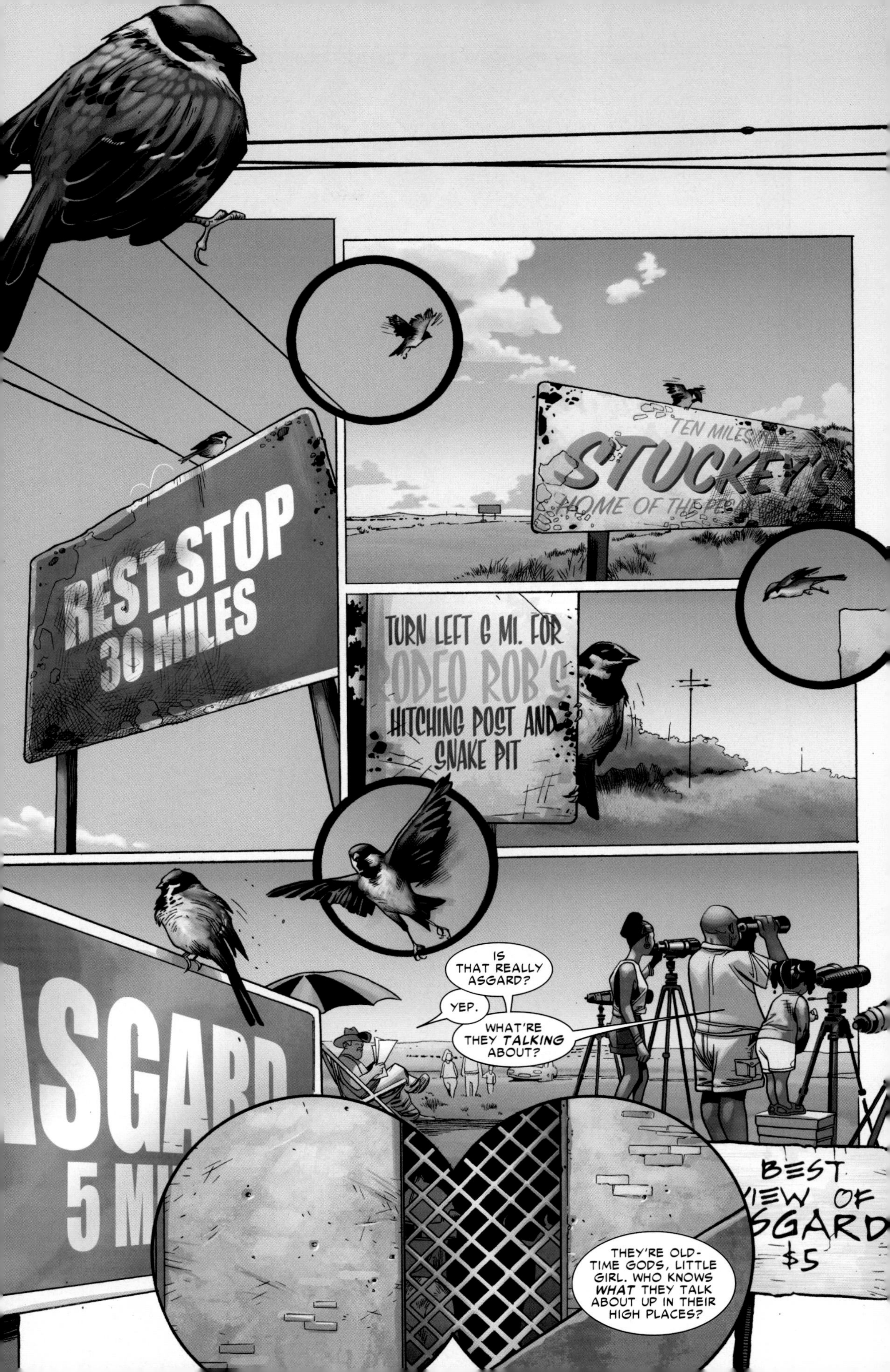

REST STOP
30 MILES
TEN MILES
STUCKEY'S
HOME OF THE PE
TURN LEFT 6 MI. FOR
ODEO ROB'S
HITCHING POST AND
SNAKE PIT
SGARD
5 MI
IS THAT REALLY ASGARD?
YEP.
WHAT'RE THEY *TALKING* ABOUT?
BEST
IEW OF
SGARD
$5
THEY'RE OLD-TIME GODS, LITTLE GIRL. WHO KNOWS *WHAT* THEY TALK ABOUT UP IN THEIR HIGH PLACES?

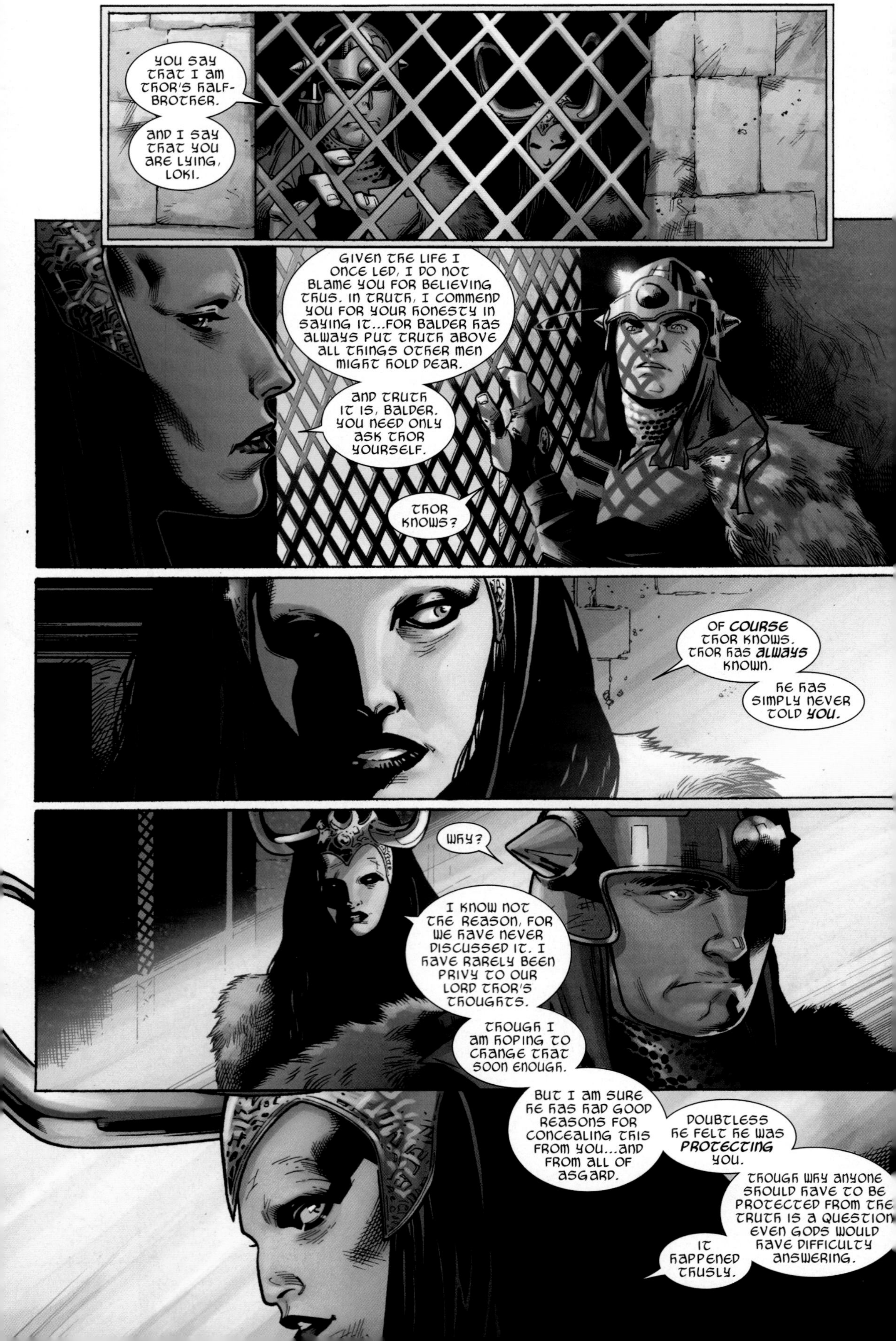
YOU SAY THAT I AM THOR'S HALF-BROTHER.
AND I SAY THAT YOU ARE LYING, LOKI.
GIVEN THE LIFE I ONCE LED, I DO NOT BLAME YOU FOR BELIEVING THUS. IN TRUTH, I COMMEND YOU FOR YOUR HONESTY IN SAYING IT...FOR BALDER HAS ALWAYS PUT TRUTH ABOVE ALL THINGS OTHER MEN MIGHT HOLD DEAR.
AND TRUTH IT IS, BALDER. YOU NEED ONLY ASK THOR YOURSELF.
THOR KNOWS?
OF COURSE THOR KNOWS. THOR HAS ALWAYS KNOWN.
HE HAS SIMPLY NEVER TOLD YOU.
WHY?
I KNOW NOT THE REASON, FOR WE HAVE NEVER DISCUSSED IT. I HAVE RARELY BEEN PRIVY TO OUR LORD THOR'S THOUGHTS.
THOUGH I AM HOPING TO CHANGE THAT SOON ENOUGH.
BUT I AM SURE HE HAS HAD GOOD REASONS FOR CONCEALING THIS FROM YOU...AND FROM ALL OF ASGARD.
DOUBTLESS HE FELT HE WAS PROTECTING YOU.
THOUGH WHY ANYONE SHOULD HAVE TO BE PROTECTED FROM THE TRUTH IS A QUESTION EVEN GODS WOULD HAVE DIFFICULTY ANSWERING.
IT HAPPENED THUSLY.

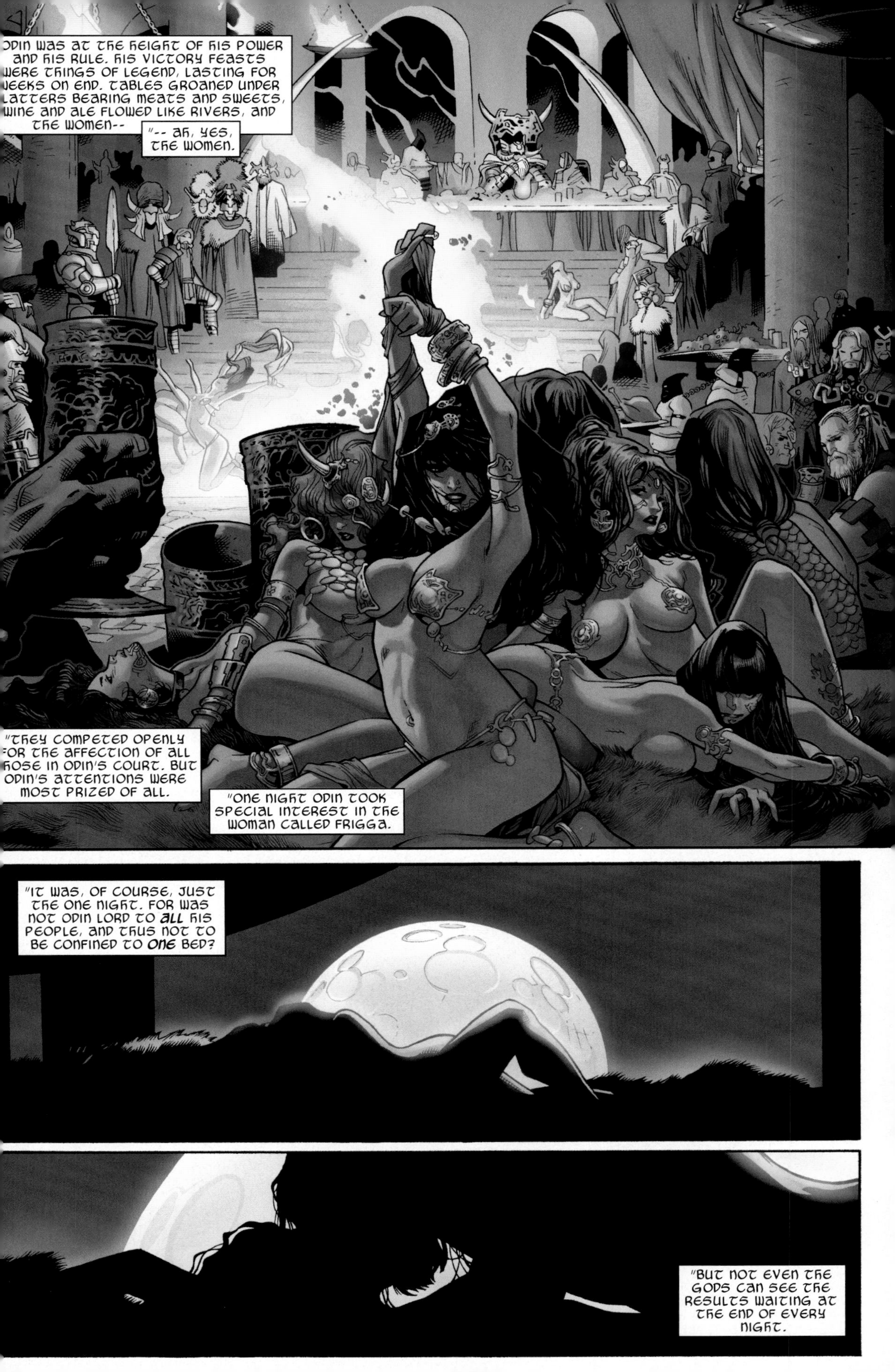
ODIN WAS AT THE HEIGHT OF HIS POWER AND HIS RULE. HIS VICTORY FEASTS WERE THINGS OF LEGEND, LASTING FOR WEEKS ON END. TABLES GROANED UNDER LATTERS BEARING MEATS AND SWEETS, WINE AND ALE FLOWED LIKE RIVERS, AND THE WOMEN--
"-- AH, YES, THE WOMEN.
"THEY COMPETED OPENLY FOR THE AFFECTION OF ALL HOSE IN ODIN'S COURT. BUT ODIN'S ATTENTIONS WERE MOST PRIZED OF ALL.
"ONE NIGHT ODIN TOOK SPECIAL INTEREST IN THE WOMAN CALLED FRIGGA.
"IT WAS, OF COURSE, JUST THE ONE NIGHT. FOR WAS NOT ODIN LORD TO ALL HIS PEOPLE, AND THUS NOT TO BE CONFINED TO ONE BED?
"BUT NOT EVEN THE GODS CAN SEE THE RESULTS WAITING AT THE END OF EVERY NIGHT.

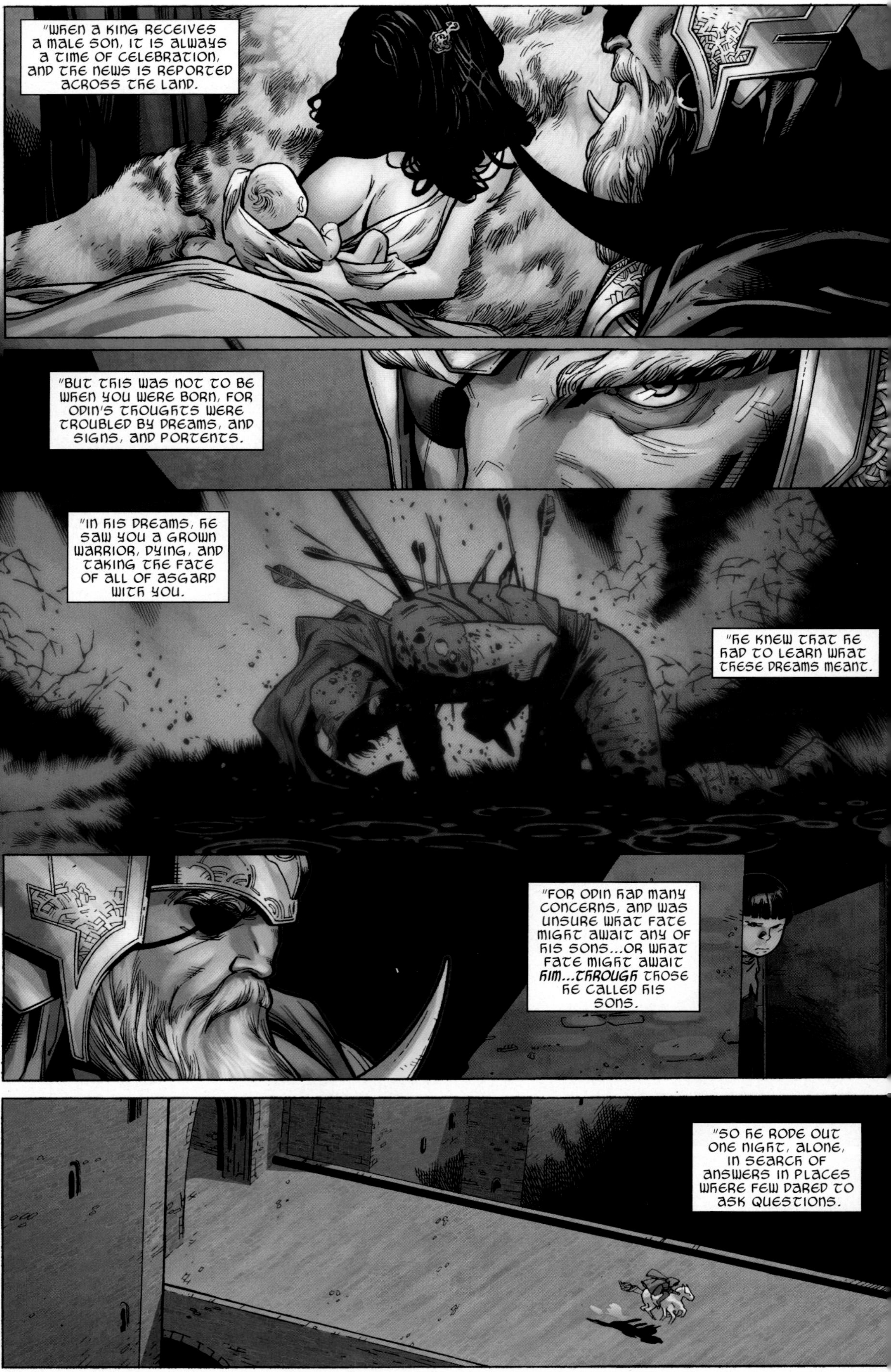
"WHEN A KING RECEIVES A MALE SON, IT IS ALWAYS A TIME OF CELEBRATION, AND THE NEWS IS REPORTED ACROSS THE LAND.
"BUT THIS WAS NOT TO BE WHEN YOU WERE BORN, FOR ODIN'S THOUGHTS WERE TROUBLED BY DREAMS, AND SIGNS, AND PORTENTS.
"IN HIS DREAMS, HE SAW YOU A GROWN WARRIOR, DYING, AND TAKING THE FATE OF ALL OF ASGARD WITH YOU.
"HE KNEW THAT HE HAD TO LEARN WHAT THESE DREAMS MEANT.
"FOR ODIN HAD MANY CONCERNS, AND WAS UNSURE WHAT FATE MIGHT AWAIT ANY OF HIS SONS...OR WHAT FATE MIGHT AWAIT HIM...THROUGH THOSE HE CALLED HIS SONS.
"SO HE RODE OUT ONE NIGHT, ALONE, IN SEARCH OF ANSWERS IN PLACES WHERE FEW DARED TO ASK QUESTIONS.

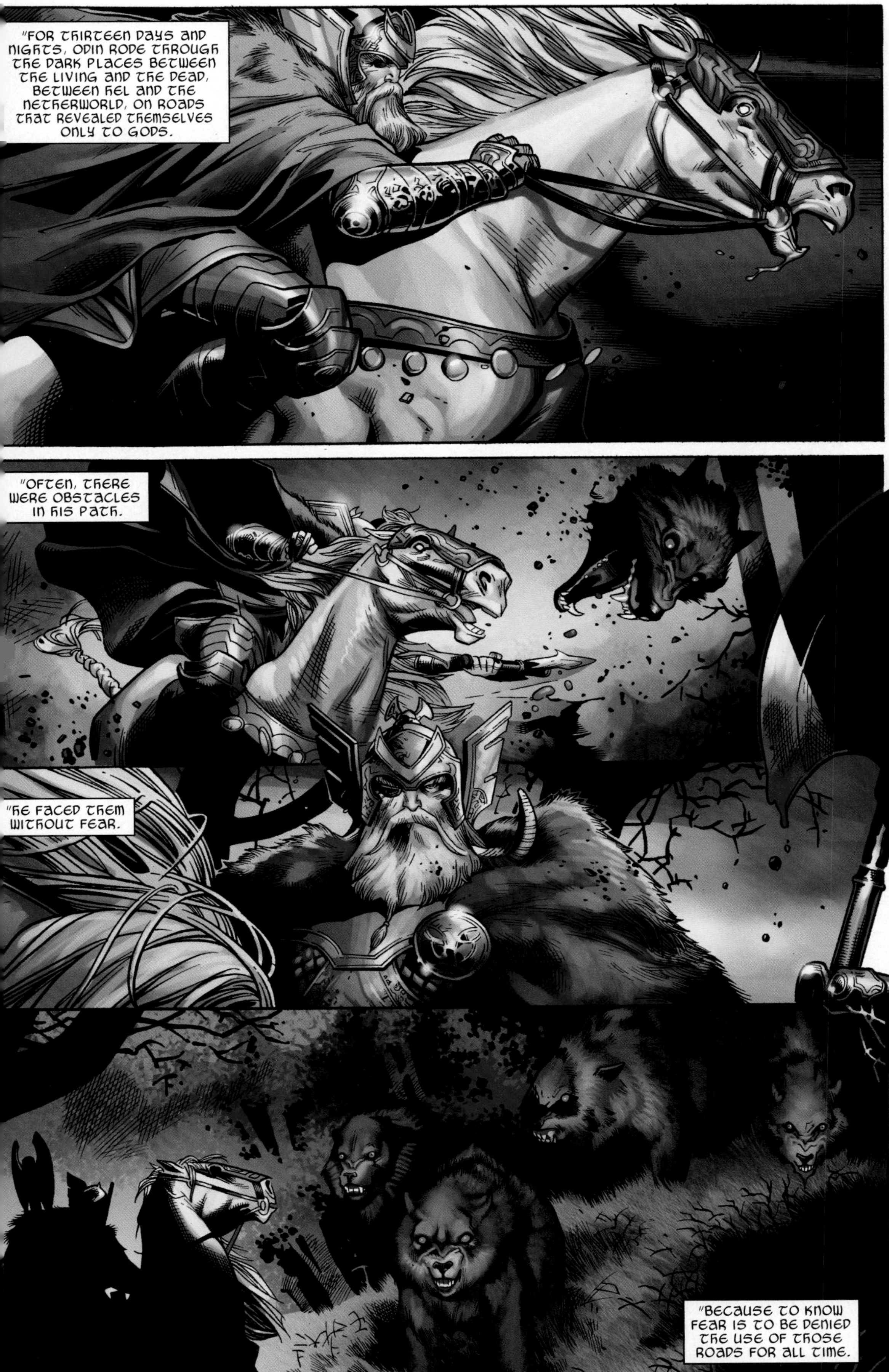
"FOR THIRTEEN DAYS AND NIGHTS, ODIN RODE THROUGH THE DARK PLACES BETWEEN THE LIVING AND THE DEAD, BETWEEN HEL AND THE NETHERWORLD, ON ROADS THAT REVEALED THEMSELVES ONLY TO GODS.
"OFTEN, THERE WERE OBSTACLES IN HIS PATH.
"HE FACED THEM WITHOUT FEAR.
"BECAUSE TO KNOW FEAR IS TO BE DENIED THE USE OF THOSE ROADS FOR ALL TIME.

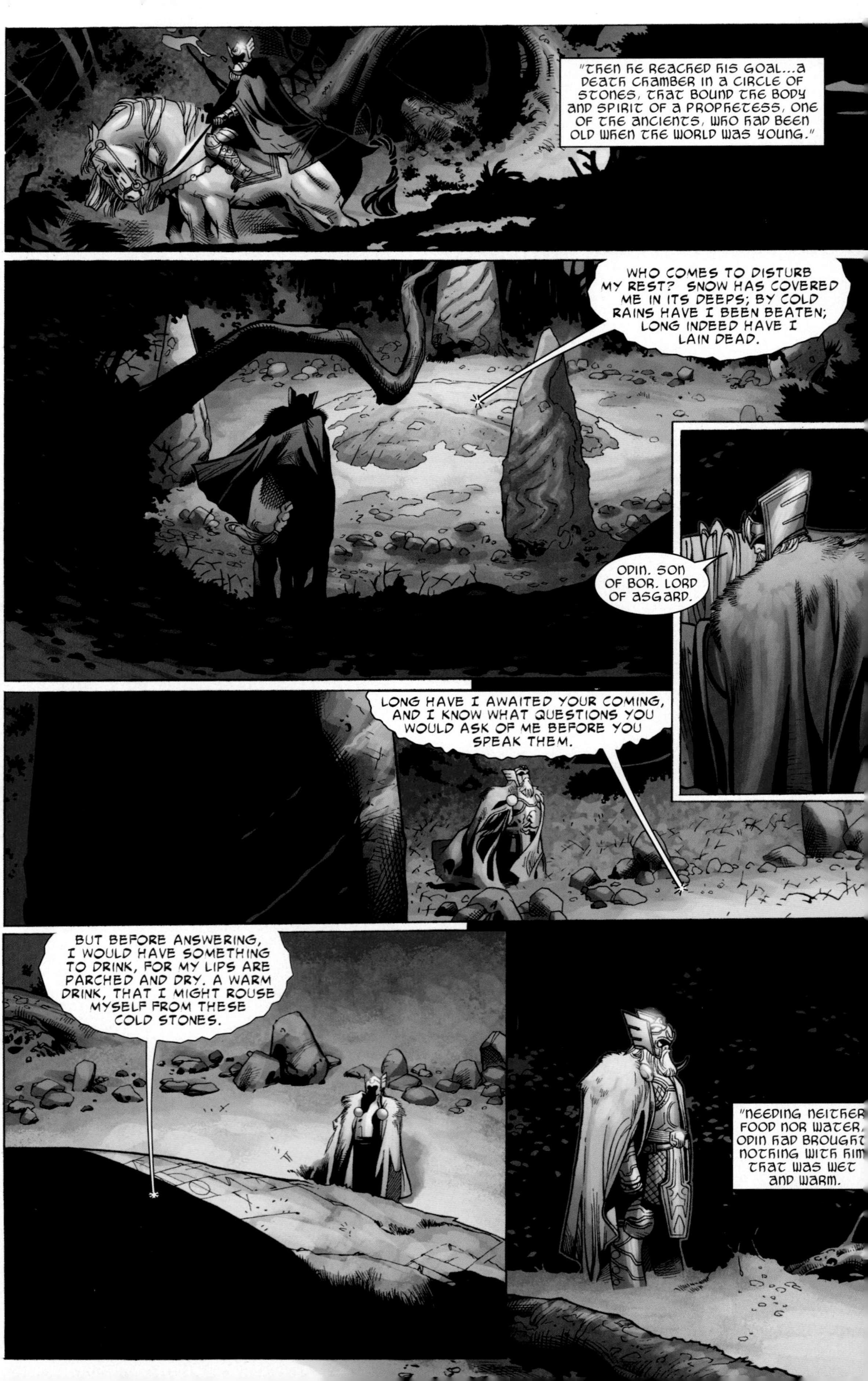
"THEN HE REACHED HIS GOAL...A DEATH CHAMBER IN A CIRCLE OF STONES, THAT BOUND THE BODY AND SPIRIT OF A PROPHETESS, ONE OF THE ANCIENTS, WHO HAD BEEN OLD WHEN THE WORLD WAS YOUNG."
WHO COMES TO DISTURB MY REST? SNOW HAS COVERED ME IN ITS DEEPS; BY COLD RAINS HAVE I BEEN BEATEN; LONG INDEED HAVE I LAIN DEAD.
ODIN. SON OF BOR. LORD OF ASGARD.
LONG HAVE I AWAITED YOUR COMING, AND I KNOW WHAT QUESTIONS YOU WOULD ASK OF ME BEFORE YOU SPEAK THEM.
BUT BEFORE ANSWERING, I WOULD HAVE SOMETHING TO DRINK, FOR MY LIPS ARE PARCHED AND DRY. A WARM DRINK, THAT I MIGHT ROUSE MYSELF FROM THESE COLD STONES.
"NEEDING NEITHER FOOD NOR WATER, ODIN HAD BROUGHT NOTHING WITH HIM THAT WAS WET AND WARM.

"NAUGHT BUT THE WARM BLOOD THAT COURSED THROUGH HIS VEINS.

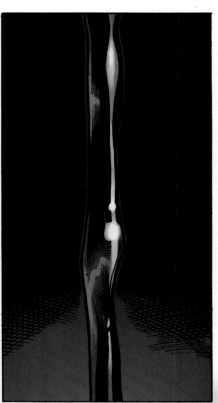

"THE GIFT OF A GOD'S BLOOD TO A RESTLESS SPIRIT OF THE DEAD.

"WHAT WAS BIRTHED IN THAT MOMENT--

--WOULD BECOME THE NIGHTMARE WHOSE CHILDREN STILL HAUNT THE MORTAL WORLD IN SEARCH OF BLOOD."

YOU HAVE FREED ME FROM THIS PLACE AND GIVEN ME STRENGTH, AND GRACE, AND POWER.

I THANK YOU NOW, WITH THE PROPHECY OF YOUR INFANT SON'S LIFE, AND DEATH, AND REBIRTH.

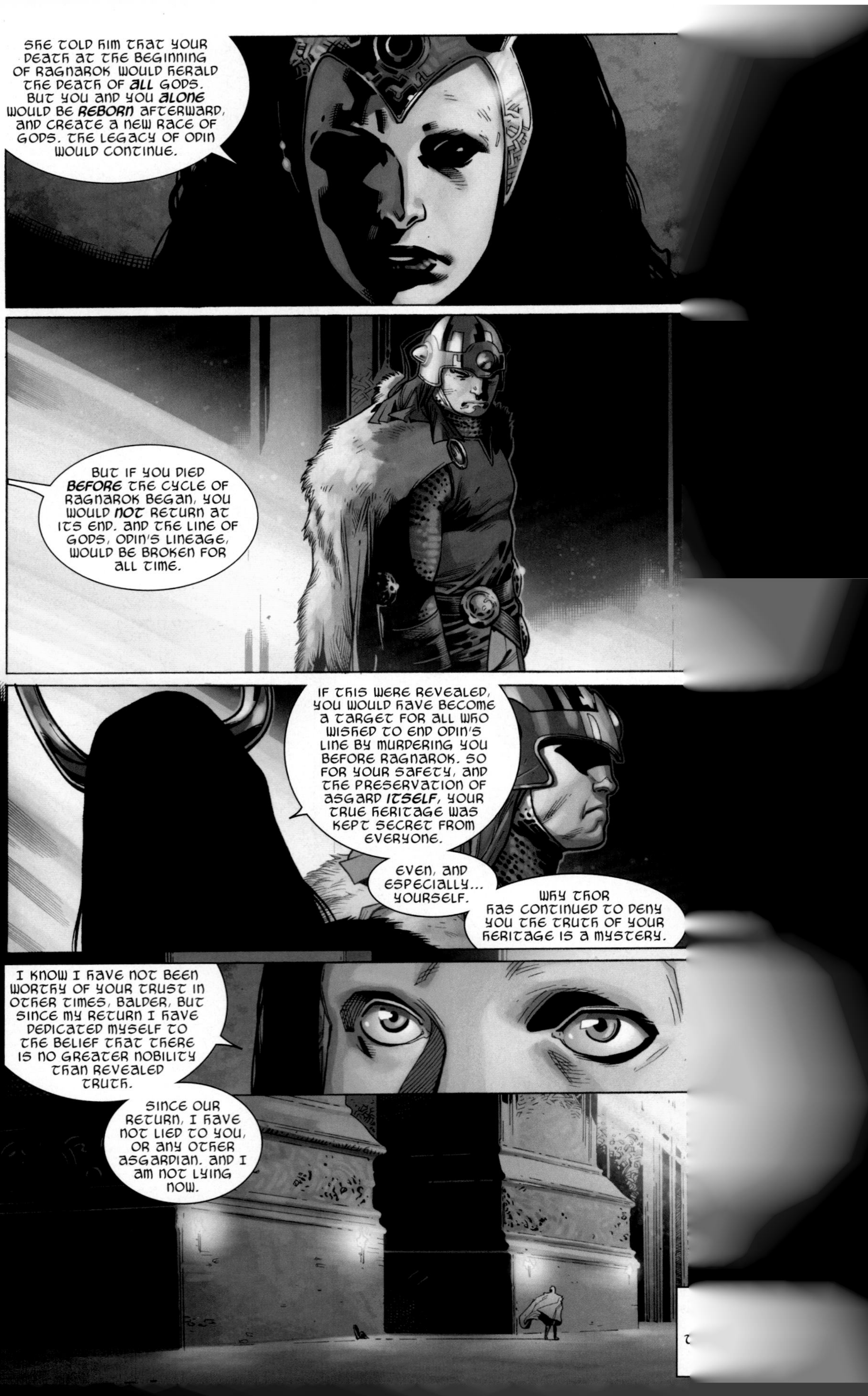
SHE TOLD HIM THAT YOUR DEATH AT THE BEGINNING OF RAGNAROK WOULD HERALD THE DEATH OF ALL GODS. BUT YOU AND YOU ALONE WOULD BE REBORN AFTERWARD, AND CREATE A NEW RACE OF GODS. THE LEGACY OF ODIN WOULD CONTINUE.
BUT IF YOU DIED BEFORE THE CYCLE OF RAGNAROK BEGAN, YOU WOULD NOT RETURN AT ITS END. AND THE LINE OF GODS, ODIN'S LINEAGE, WOULD BE BROKEN FOR ALL TIME.
IF THIS WERE REVEALED, YOU WOULD HAVE BECOME A TARGET FOR ALL WHO WISHED TO END ODIN'S LINE BY MURDERING YOU BEFORE RAGNAROK. SO FOR YOUR SAFETY, AND THE PRESERVATION OF ASGARD ITSELF, YOUR TRUE HERITAGE WAS KEPT SECRET FROM EVERYONE.
EVEN, AND ESPECIALLY... YOURSELF.
WHY THOR HAS CONTINUED TO DENY YOU THE TRUTH OF YOUR HERITAGE IS A MYSTERY.
I KNOW I HAVE NOT BEEN WORTHY OF YOUR TRUST IN OTHER TIMES, BALDER, BUT SINCE MY RETURN I HAVE DEDICATED MYSELF TO THE BELIEF THAT THERE IS NO GREATER NOBILITY THAN REVEALED TRUTH.
SINCE OUR RETURN, I HAVE NOT LIED TO YOU, OR ANY OTHER ASGARDIAN. AND I AM NOT LYING NOW.

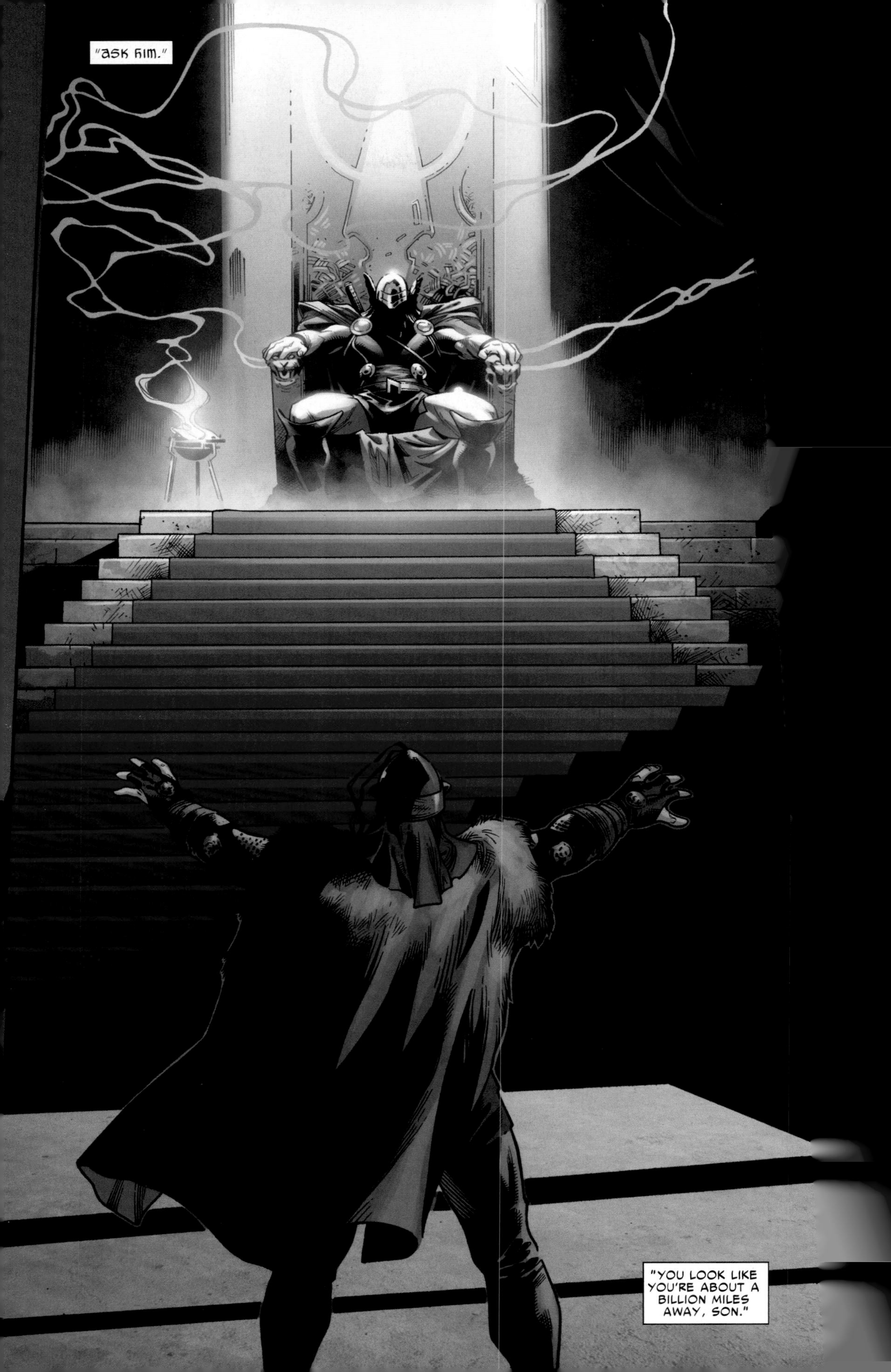
"ASK HIM."
"YOU LOOK LIKE YOU'RE ABOUT A BILLION MILES AWAY, SON."

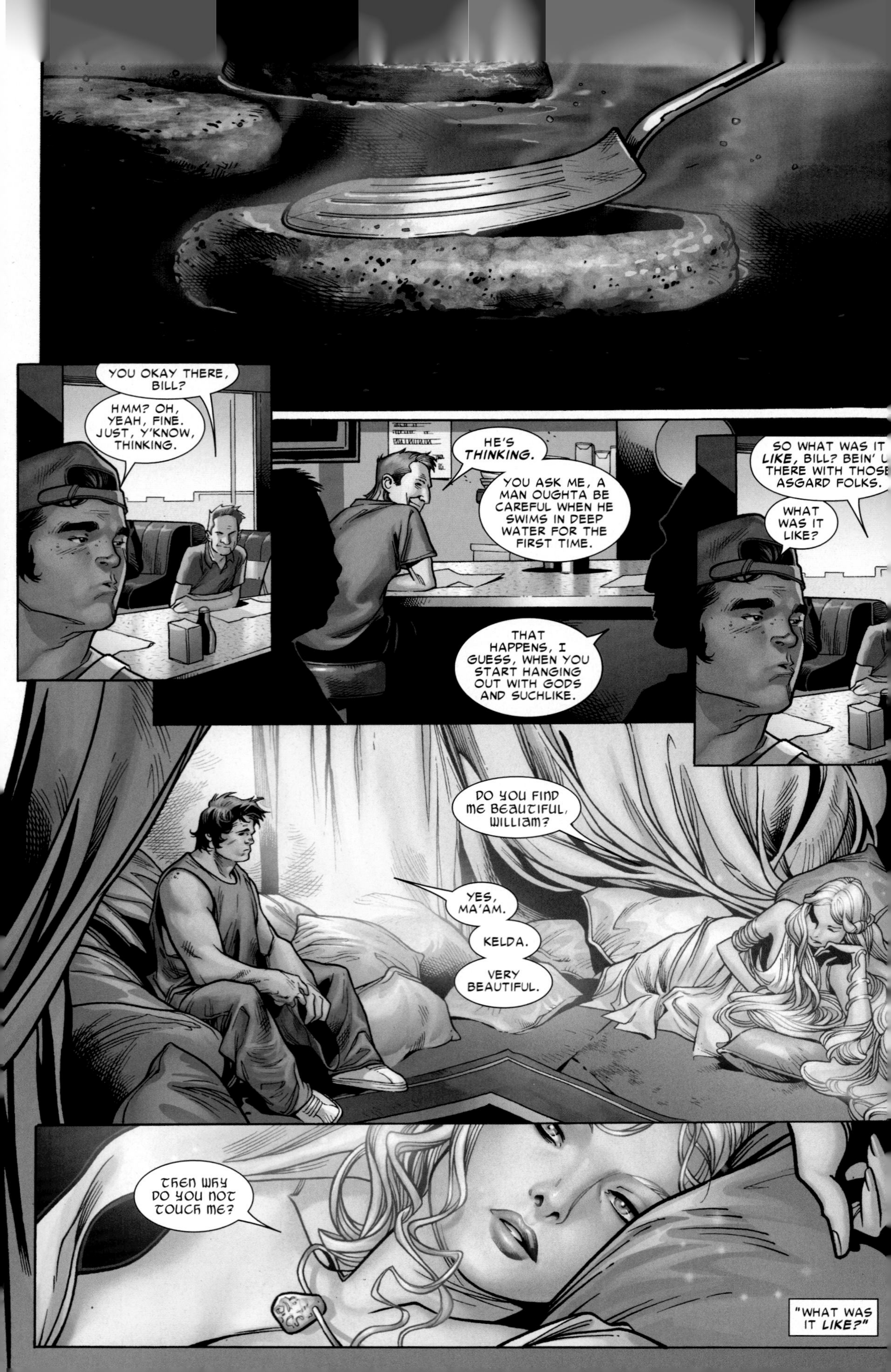

YOU OKAY THERE, BILL?
HMM? OH, YEAH, FINE. JUST, Y'KNOW, THINKING.
HE'S *THINKING.*
YOU ASK ME, A MAN OUGHTA BE CAREFUL WHEN HE SWIMS IN DEEP WATER FOR THE FIRST TIME.
THAT HAPPENS, I GUESS, WHEN YOU START HANGING OUT WITH GODS AND SUCHLIKE.
SO WHAT WAS IT *LIKE,* BILL? BEIN' U THERE WITH THOSE ASGARD FOLKS.
WHAT WAS IT LIKE?
DO YOU FIND ME BEAUTIFUL, WILLIAM?
YES, MA'AM.
KELDA.
VERY BEAUTIFUL.
THEN WHY DO YOU NOT TOUCH ME?
"WHAT WAS IT *LIKE?*"

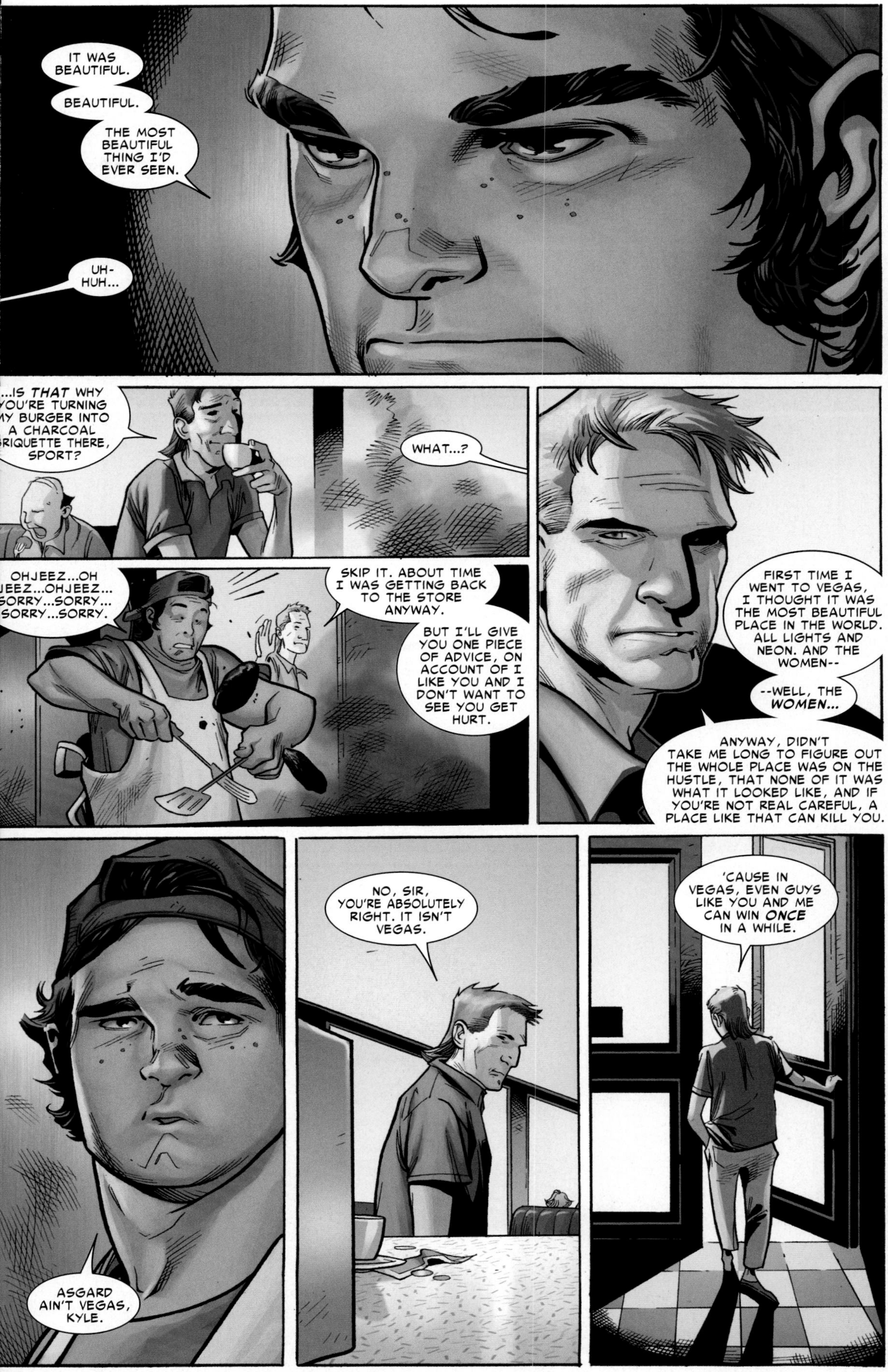
IT WAS BEAUTIFUL.
BEAUTIFUL.
THE MOST BEAUTIFUL THING I'D EVER SEEN.
UH-HUH...
...IS THAT WHY YOU'RE TURNING MY BURGER INTO A CHARCOAL BRIQUETTE THERE, SPORT?
WHAT...?
OHJEEZ...OH JEEZ...OHJEEZ... SORRY...SORRY... SORRY...SORRY.
SKIP IT. ABOUT TIME I WAS GETTING BACK TO THE STORE ANYWAY.
BUT I'LL GIVE YOU ONE PIECE OF ADVICE, ON ACCOUNT OF I LIKE YOU AND I DON'T WANT TO SEE YOU GET HURT.
FIRST TIME I WENT TO VEGAS, I THOUGHT IT WAS THE MOST BEAUTIFUL PLACE IN THE WORLD. ALL LIGHTS AND NEON. AND THE WOMEN--
--WELL, THE *WOMEN...*
ANYWAY, DIDN'T TAKE ME LONG TO FIGURE OUT THE WHOLE PLACE WAS ON THE HUSTLE, THAT NONE OF IT WAS WHAT IT LOOKED LIKE, AND IF YOU'RE NOT REAL CAREFUL, A PLACE LIKE THAT CAN KILL YOU.
ASGARD AIN'T VEGAS, KYLE.
NO, SIR, YOU'RE ABSOLUTELY RIGHT. IT ISN'T VEGAS.
'CAUSE IN VEGAS, EVEN GUYS LIKE YOU AND ME CAN WIN *ONCE* IN A WHILE.

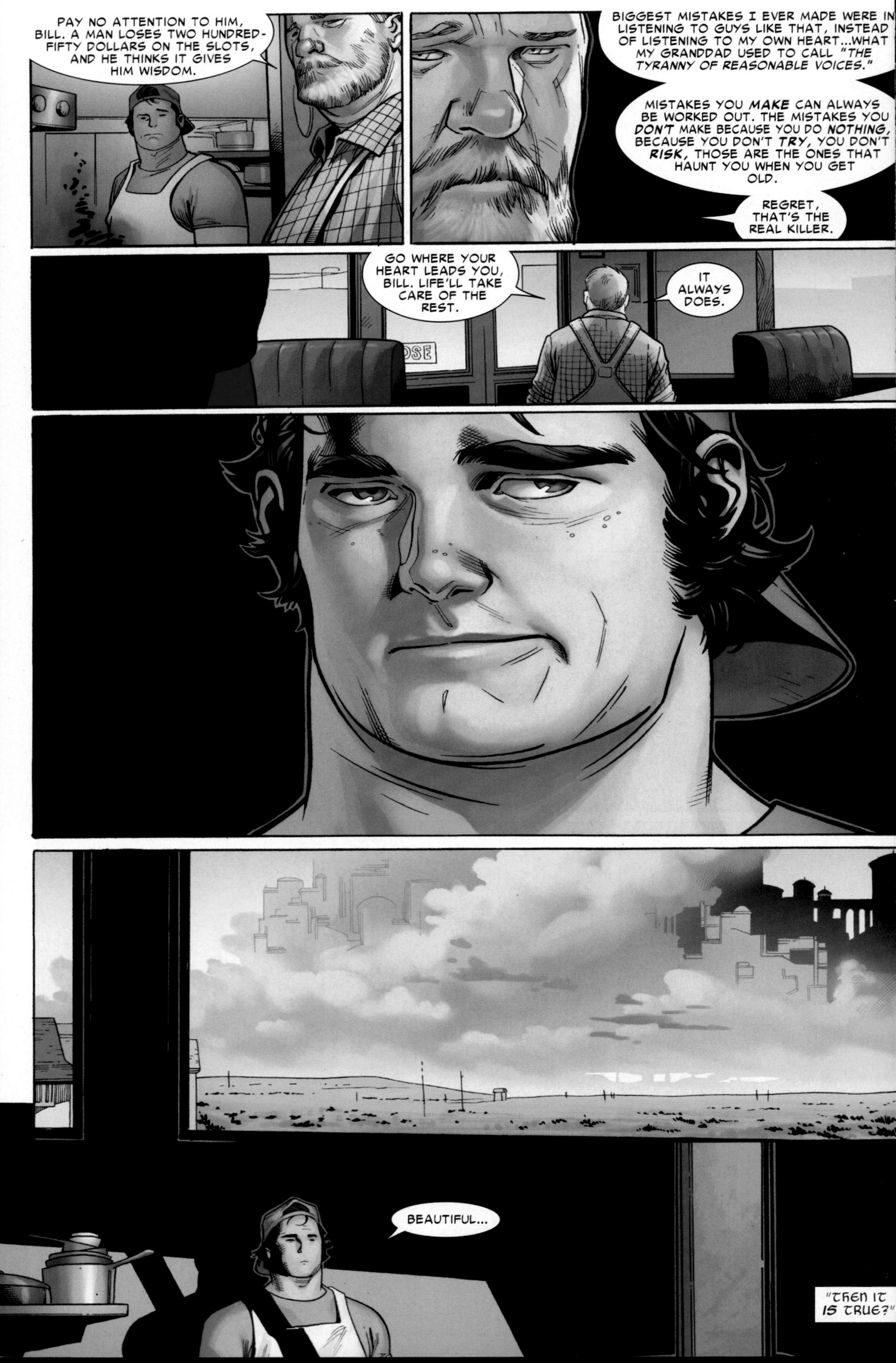
PAY NO ATTENTION TO HIM, BILL. A MAN LOSES TWO HUNDRED-FIFTY DOLLARS ON THE SLOTS, AND HE THINKS IT GIVES HIM WISDOM.
BIGGEST MISTAKES I EVER MADE WERE IN LISTENING TO GUYS LIKE THAT, INSTEAD OF LISTENING TO MY OWN HEART...WHAT MY GRANDDAD USED TO CALL "THE TYRANNY OF REASONABLE VOICES."
MISTAKES YOU MAKE CAN ALWAYS BE WORKED OUT. THE MISTAKES YOU DON'T MAKE BECAUSE YOU DO NOTHING, BECAUSE YOU DON'T TRY, YOU DON'T RISK, THOSE ARE THE ONES THAT HAUNT YOU WHEN YOU GET OLD.
REGRET, THAT'S THE REAL KILLER.
GO WHERE YOUR HEART LEADS YOU, BILL. LIFE'LL TAKE CARE OF THE REST.
IT ALWAYS DOES.
BEAUTIFUL...
"THEN IT IS TRUE?"

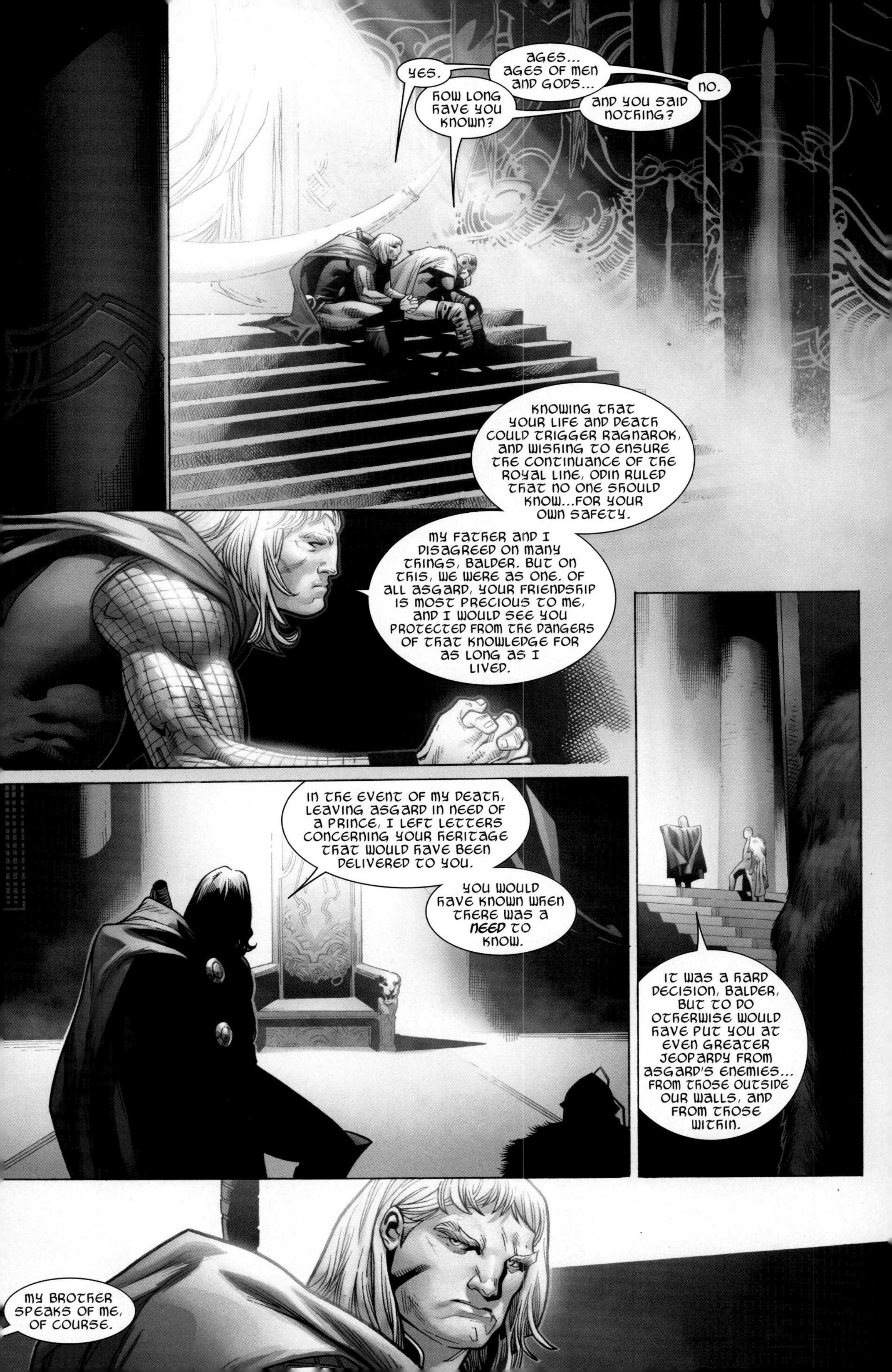
AGES... AGES OF MEN AND GODS...
YES.
NO.
HOW LONG HAVE YOU KNOWN?
AND YOU SAID NOTHING?
KNOWING THAT YOUR LIFE AND DEATH COULD TRIGGER RAGNAROK, AND WISHING TO ENSURE THE CONTINUANCE OF THE ROYAL LINE, ODIN RULED THAT NO ONE SHOULD KNOW...FOR YOUR OWN SAFETY.
MY FATHER AND I DISAGREED ON MANY THINGS, BALDER. BUT ON THIS, WE WERE AS ONE. OF ALL ASGARD, YOUR FRIENDSHIP IS MOST PRECIOUS TO ME, AND I WOULD SEE YOU PROTECTED FROM THE DANGERS OF THAT KNOWLEDGE FOR AS LONG AS I LIVED.
IT WAS A HARD DECISION, BALDER, BUT TO DO OTHERWISE WOULD HAVE PUT YOU AT EVEN GREATER JEOPARDY FROM ASGARD'S ENEMIES... FROM THOSE OUTSIDE OUR WALLS, AND FROM THOSE WITHIN.
IN THE EVENT OF MY DEATH, LEAVING ASGARD IN NEED OF A PRINCE, I LEFT LETTERS CONCERNING YOUR HERITAGE THAT WOULD HAVE BEEN DELIVERED TO YOU.
YOU WOULD HAVE KNOWN WHEN THERE WAS A NEED TO KNOW.
MY BROTHER SPEAKS OF ME, OF COURSE.

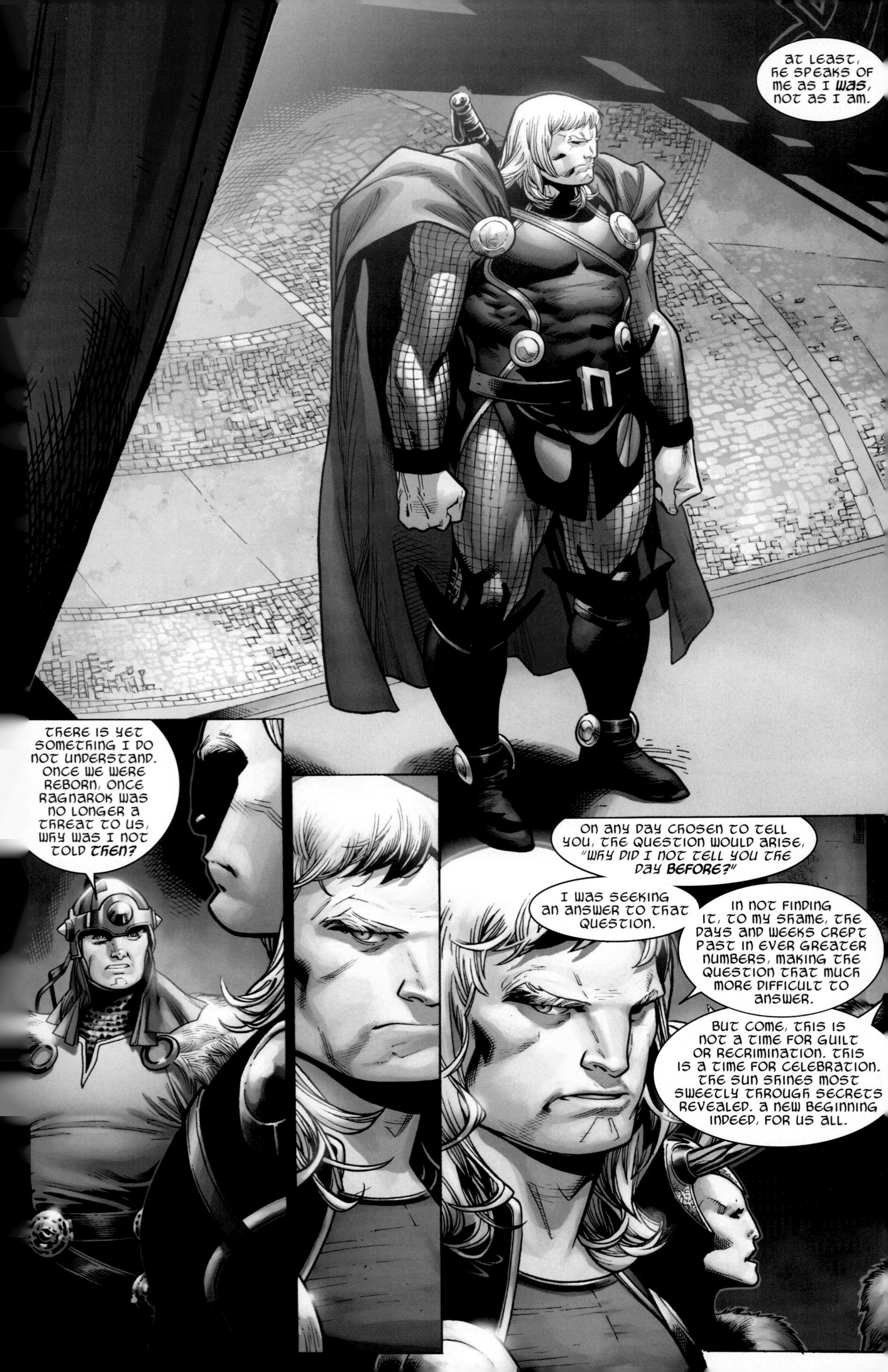
AT LEAST, HE SPEAKS OF ME AS I WAS, NOT AS I AM.
THERE IS YET SOMETHING I DO NOT UNDERSTAND. ONCE WE WERE REBORN, ONCE RAGNAROK WAS NO LONGER A THREAT TO US, WHY WAS I NOT TOLD THEN?
ON ANY DAY CHOSEN TO TELL YOU, THE QUESTION WOULD ARISE, "WHY DID I NOT TELL YOU THE DAY BEFORE?"
I WAS SEEKING AN ANSWER TO THAT QUESTION.
IN NOT FINDING IT, TO MY SHAME, THE DAYS AND WEEKS CREPT PAST IN EVER GREATER NUMBERS, MAKING THE QUESTION THAT MUCH MORE DIFFICULT TO ANSWER.
BUT COME, THIS IS NOT A TIME FOR GUILT OR RECRIMINATION. THIS IS A TIME FOR CELEBRATION. THE SUN SHINES MOST SWEETLY THROUGH SECRETS REVEALED. A NEW BEGINNING INDEED, FOR US ALL.

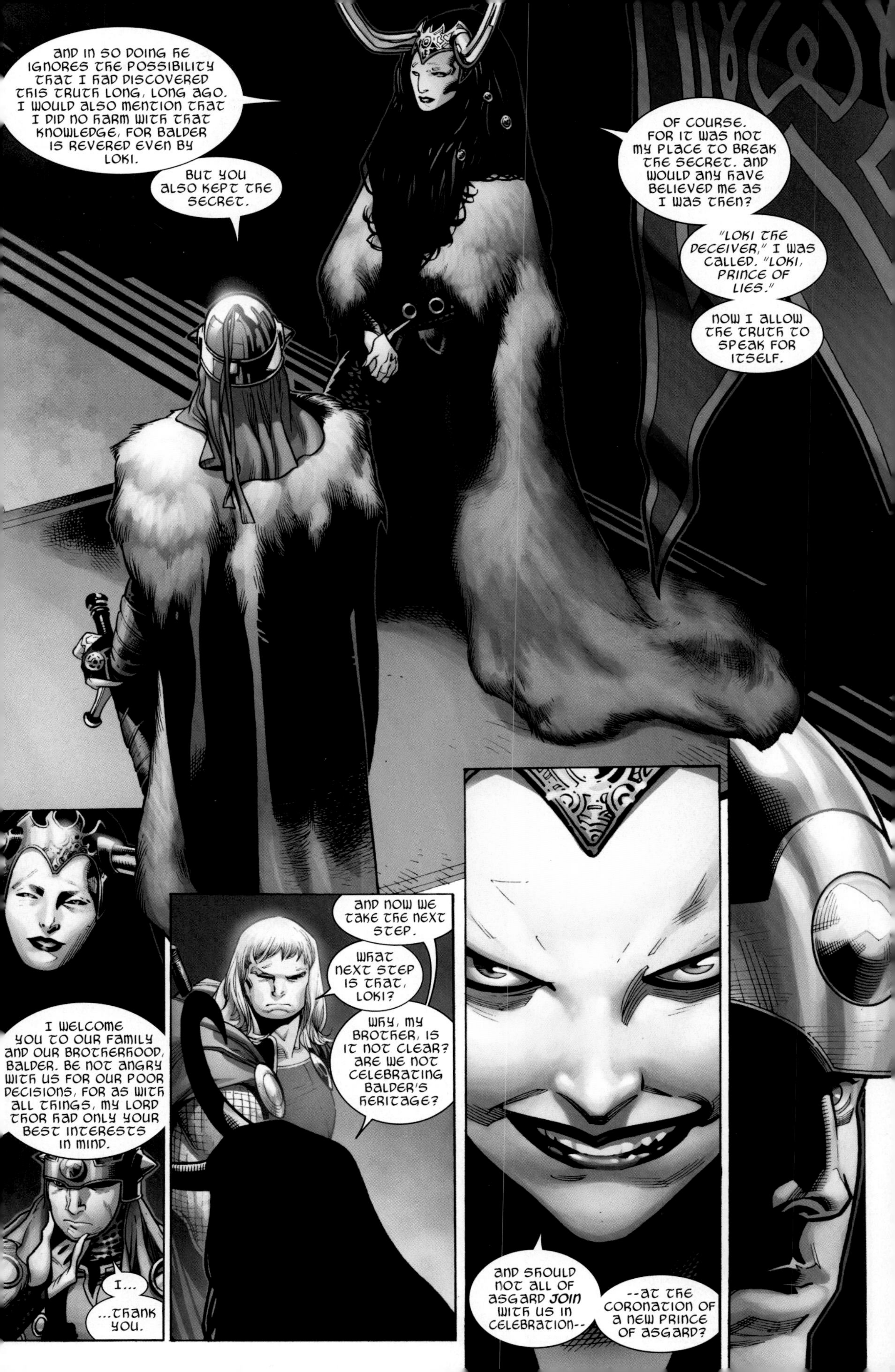
AND IN SO DOING HE IGNORES THE POSSIBILITY THAT I HAD DISCOVERED THIS TRUTH LONG, LONG AGO. I WOULD ALSO MENTION THAT I DID NO HARM WITH THAT KNOWLEDGE, FOR BALDER IS REVERED EVEN BY LOKI.
BUT YOU ALSO KEPT THE SECRET.
OF COURSE. FOR IT WAS NOT MY PLACE TO BREAK THE SECRET. AND WOULD ANY HAVE BELIEVED ME AS I WAS THEN?
"LOKI THE DECEIVER," I WAS CALLED. "LOKI, PRINCE OF LIES."
NOW I ALLOW THE TRUTH TO SPEAK FOR ITSELF.
I WELCOME YOU TO OUR FAMILY AND OUR BROTHERHOOD, BALDER. BE NOT ANGRY WITH US FOR OUR POOR DECISIONS, FOR AS WITH ALL THINGS, MY LORD THOR HAD ONLY YOUR BEST INTERESTS IN MIND.
I...
...THANK YOU.
AND NOW WE TAKE THE NEXT STEP.
WHAT NEXT STEP IS THAT, LOKI?
WHY, MY BROTHER, IS IT NOT CLEAR? ARE WE NOT CELEBRATING BALDER'S HERITAGE?
AND SHOULD NOT ALL OF ASGARD JOIN WITH US IN CELEBRATION--
--AT THE CORONATION OF A NEW PRINCE OF ASGARD?

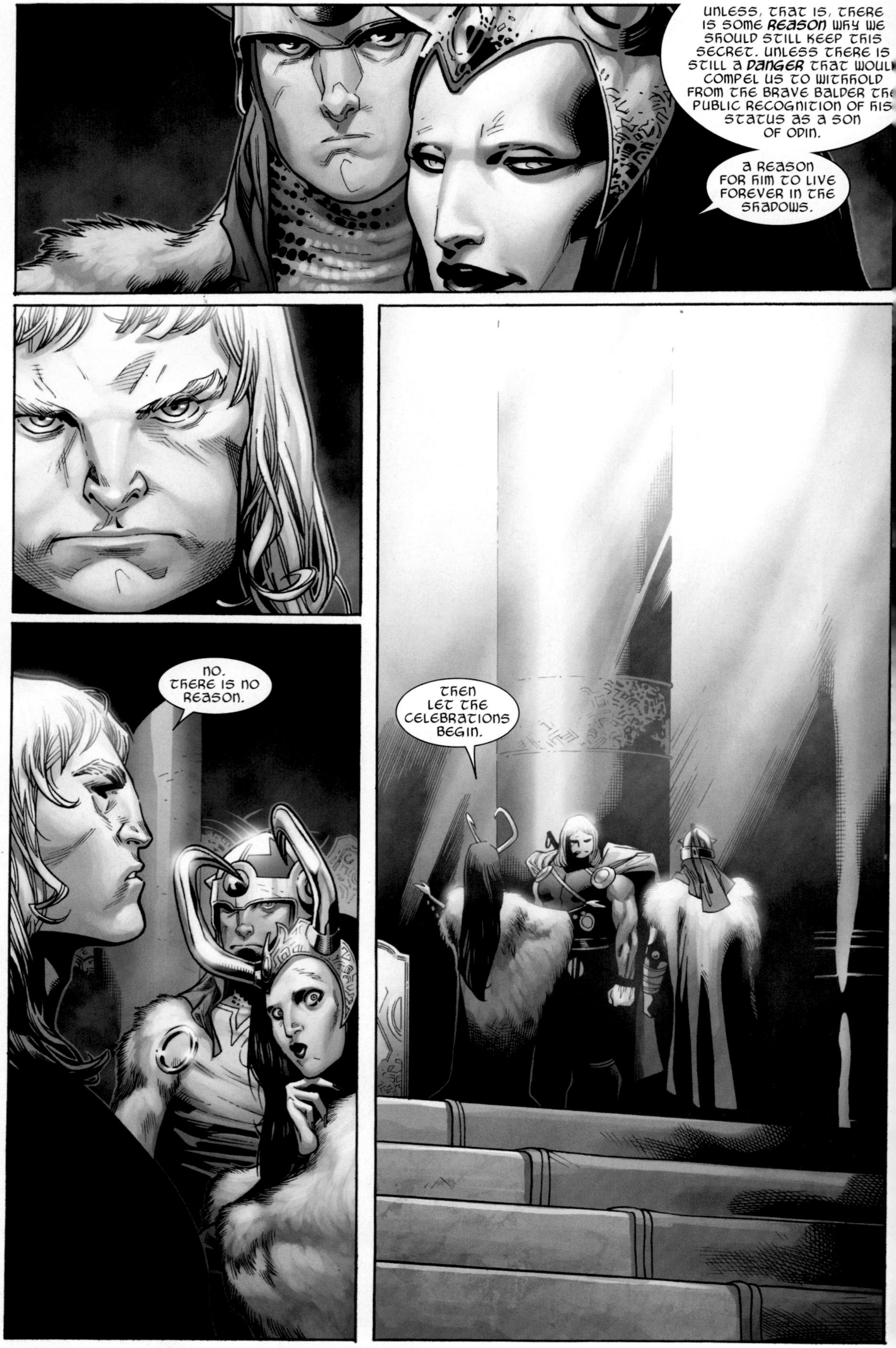
UNLESS, THAT IS, THERE IS SOME REASON WHY WE SHOULD STILL KEEP THIS SECRET. UNLESS THERE IS STILL A DANGER THAT WOULD COMPEL US TO WITHHOLD FROM THE BRAVE BALDER THE PUBLIC RECOGNITION OF HIS STATUS AS A SON OF ODIN.
A REASON FOR HIM TO LIVE FOREVER IN THE SHADOWS.
NO. THERE IS NO REASON.
THEN LET THE CELEBRATIONS BEGIN.

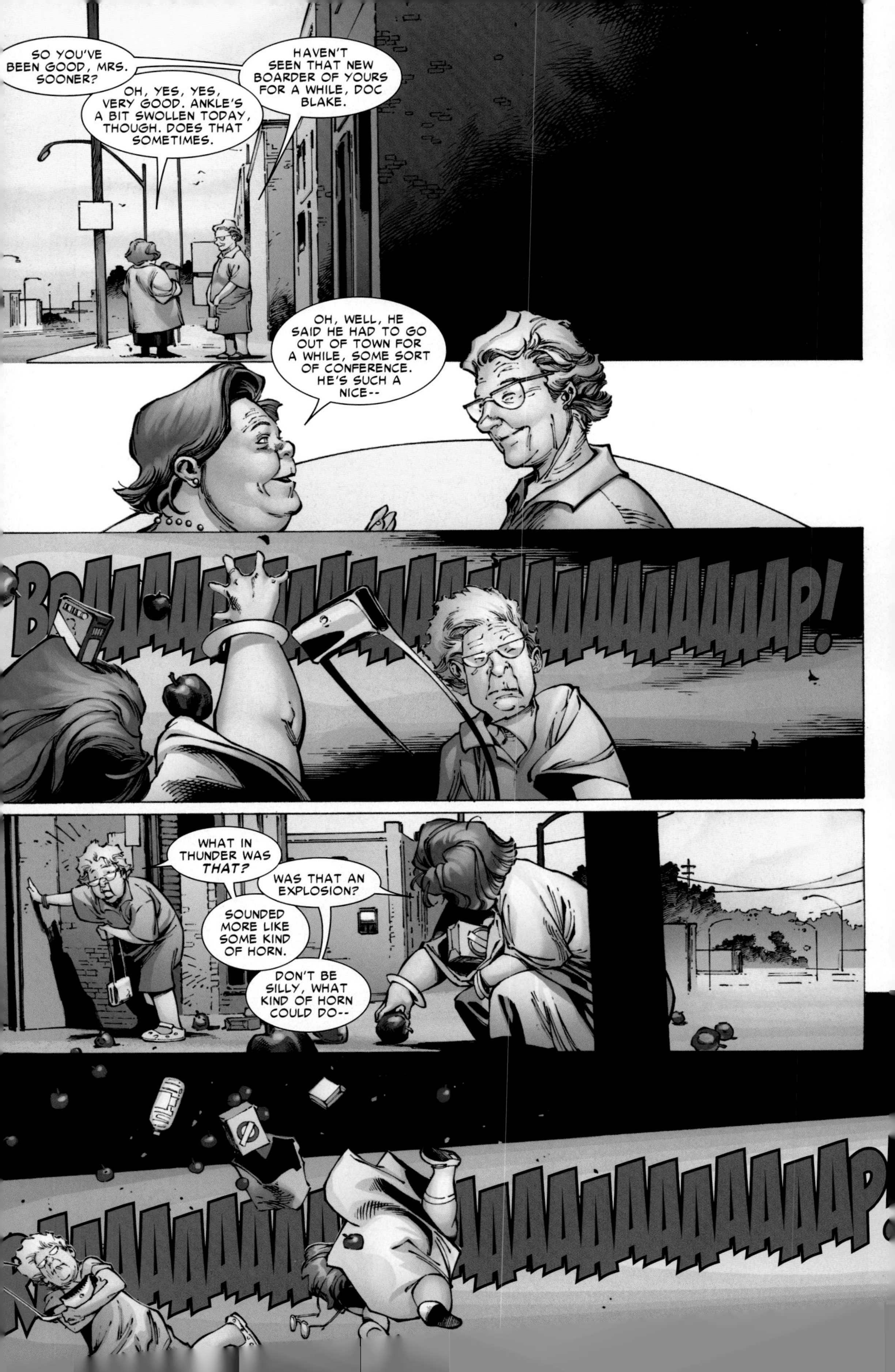
SO YOU'VE BEEN GOOD, MRS. SOONER?
OH, YES, YES, VERY GOOD. ANKLE'S A BIT SWOLLEN TODAY, THOUGH. DOES THAT SOMETIMES.
HAVEN'T SEEN THAT NEW BOARDER OF YOURS FOR A WHILE, DOC BLAKE.
OH, WELL, HE SAID HE HAD TO GO OUT OF TOWN FOR A WHILE, SOME SORT OF CONFERENCE. HE'S SUCH A NICE--
WHAT IN THUNDER WAS THAT?
WAS THAT AN EXPLOSION?
SOUNDED MORE LIKE SOME KIND OF HORN.
DON'T BE SILLY, WHAT KIND OF HORN COULD DO--

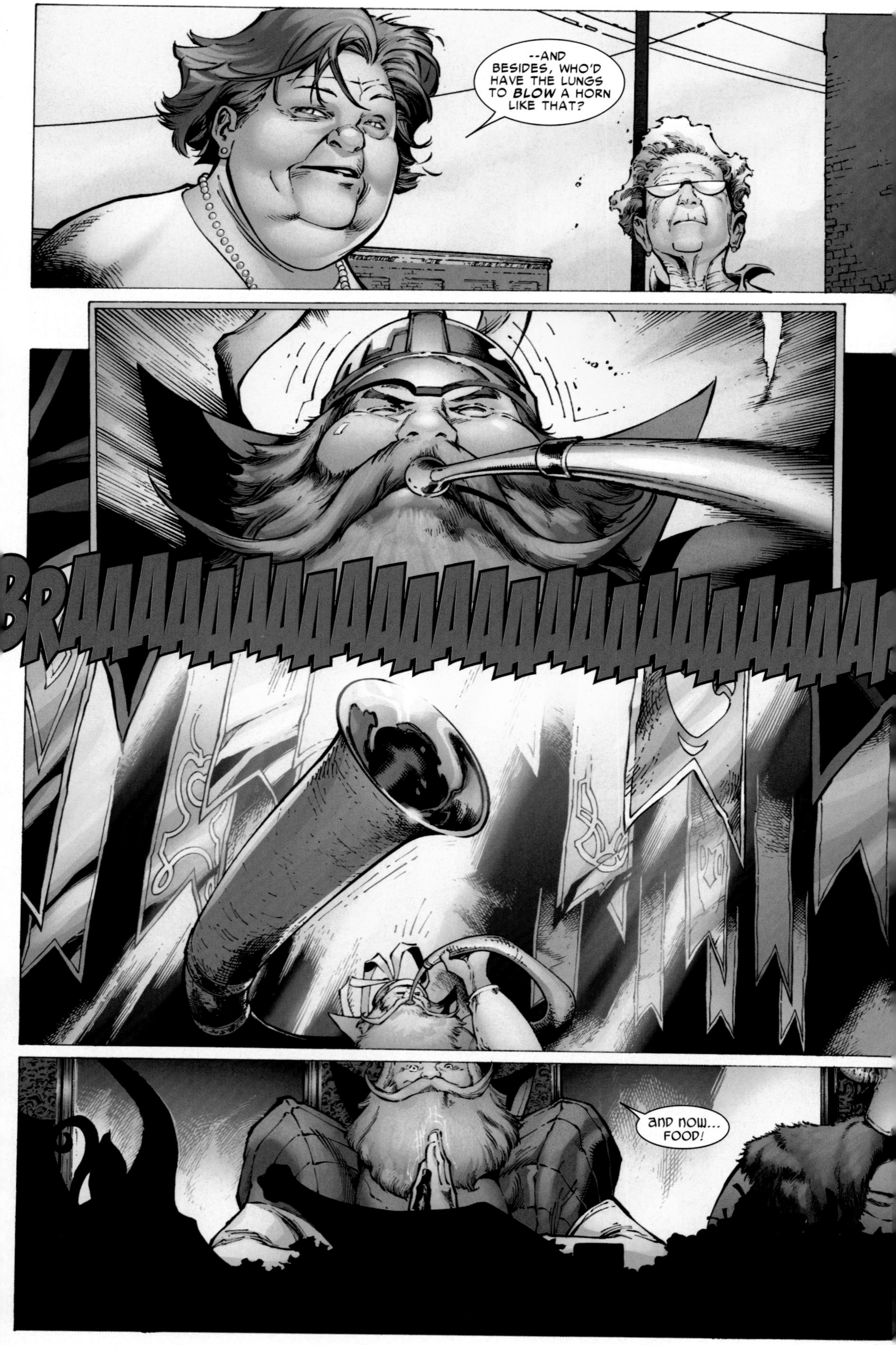
--AND BESIDES, WHO'D HAVE THE LUNGS TO *BLOW* A HORN LIKE THAT?
BRAAAAAAAAAAAAAAAAAAAAAAAAP
AND NOW... FOOD!

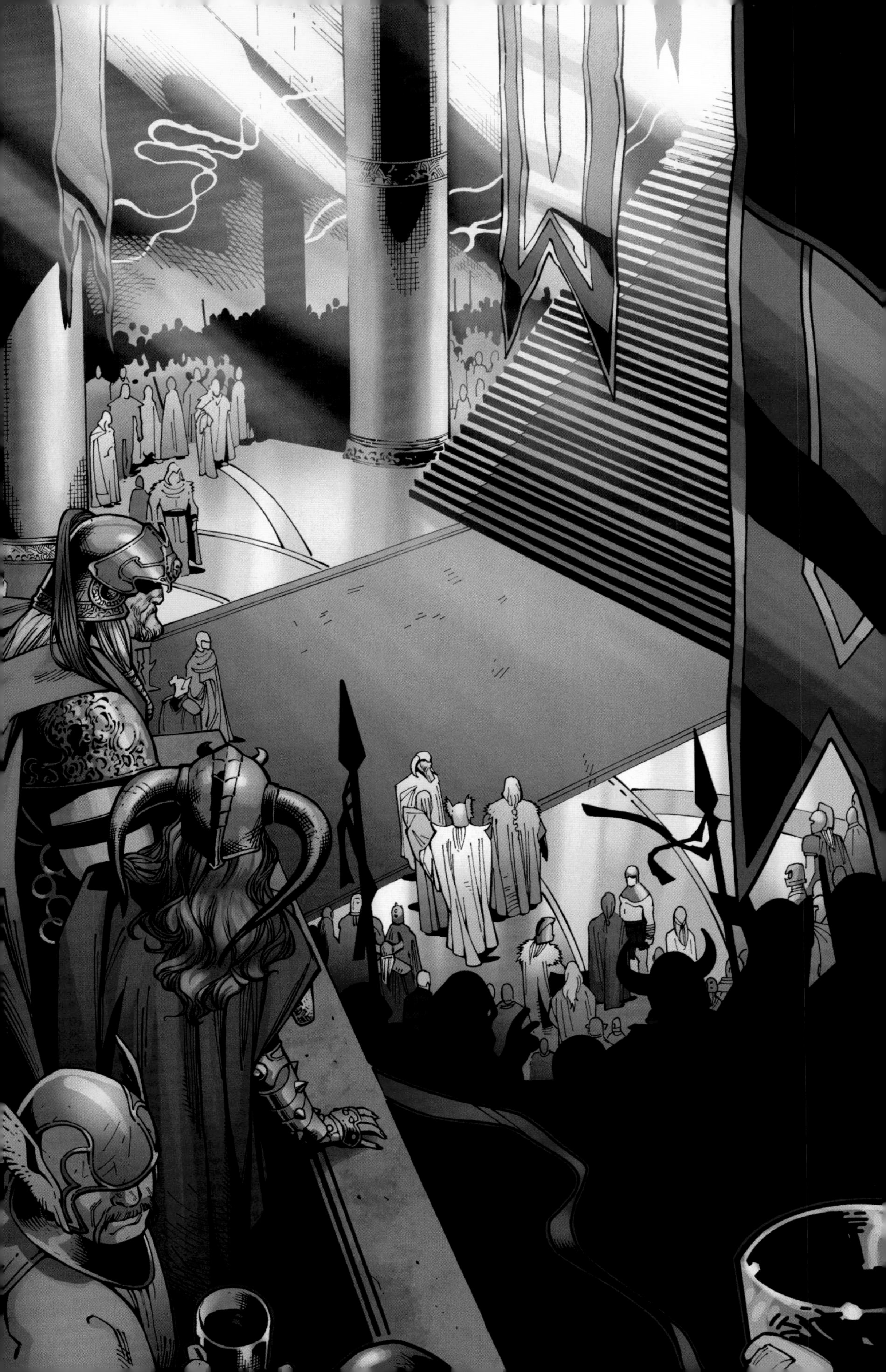

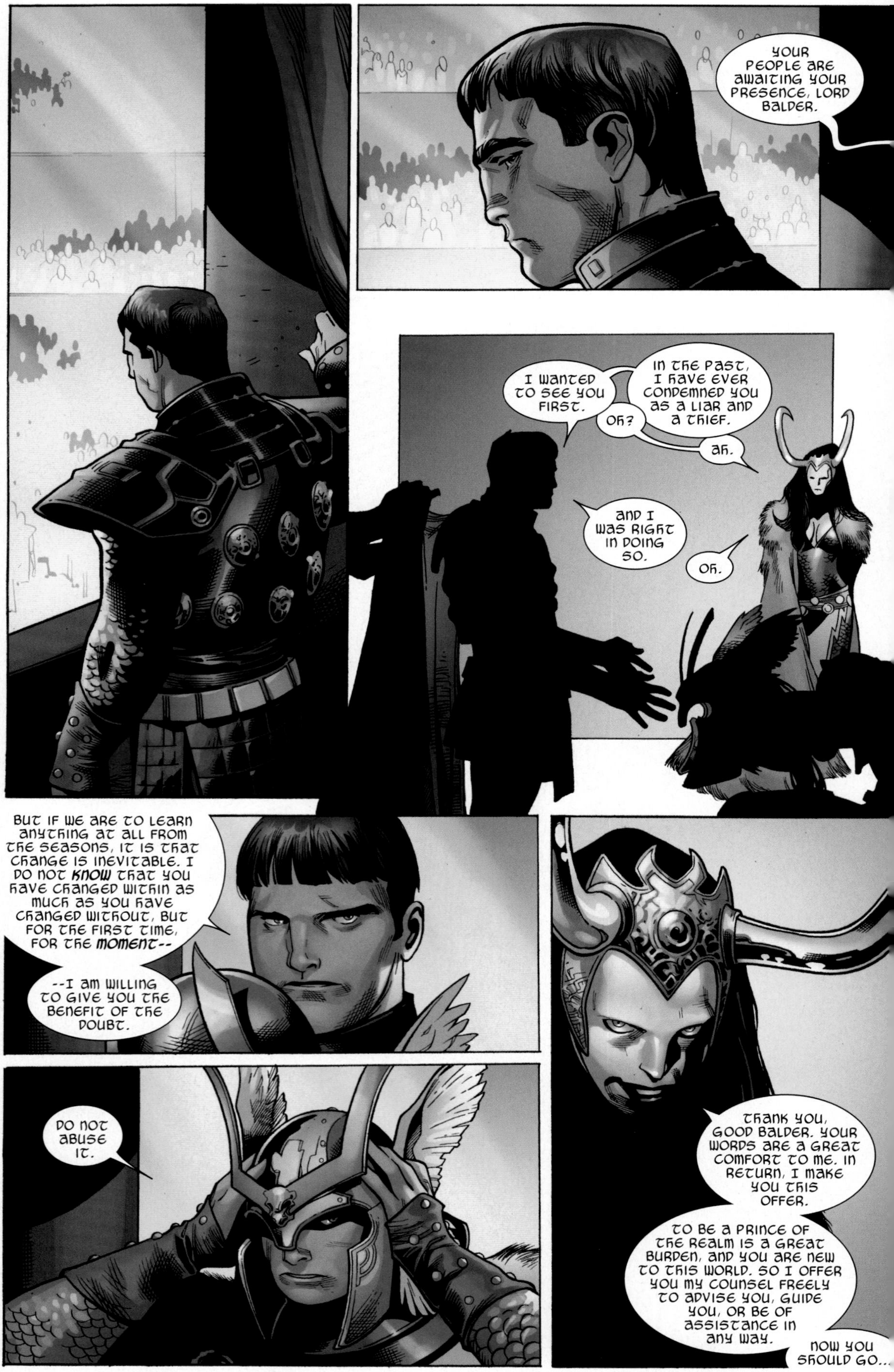
YOUR PEOPLE ARE AWAITING YOUR PRESENCE, LORD BALDER.
I WANTED TO SEE YOU FIRST.
OH?
IN THE PAST, I HAVE EVER CONDEMNED YOU AS A LIAR AND A THIEF.
AH.
AND I WAS RIGHT IN DOING SO.
OH.
BUT IF WE ARE TO LEARN ANYTHING AT ALL FROM THE SEASONS, IT IS THAT CHANGE IS INEVITABLE. I DO NOT KNOW THAT YOU HAVE CHANGED WITHIN AS MUCH AS YOU HAVE CHANGED WITHOUT, BUT FOR THE FIRST TIME, FOR THE MOMENT--
--I AM WILLING TO GIVE YOU THE BENEFIT OF THE DOUBT.
DO NOT ABUSE IT.
THANK YOU, GOOD BALDER. YOUR WORDS ARE A GREAT COMFORT TO ME. IN RETURN, I MAKE YOU THIS OFFER.
TO BE A PRINCE OF THE REALM IS A GREAT BURDEN, AND YOU ARE NEW TO THIS WORLD. SO I OFFER YOU MY COUNSEL FREELY TO ADVISE YOU, GUIDE YOU, OR BE OF ASSISTANCE IN ANY WAY.
NOW YOU SHOULD GO...

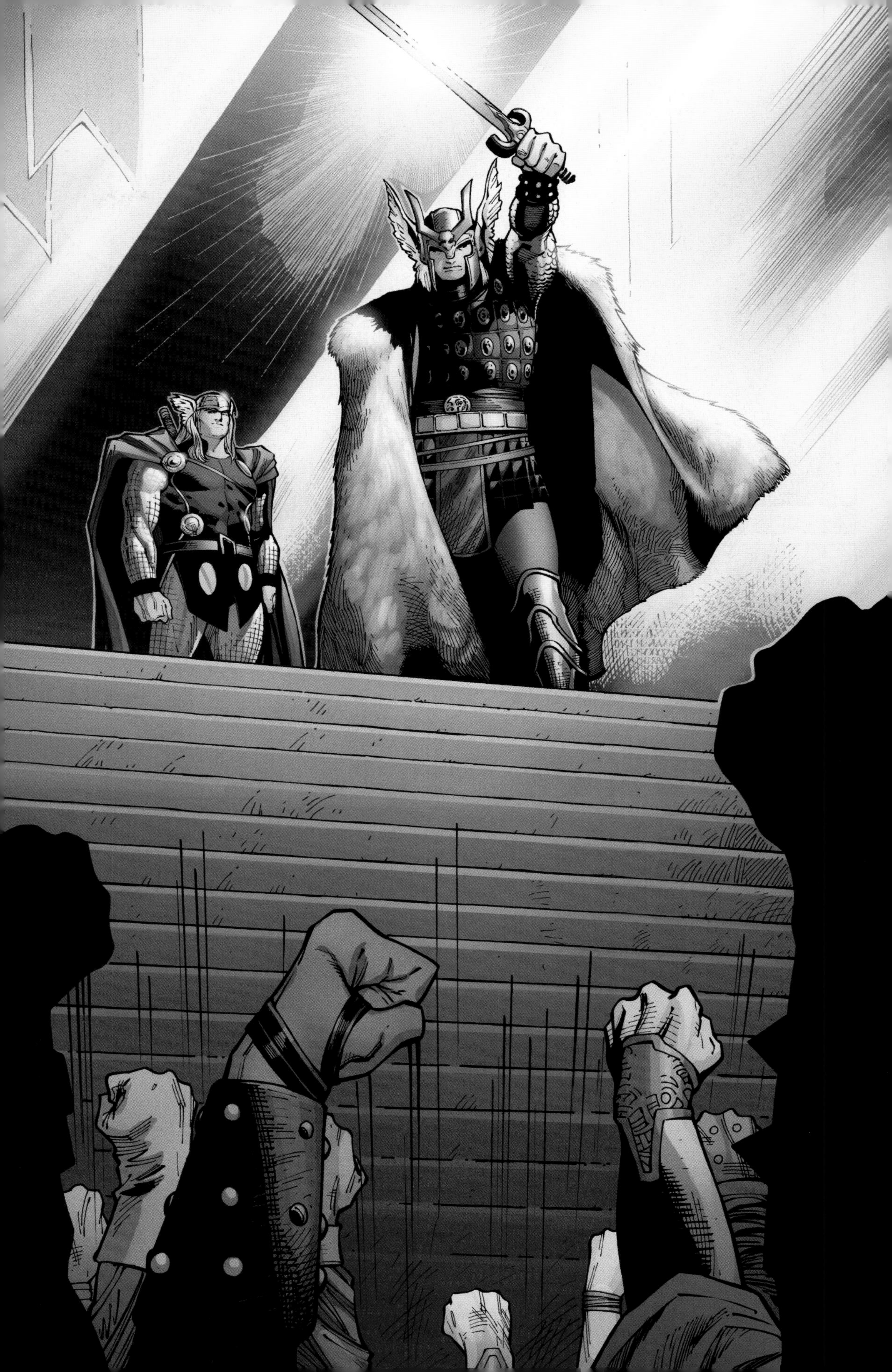

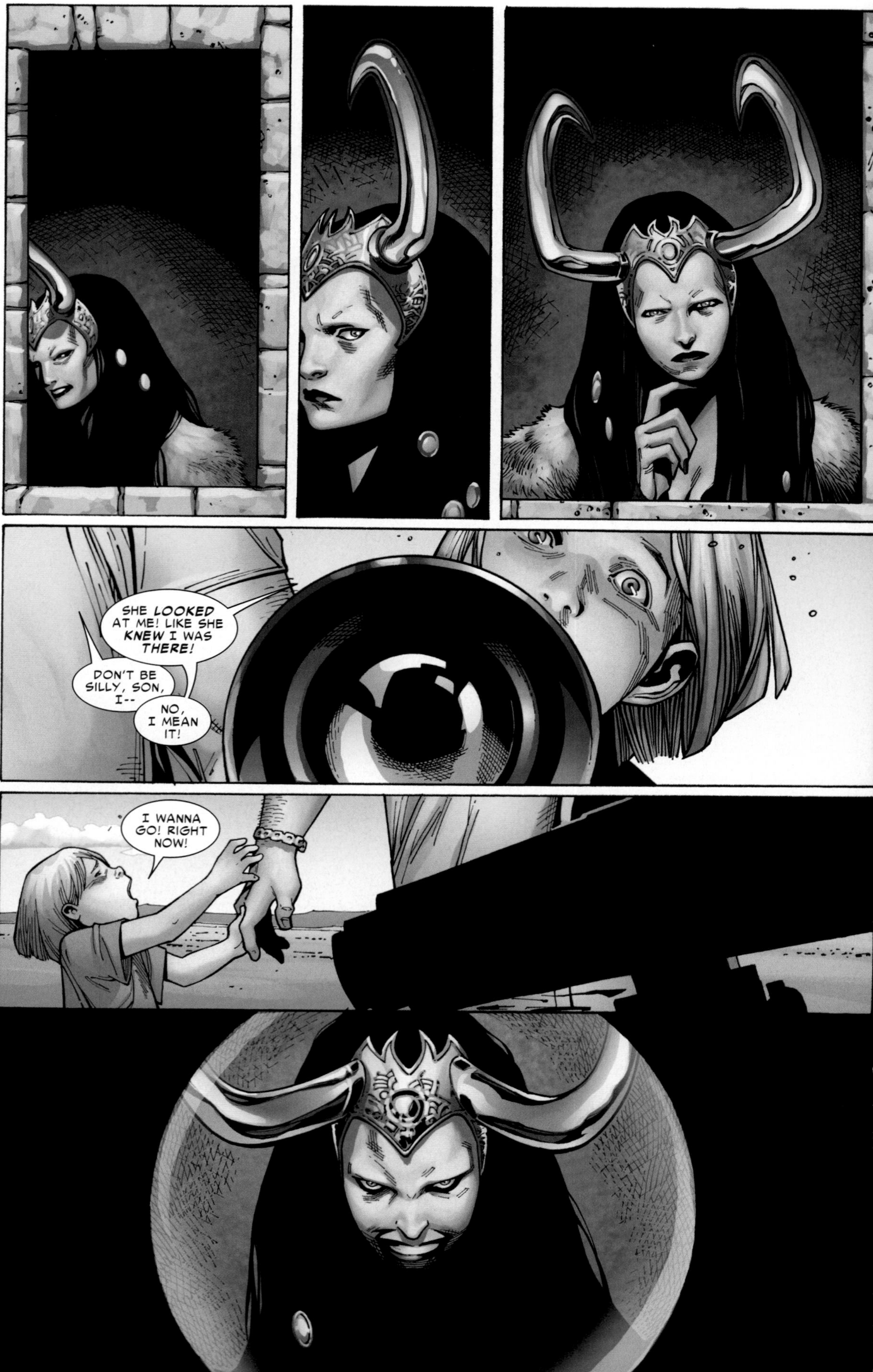
SHE *LOOKED* AT ME! LIKE SHE *KNEW* I WAS *THERE!*
DON'T BE SILLY, SON, I--
NO, I MEAN IT!
I WANNA GO! RIGHT NOW!

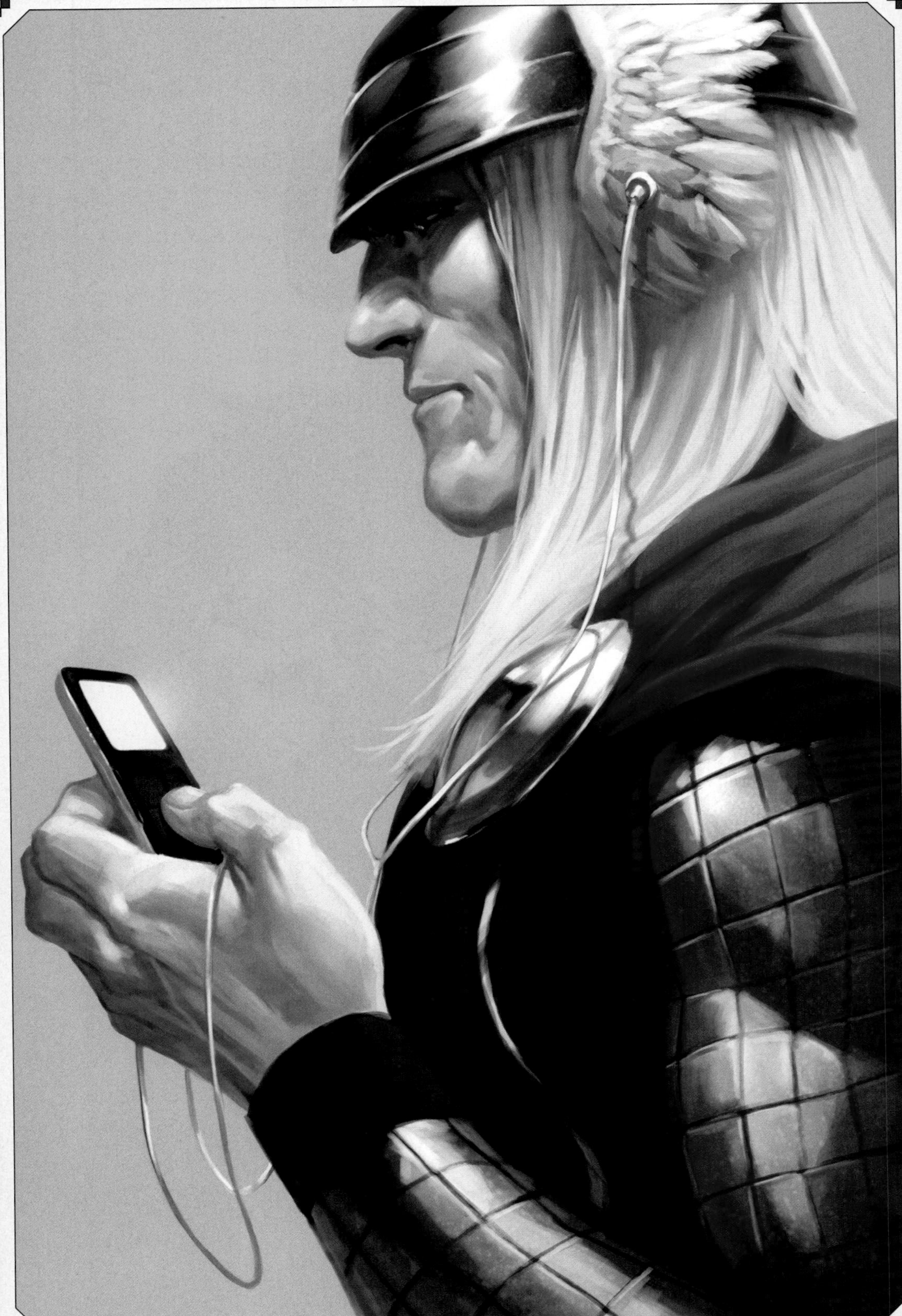

Thor #601 variant by Marko Djurdjević

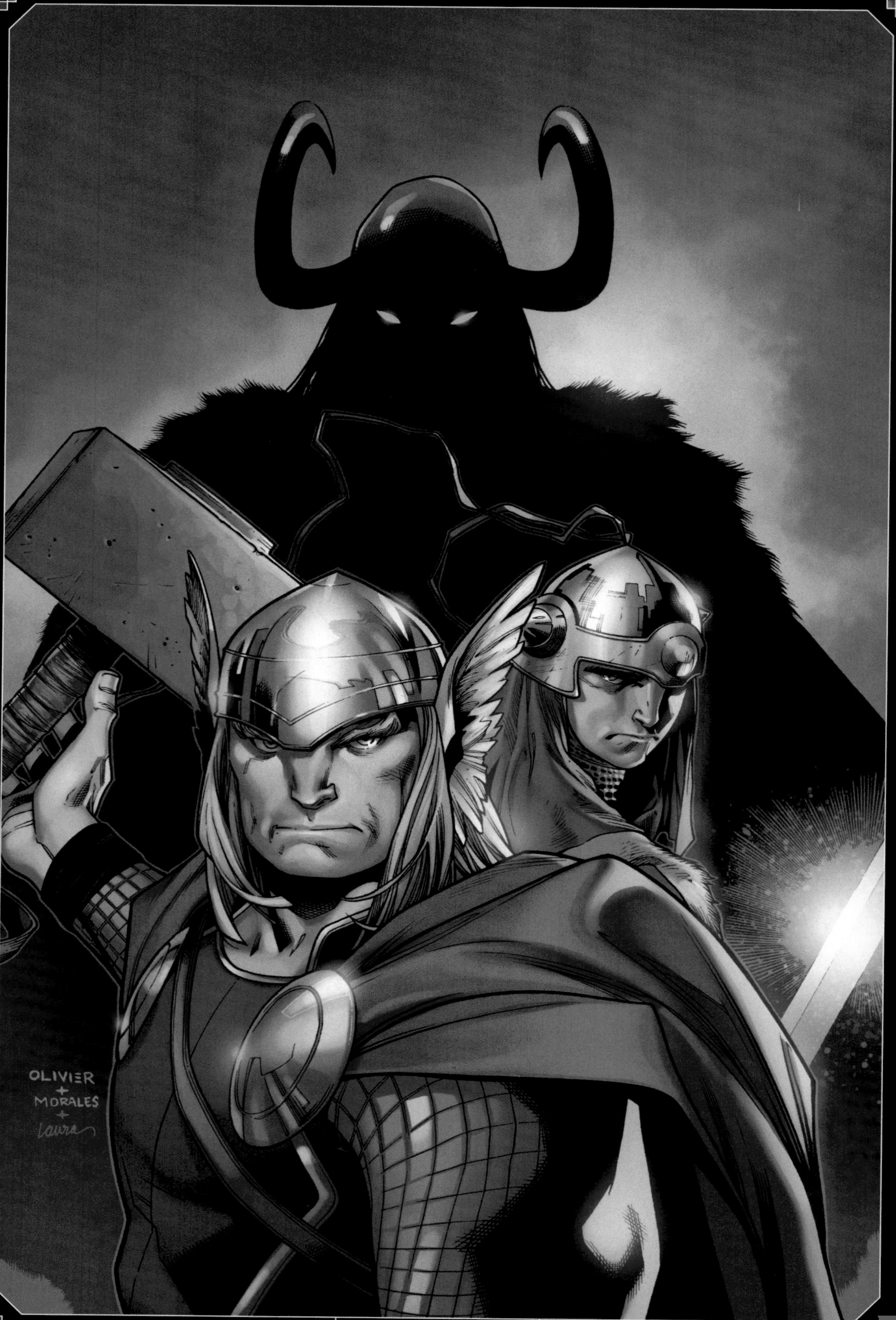
OLIVIER
+
MORALES
+
Laura

THOR #12

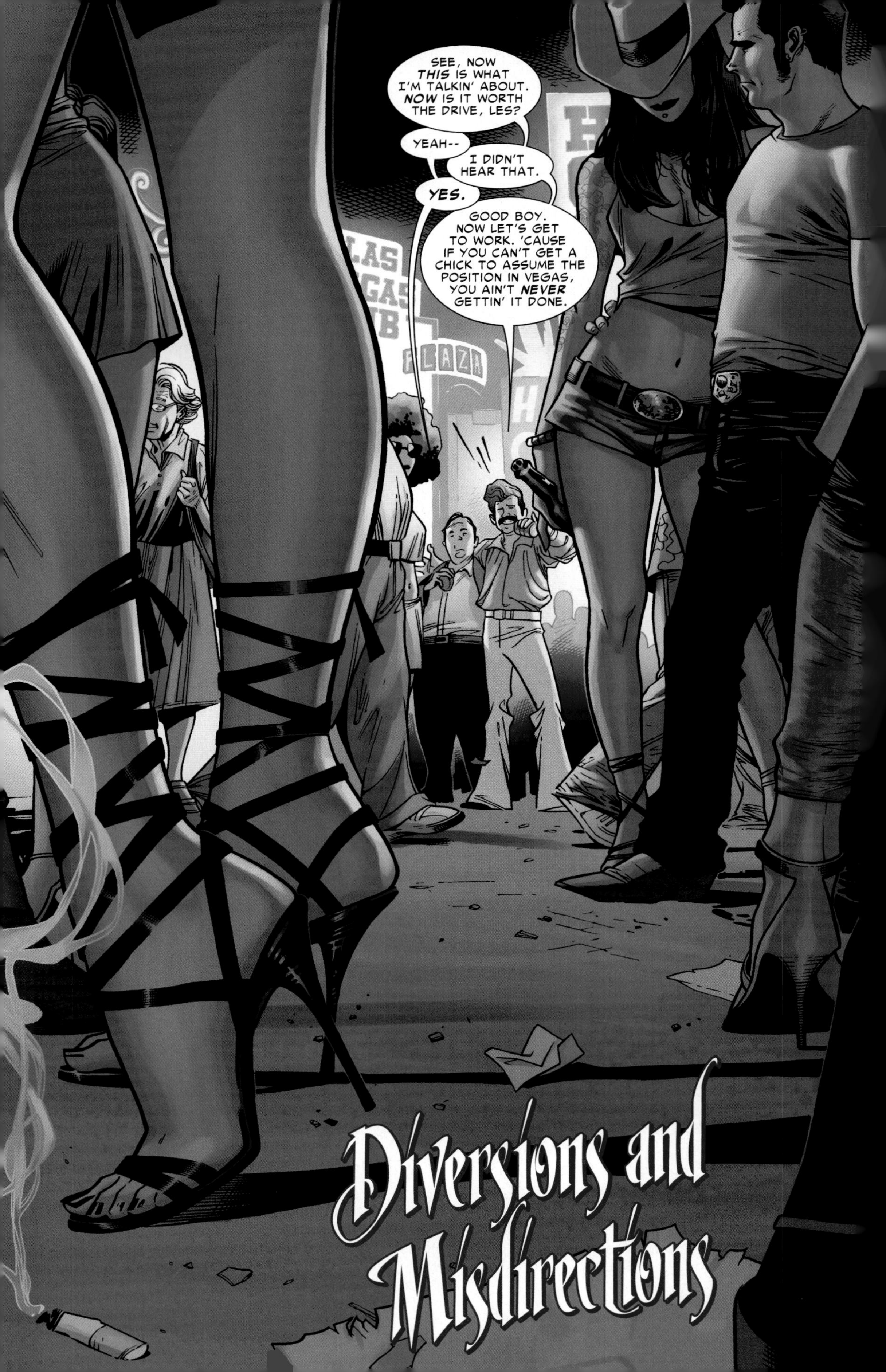
SEE, NOW THIS IS WHAT I'M TALKIN' ABOUT. NOW IS IT WORTH THE DRIVE, LES?
YEAH--
I DIDN'T HEAR THAT.
YES.
GOOD BOY. NOW LET'S GET TO WORK. 'CAUSE IF YOU CAN'T GET A CHICK TO ASSUME THE POSITION IN VEGAS, YOU AIN'T NEVER GETTIN' IT DONE.
PLAZA
Diversions and Misdirections

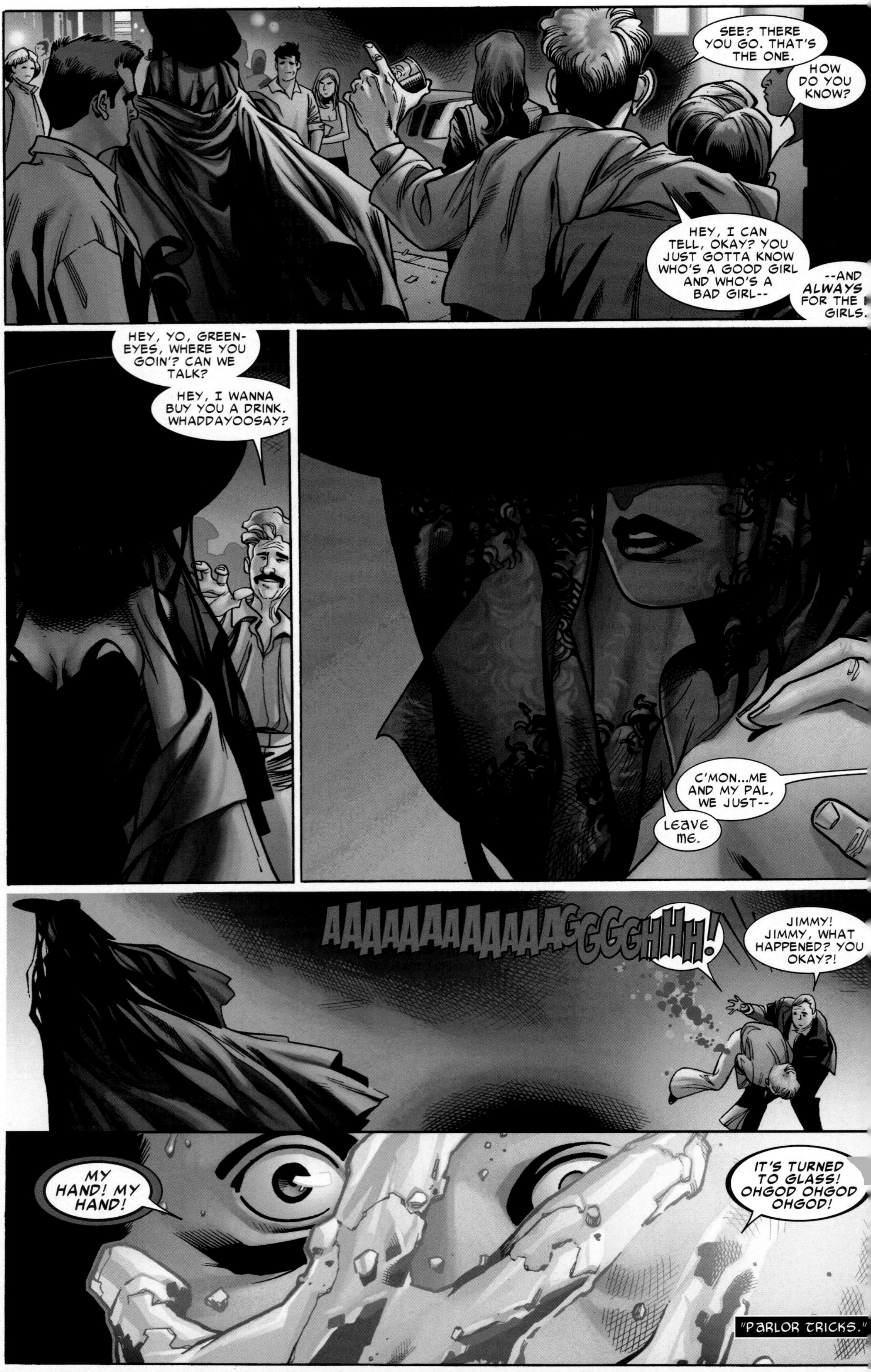
SEE? THERE YOU GO. THAT'S THE ONE.
HOW DO YOU KNOW?
HEY, I CAN TELL, OKAY? YOU JUST GOTTA KNOW WHO'S A GOOD GIRL AND WHO'S A BAD GIRL--
--AND ALWAYS FOR THE GIRLS.
HEY, YO, GREEN-EYES, WHERE YOU GOIN'? CAN WE TALK?
HEY, I WANNA BUY YOU A DRINK. WHADDAYOOSAY?
C'MON...ME AND MY PAL, WE JUST--
LEAVE ME.
AAAAAAAAAAAAGGGGHHH!
JIMMY! JIMMY, WHAT HAPPENED? YOU OKAY?!
MY HAND! MY HAND!
IT'S TURNED TO GLASS! OHGOD OHGOD OHGOD!
"PARLOR TRICKS."

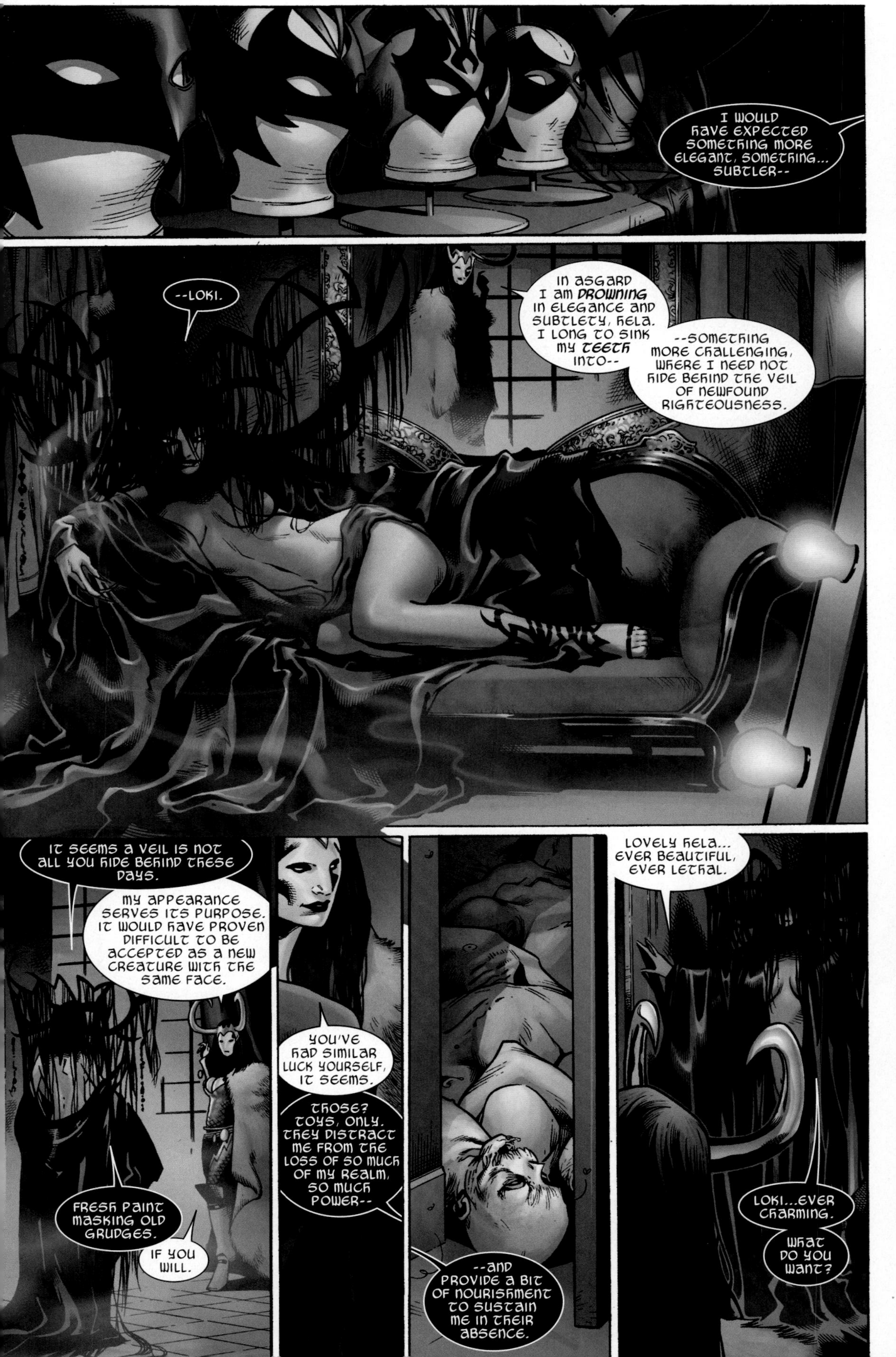
I WOULD HAVE EXPECTED SOMETHING MORE ELEGANT, SOMETHING... SUBTLER--
--LOKI.
IN ASGARD I AM DROWNING IN ELEGANCE AND SUBTLETY, HELA. I LONG TO SINK MY TEETH INTO--
--SOMETHING MORE CHALLENGING, WHERE I NEED NOT HIDE BEHIND THE VEIL OF NEWFOUND RIGHTEOUSNESS.
IT SEEMS A VEIL IS NOT ALL YOU HIDE BEHIND THESE DAYS.
MY APPEARANCE SERVES ITS PURPOSE. IT WOULD HAVE PROVEN DIFFICULT TO BE ACCEPTED AS A NEW CREATURE WITH THE SAME FACE.
FRESH PAINT MASKING OLD GRUDGES.
IF YOU WILL.
YOU'VE HAD SIMILAR LUCK YOURSELF, IT SEEMS.
THOSE? TOYS, ONLY. THEY DISTRACT ME FROM THE LOSS OF SO MUCH OF MY REALM, SO MUCH POWER--
--AND PROVIDE A BIT OF NOURISHMENT TO SUSTAIN ME IN THEIR ABSENCE.
LOVELY HELA... EVER BEAUTIFUL, EVER LETHAL.
LOKI...EVER CHARMING.
WHAT DO YOU WANT?

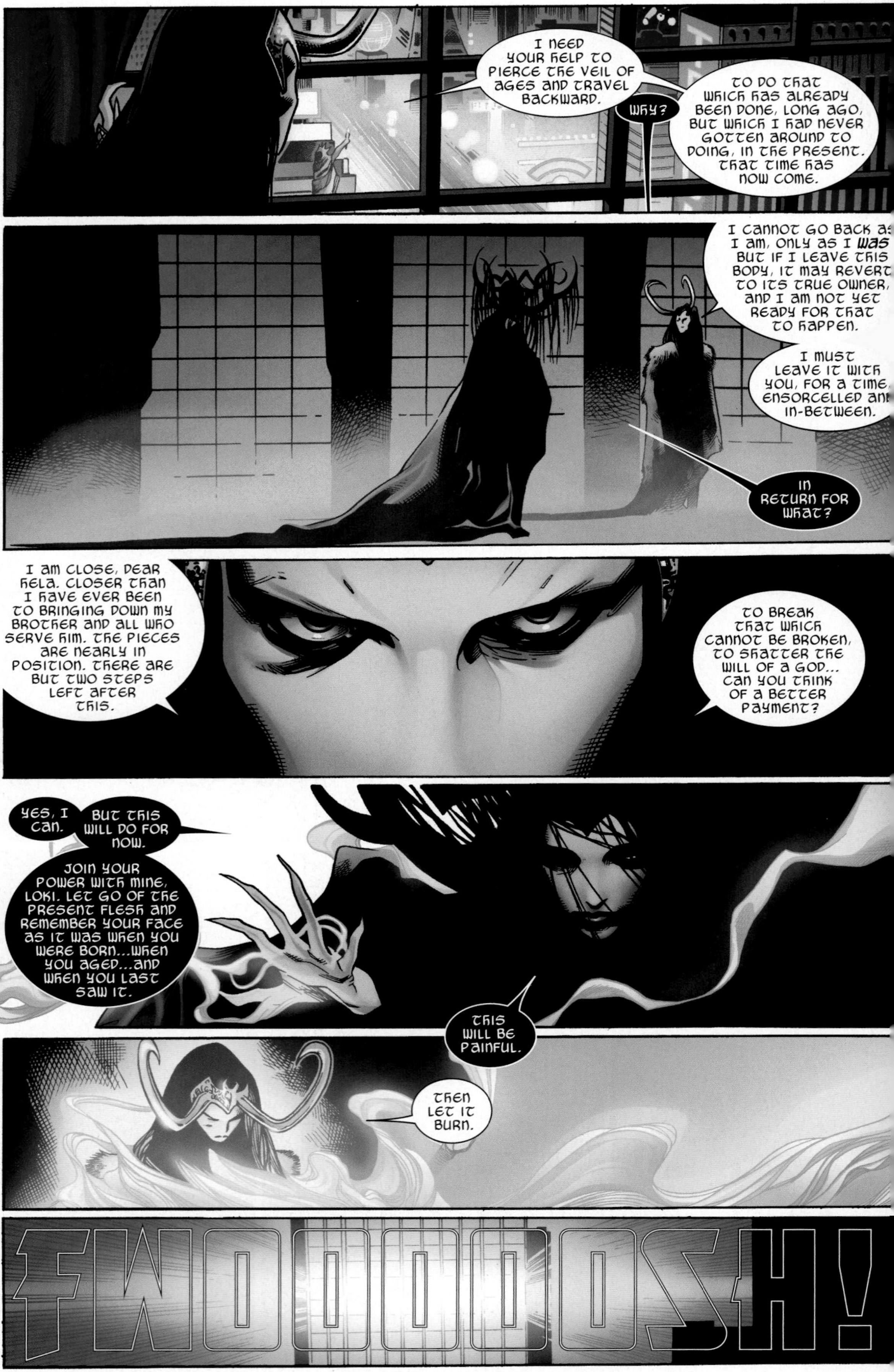
I NEED YOUR HELP TO PIERCE THE VEIL OF AGES AND TRAVEL BACKWARD.
WHY?
TO DO THAT WHICH HAS ALREADY BEEN DONE, LONG AGO, BUT WHICH I HAD NEVER GOTTEN AROUND TO DOING, IN THE PRESENT. THAT TIME HAS NOW COME.
I CANNOT GO BACK AS I AM, ONLY AS I *WAS* BUT IF I LEAVE THIS BODY, IT MAY REVERT TO ITS TRUE OWNER, AND I AM NOT YET READY FOR THAT TO HAPPEN.
I MUST LEAVE IT WITH YOU, FOR A TIME, ENSORCELLED AND IN-BETWEEN.
IN RETURN FOR WHAT?
I AM CLOSE, DEAR HELA. CLOSER THAN I HAVE EVER BEEN TO BRINGING DOWN MY BROTHER AND ALL WHO SERVE HIM. THE PIECES ARE NEARLY IN POSITION. THERE ARE BUT TWO STEPS LEFT AFTER THIS.
TO BREAK THAT WHICH CANNOT BE BROKEN, TO SHATTER THE WILL OF A GOD... CAN YOU THINK OF A BETTER PAYMENT?
YES, I CAN.
BUT THIS WILL DO FOR NOW.
JOIN YOUR POWER WITH MINE, LOKI. LET GO OF THE PRESENT FLESH AND REMEMBER YOUR FACE AS IT WAS WHEN YOU WERE BORN...WHEN YOU AGED...AND WHEN YOU LAST SAW IT.
THIS WILL BE PAINFUL.
THEN LET IT BURN.
FWOOOOOSH!

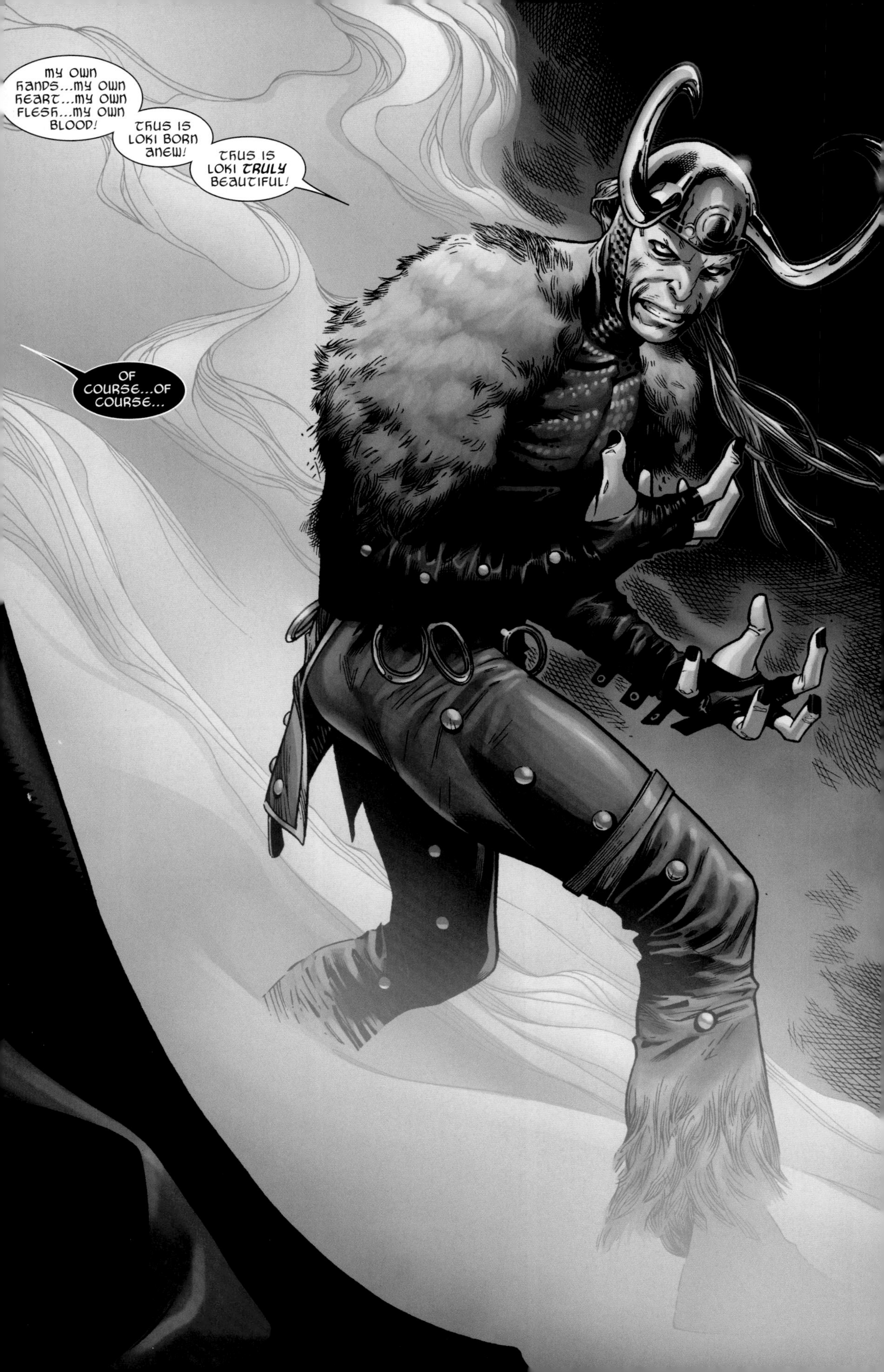
MY OWN HANDS...MY OWN HEART...MY OWN FLESH...MY OWN BLOOD!
THUS IS LOKI BORN ANEW!
THUS IS LOKI *TRULY* BEAUTIFUL!
OF COURSE...OF COURSE...

THERE IS SOMETHING ABOUT THIS BODY THAT FEELS...FAMILIAR TO ME.

I WOULD NOT BE AT ALL SURPRISED. LET'S JUST SAY FOR NOW THAT I *BORROWED* IT FROM SOMEONE WHO WILL HAVE NO USE FOR IT VERY SOON.

NOW...WE MUST MOVE QUICKLY. THE SKIN CANNOT LONG SURVIVE WITHOUT A HOST.

THEN PREPARE YOURSELF, LOKI.

MY POWER IS YOUR POWER...MY VOICE, YOUR VOICE...MY STRENGTH, YOUR STRENGTH...TO PIERCE THE VEIL OF TIME AND SPACE.

DO WHAT YOU MUST AND DO NOT TARRY, LOKI. CALL MY NAME WHEN YOU ARE READY TO RETURN.

I SHALL.

YOU SHALL BE WELL REPAID FOR THIS KINDNESS, HELA...YOU SHALL BE...

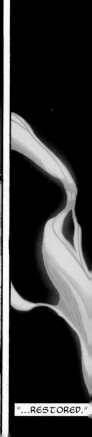

"...RESTORED."

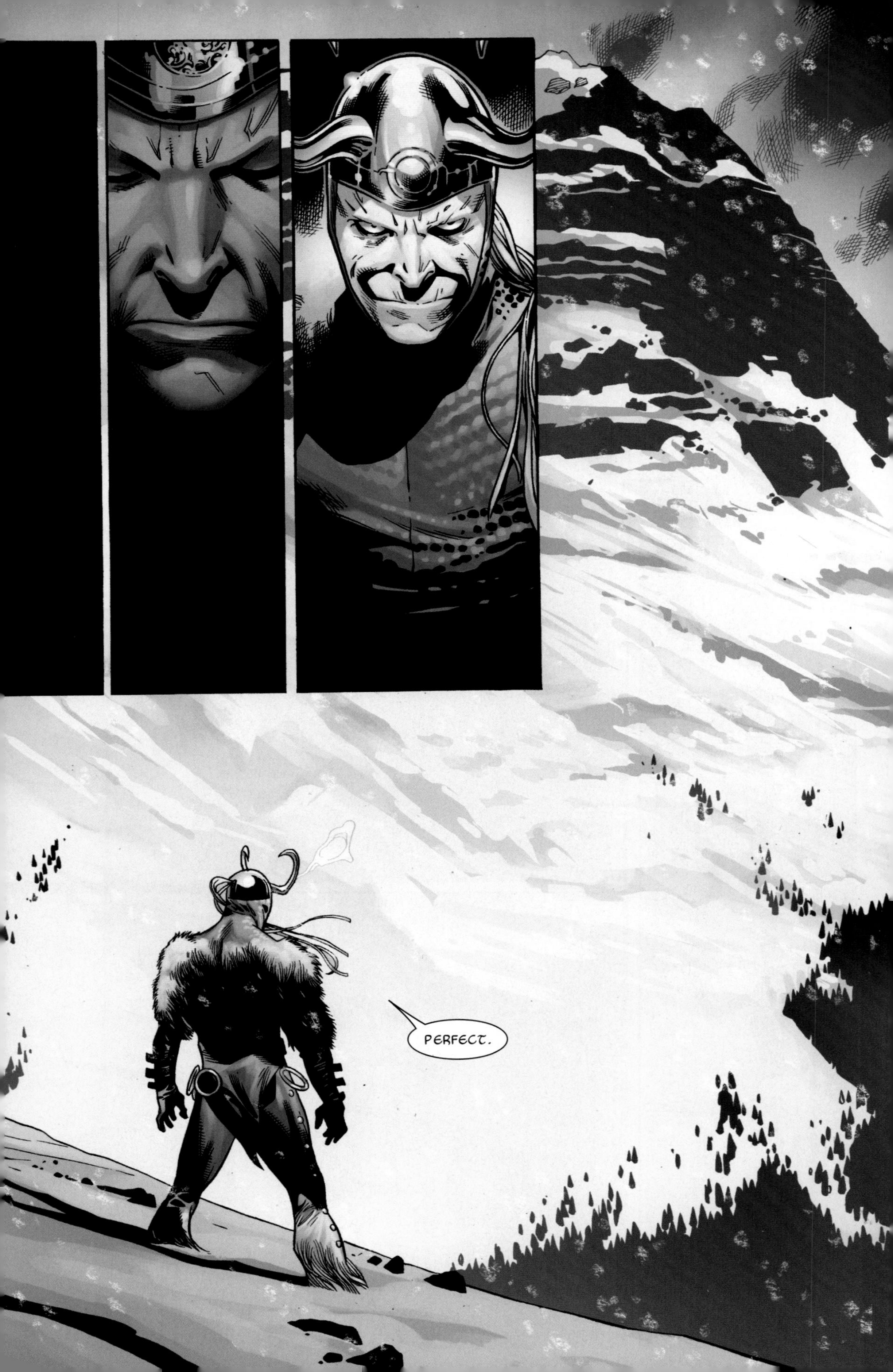
PERFECT.

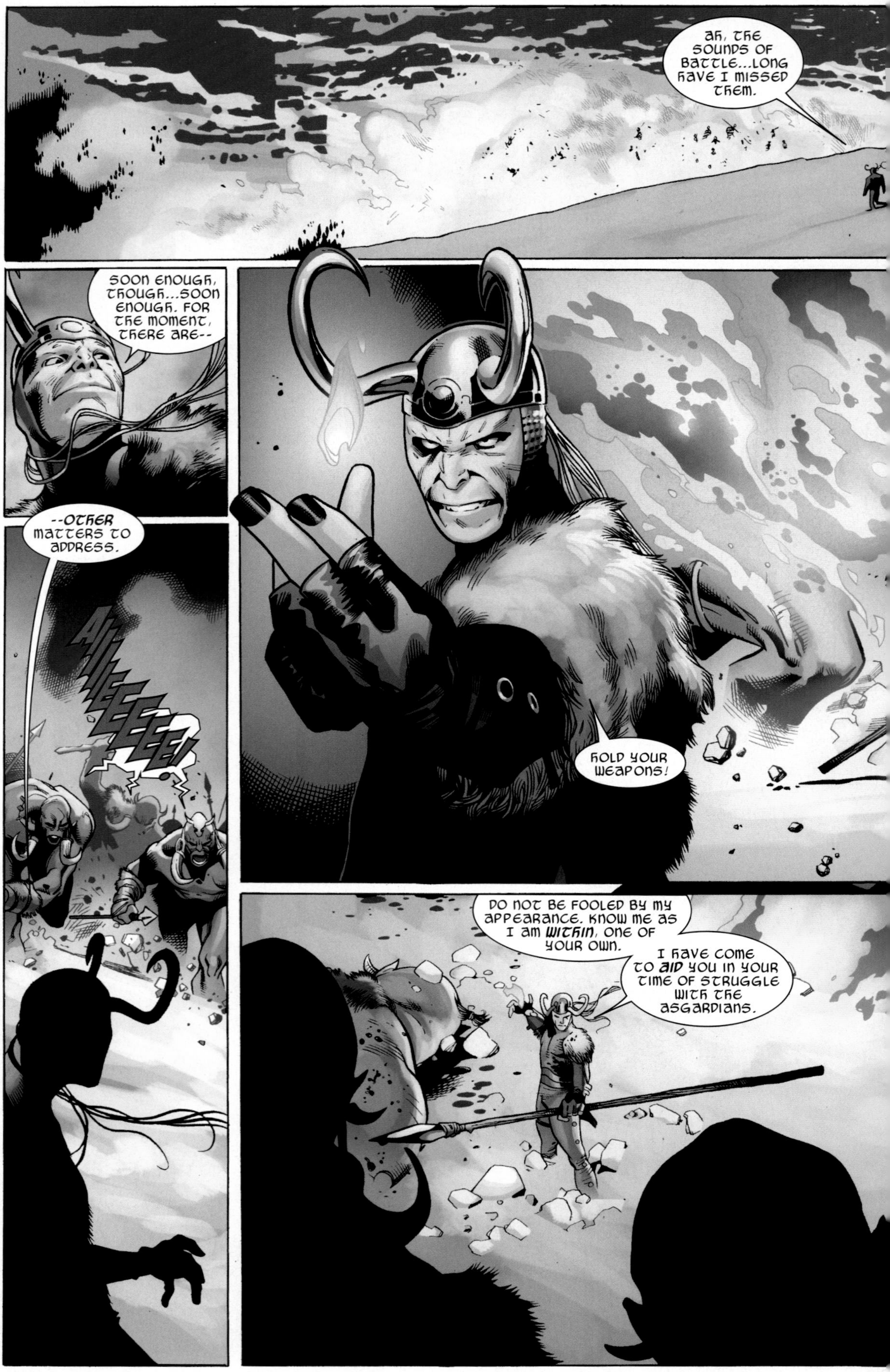
AH, THE SOUNDS OF BATTLE...LONG HAVE I MISSED THEM.
SOON ENOUGH, THOUGH...SOON ENOUGH. FOR THE MOMENT, THERE ARE--
--OTHER MATTERS TO ADDRESS.
AIIEEEEEEE!
HOLD YOUR WEAPONS!
DO NOT BE FOOLED BY MY APPEARANCE. KNOW ME AS I AM WITHIN, ONE OF YOUR OWN.
I HAVE COME TO AID YOU IN YOUR TIME OF STRUGGLE WITH THE ASGARDIANS.

I SAID--

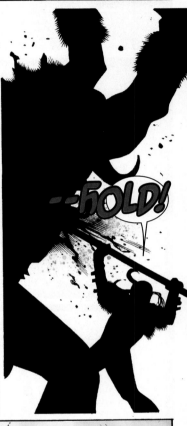

--HOLD!

I SMELL IN YOU THE BLOOD THAT RUNS THROUGH MY VEINS.

WHAT DO YOU WANT FROM US?

A MOMENT ONLY. A FLICKER OF TIME.

A CLOAK, THAT I MAY CONCEAL MY APPEARANCE.

AND YOUR FASTEST RUNNER.

"ONE WHOSE SPEED AND SKILL WILL DRAW THE ATTENTION OF THE LORD OF ASGARD--

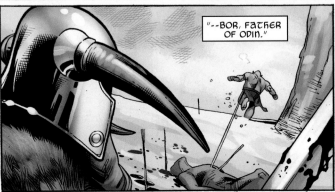

"--BOR, FATHER OF ODIN."

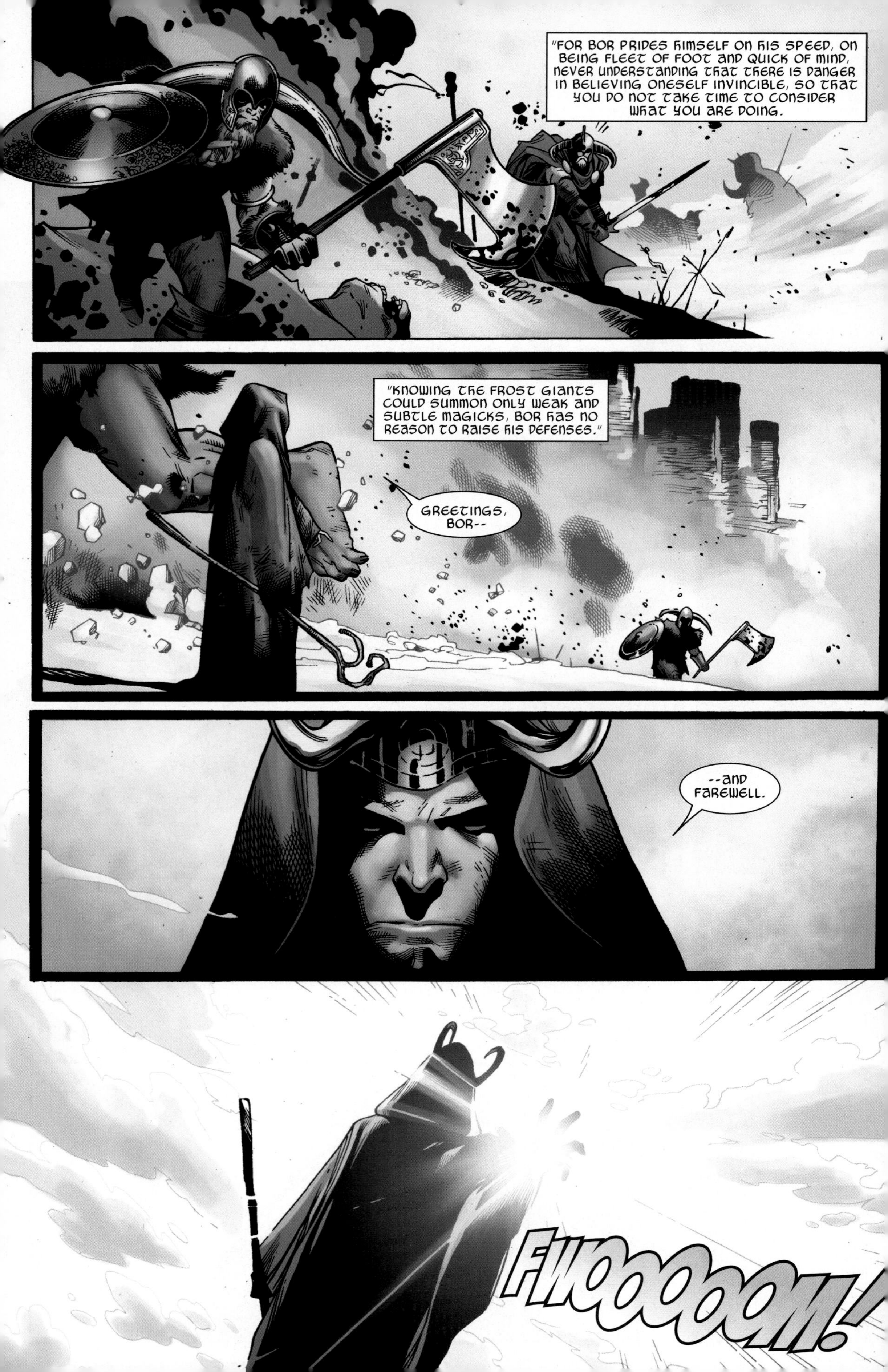
"FOR BOR PRIDES HIMSELF ON HIS SPEED, ON BEING FLEET OF FOOT AND QUICK OF MIND, NEVER UNDERSTANDING THAT THERE IS DANGER IN BELIEVING ONESELF INVINCIBLE, SO THAT YOU DO NOT TAKE TIME TO CONSIDER WHAT YOU ARE DOING.
"KNOWING THE FROST GIANTS COULD SUMMON ONLY WEAK AND SUBTLE MAGICKS, BOR HAS NO REASON TO RAISE HIS DEFENSES."
GREETINGS, BOR--
--AND FAREWELL.
FWOOOOOM!

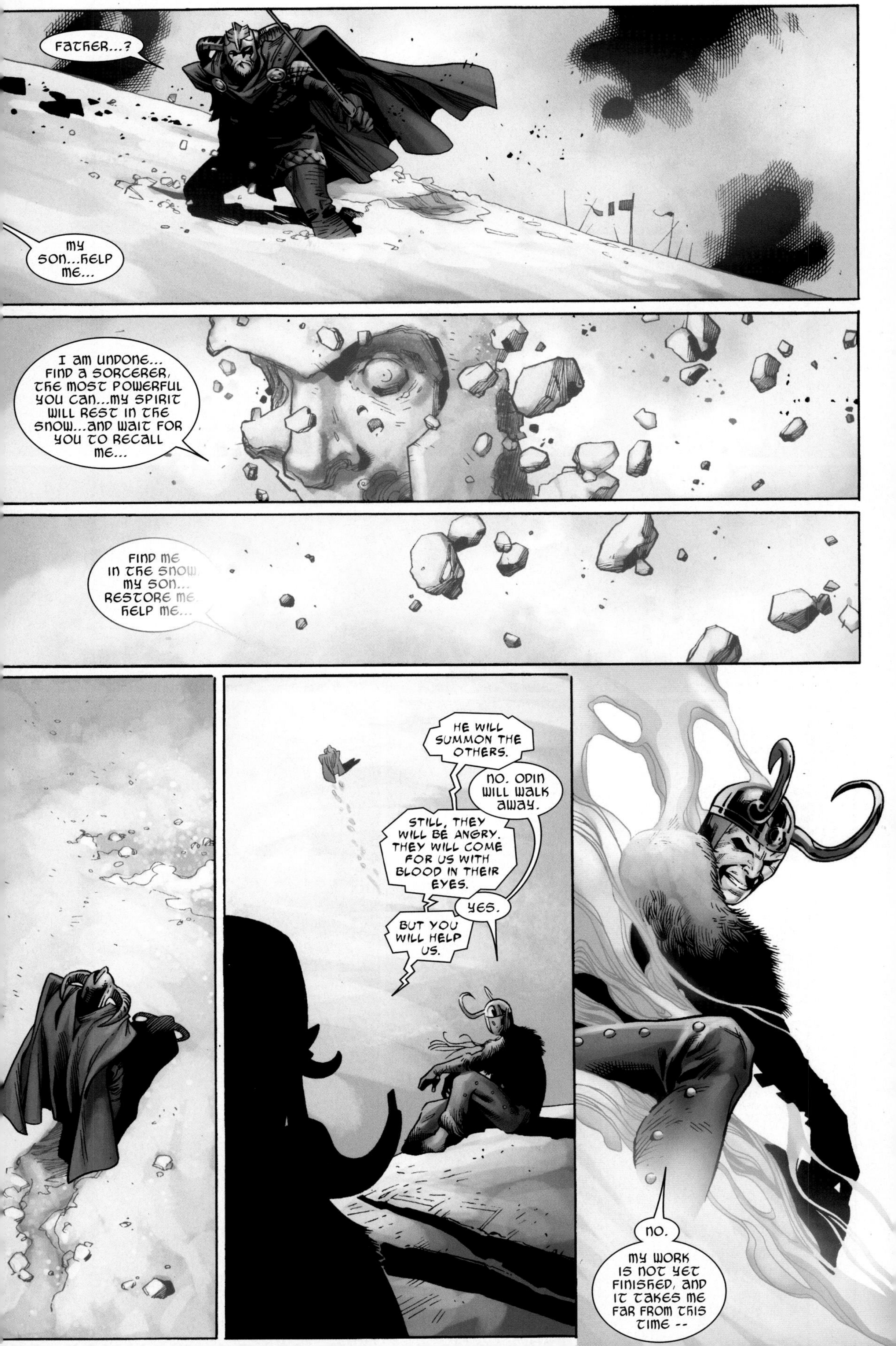
FATHER...?
MY SON...HELP ME...
I AM UNDONE... FIND A SORCERER, THE MOST POWERFUL YOU CAN...MY SPIRIT WILL REST IN THE SNOW...AND WAIT FOR YOU TO RECALL ME...
FIND ME IN THE SNOW, MY SON... RESTORE ME. HELP ME...
HE WILL SUMMON THE OTHERS.
NO. ODIN WILL WALK AWAY.
STILL, THEY WILL BE ANGRY. THEY WILL COME FOR US WITH BLOOD IN THEIR EYES.
YES.
BUT YOU WILL HELP US.
NO.
MY WORK IS NOT YET FINISHED, AND IT TAKES ME FAR FROM THIS TIME --

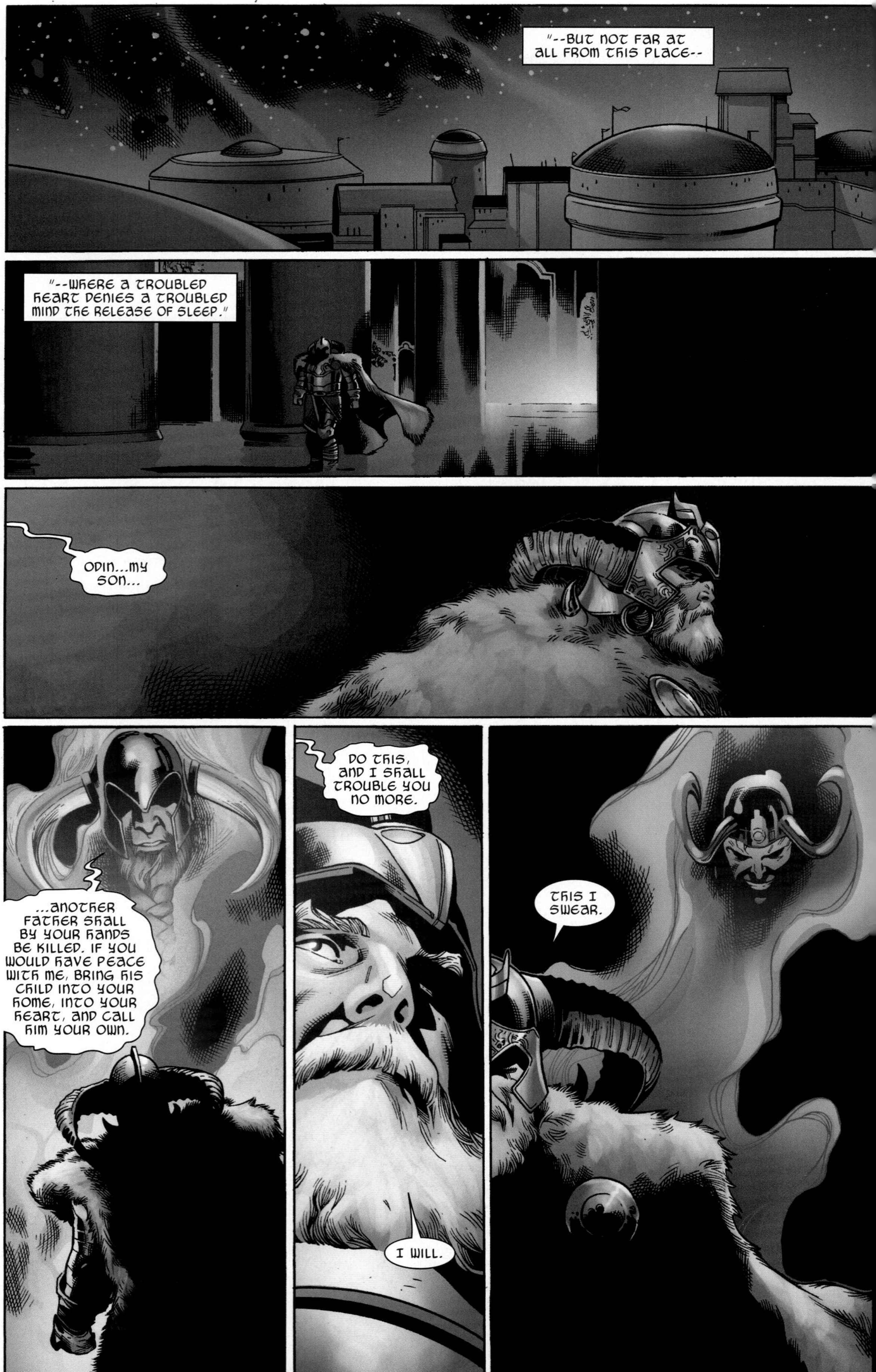
"--BUT NOT FAR AT ALL FROM THIS PLACE--
"--WHERE A TROUBLED HEART DENIES A TROUBLED MIND THE RELEASE OF SLEEP."
ODIN...MY SON...
...ANOTHER FATHER SHALL BY YOUR HANDS BE KILLED. IF YOU WOULD HAVE PEACE WITH ME, BRING HIS CHILD INTO YOUR HOME, INTO YOUR HEART, AND CALL HIM YOUR OWN.
DO THIS, AND I SHALL TROUBLE YOU NO MORE.
I WILL.
THIS I SWEAR.

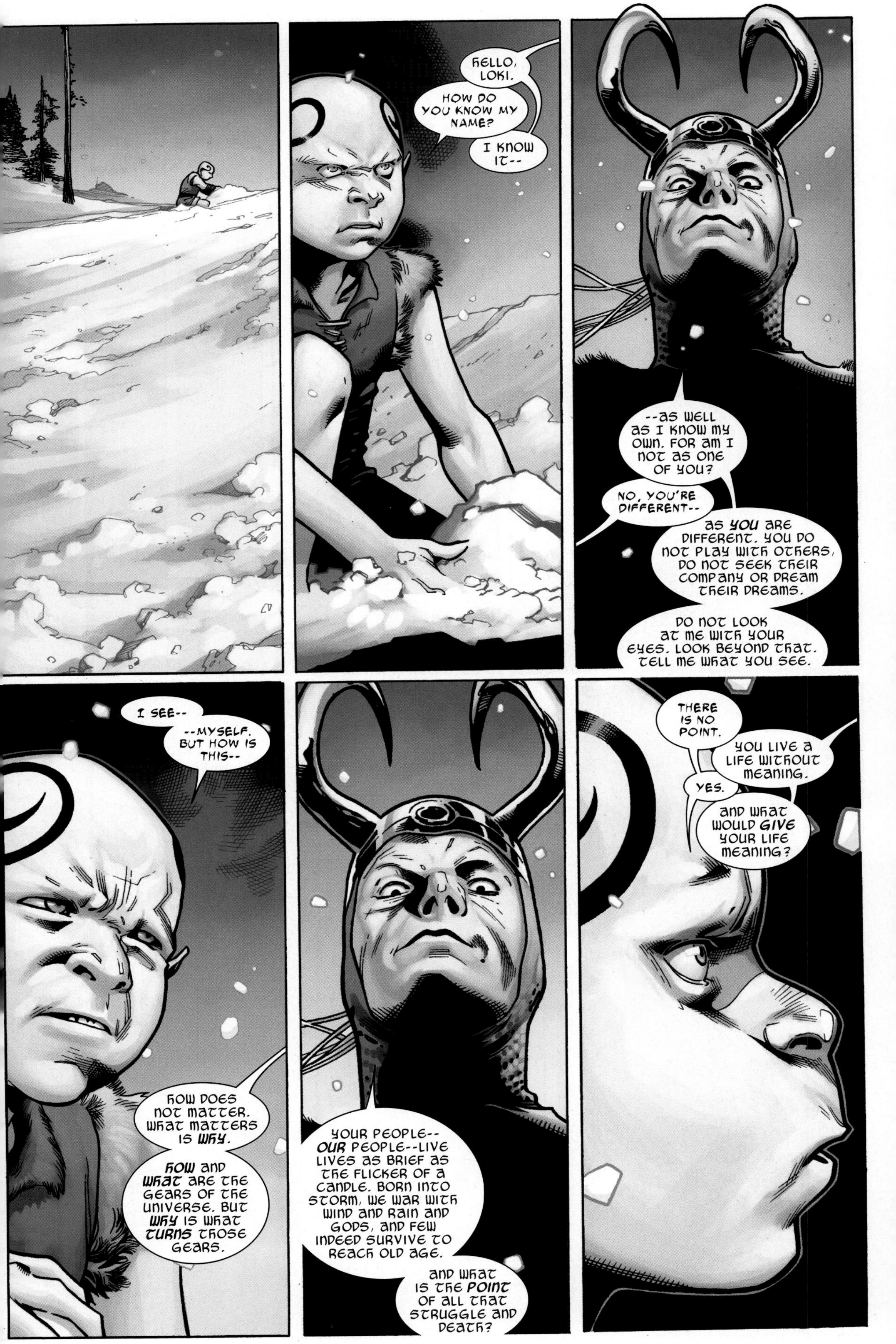
HELLO, LOKI.
HOW DO YOU KNOW MY NAME?
I KNOW IT--
--AS WELL AS I KNOW MY OWN. FOR AM I NOT AS ONE OF YOU?
NO, YOU'RE DIFFERENT--
AS YOU ARE DIFFERENT. YOU DO NOT PLAY WITH OTHERS, DO NOT SEEK THEIR COMPANY OR DREAM THEIR DREAMS.
DO NOT LOOK AT ME WITH YOUR EYES. LOOK BEYOND THAT. TELL ME WHAT YOU SEE.
I SEE--
--MYSELF. BUT HOW IS THIS--
HOW DOES NOT MATTER. WHAT MATTERS IS WHY.
HOW AND WHAT ARE THE GEARS OF THE UNIVERSE. BUT WHY IS WHAT TURNS THOSE GEARS.
YOUR PEOPLE-- OUR PEOPLE--LIVE LIVES AS BRIEF AS THE FLICKER OF A CANDLE. BORN INTO STORM, WE WAR WITH WIND AND RAIN AND GODS, AND FEW INDEED SURVIVE TO REACH OLD AGE.
AND WHAT IS THE POINT OF ALL THAT STRUGGLE AND DEATH?
THERE IS NO POINT.
YOU LIVE A LIFE WITHOUT MEANING.
YES.
AND WHAT WOULD GIVE YOUR LIFE MEANING?

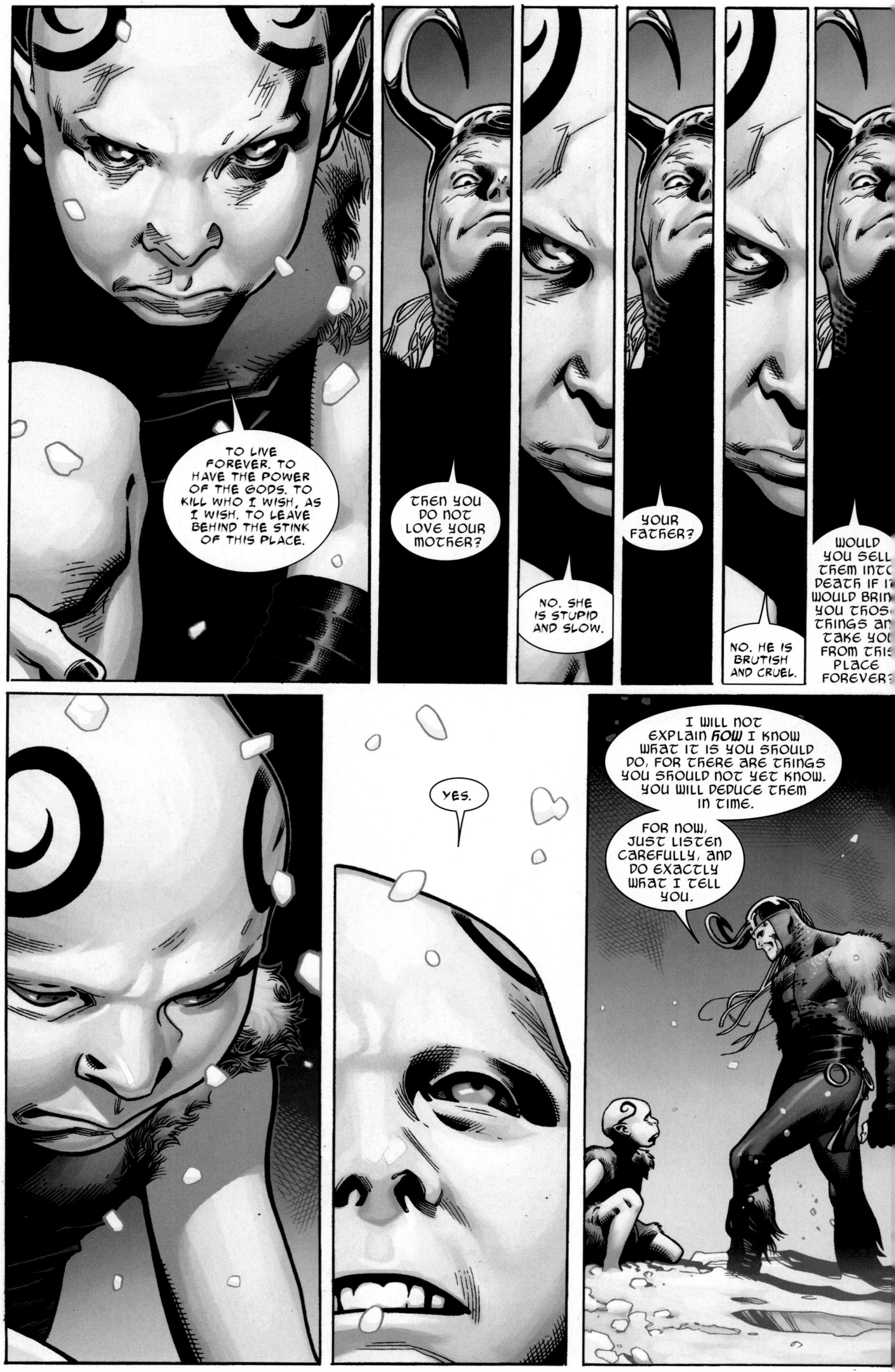
TO LIVE FOREVER. TO HAVE THE POWER OF THE GODS. TO KILL WHO I WISH, AS I WISH. TO LEAVE BEHIND THE STINK OF THIS PLACE.
THEN YOU DO NOT LOVE YOUR MOTHER?
NO. SHE IS STUPID AND SLOW.
YOUR FATHER?
NO. HE IS BRUTISH AND CRUEL.
WOULD YOU SELL THEM INTO DEATH IF IT WOULD BRING YOU THOSE THINGS AND TAKE YOU FROM THIS PLACE FOREVER?
YES.
I WILL NOT EXPLAIN HOW I KNOW WHAT IT IS YOU SHOULD DO, FOR THERE ARE THINGS YOU SHOULD NOT YET KNOW. YOU WILL DEDUCE THEM IN TIME.
FOR NOW, JUST LISTEN CAREFULLY, AND DO EXACTLY WHAT I TELL YOU.

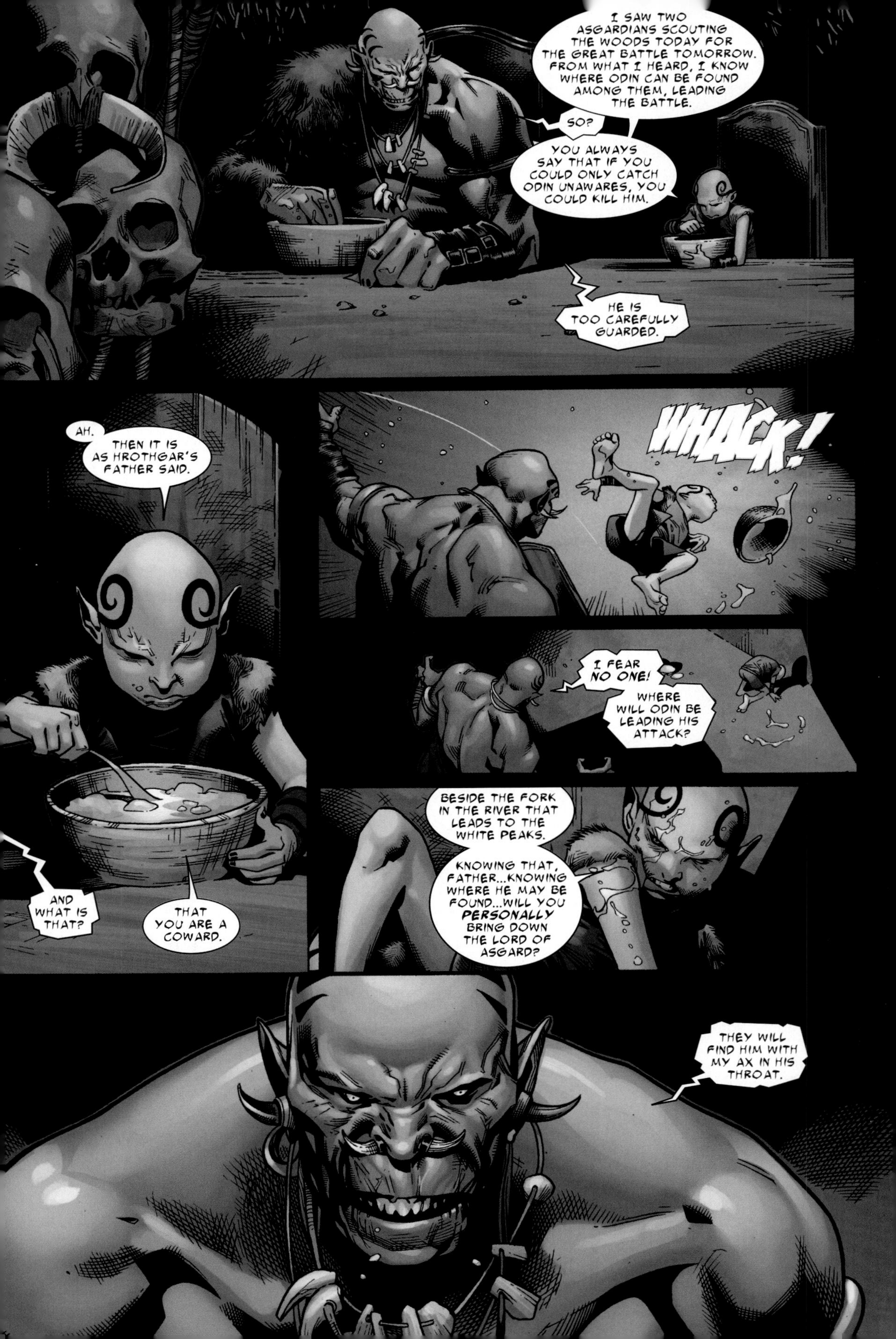
I SAW TWO ASGARDIANS SCOUTING THE WOODS TODAY FOR THE GREAT BATTLE TOMORROW. FROM WHAT I HEARD, I KNOW WHERE ODIN CAN BE FOUND AMONG THEM, LEADING THE BATTLE.
SO?
YOU ALWAYS SAY THAT IF YOU COULD ONLY CATCH ODIN UNAWARES, YOU COULD KILL HIM.
HE IS TOO CAREFULLY GUARDED.
AH.
THEN IT IS AS HROTHGAR'S FATHER SAID.
AND WHAT IS THAT?
THAT YOU ARE A COWARD.
WHACK!
I FEAR NO ONE!
WHERE WILL ODIN BE LEADING HIS ATTACK?
BESIDE THE FORK IN THE RIVER THAT LEADS TO THE WHITE PEAKS.
KNOWING THAT, FATHER...KNOWING WHERE HE MAY BE FOUND...WILL YOU PERSONALLY BRING DOWN THE LORD OF ASGARD?
THEY WILL FIND HIM WITH MY AX IN HIS THROAT.

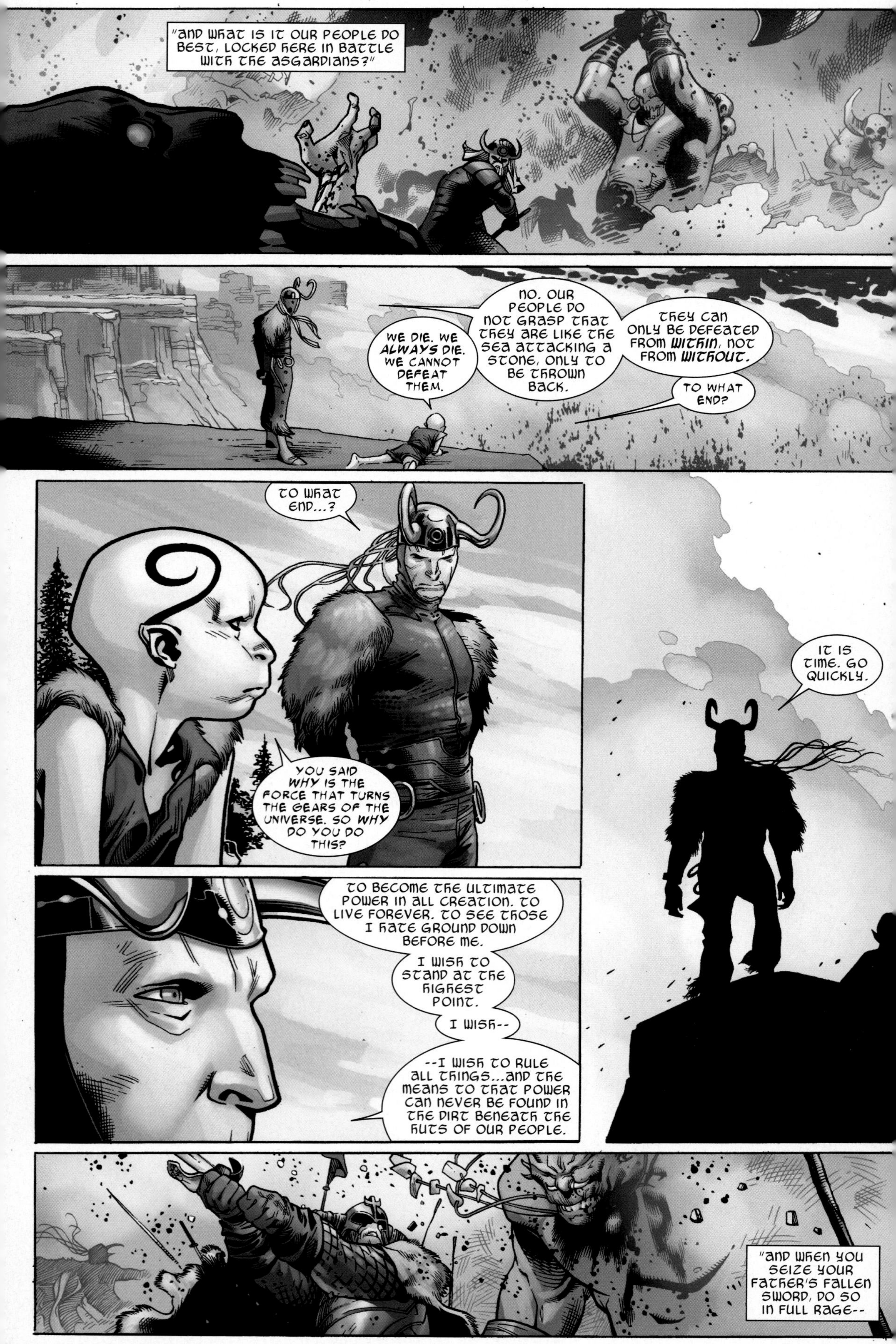
"AND WHAT IS IT OUR PEOPLE DO BEST, LOCKED HERE IN BATTLE WITH THE ASGARDIANS?"
WE DIE. WE ALWAYS DIE. WE CANNOT DEFEAT THEM.
NO. OUR PEOPLE DO NOT GRASP THAT THEY ARE LIKE THE SEA ATTACKING A STONE, ONLY TO BE THROWN BACK.
THEY CAN ONLY BE DEFEATED FROM WITHIN, NOT FROM WITHOUT.
TO WHAT END?
TO WHAT END...?
YOU SAID WHY IS THE FORCE THAT TURNS THE GEARS OF THE UNIVERSE. SO WHY DO YOU DO THIS?
IT IS TIME. GO QUICKLY.
TO BECOME THE ULTIMATE POWER IN ALL CREATION. TO LIVE FOREVER. TO SEE THOSE I HATE GROUND DOWN BEFORE ME.
I WISH TO STAND AT THE HIGHEST POINT.
I WISH--
--I WISH TO RULE ALL THINGS...AND THE MEANS TO THAT POWER CAN NEVER BE FOUND IN THE DIRT BENEATH THE HUTS OF OUR PEOPLE.
"AND WHEN YOU SEIZE YOUR FATHER'S FALLEN SWORD, DO SO IN FULL RAGE--

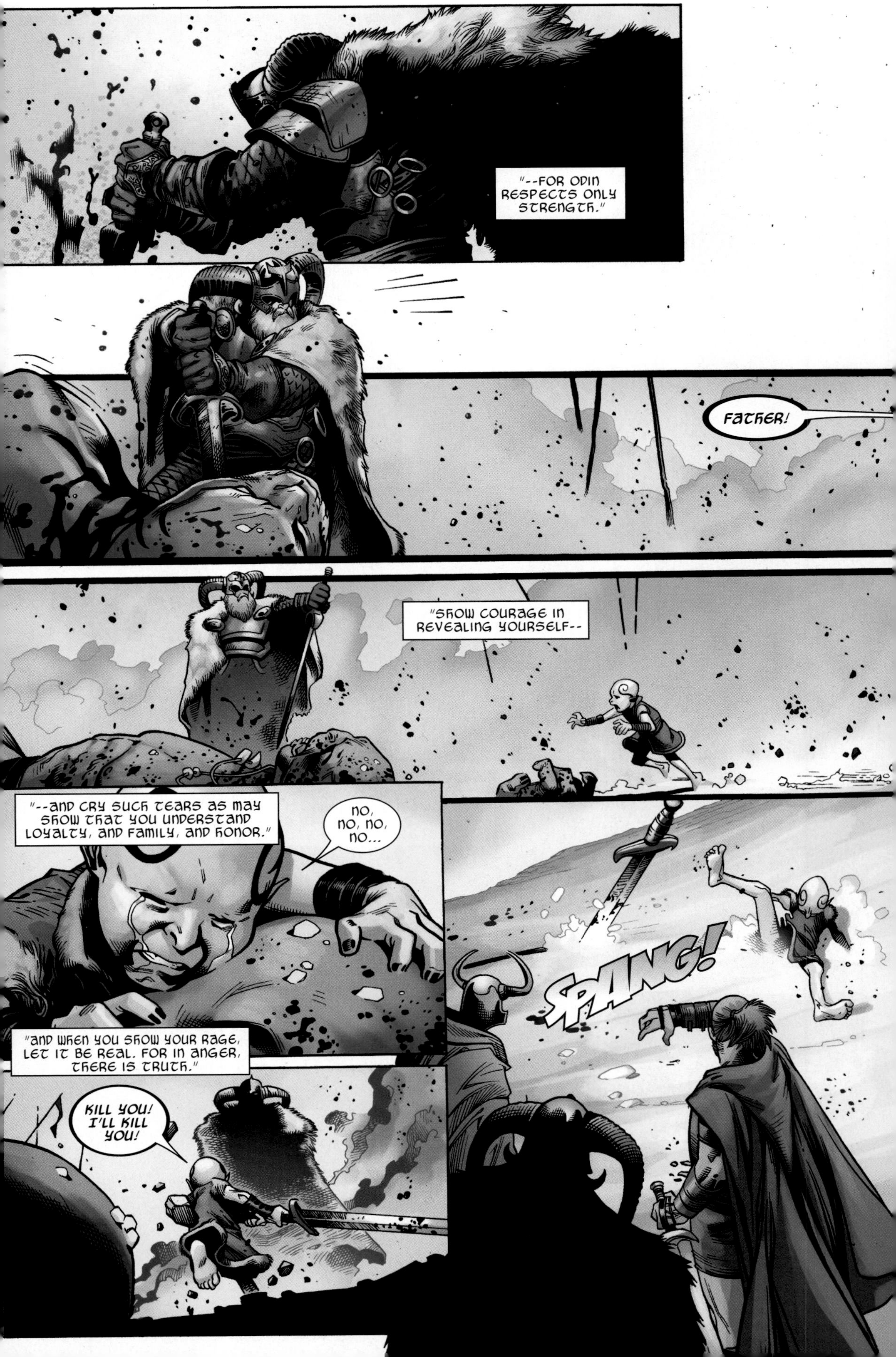

"--FOR ODIN RESPECTS ONLY STRENGTH."
FATHER!
"SHOW COURAGE IN REVEALING YOURSELF--
"--AND CRY SUCH TEARS AS MAY SHOW THAT YOU UNDERSTAND LOYALTY, AND FAMILY, AND HONOR."
NO, NO, NO, NO...
"AND WHEN YOU SHOW YOUR RAGE, LET IT BE REAL. FOR IN ANGER, THERE IS TRUTH."
KILL YOU! I'LL KILL YOU!
SPANG!

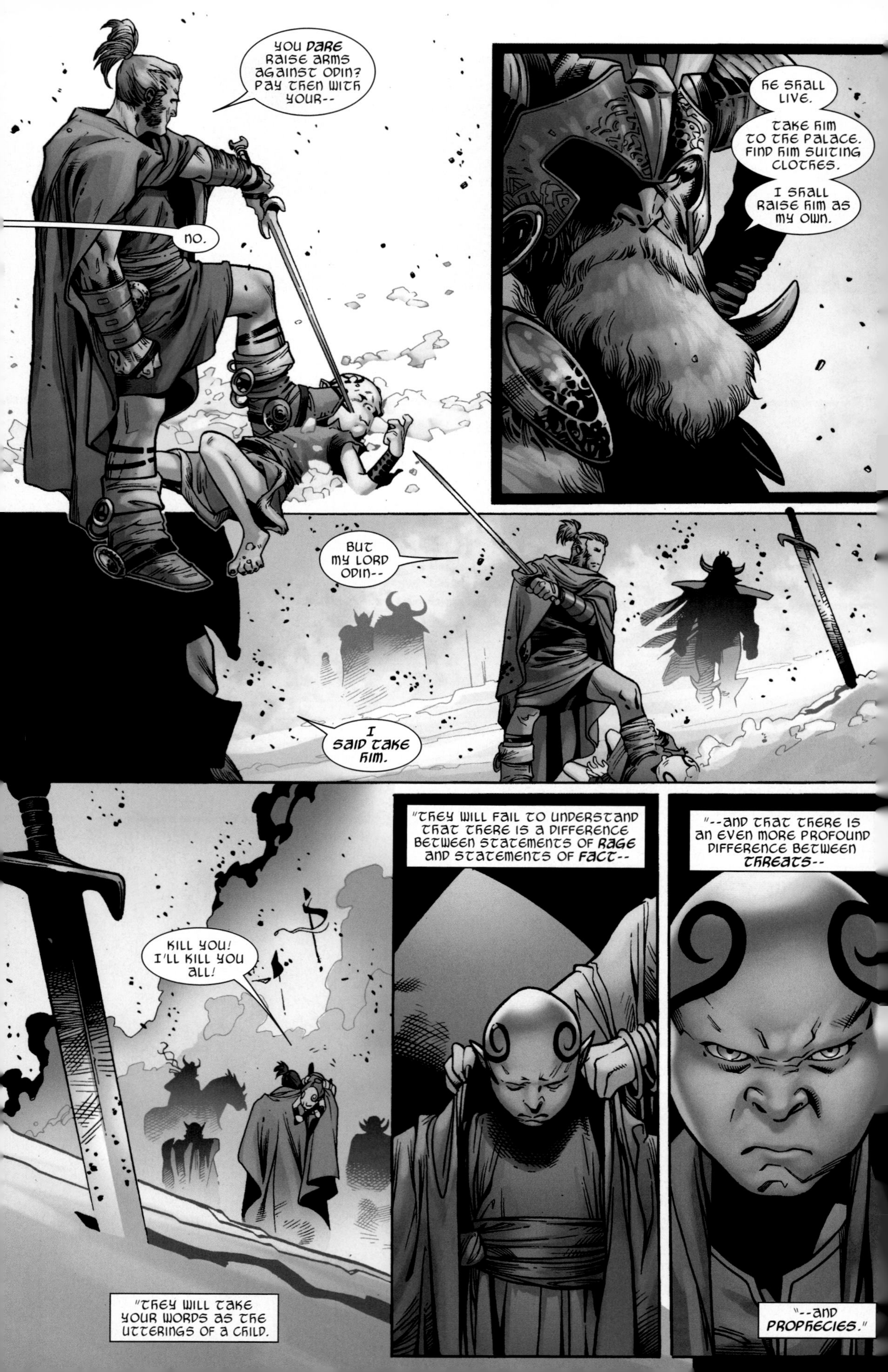
YOU DARE RAISE ARMS AGAINST ODIN? PAY THEN WITH YOUR--
NO.
HE SHALL LIVE.
TAKE HIM TO THE PALACE. FIND HIM SUITING CLOTHES.
I SHALL RAISE HIM AS MY OWN.
BUT MY LORD ODIN--
I SAID TAKE HIM.
KILL YOU! I'LL KILL YOU ALL!
"THEY WILL TAKE YOUR WORDS AS THE UTTERINGS OF A CHILD.
"THEY WILL FAIL TO UNDERSTAND THAT THERE IS A DIFFERENCE BETWEEN STATEMENTS OF RAGE AND STATEMENTS OF FACT--
"--AND THAT THERE IS AN EVEN MORE PROFOUND DIFFERENCE BETWEEN THREATS--
"--AND PROPHECIES."

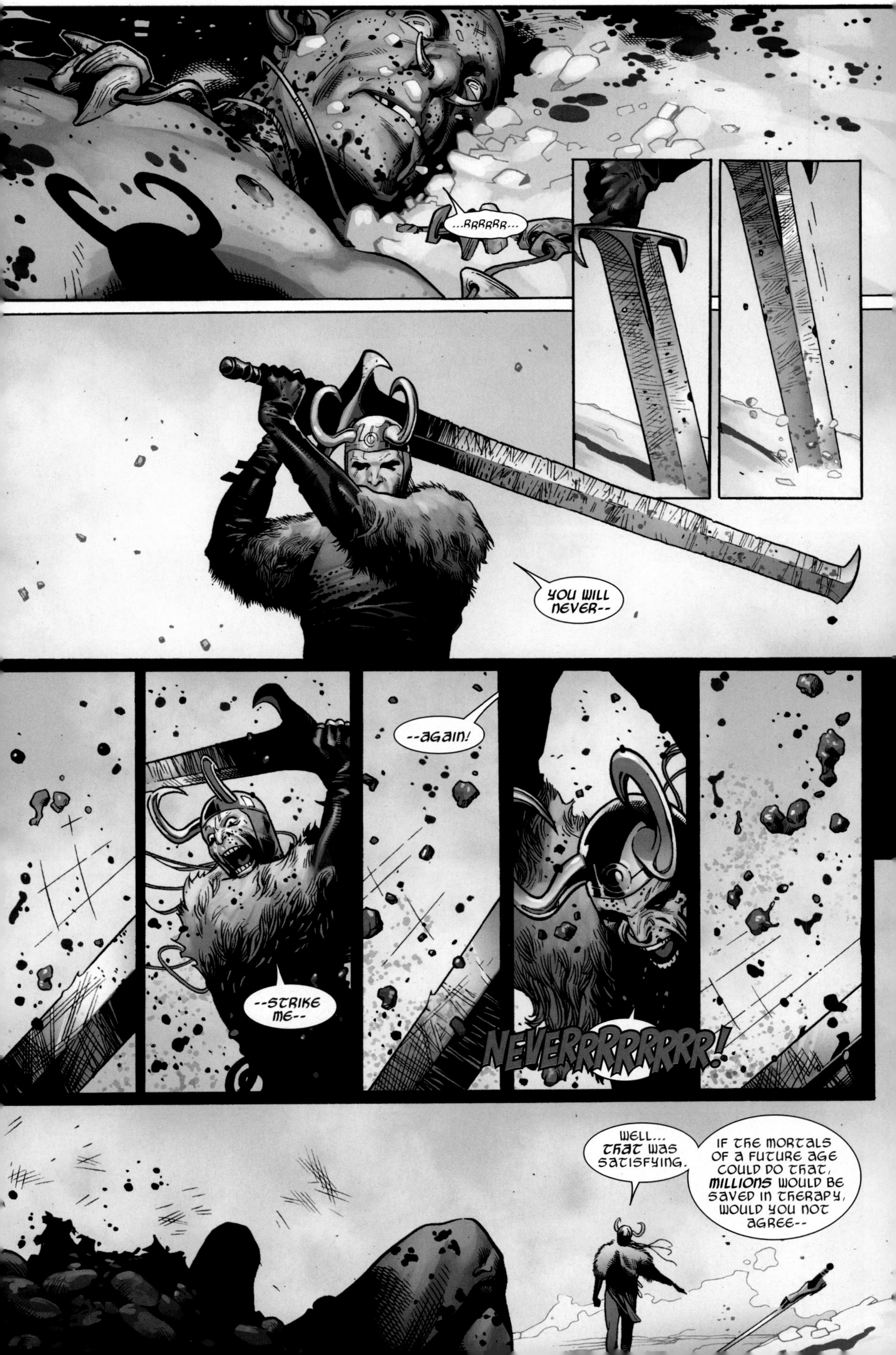
...RRRRRR...
YOU WILL NEVER--
--STRIKE ME--
--AGAIN!
NEVERRRRRRRR!
WELL... THAT WAS SATISFYING.
IF THE MORTALS OF A FUTURE AGE COULD DO THAT, MILLIONS WOULD BE SAVED IN THERAPY, WOULD YOU NOT AGREE--

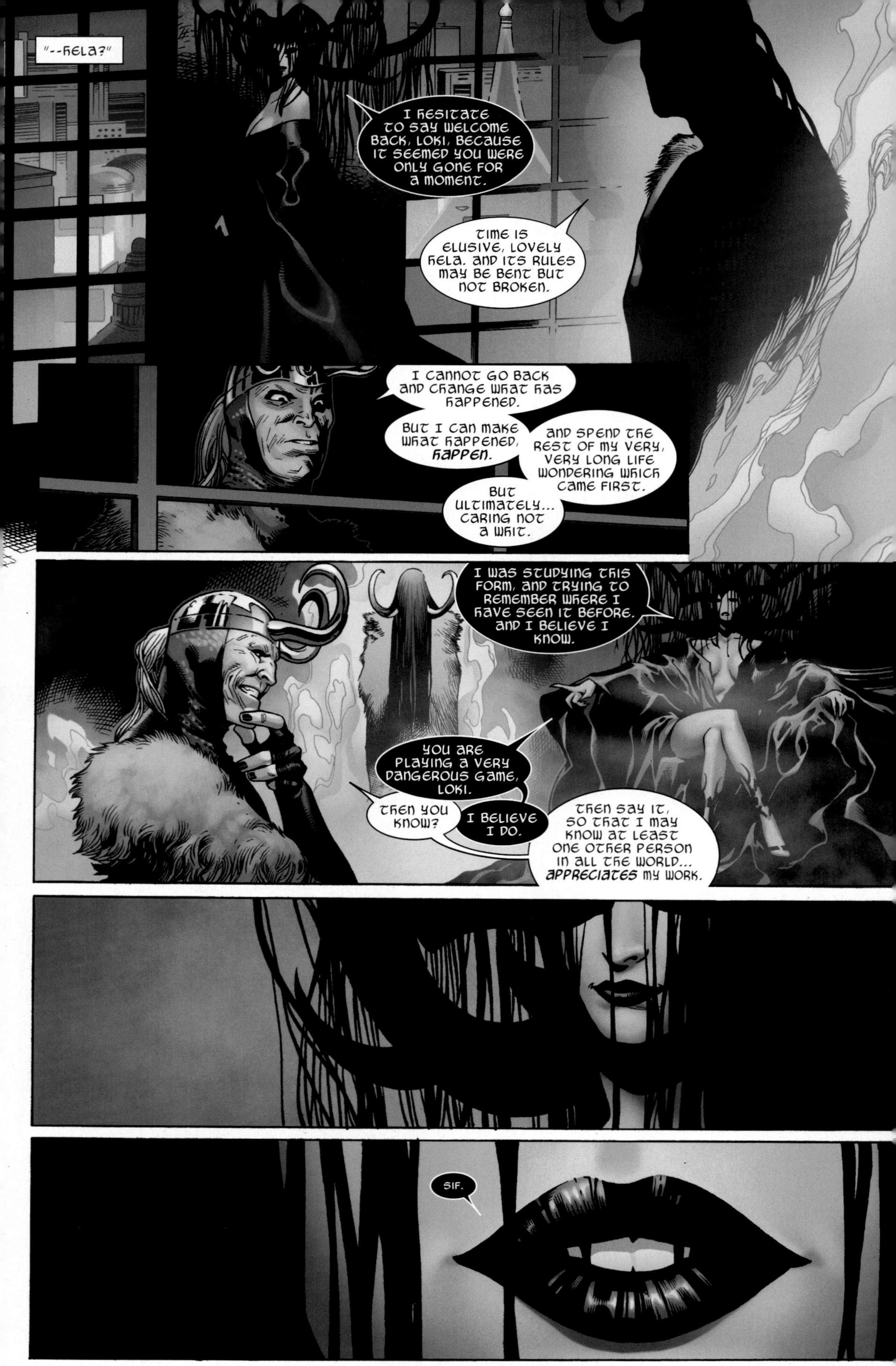
"--HELA?"
I HESITATE TO SAY WELCOME BACK, LOKI, BECAUSE IT SEEMED YOU WERE ONLY GONE FOR A MOMENT.
TIME IS ELUSIVE, LOVELY HELA. AND ITS RULES MAY BE BENT BUT NOT BROKEN.
I CANNOT GO BACK AND CHANGE WHAT HAS HAPPENED.
BUT I CAN MAKE WHAT HAPPENED, HAPPEN.
AND SPEND THE REST OF MY VERY, VERY LONG LIFE WONDERING WHICH CAME FIRST.
BUT ULTIMATELY... CARING NOT A WHIT.
I WAS STUDYING THIS FORM, AND TRYING TO REMEMBER WHERE I HAVE SEEN IT BEFORE. AND I BELIEVE I KNOW.
YOU ARE PLAYING A VERY DANGEROUS GAME, LOKI.
THEN YOU KNOW?
I BELIEVE I DO.
THEN SAY IT, SO THAT I MAY KNOW AT LEAST ONE OTHER PERSON IN ALL THE WORLD... APPRECIATES MY WORK.
SIF.

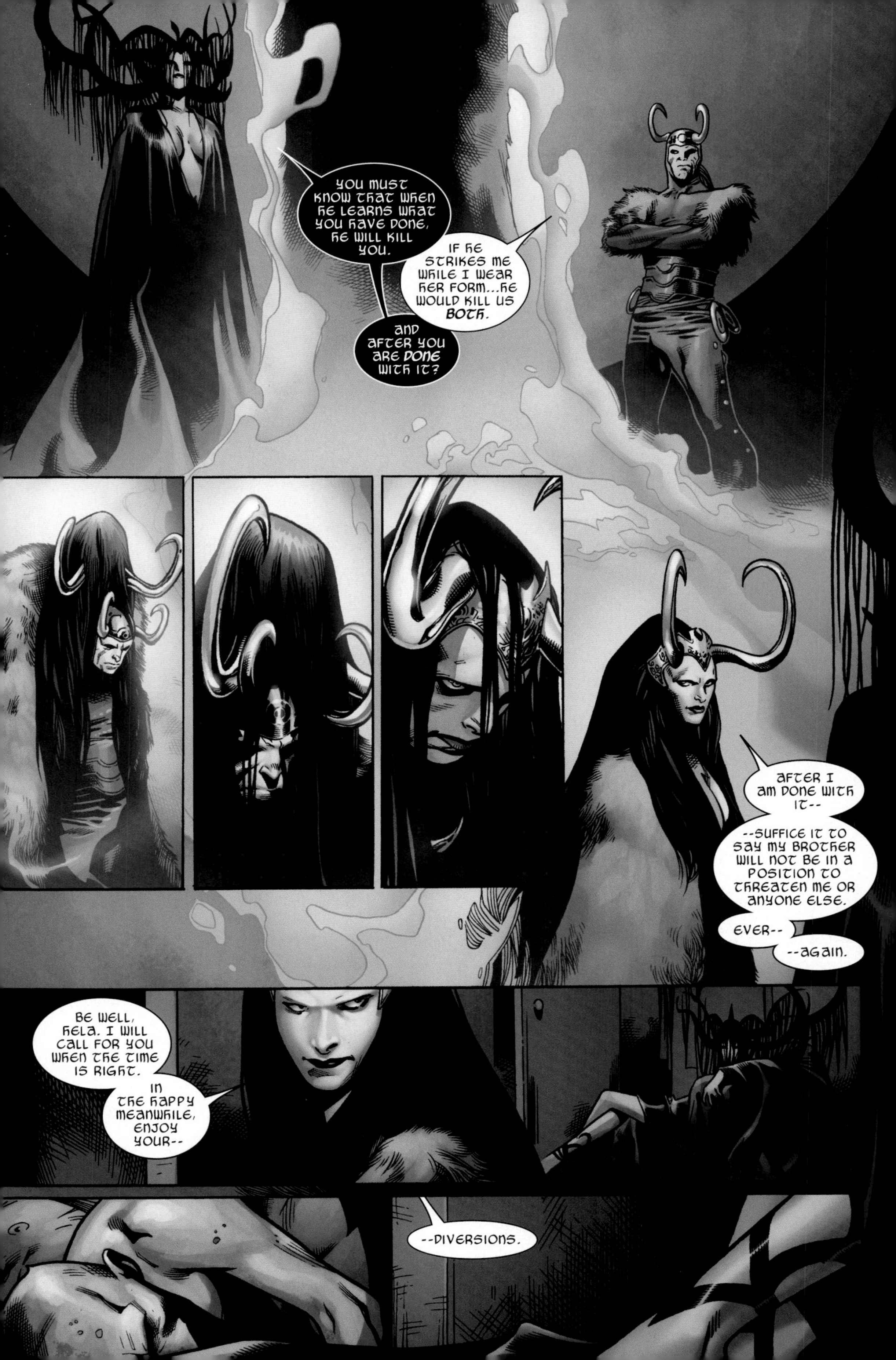
YOU MUST KNOW THAT WHEN HE LEARNS WHAT YOU HAVE DONE, HE WILL KILL YOU.
IF HE STRIKES ME WHILE I WEAR HER FORM...HE WOULD KILL US BOTH.
AND AFTER YOU ARE DONE WITH IT?
AFTER I AM DONE WITH IT--
--SUFFICE IT TO SAY MY BROTHER WILL NOT BE IN A POSITION TO THREATEN ME OR ANYONE ELSE.
EVER--
--AGAIN.
BE WELL, HELA. I WILL CALL FOR YOU WHEN THE TIME IS RIGHT.
IN THE HAPPY MEANWHILE, ENJOY YOUR--
--DIVERSIONS.

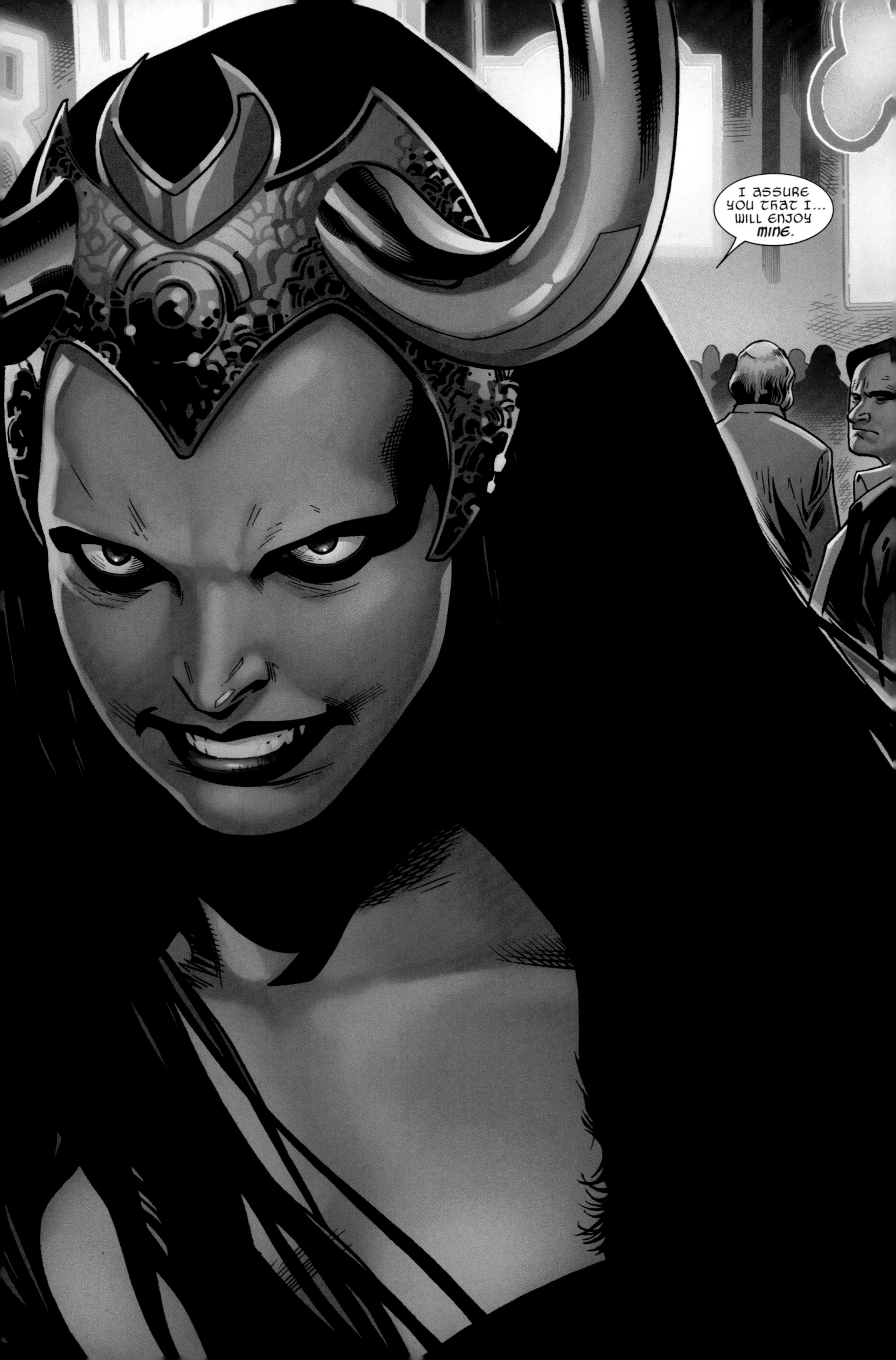
I ASSURE YOU THAT I... WILL ENJOY MINE.

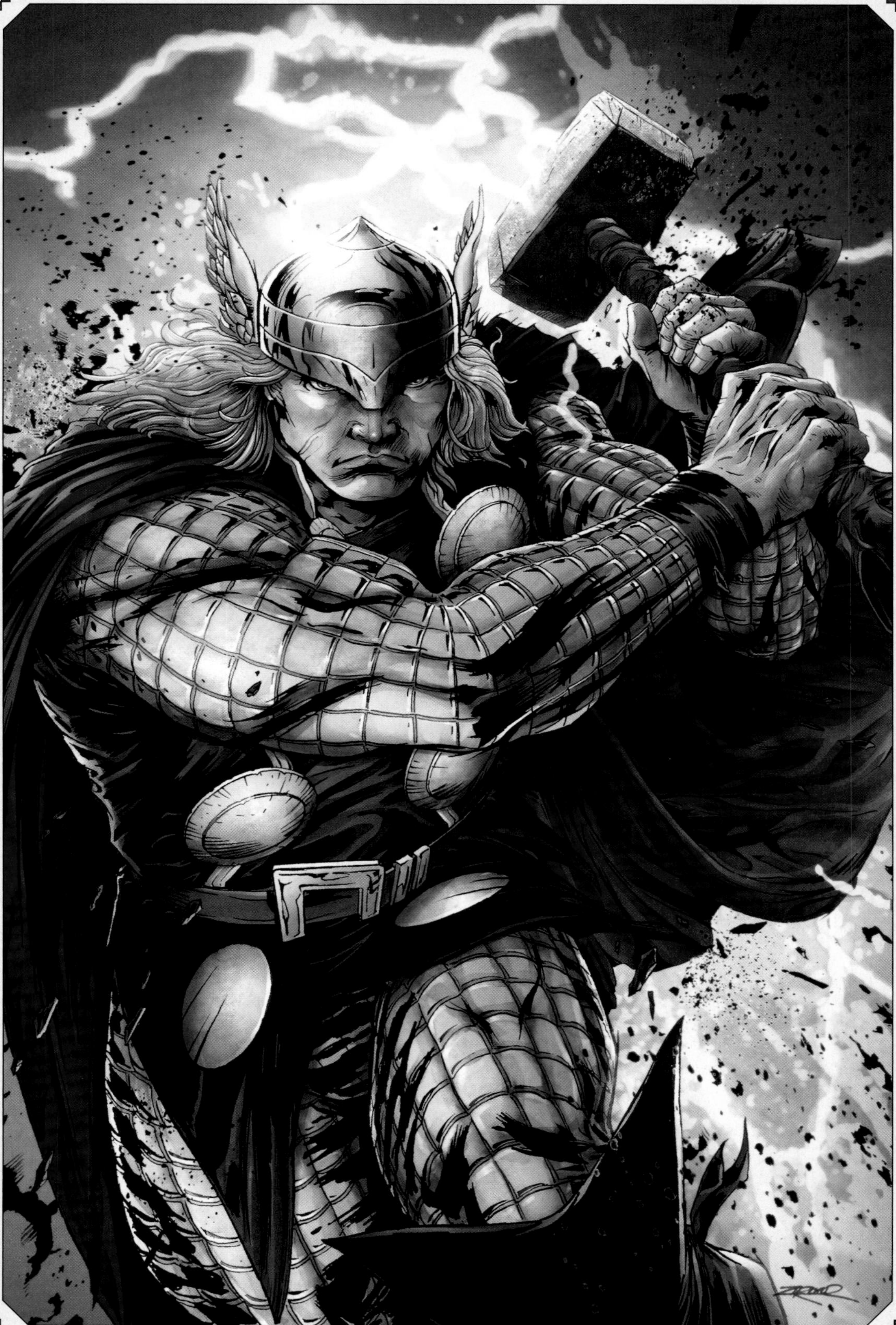

Thor #600 variant by Patch Zircher & June Chung

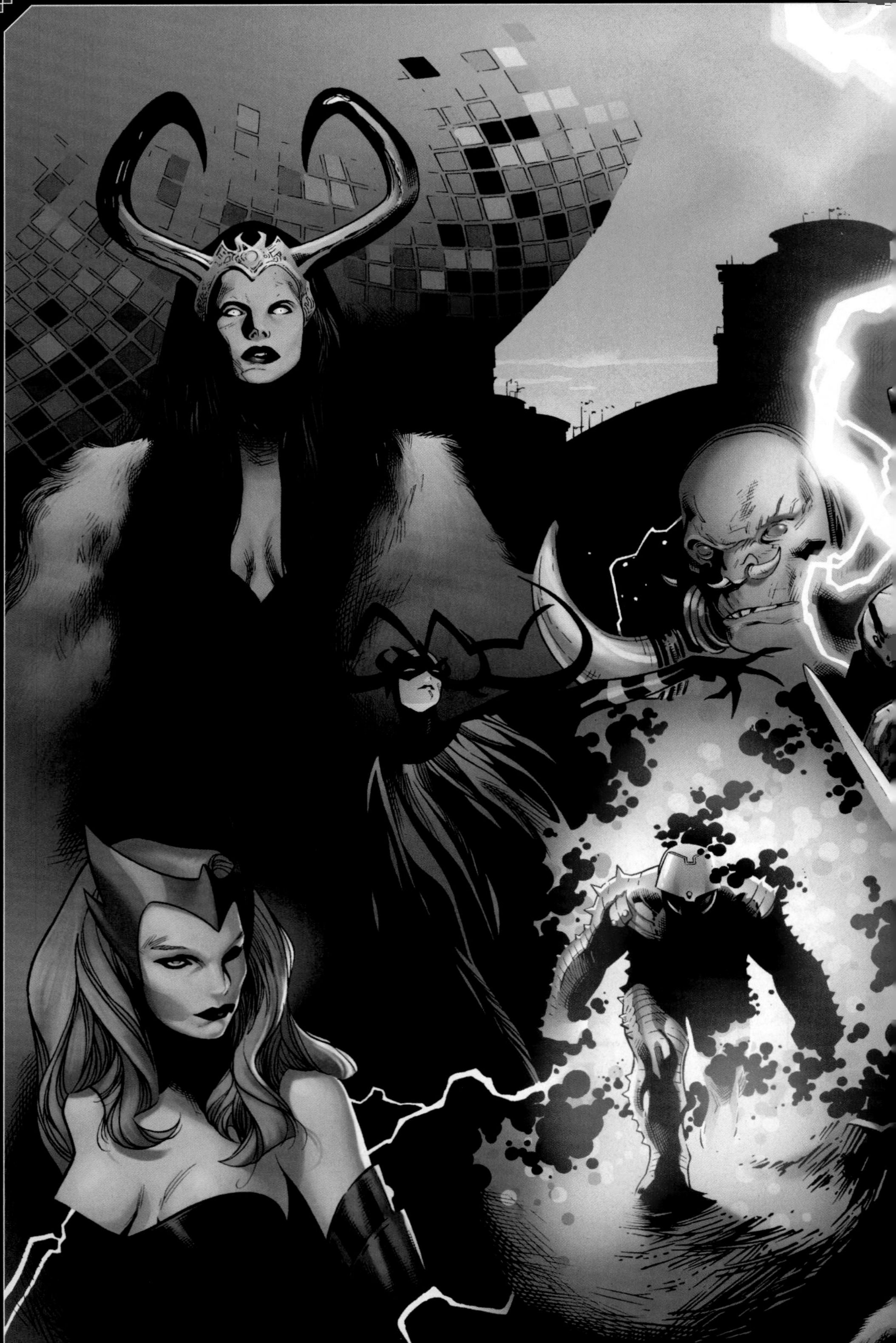

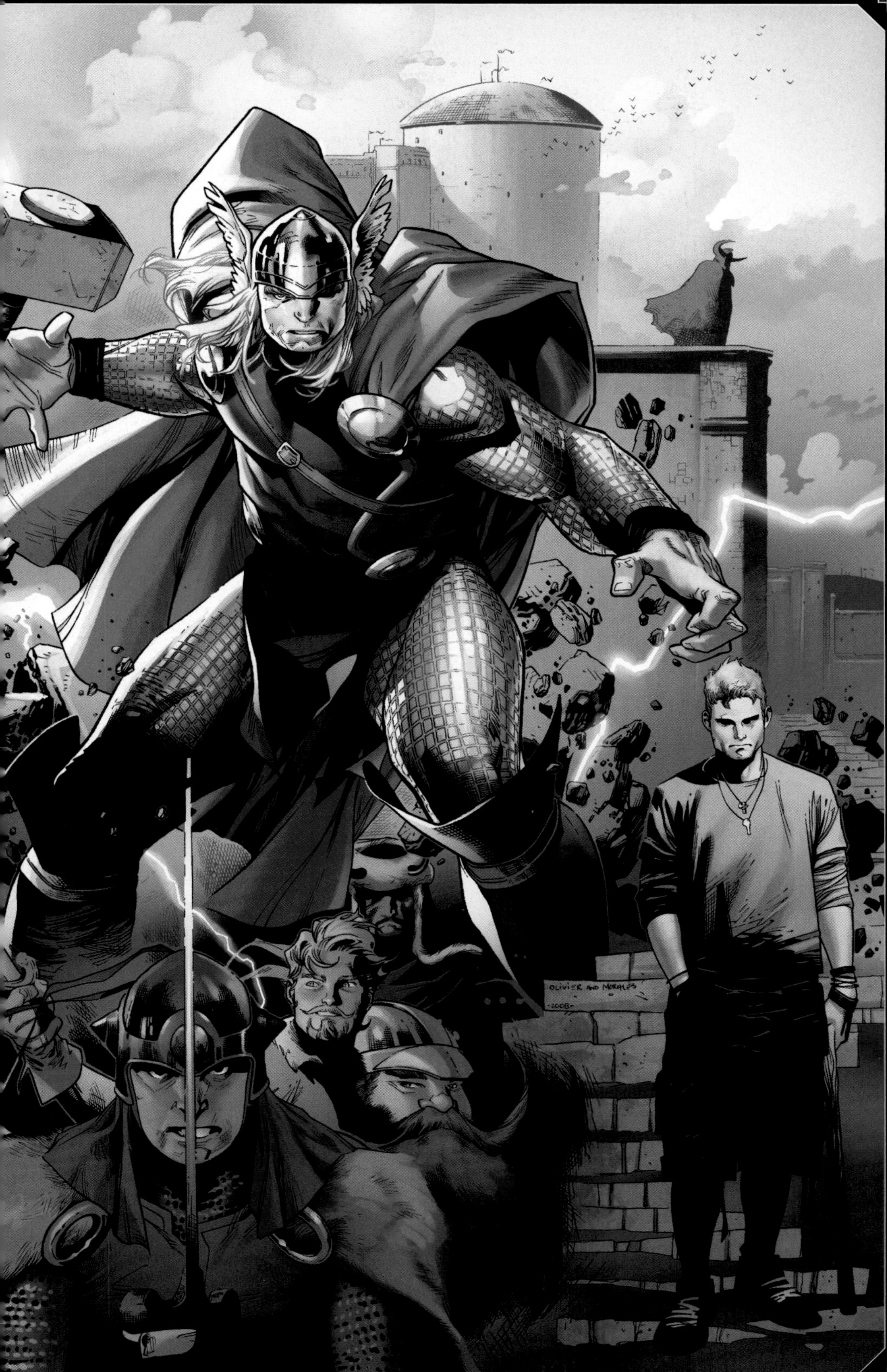
OLIVIER AND MORALES
-2008-

THOR #600

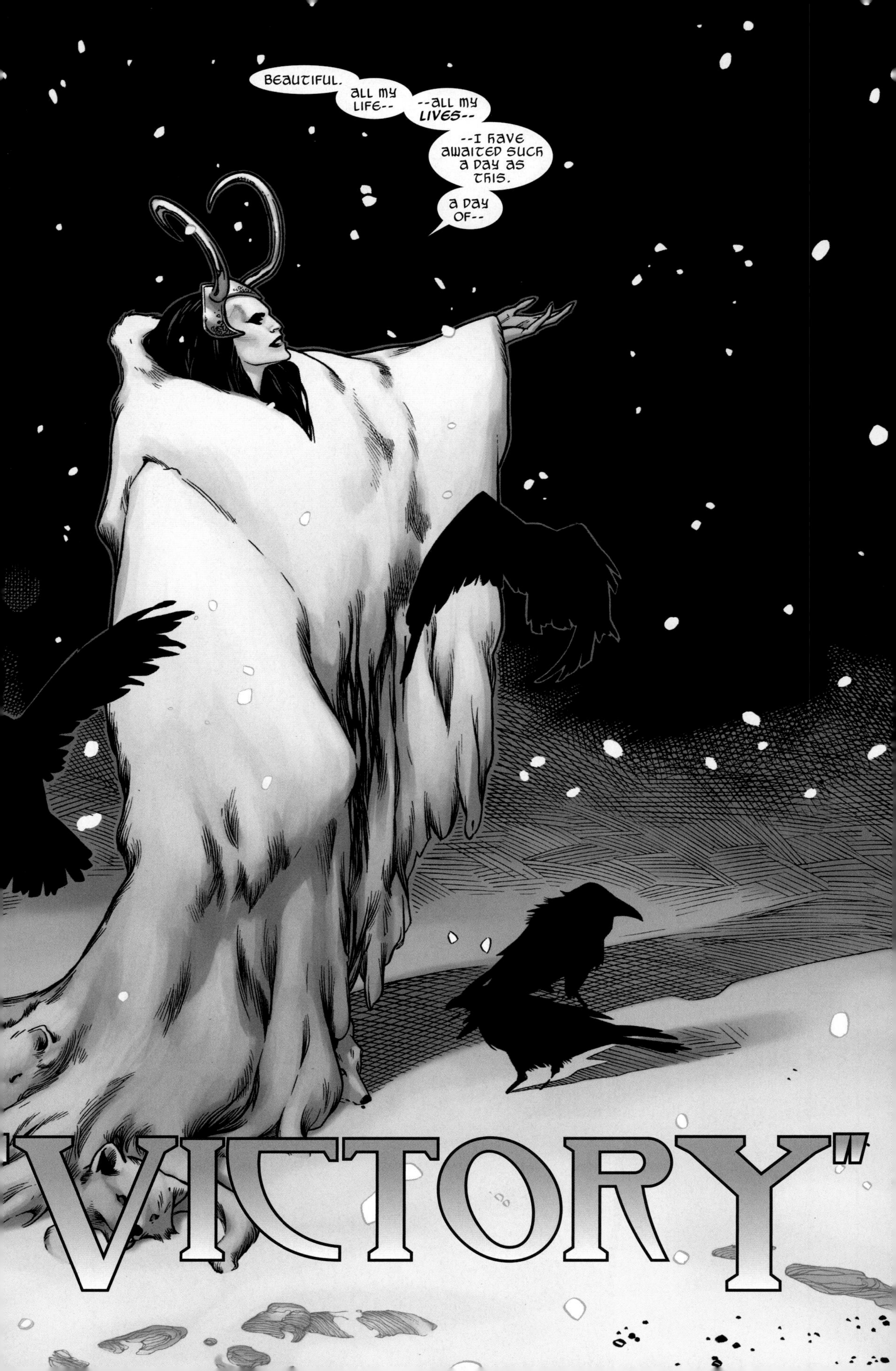
BEAUTIFUL.
ALL MY LIFE--
--ALL MY LIVES--
--I HAVE AWAITED SUCH A DAY AS THIS.
A DAY OF--
VICTORY"

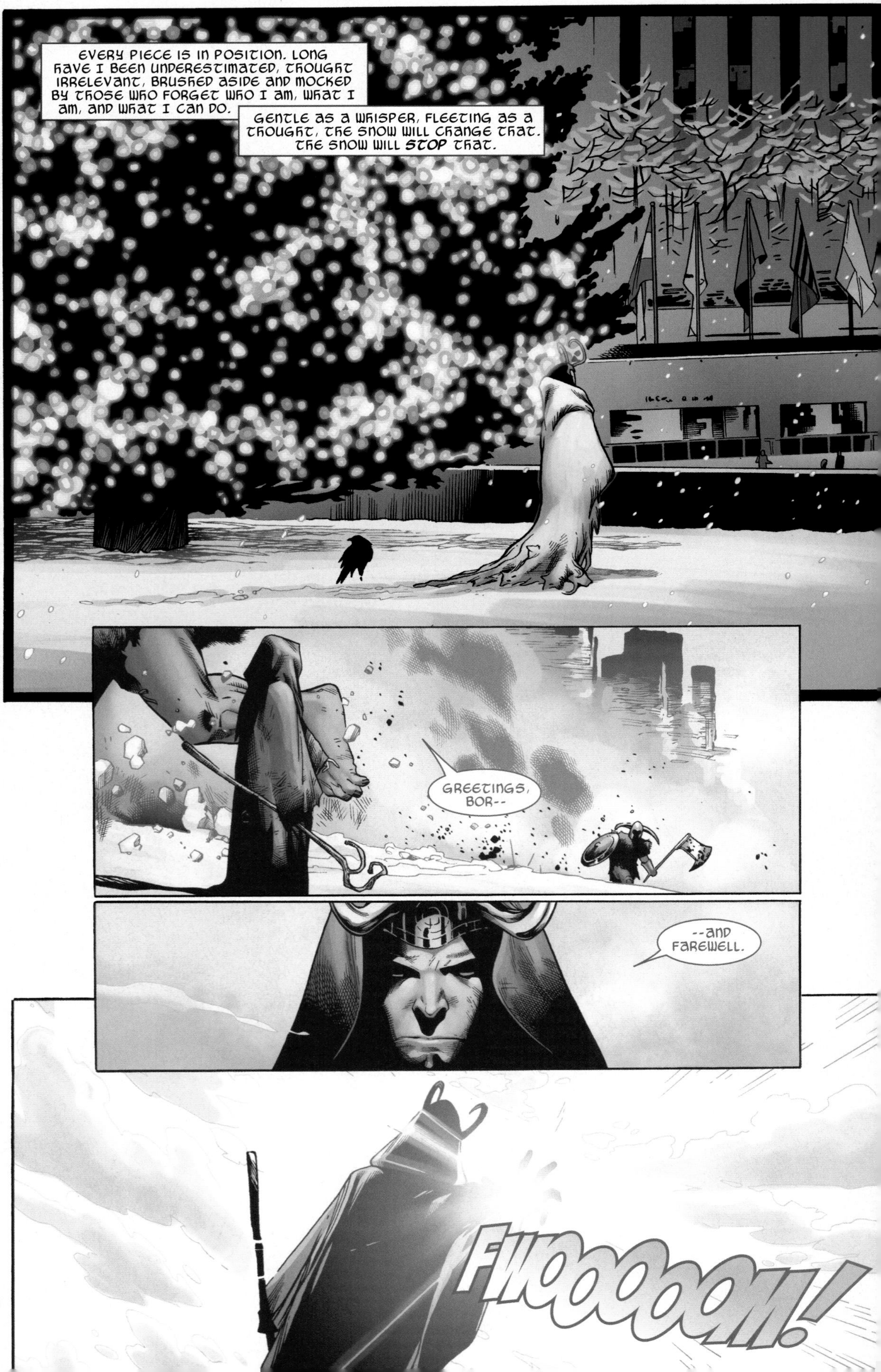

EVERY PIECE IS IN POSITION. LONG HAVE I BEEN UNDERESTIMATED, THOUGHT IRRELEVANT, BRUSHED ASIDE AND MOCKED BY THOSE WHO FORGET WHO I AM, WHAT I AM, AND WHAT I CAN DO.
GENTLE AS A WHISPER, FLEETING AS A THOUGHT, THE SNOW WILL CHANGE THAT. THE SNOW WILL STOP THAT.
GREETINGS, BOR--
--AND FAREWELL.
FWOOOOOM!

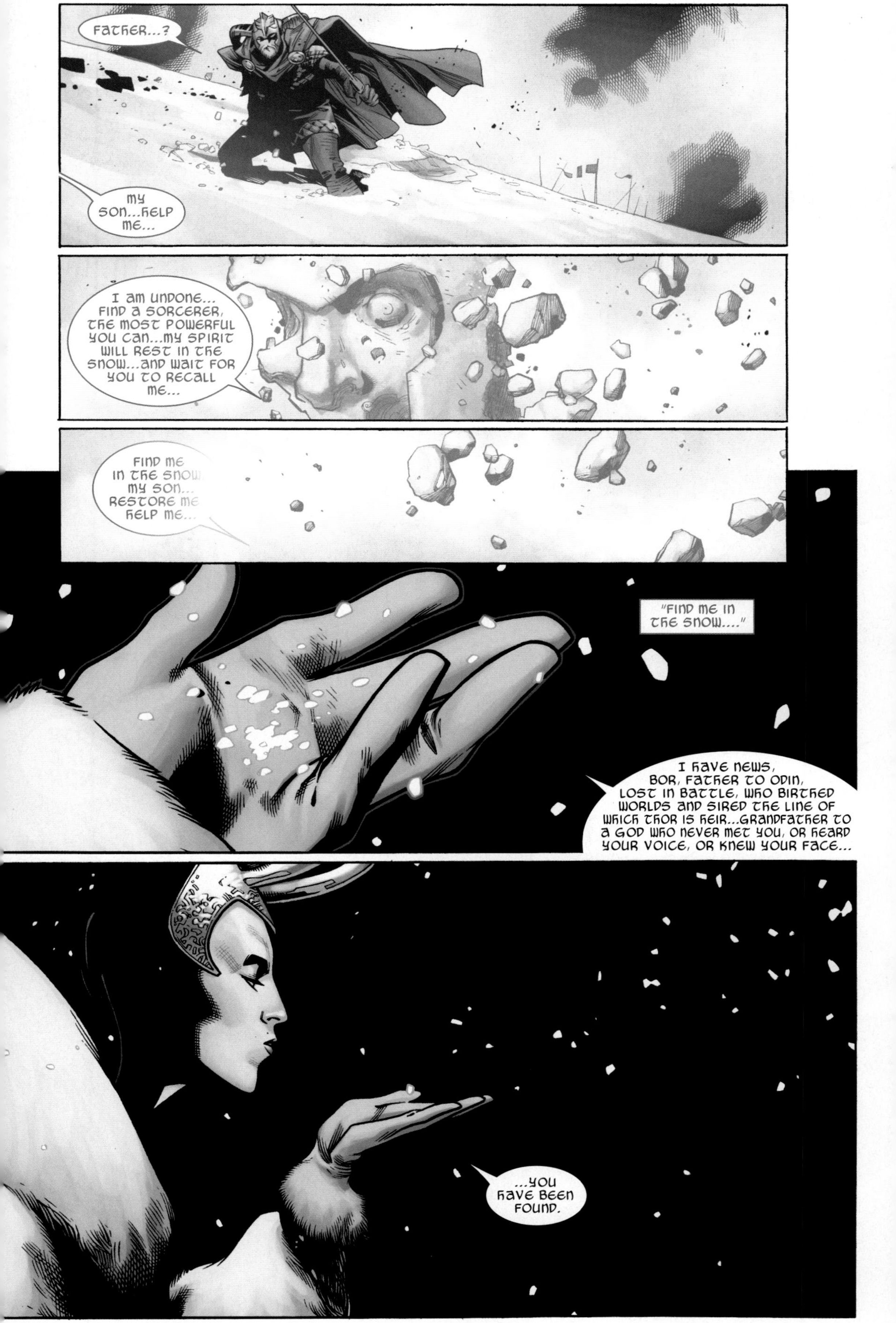
FATHER...?
MY SON...HELP ME...
I AM UNDONE... FIND A SORCERER, THE MOST POWERFUL YOU CAN...MY SPIRIT WILL REST IN THE SNOW...AND WAIT FOR YOU TO RECALL ME...
FIND ME IN THE SNOW, MY SON... RESTORE ME... HELP ME...
"FIND ME IN THE SNOW...."
I HAVE NEWS, BOR, FATHER TO ODIN, LOST IN BATTLE, WHO BIRTHED WORLDS AND SIRED THE LINE OF WHICH THOR IS HEIR...GRANDFATHER TO A GOD WHO NEVER MET YOU, OR HEARD YOUR VOICE, OR KNEW YOUR FACE...
...YOU HAVE BEEN FOUND.

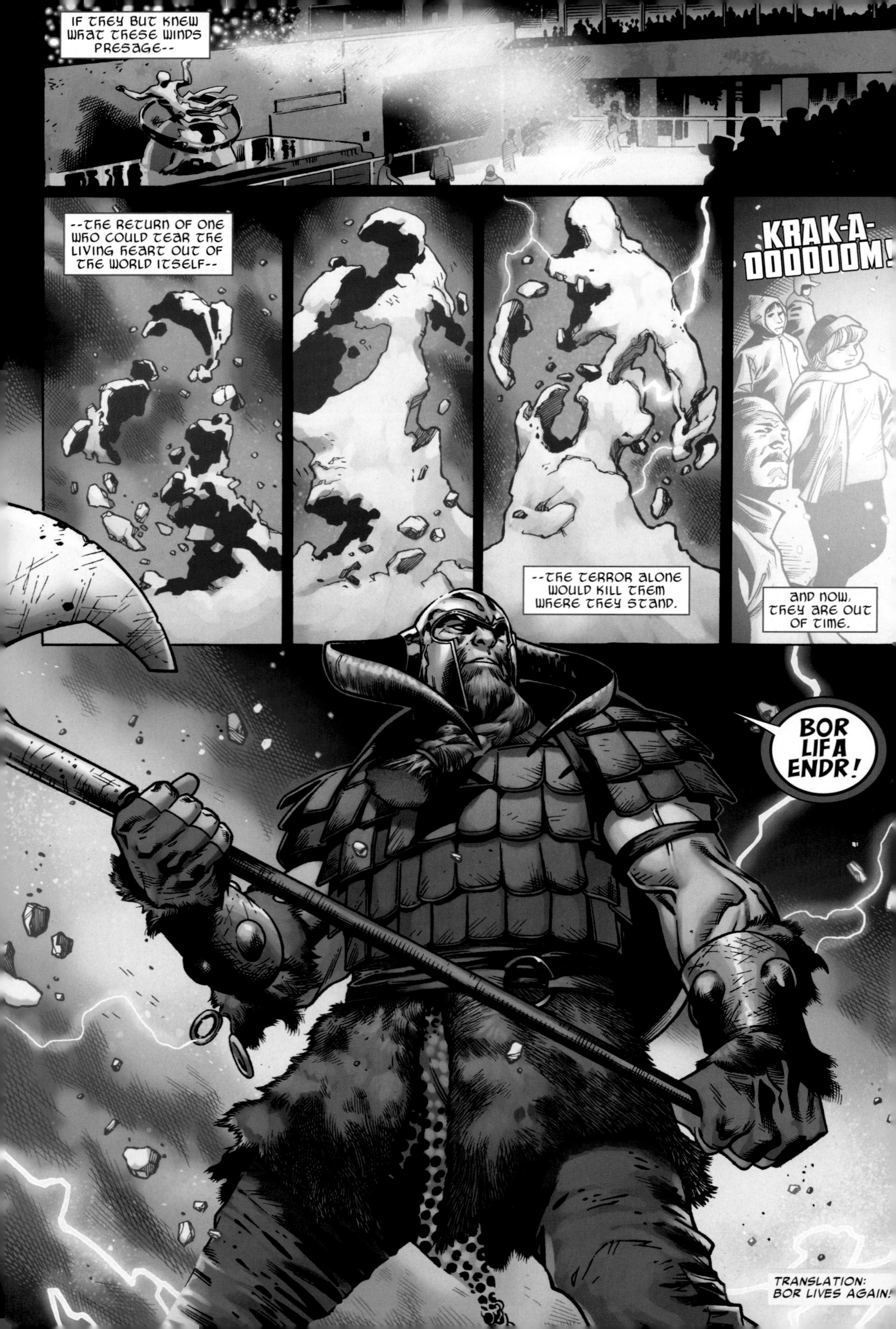
IF THEY BUT KNEW WHAT THESE WINDS PRESAGE--
--THE RETURN OF ONE WHO COULD TEAR THE LIVING HEART OUT OF THE WORLD ITSELF--
--THE TERROR ALONE WOULD KILL THEM WHERE THEY STAND.
KRAK-A-DOOOOOOM!
AND NOW, THEY ARE OUT OF TIME.
BOR LIFA ENDR!
TRANSLATION: BOR LIVES AGAIN!

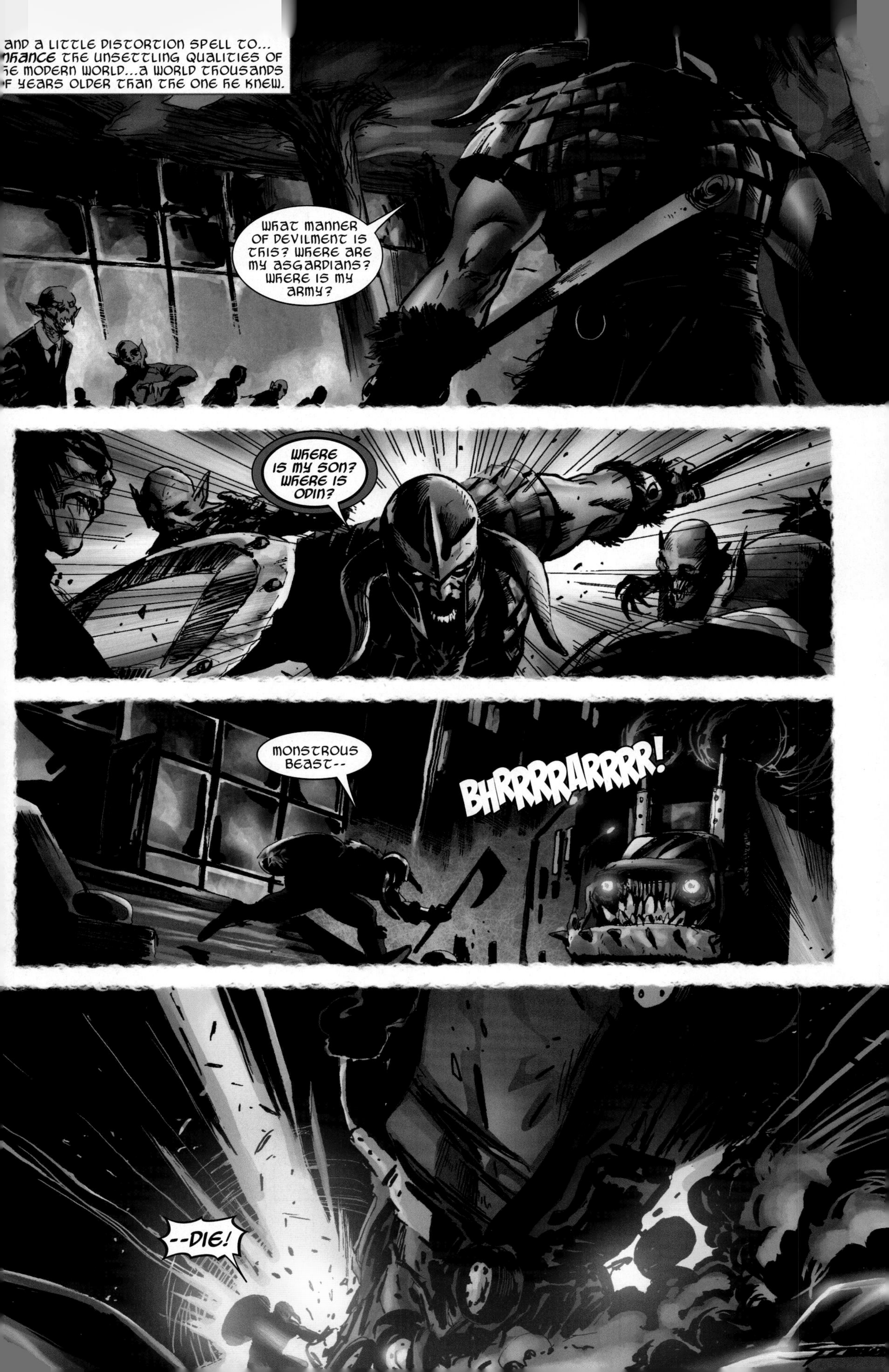

AND A LITTLE DISTORTION SPELL TO...
NHANCE THE UNSETTLING QUALITIES OF
E MODERN WORLD...A WORLD THOUSANDS
F YEARS OLDER THAN THE ONE HE KNEW.
WHAT MANNER OF DEVILMENT IS THIS? WHERE ARE MY ASGARDIANS? WHERE IS MY ARMY?
WHERE IS MY SON? WHERE IS ODIN?
MONSTROUS BEAST--
BHRRRRARRRR!
--DIE!

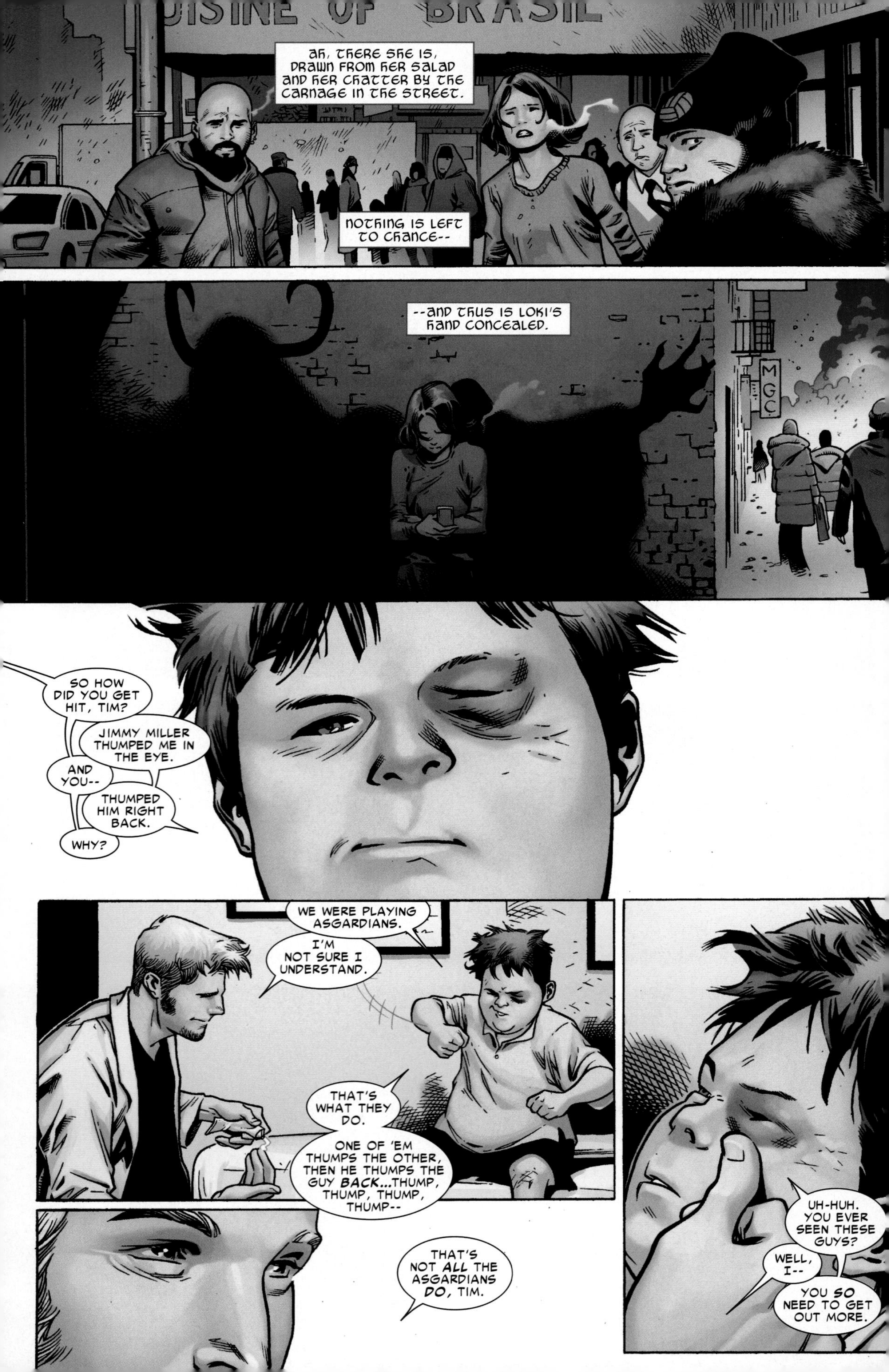
UISINE OF BRASIL
AH, THERE SHE IS, DRAWN FROM HER SALAD AND HER CHATTER BY THE CARNAGE IN THE STREET.
NOTHING IS LEFT TO CHANCE--
--AND THUS IS LOKI'S HAND CONCEALED.
MGC
SO HOW DID YOU GET HIT, TIM?
JIMMY MILLER THUMPED ME IN THE EYE.
AND YOU--
THUMPED HIM RIGHT BACK.
WHY?
WE WERE PLAYING ASGARDIANS.
I'M NOT SURE I UNDERSTAND.
THAT'S WHAT THEY DO.
ONE OF 'EM THUMPS THE OTHER, THEN HE THUMPS THE GUY BACK...THUMP, THUMP, THUMP, THUMP--
THAT'S NOT ALL THE ASGARDIANS DO, TIM.
UH-HUH. YOU EVER SEEN THESE GUYS?
WELL, I--
YOU SO NEED TO GET OUT MORE.

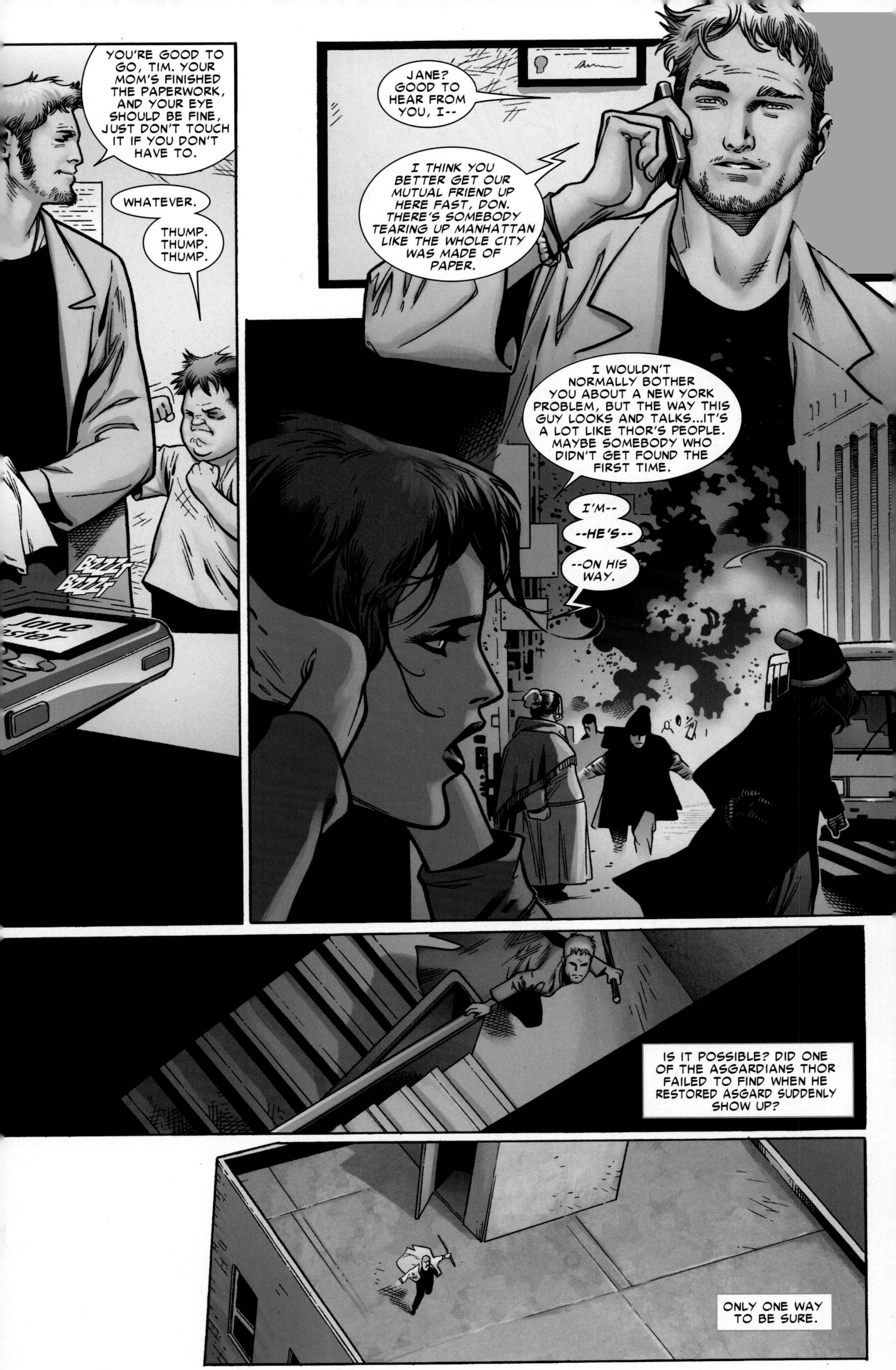
YOU'RE GOOD TO GO, TIM. YOUR MOM'S FINISHED THE PAPERWORK, AND YOUR EYE SHOULD BE FINE, JUST DON'T TOUCH IT IF YOU DON'T HAVE TO.
WHATEVER.
THUMP. THUMP. THUMP.
BZZZT BZZZT
JANE? GOOD TO HEAR FROM YOU, I--
I THINK YOU BETTER GET OUR MUTUAL FRIEND UP HERE FAST, DON. THERE'S SOMEBODY TEARING UP MANHATTAN LIKE THE WHOLE CITY WAS MADE OF PAPER.
I WOULDN'T NORMALLY BOTHER YOU ABOUT A NEW YORK PROBLEM, BUT THE WAY THIS GUY LOOKS AND TALKS...IT'S A LOT LIKE THOR'S PEOPLE. MAYBE SOMEBODY WHO DIDN'T GET FOUND THE FIRST TIME.
I'M--
--HE'S--
--ON HIS WAY.
IS IT POSSIBLE? DID ONE OF THE ASGARDIANS THOR FAILED TO FIND WHEN HE RESTORED ASGARD SUDDENLY SHOW UP?
ONLY ONE WAY TO BE SURE.

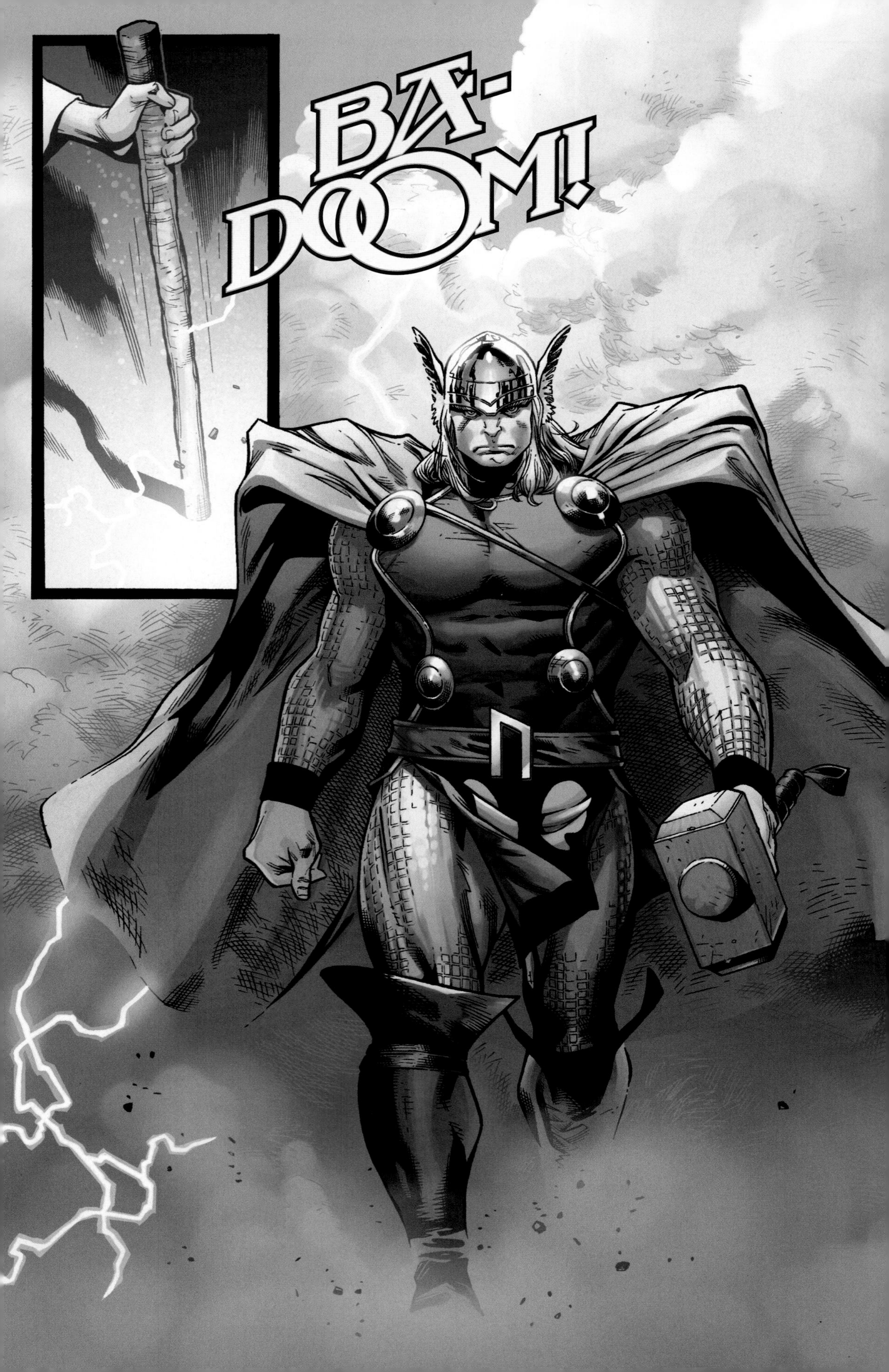
BA-DOOM!

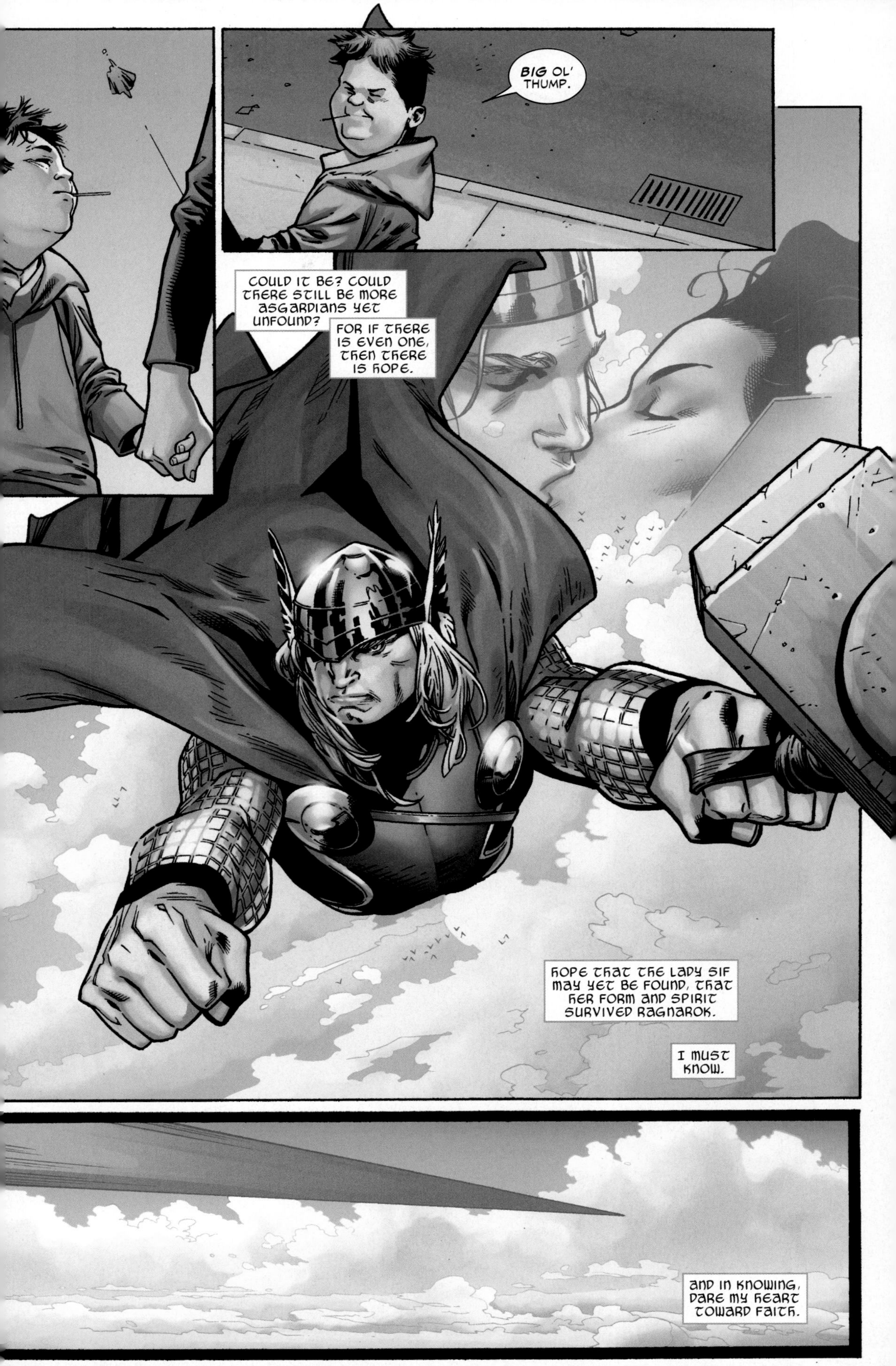
BIG OL' THUMP.
COULD IT BE? COULD THERE STILL BE MORE ASGARDIANS YET UNFOUND?
FOR IF THERE IS EVEN ONE, THEN THERE IS HOPE.
HOPE THAT THE LADY SIF MAY YET BE FOUND, THAT HER FORM AND SPIRIT SURVIVED RAGNAROK.
I MUST KNOW.
AND IN KNOWING, DARE MY HEART TOWARD FAITH.

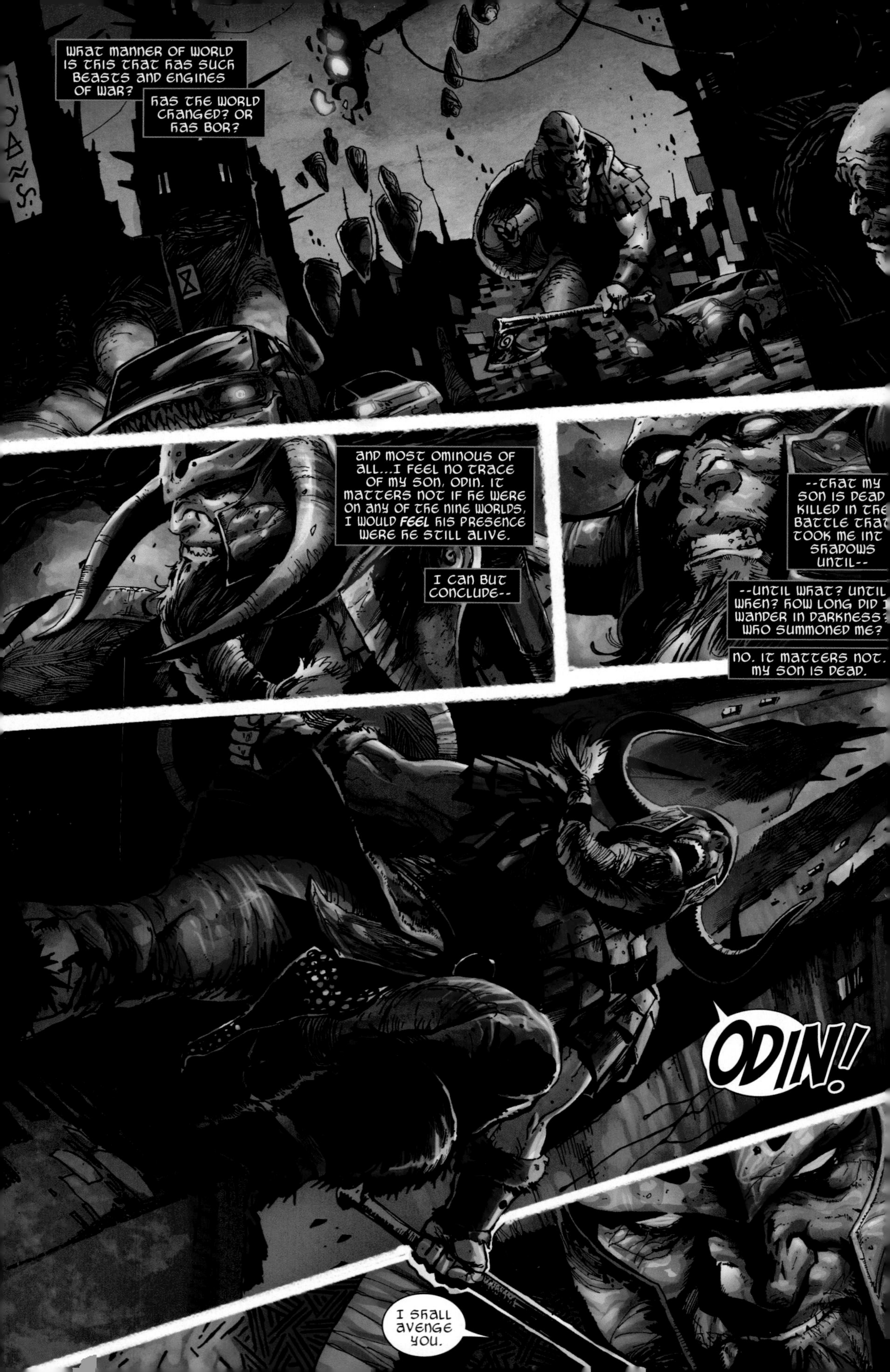
WHAT MANNER OF WORLD IS THIS THAT HAS SUCH BEASTS AND ENGINES OF WAR?
HAS THE WORLD CHANGED? OR HAS BOR?
AND MOST OMINOUS OF ALL...I FEEL NO TRACE OF MY SON, ODIN. IT MATTERS NOT IF HE WERE ON ANY OF THE NINE WORLDS, I WOULD FEEL HIS PRESENCE WERE HE STILL ALIVE.
I CAN BUT CONCLUDE--
--THAT MY SON IS DEAD KILLED IN THE BATTLE THAT TOOK ME INT SHADOWS UNTIL--
--UNTIL WHAT? UNTIL WHEN? HOW LONG DID I WANDER IN DARKNESS? WHO SUMMONED ME?
NO. IT MATTERS NOT. MY SON IS DEAD.
ODIN!
I SHALL AVENGE YOU.

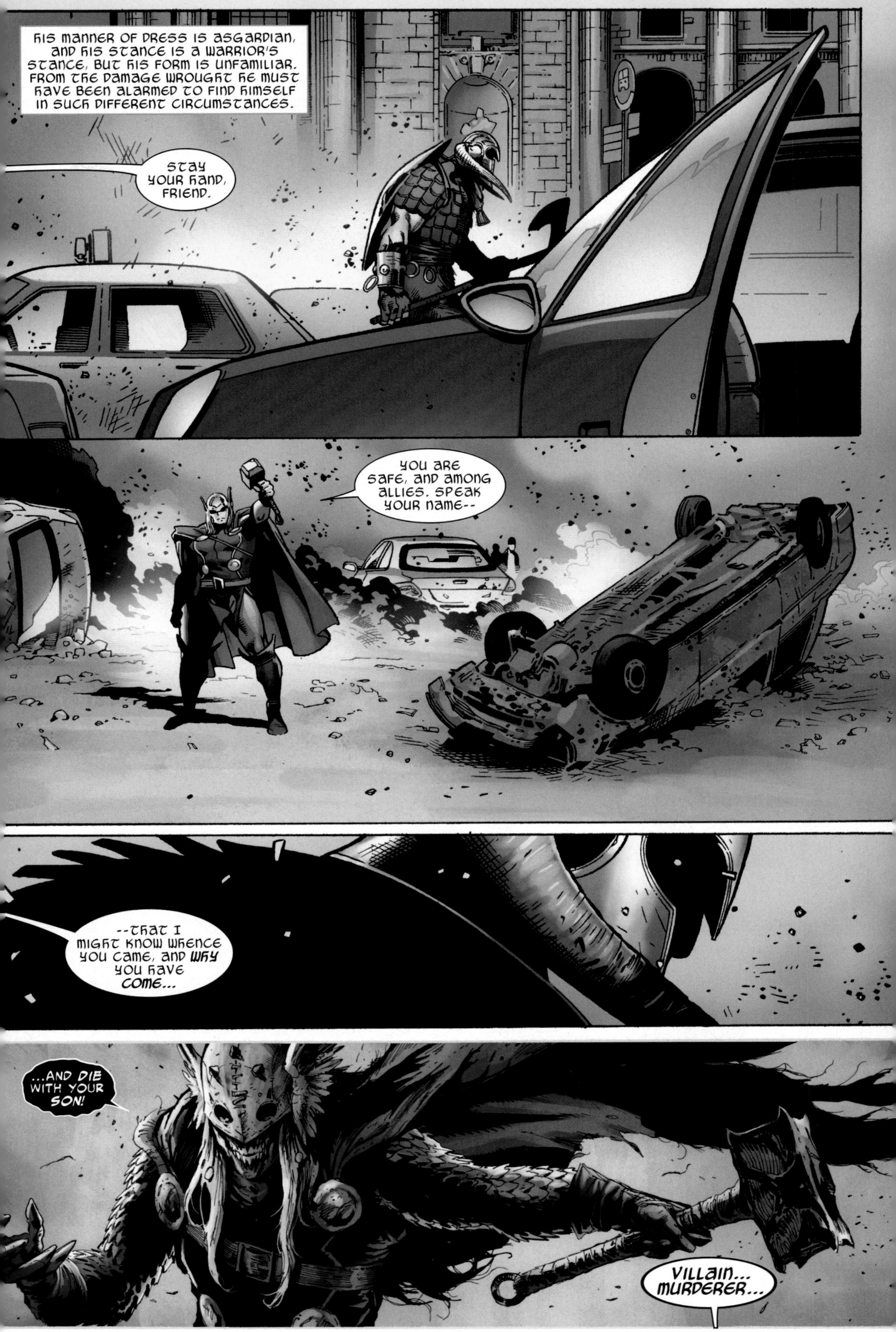
HIS MANNER OF DRESS IS ASGARDIAN, AND HIS STANCE IS A WARRIOR'S STANCE, BUT HIS FORM IS UNFAMILIAR. FROM THE DAMAGE WROUGHT HE MUST HAVE BEEN ALARMED TO FIND HIMSELF IN SUCH DIFFERENT CIRCUMSTANCES.
STAY YOUR HAND, FRIEND.
YOU ARE SAFE, AND AMONG ALLIES. SPEAK YOUR NAME--
--THAT I MIGHT KNOW WHENCE YOU CAME, AND WHY YOU HAVE COME...
...AND DIE WITH YOUR SON!
VILLAIN... MURDERER...

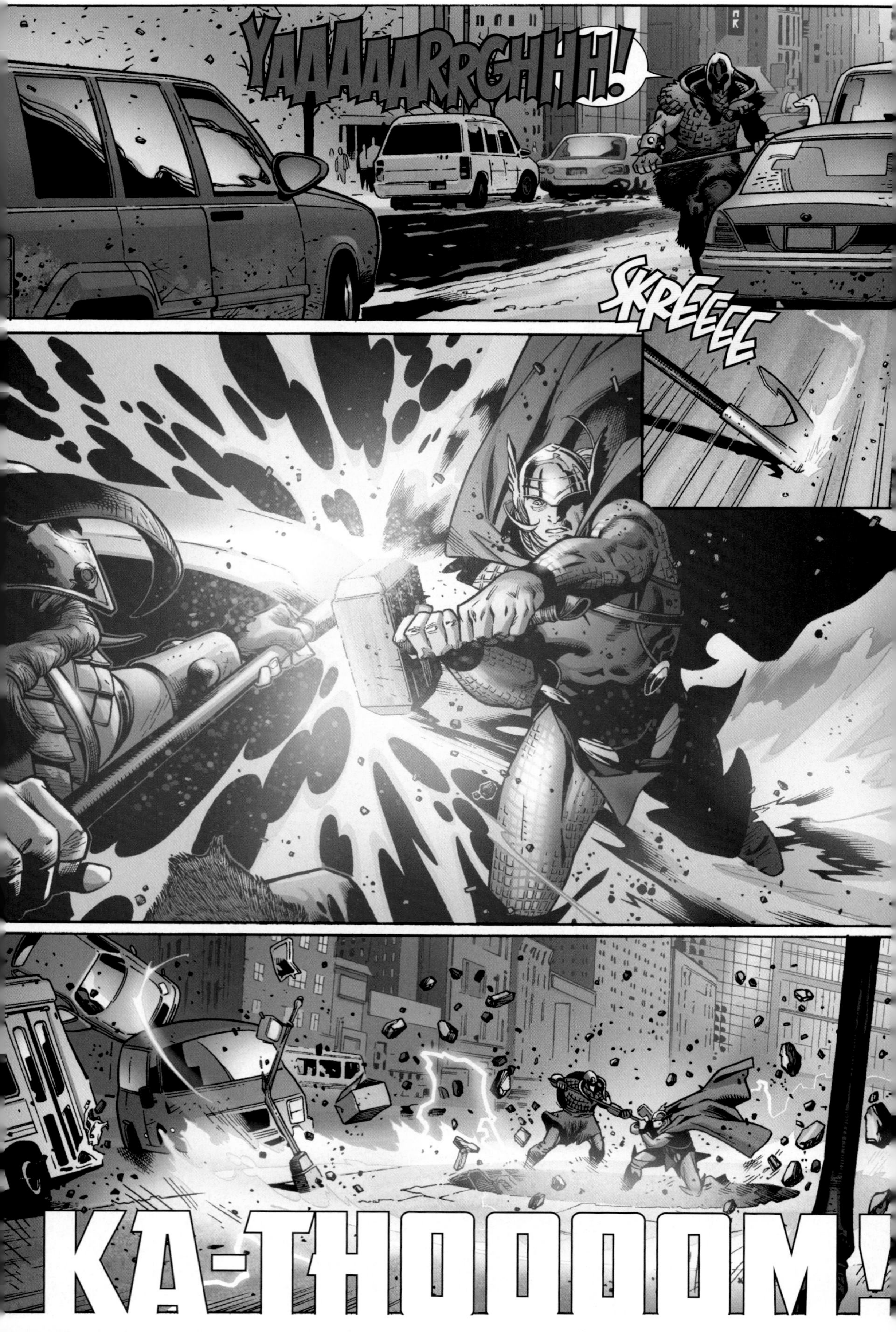

YAAAAARRGHHH!
SKREEEEE
KA-THOOOOM!

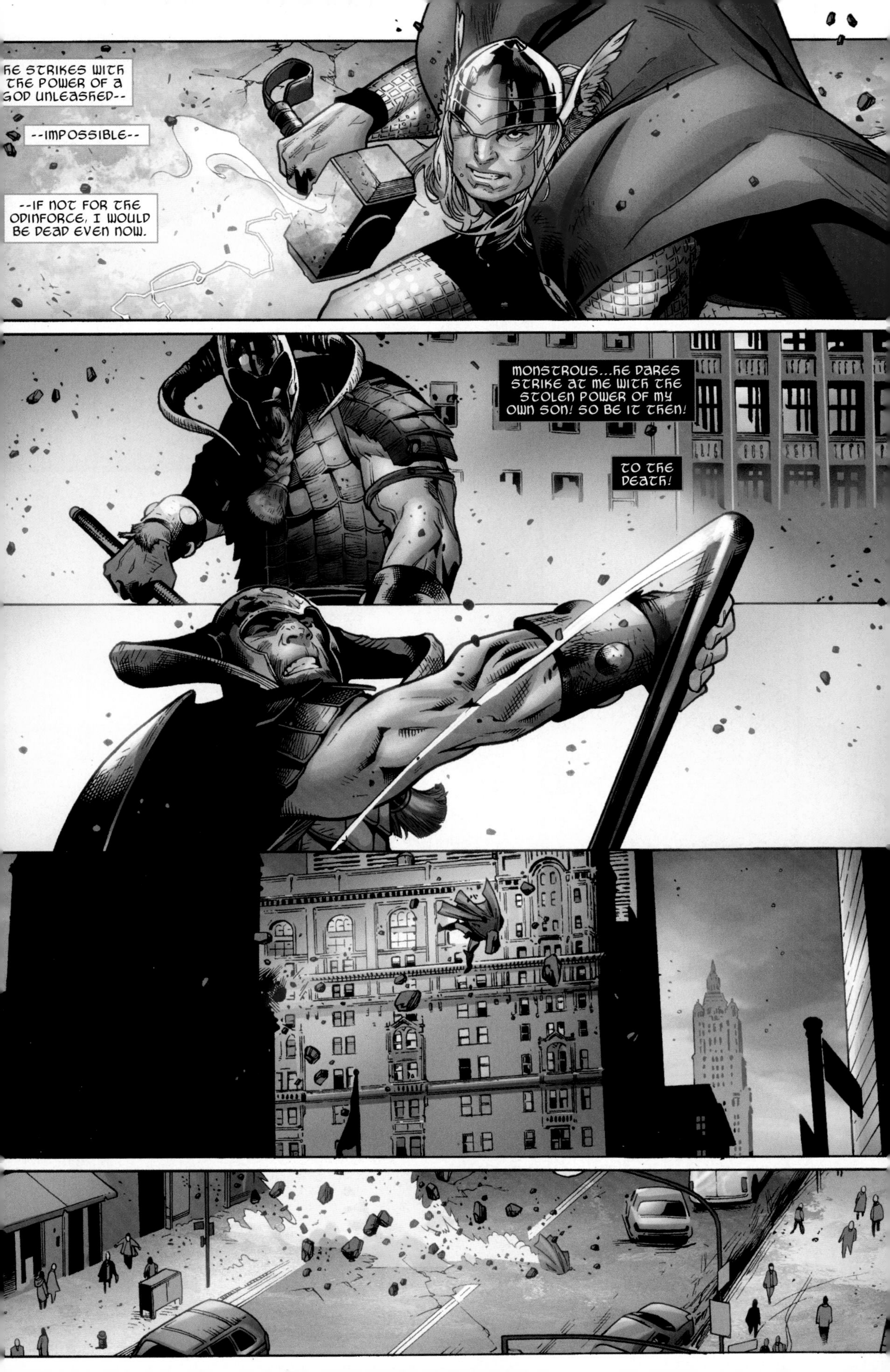
HE STRIKES WITH THE POWER OF A GOD UNLEASHED--
--IMPOSSIBLE--
--IF NOT FOR THE ODINFORCE, I WOULD BE DEAD EVEN NOW.
MONSTROUS...HE DARES STRIKE AT ME WITH THE STOLEN POWER OF MY OWN SON! SO BE IT THEN!
TO THE DEATH!

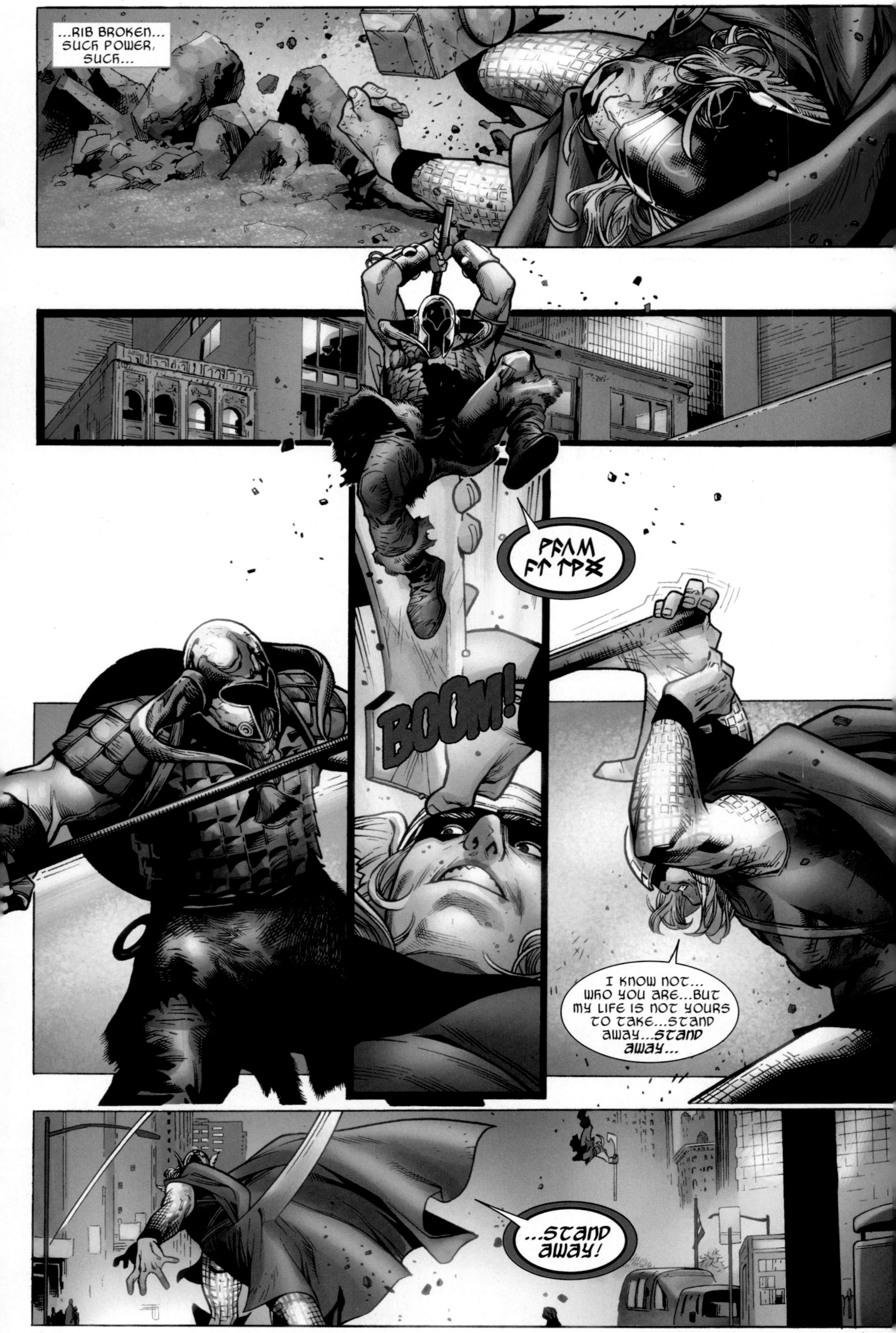
...RIB BROKEN... SUCH POWER, SUCH...
BOOM!
I KNOW NOT... WHO YOU ARE...BUT MY LIFE IS NOT YOURS TO TAKE...STAND AWAY...***STAND AWAY***...
...***STAND AWAY!***

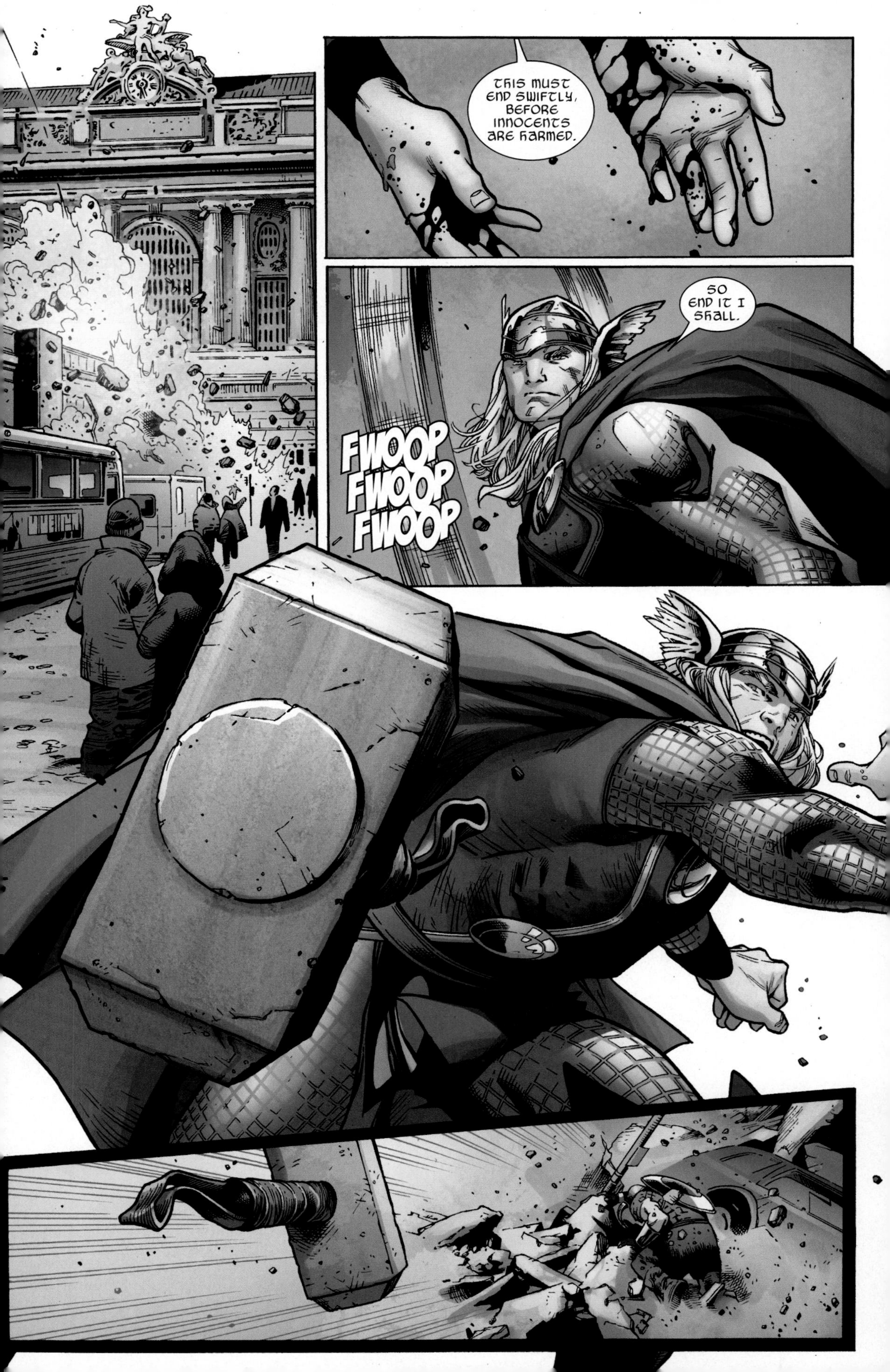

THIS MUST END SWIFTLY, BEFORE INNOCENTS ARE HARMED.
SO END IT I SHALL.
FWOOP
FWOOP
FWOOP

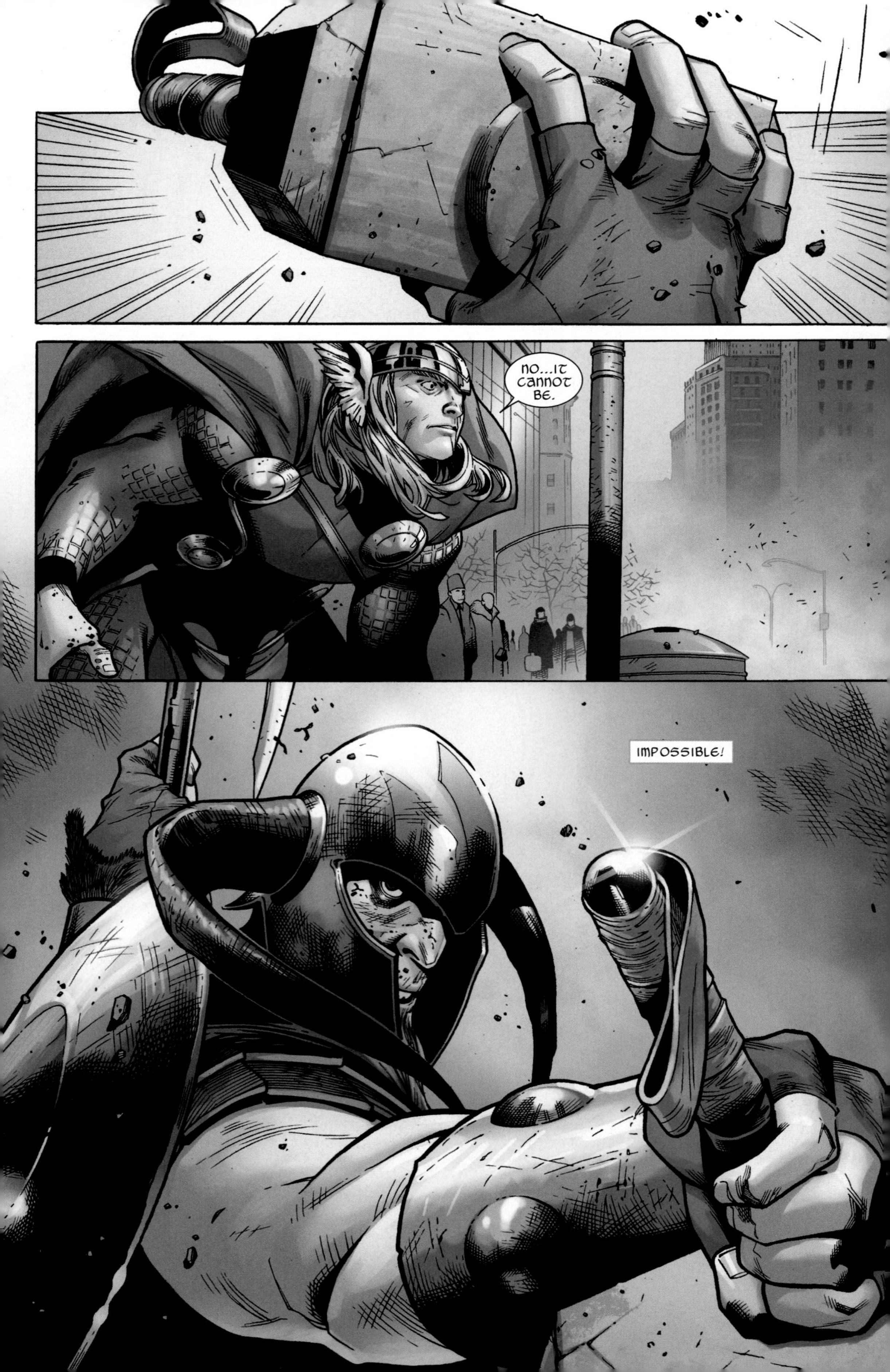
NO...IT CANNOT BE.
IMPOSSIBLE!

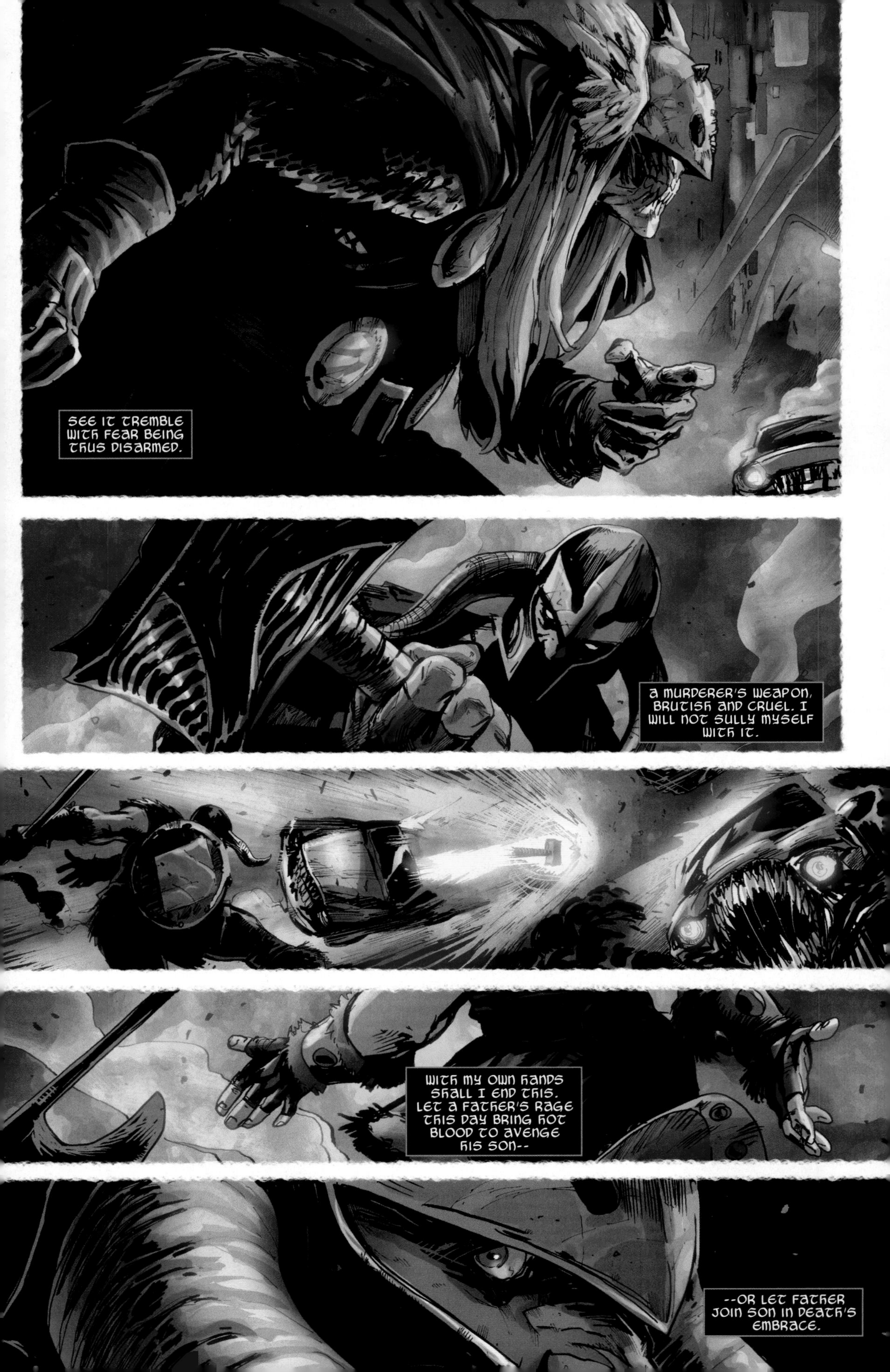
SEE IT TREMBLE WITH FEAR BEING THUS DISARMED.
A MURDERER'S WEAPON, BRUTISH AND CRUEL. I WILL NOT SULLY MYSELF WITH IT.
WITH MY OWN HANDS SHALL I END THIS. LET A FATHER'S RAGE THIS DAY BRING HOT BLOOD TO AVENGE HIS SON--
--OR LET FATHER JOIN SON IN DEATH'S EMBRACE.

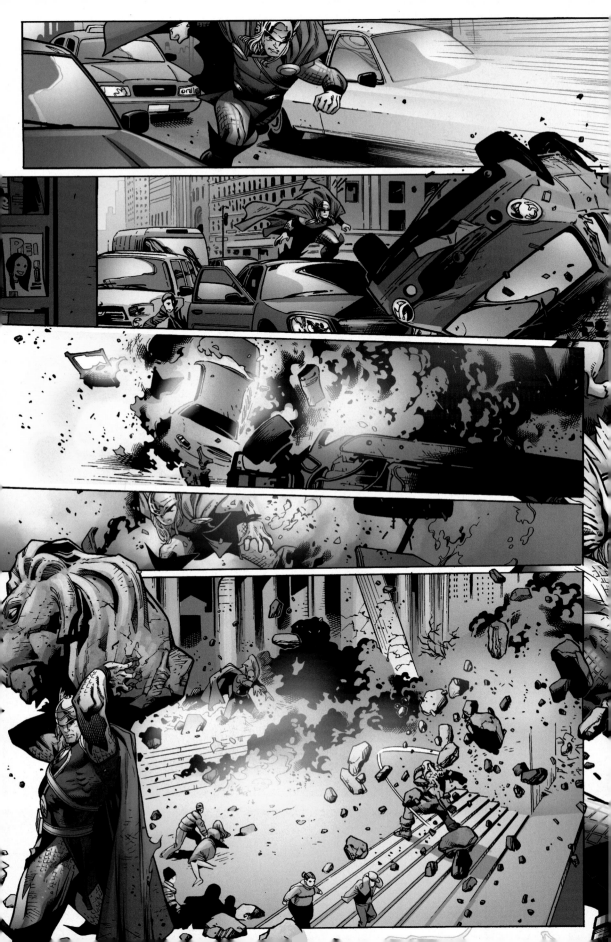

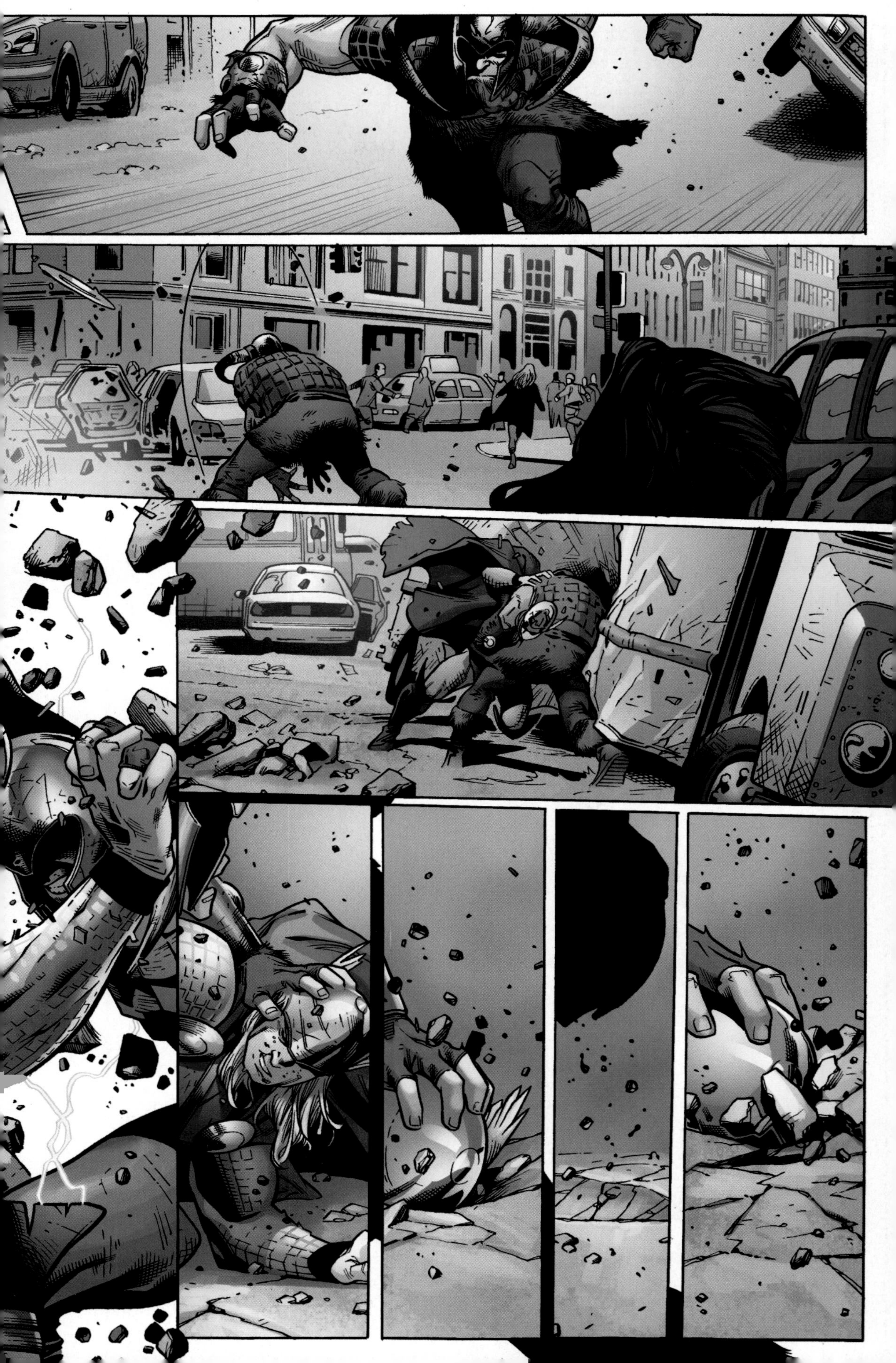

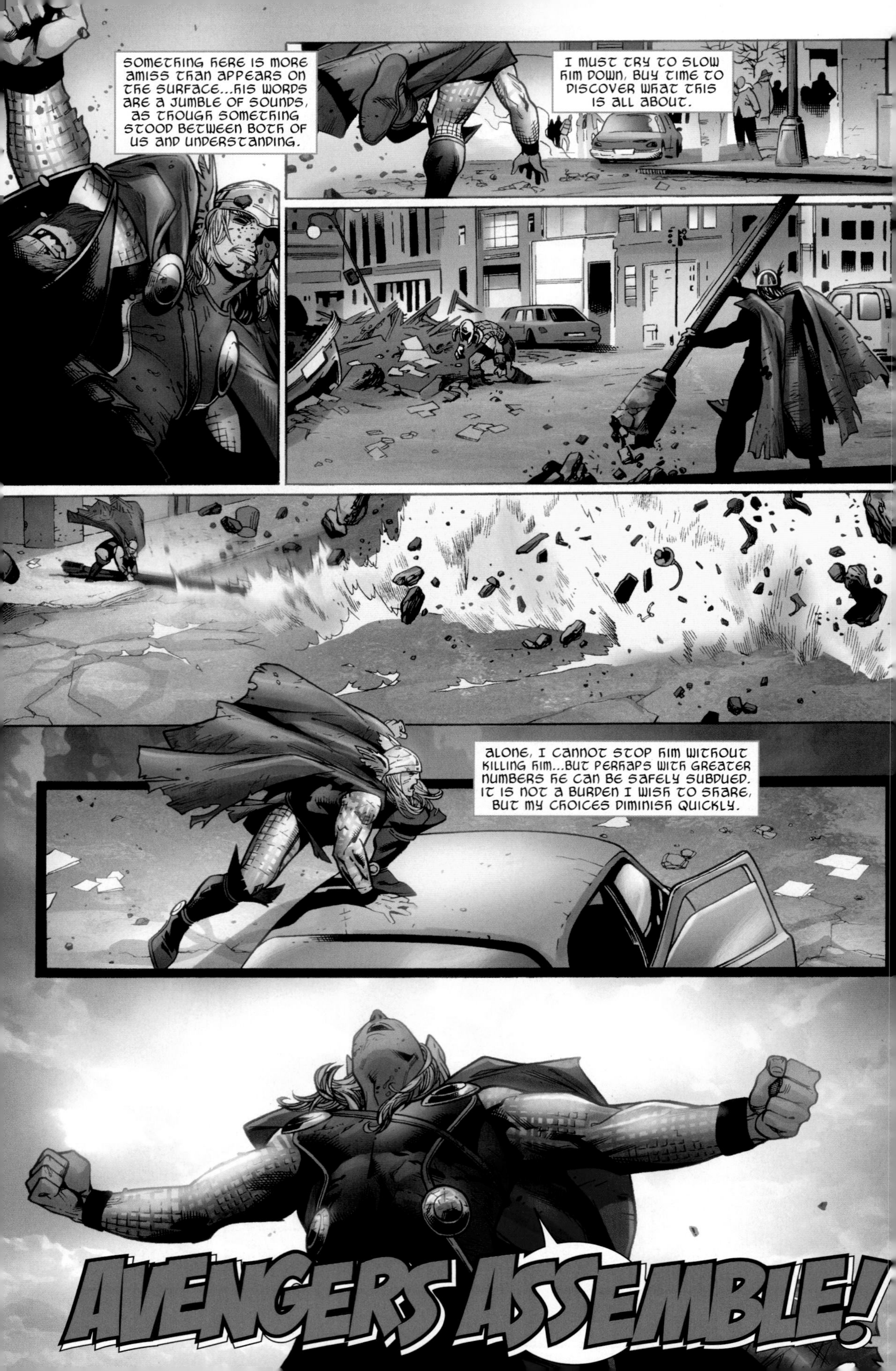

SOMETHING HERE IS MORE AMISS THAN APPEARS ON THE SURFACE...HIS WORDS ARE A JUMBLE OF SOUNDS, AS THOUGH SOMETHING STOOD BETWEEN BOTH OF US AND UNDERSTANDING.
I MUST TRY TO SLOW HIM DOWN, BUY TIME TO DISCOVER WHAT THIS IS ALL ABOUT.
ALONE, I CANNOT STOP HIM WITHOUT KILLING HIM...BUT PERHAPS WITH GREATER NUMBERS HE CAN BE SAFELY SUBDUED. IT IS NOT A BURDEN I WISH TO SHARE, BUT MY CHOICES DIMINISH QUICKLY.
AVENGERS ASSEMBLE!

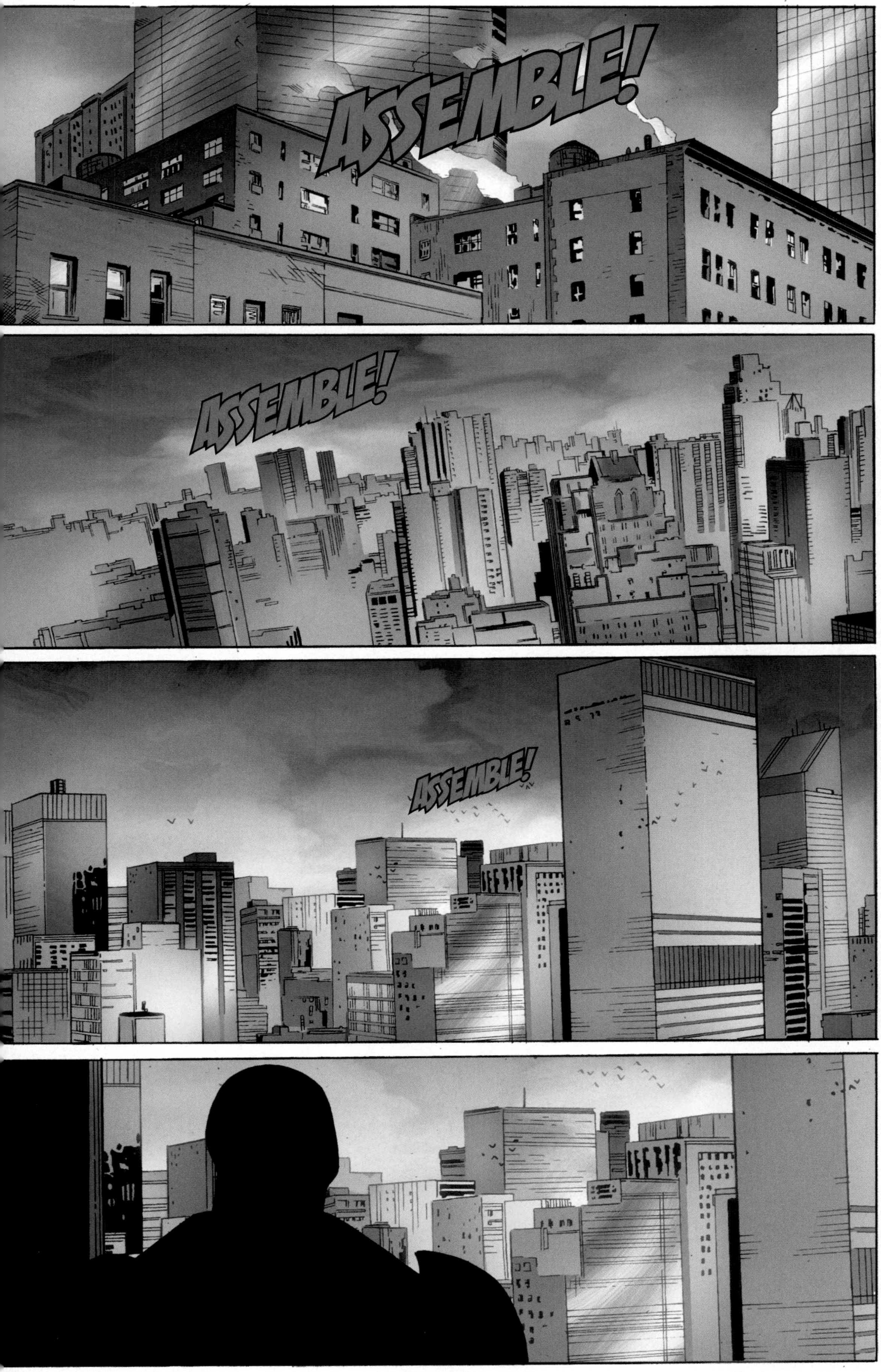
ASSEMBLE!
ASSEMBLE!
ASSEMBLE!

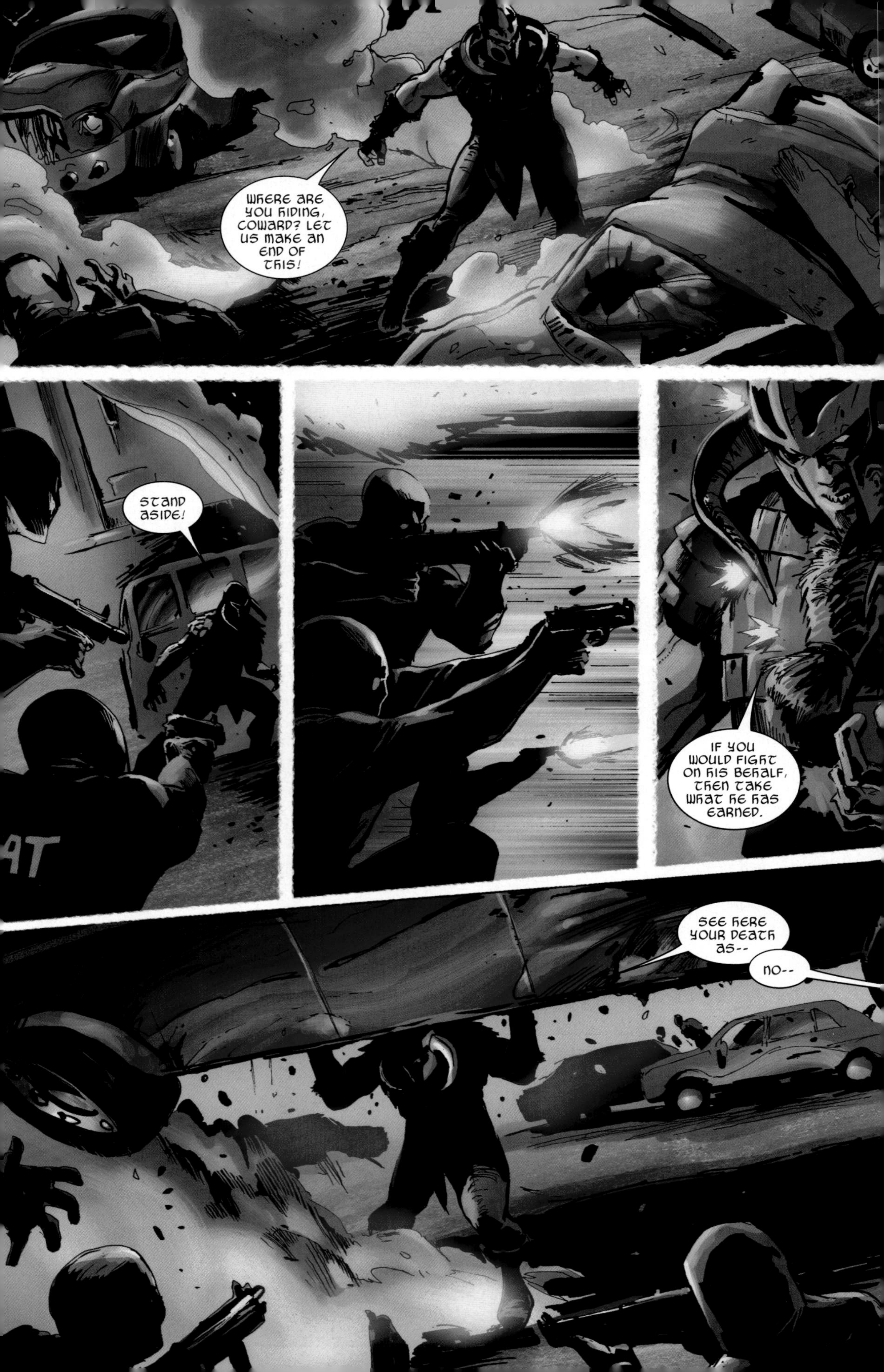
WHERE ARE YOU HIDING, COWARD? LET US MAKE AN END OF THIS!
STAND ASIDE!
IF YOU WOULD FIGHT ON HIS BEHALF, THEN TAKE WHAT HE HAS EARNED.
SEE HERE YOUR DEATH AS--
NO--

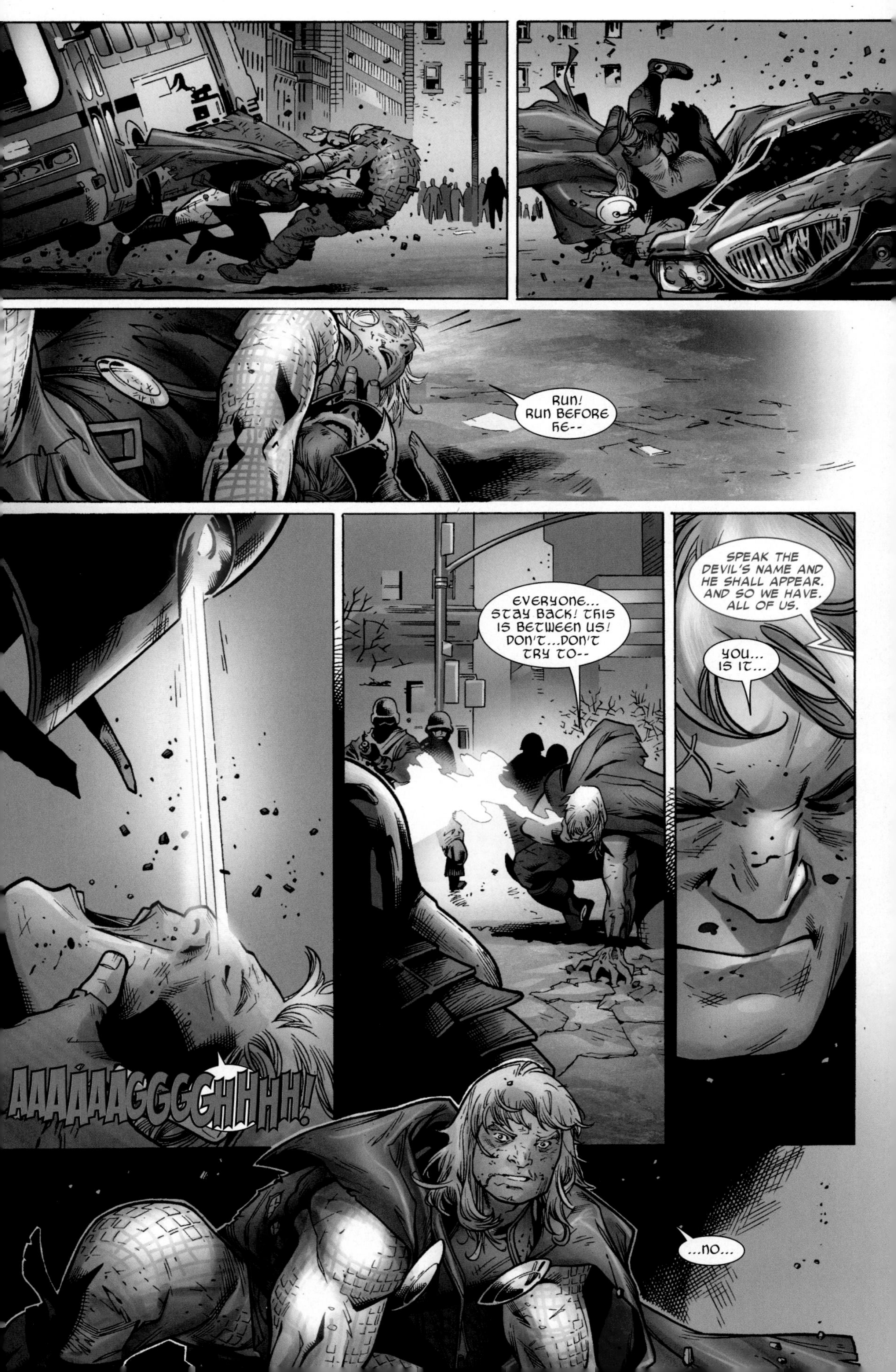

RUN! RUN BEFORE HE--
EVERYONE... STAY BACK! THIS IS BETWEEN US! DON'T...DON'T TRY TO--
SPEAK THE DEVIL'S NAME AND HE SHALL APPEAR. AND SO WE HAVE. ALL OF US.
YOU... IS IT...
AAAAAAGGGGHHHH!
...NO...

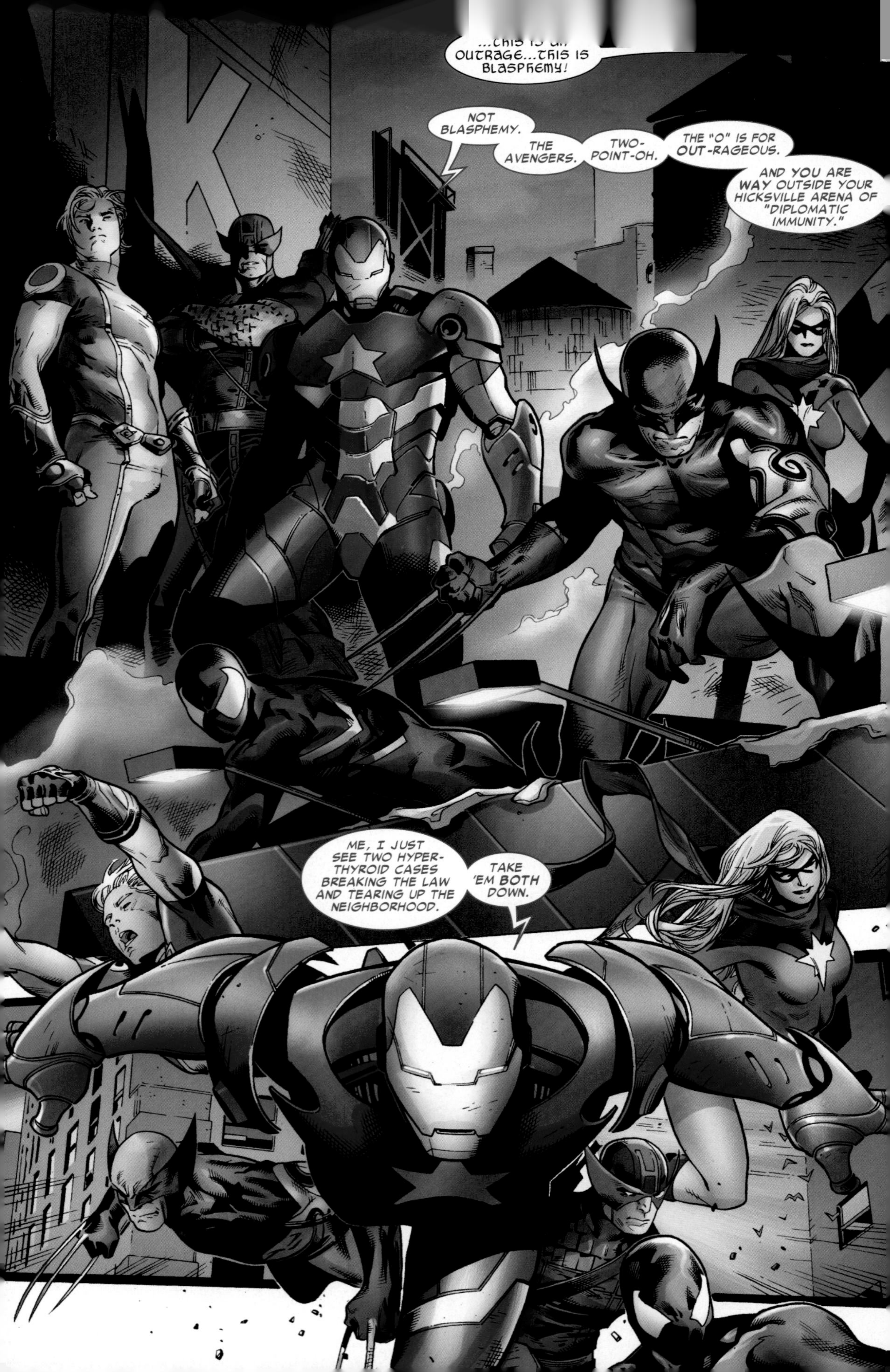

OUTRAGE...THIS IS BLASPHEMY!
NOT BLASPHEMY.
THE AVENGERS.
TWO-POINT-OH.
THE "O" IS FOR OUT-RAGEOUS.
AND YOU ARE WAY OUTSIDE YOUR HICKSVILLE ARENA OF "DIPLOMATIC IMMUNITY."
ME, I JUST SEE TWO HYPER-THYROID CASES BREAKING THE LAW AND TEARING UP THE NEIGHBORHOOD.
TAKE 'EM BOTH DOWN.

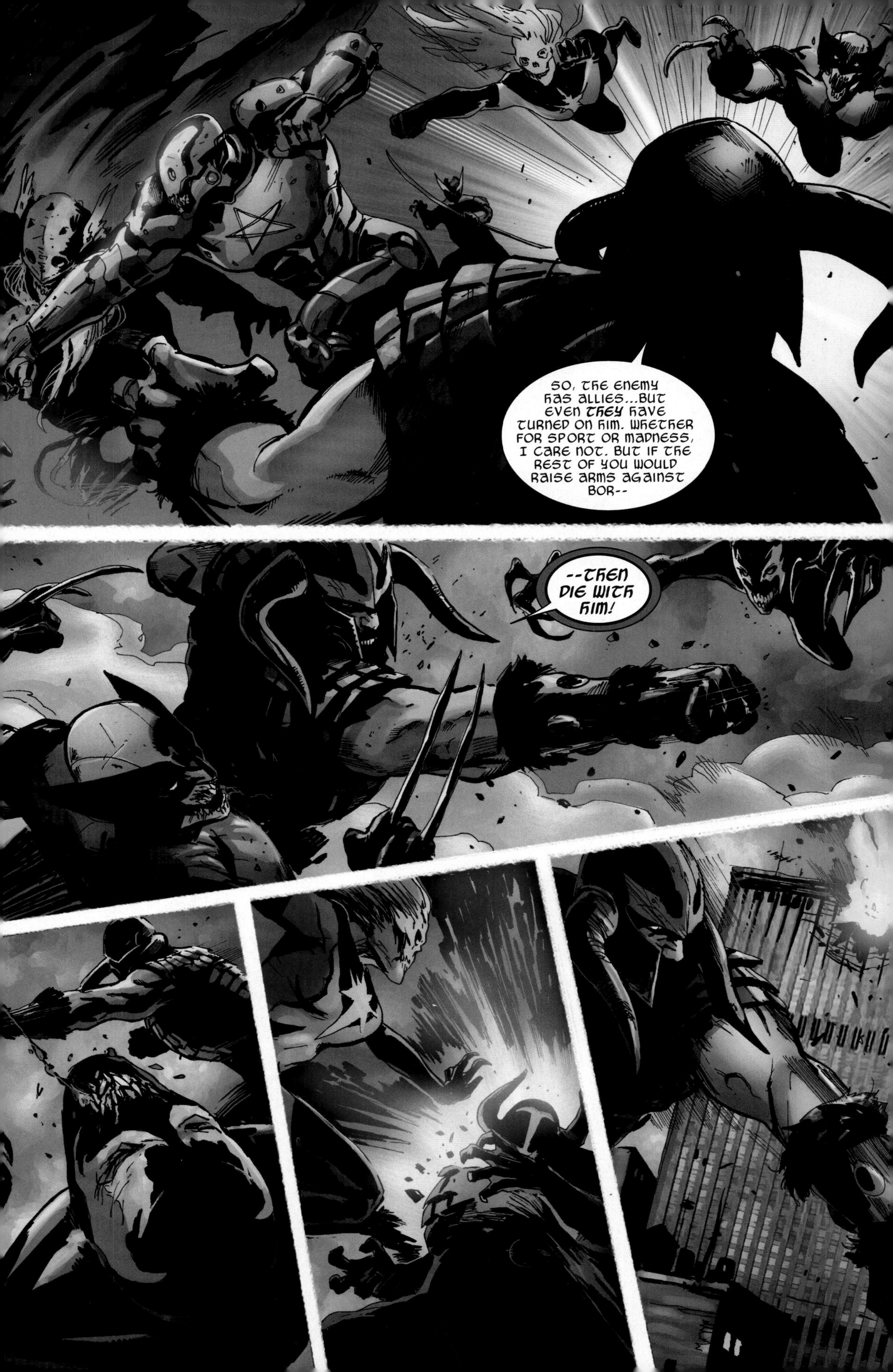
SO, THE ENEMY HAS ALLIES...BUT EVEN THEY HAVE TURNED ON HIM. WHETHER FOR SPORT OR MADNESS, I CARE NOT. BUT IF THE REST OF YOU WOULD RAISE ARMS AGAINST BOR--
--THEN DIE WITH HIM!

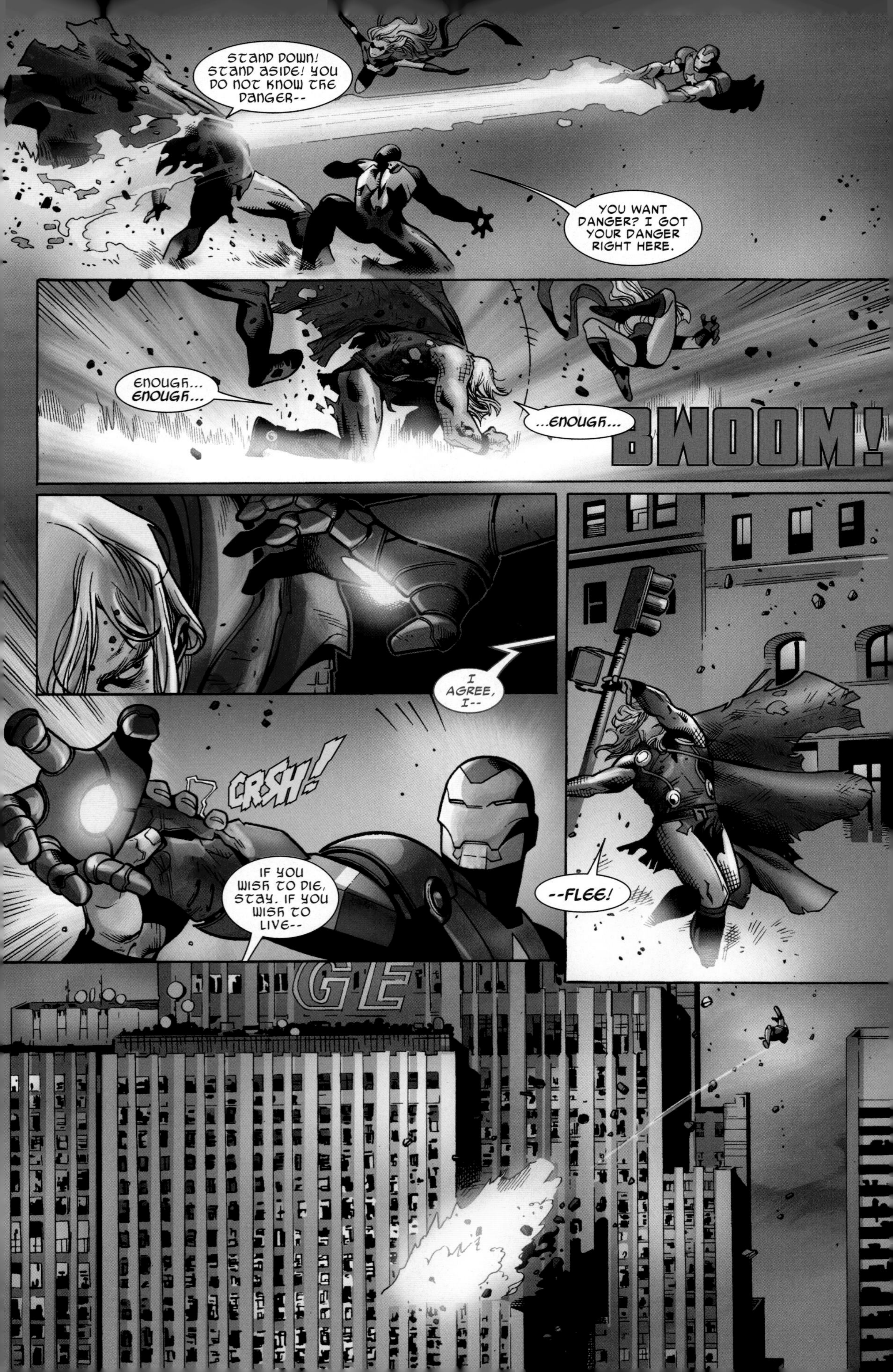
STAND DOWN! STAND ASIDE! YOU DO NOT KNOW THE DANGER--
YOU WANT DANGER? I GOT YOUR DANGER RIGHT HERE.
ENOUGH... ENOUGH...
...ENOUGH...
BWOOM!
I AGREE, I--
CRSH!
IF YOU WISH TO DIE, STAY. IF YOU WISH TO LIVE--
--FLEE!

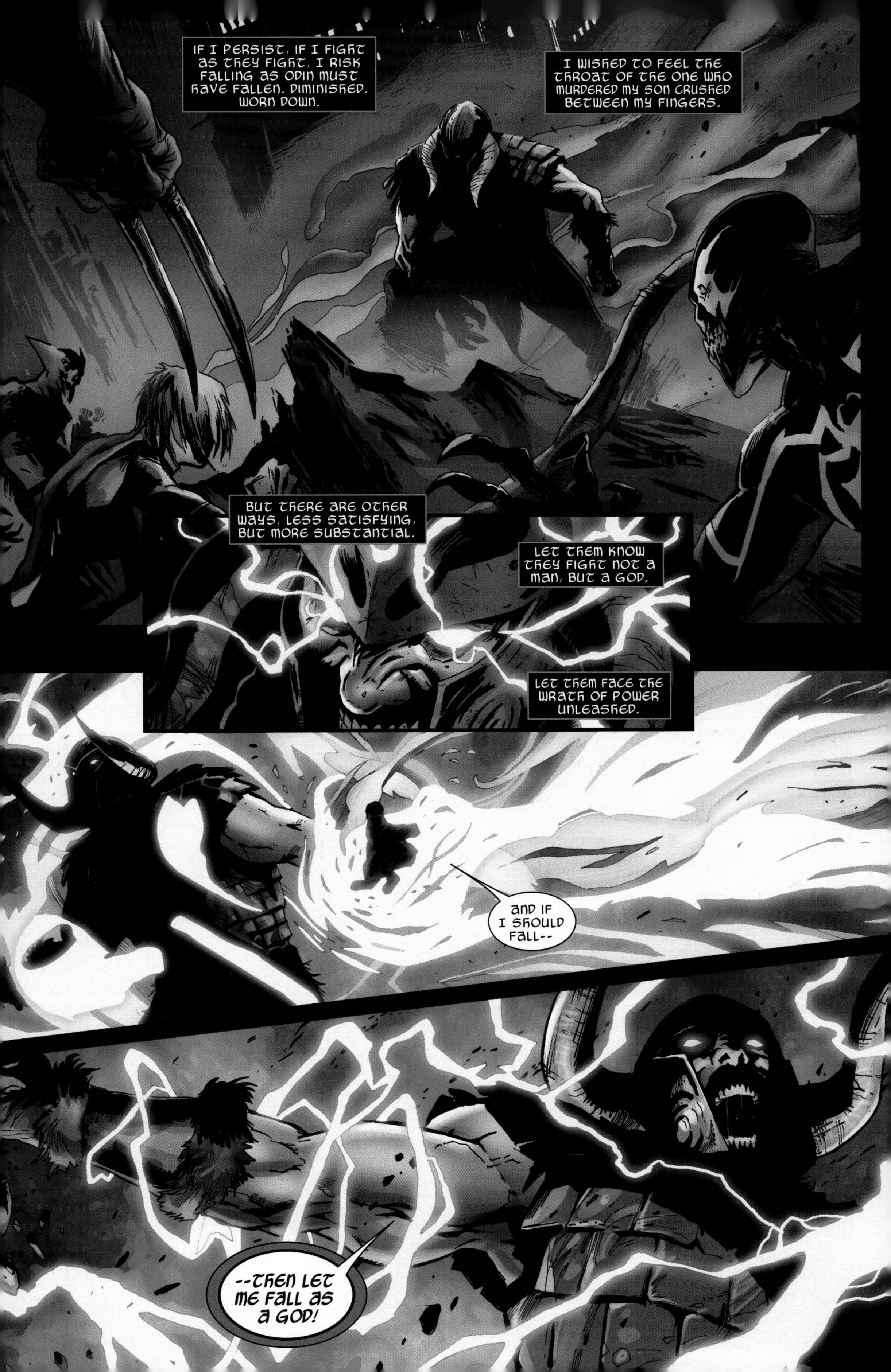
IF I PERSIST, IF I FIGHT AS THEY FIGHT, I RISK FALLING AS ODIN MUST HAVE FALLEN. DIMINISHED. WORN DOWN.
I WISHED TO FEEL THE THROAT OF THE ONE WHO MURDERED MY SON CRUSHED BETWEEN MY FINGERS.
BUT THERE ARE OTHER WAYS, LESS SATISFYING, BUT MORE SUBSTANTIAL.
LET THEM KNOW THEY FIGHT NOT A MAN, BUT A GOD.
LET THEM FACE THE WRATH OF POWER UNLEASHED.
AND IF I SHOULD FALL--
--THEN LET ME FALL AS A GOD!

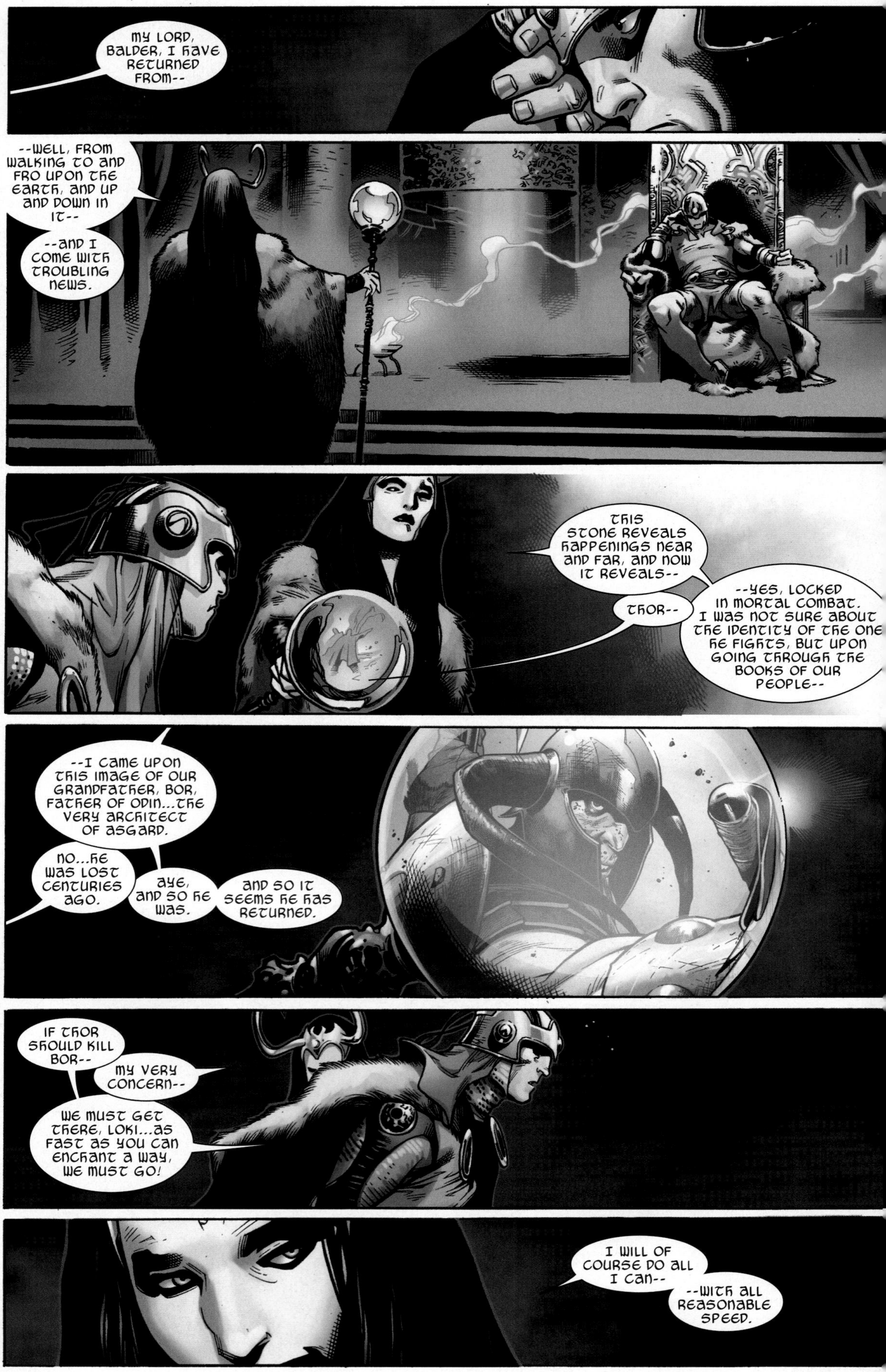
MY LORD, BALDER, I HAVE RETURNED FROM--
--WELL, FROM WALKING TO AND FRO UPON THE EARTH, AND UP AND DOWN IN IT--
--AND I COME WITH TROUBLING NEWS.
THIS STONE REVEALS HAPPENINGS NEAR AND FAR, AND NOW IT REVEALS--
THOR--
--YES, LOCKED IN MORTAL COMBAT. I WAS NOT SURE ABOUT THE IDENTITY OF THE ONE HE FIGHTS, BUT UPON GOING THROUGH THE BOOKS OF OUR PEOPLE--
--I CAME UPON THIS IMAGE OF OUR GRANDFATHER, BOR, FATHER OF ODIN...THE VERY ARCHITECT OF ASGARD.
NO...HE WAS LOST CENTURIES AGO.
AYE, AND SO HE WAS.
AND SO IT SEEMS HE HAS RETURNED.
IF THOR SHOULD KILL BOR--
MY VERY CONCERN--
WE MUST GET THERE, LOKI...AS FAST AS YOU CAN ENCHANT A WAY, WE MUST GO!
I WILL OF COURSE DO ALL I CAN--
--WITH ALL REASONABLE SPEED.

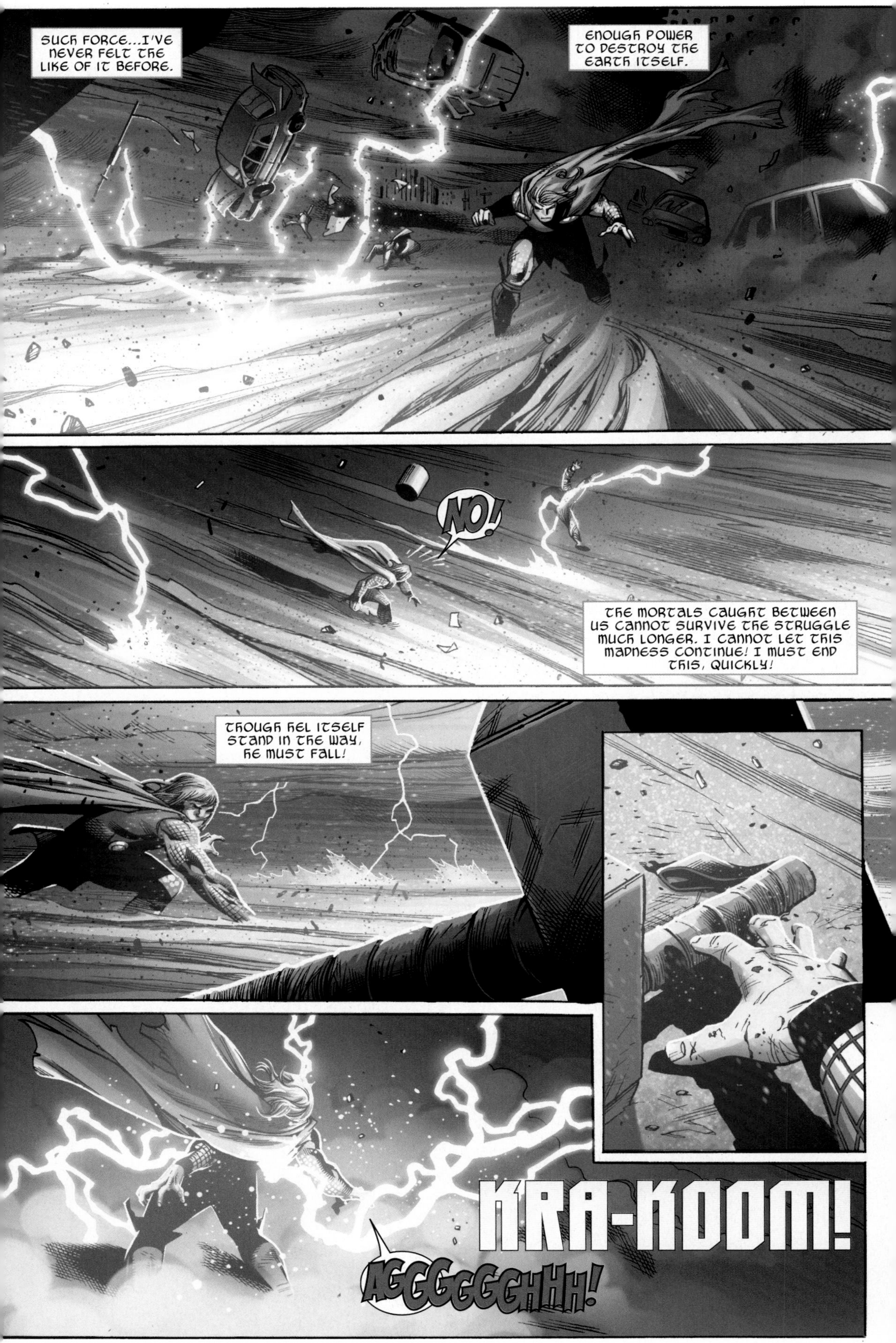

SUCH FORCE...I'VE NEVER FELT THE LIKE OF IT BEFORE.
ENOUGH POWER TO DESTROY THE EARTH ITSELF.
NO!
THE MORTALS CAUGHT BETWEEN US CANNOT SURVIVE THE STRUGGLE MUCH LONGER. I CANNOT LET THIS MADNESS CONTINUE! I MUST END THIS, QUICKLY!
THOUGH HEL ITSELF STAND IN THE WAY, HE MUST FALL!
KRA-KOOM!
AGGGGGGHHH!

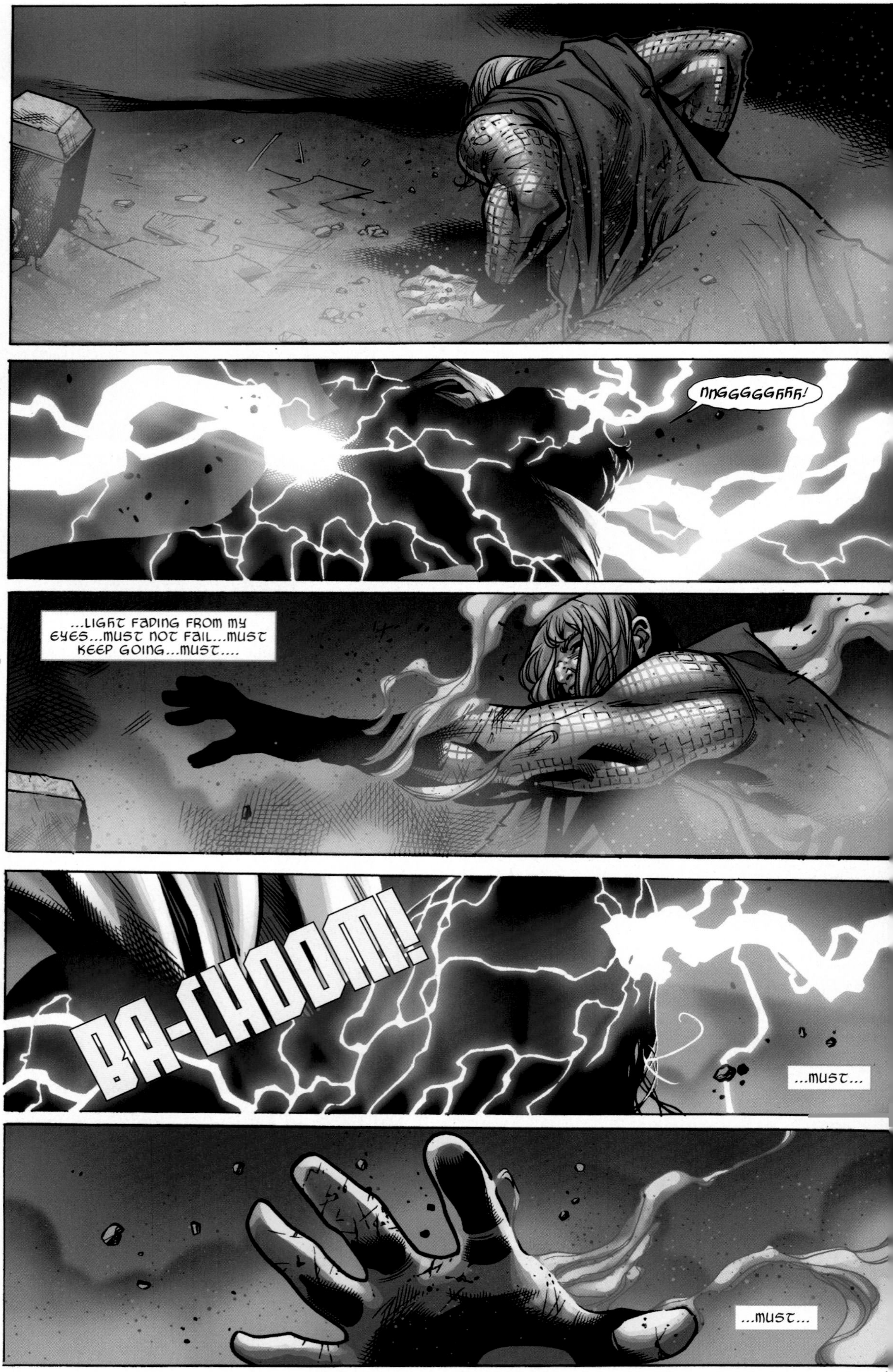

NNGGGGGHHH!
...LIGHT FADING FROM MY EYES...MUST NOT FAIL...MUST KEEP GOING...MUST....
BA-CHOOM!
...MUST...
...MUST...

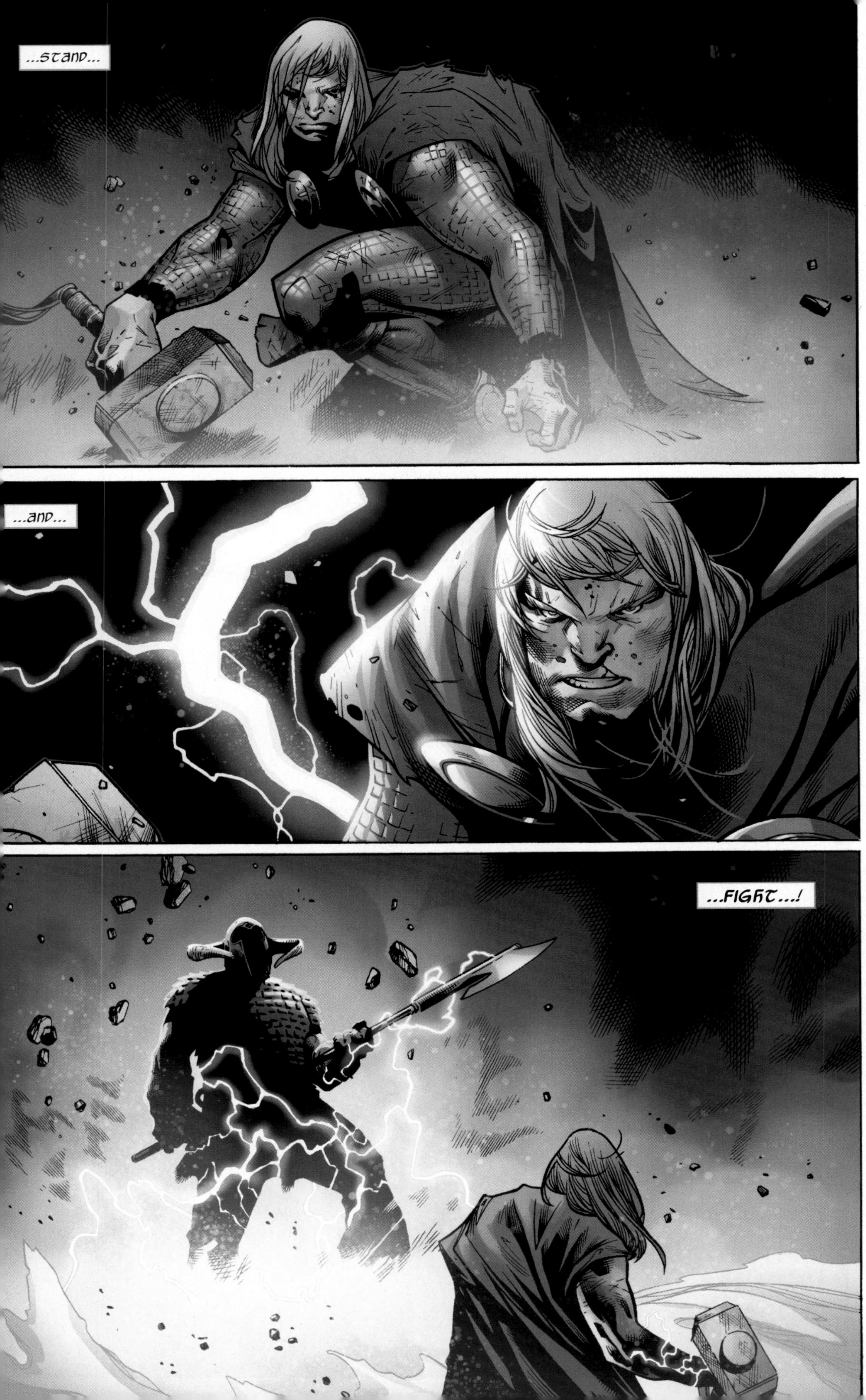
...STAND...
...AND...
...FIGHT...!

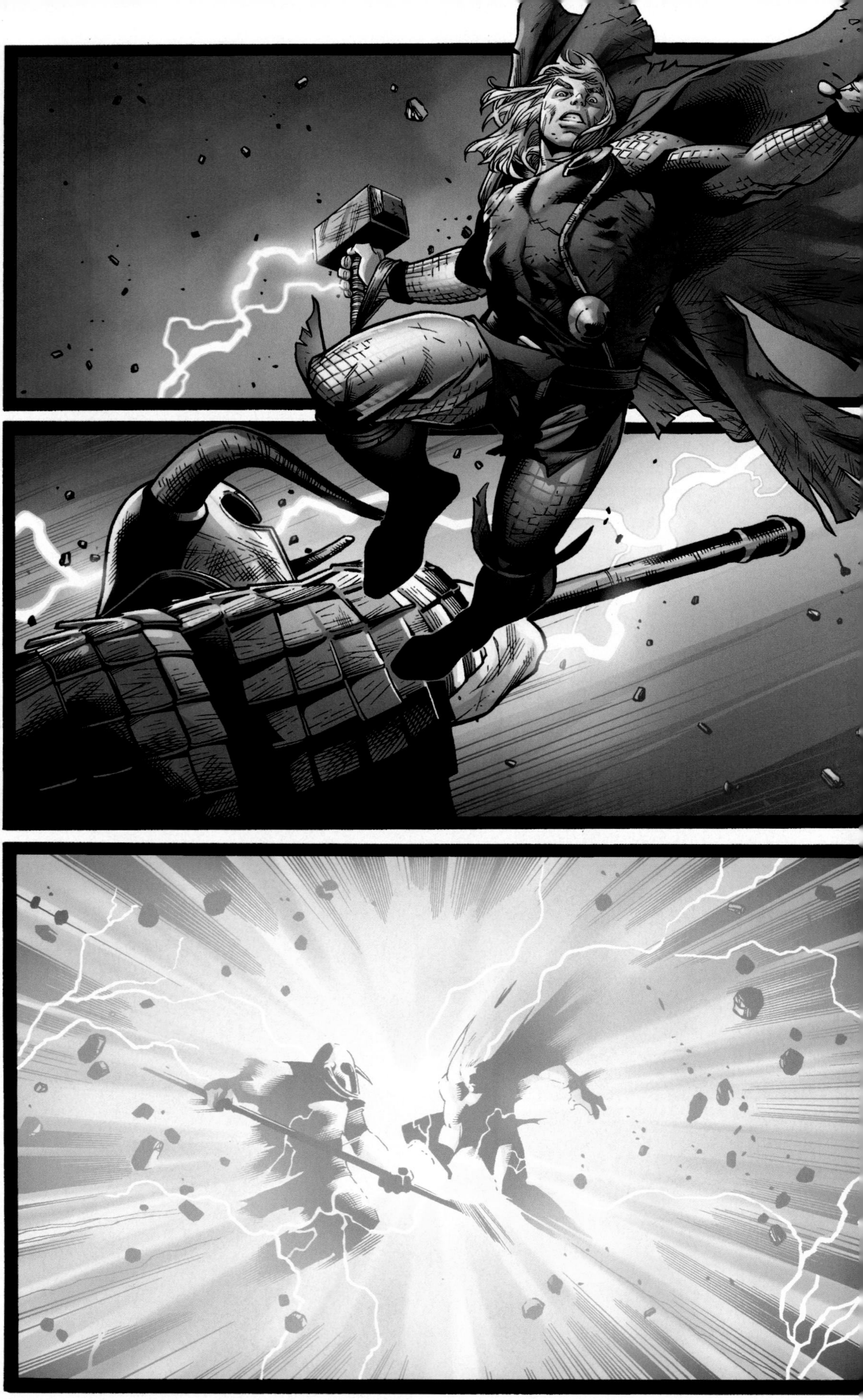

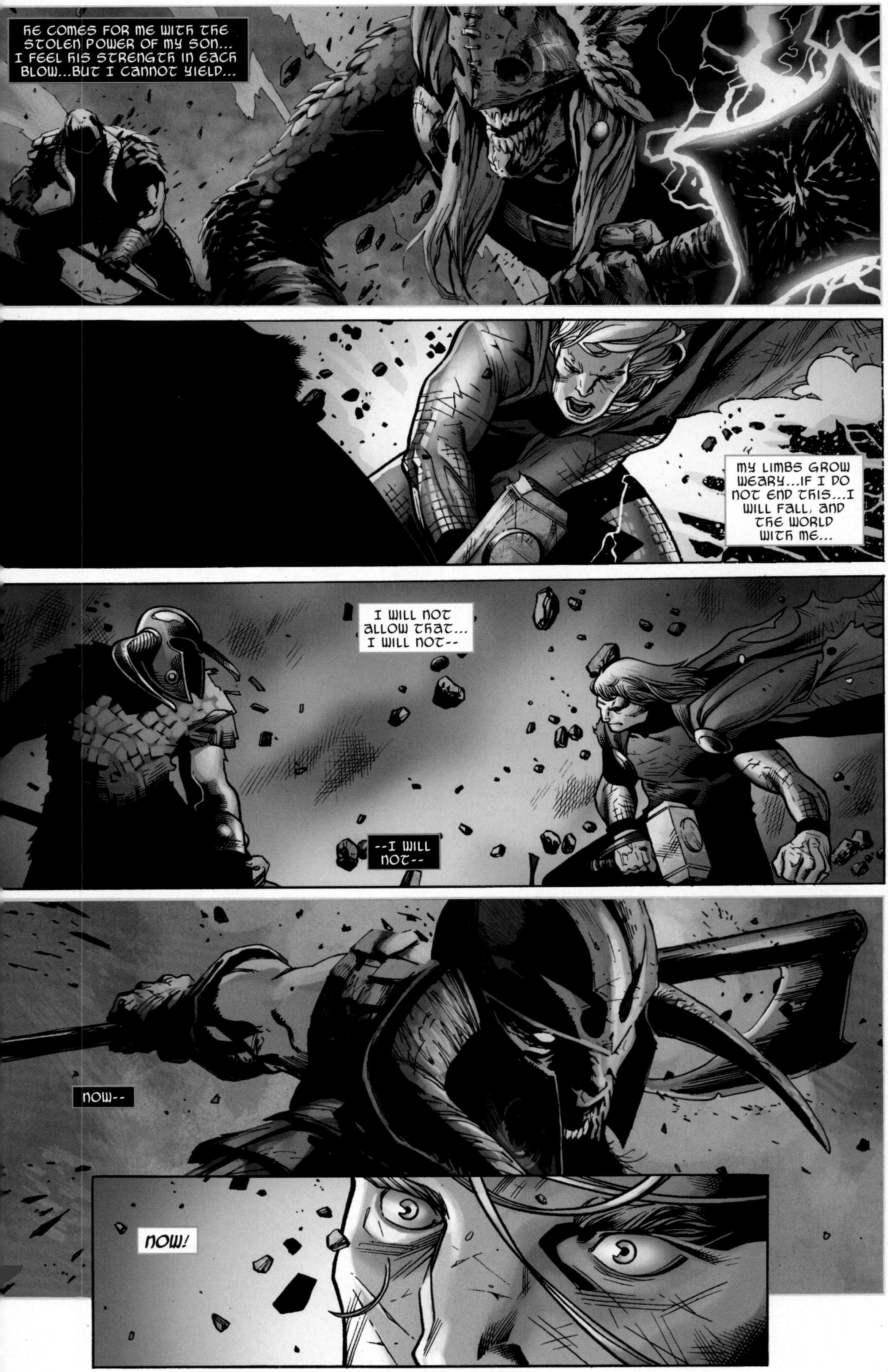
HE COMES FOR ME WITH THE STOLEN POWER OF MY SON... I FEEL HIS STRENGTH IN EACH BLOW...BUT I CANNOT YIELD...
MY LIMBS GROW WEARY...IF I DO NOT END THIS...I WILL FALL, AND THE WORLD WITH ME...
I WILL NOT ALLOW THAT... I WILL NOT--
--I WILL NOT--
NOW--
NOW!

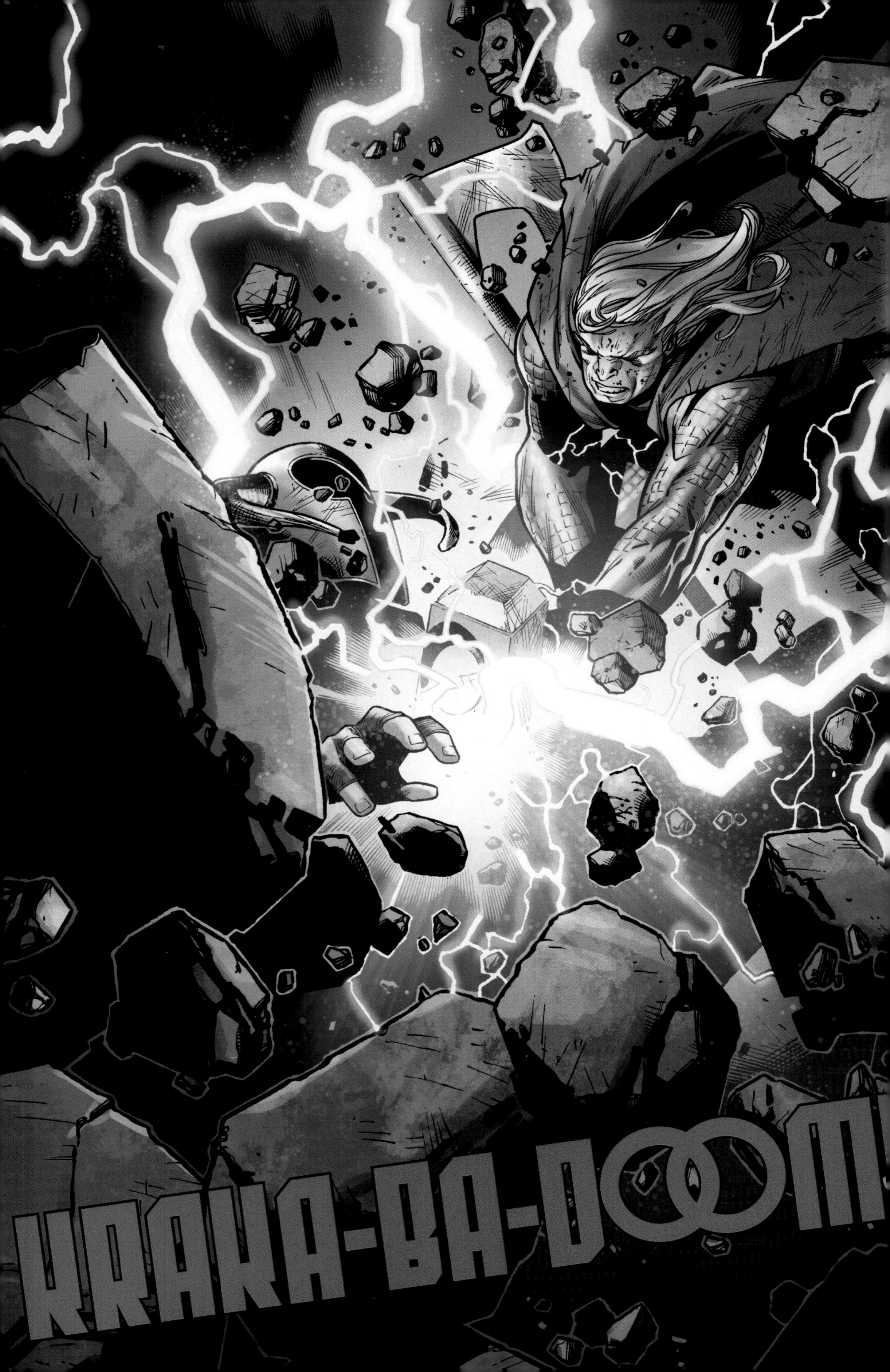
KRAKA-BA-DOOM!

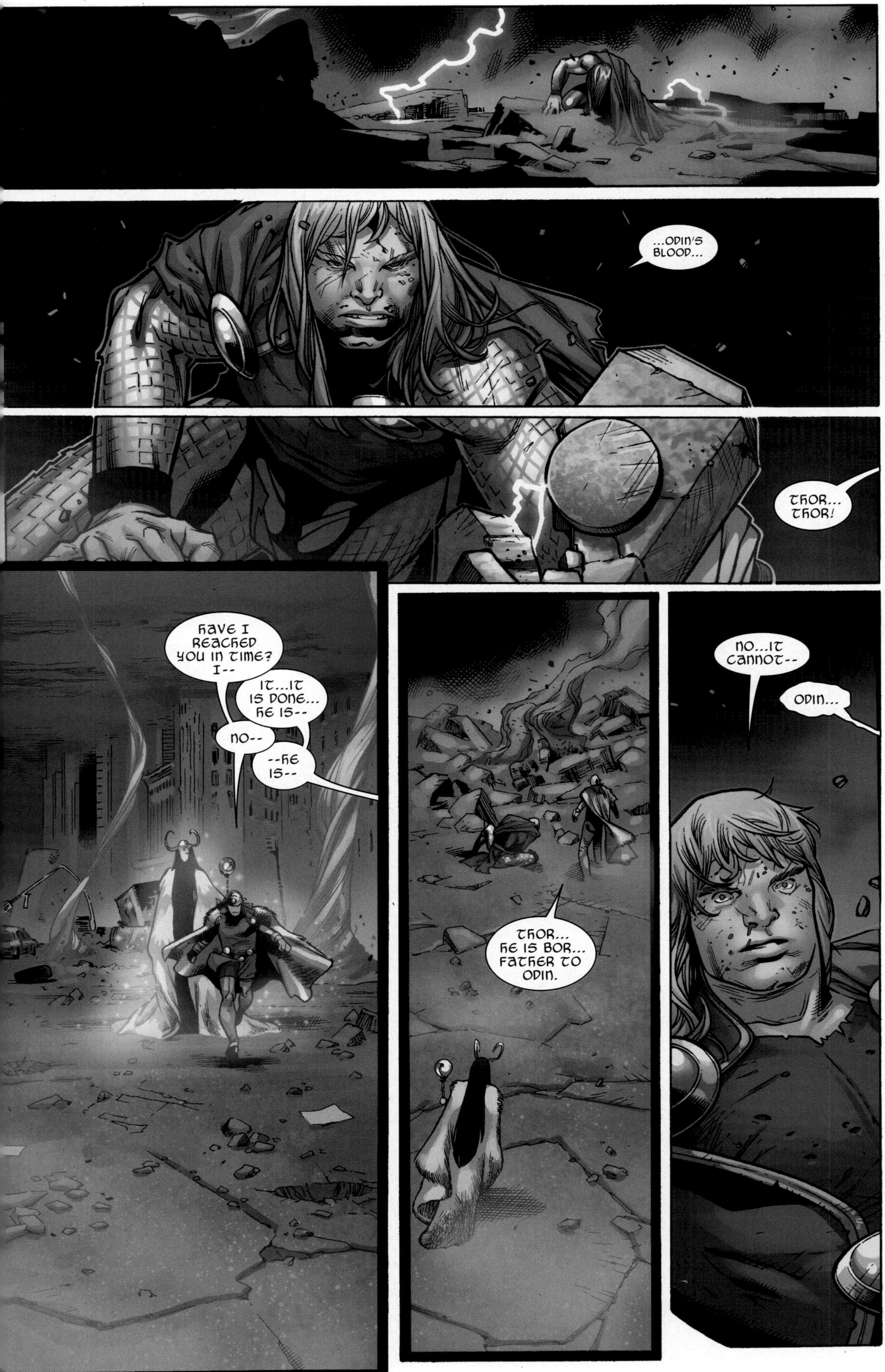
...ODIN'S BLOOD...
THOR... THOR!
HAVE I REACHED YOU IN TIME? I--
IT...IT IS DONE... HE IS--
NO--
--HE IS--
THOR... HE IS BOR... FATHER TO ODIN.
NO...IT CANNOT--
ODIN...

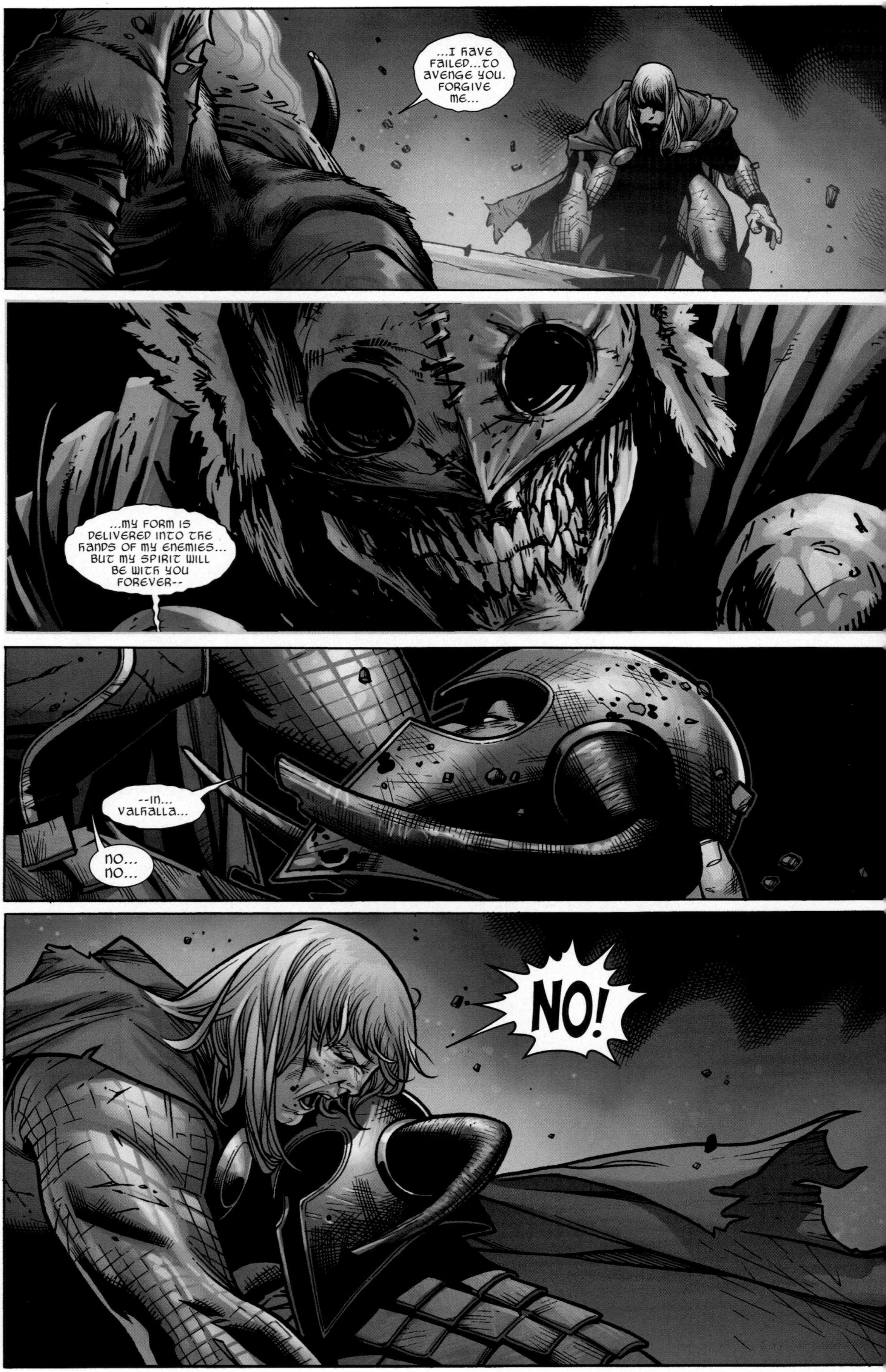
...I HAVE FAILED...TO AVENGE YOU. FORGIVE ME...
...MY FORM IS DELIVERED INTO THE HANDS OF MY ENEMIES... BUT MY SPIRIT WILL BE WITH YOU FOREVER--
--IN... VALHALLA...
NO... NO...
NO!

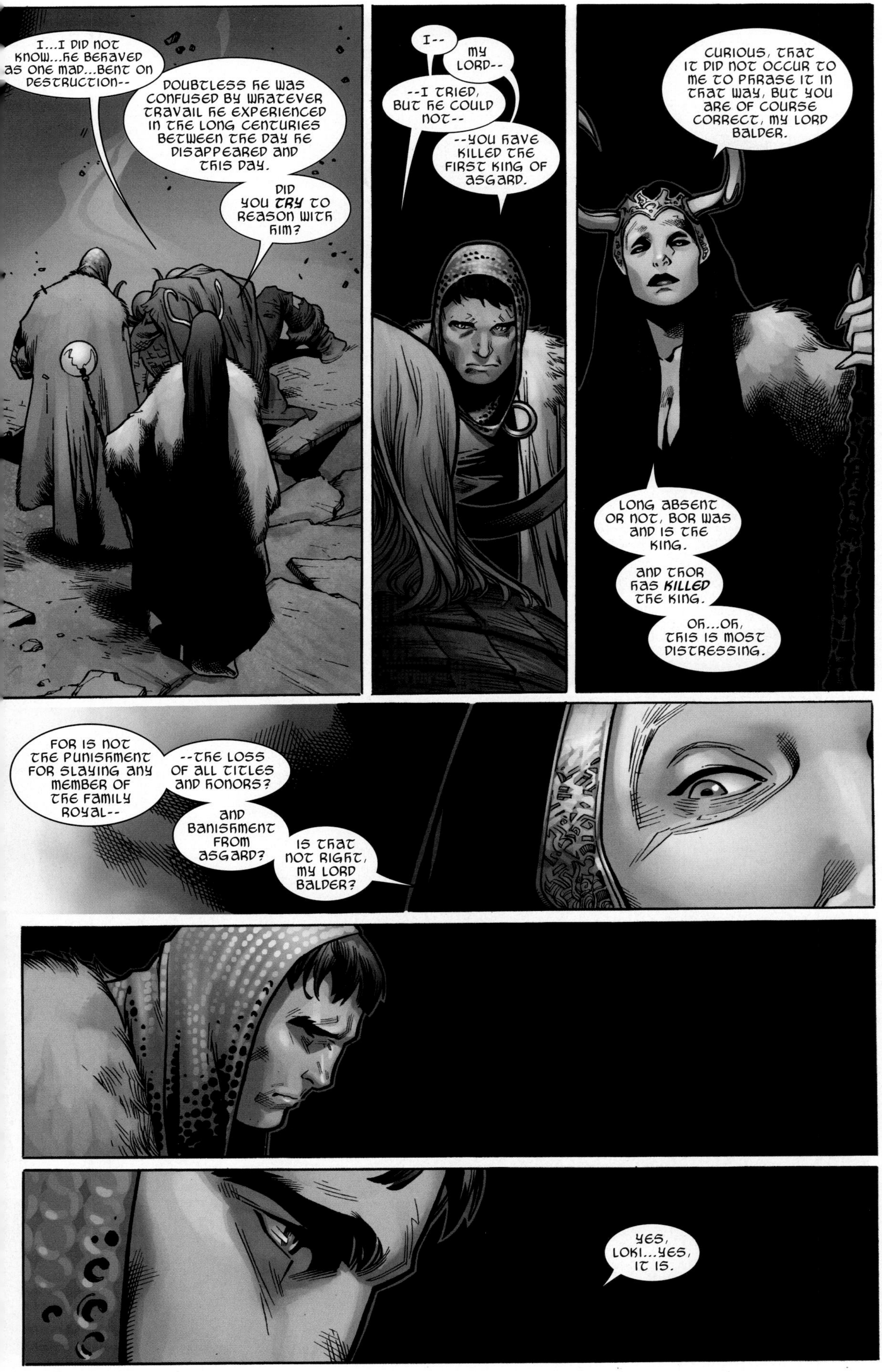
I...I DID NOT KNOW...HE BEHAVED AS ONE MAD...BENT ON DESTRUCTION--
DOUBTLESS HE WAS CONFUSED BY WHATEVER TRAVAIL HE EXPERIENCED IN THE LONG CENTURIES BETWEEN THE DAY HE DISAPPEARED AND THIS DAY.
DID YOU TRY TO REASON WITH HIM?
I--
MY LORD--
--I TRIED, BUT HE COULD NOT--
--YOU HAVE KILLED THE FIRST KING OF ASGARD.
CURIOUS, THAT IT DID NOT OCCUR TO ME TO PHRASE IT IN THAT WAY, BUT YOU ARE OF COURSE CORRECT, MY LORD BALDER.
LONG ABSENT OR NOT, BOR WAS AND IS THE KING.
AND THOR HAS KILLED THE KING.
OH...OH, THIS IS MOST DISTRESSING.
FOR IS NOT THE PUNISHMENT FOR SLAYING ANY MEMBER OF THE FAMILY ROYAL--
--THE LOSS OF ALL TITLES AND HONORS?
AND BANISHMENT FROM ASGARD?
IS THAT NOT RIGHT, MY LORD BALDER?
YES, LOKI...YES, IT IS.

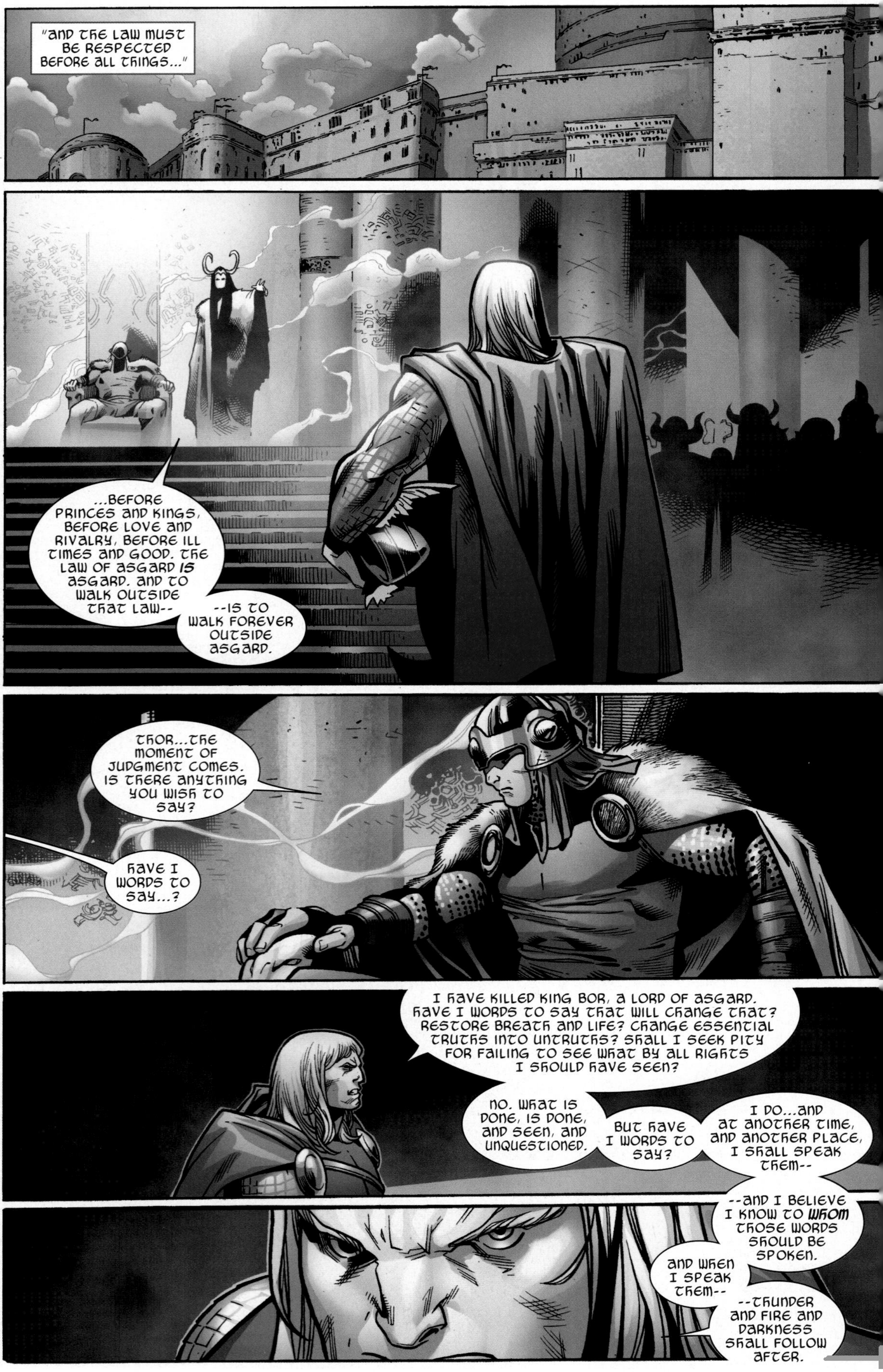
"AND THE LAW MUST BE RESPECTED BEFORE ALL THINGS..."
...BEFORE PRINCES AND KINGS, BEFORE LOVE AND RIVALRY, BEFORE ILL TIMES AND GOOD. THE LAW OF ASGARD *IS* ASGARD. AND TO WALK OUTSIDE THAT LAW--
--IS TO WALK FOREVER OUTSIDE ASGARD.
THOR...THE MOMENT OF JUDGMENT COMES. IS THERE ANYTHING YOU WISH TO SAY?
HAVE I WORDS TO SAY...?
I HAVE KILLED KING BOR, A LORD OF ASGARD. HAVE I WORDS TO SAY THAT WILL CHANGE THAT? RESTORE BREATH AND LIFE? CHANGE ESSENTIAL TRUTHS INTO UNTRUTHS? SHALL I SEEK PITY FOR FAILING TO SEE WHAT BY ALL RIGHTS I SHOULD HAVE SEEN?
NO. WHAT IS DONE, IS DONE, AND SEEN, AND UNQUESTIONED.
BUT HAVE I WORDS TO SAY?
I DO...AND AT ANOTHER TIME, AND ANOTHER PLACE, I SHALL SPEAK THEM--
--AND I BELIEVE I KNOW TO *WHOM* THOSE WORDS SHOULD BE SPOKEN.
AND WHEN I SPEAK THEM--
--THUNDER AND FIRE AND DARKNESS SHALL FOLLOW AFTER.

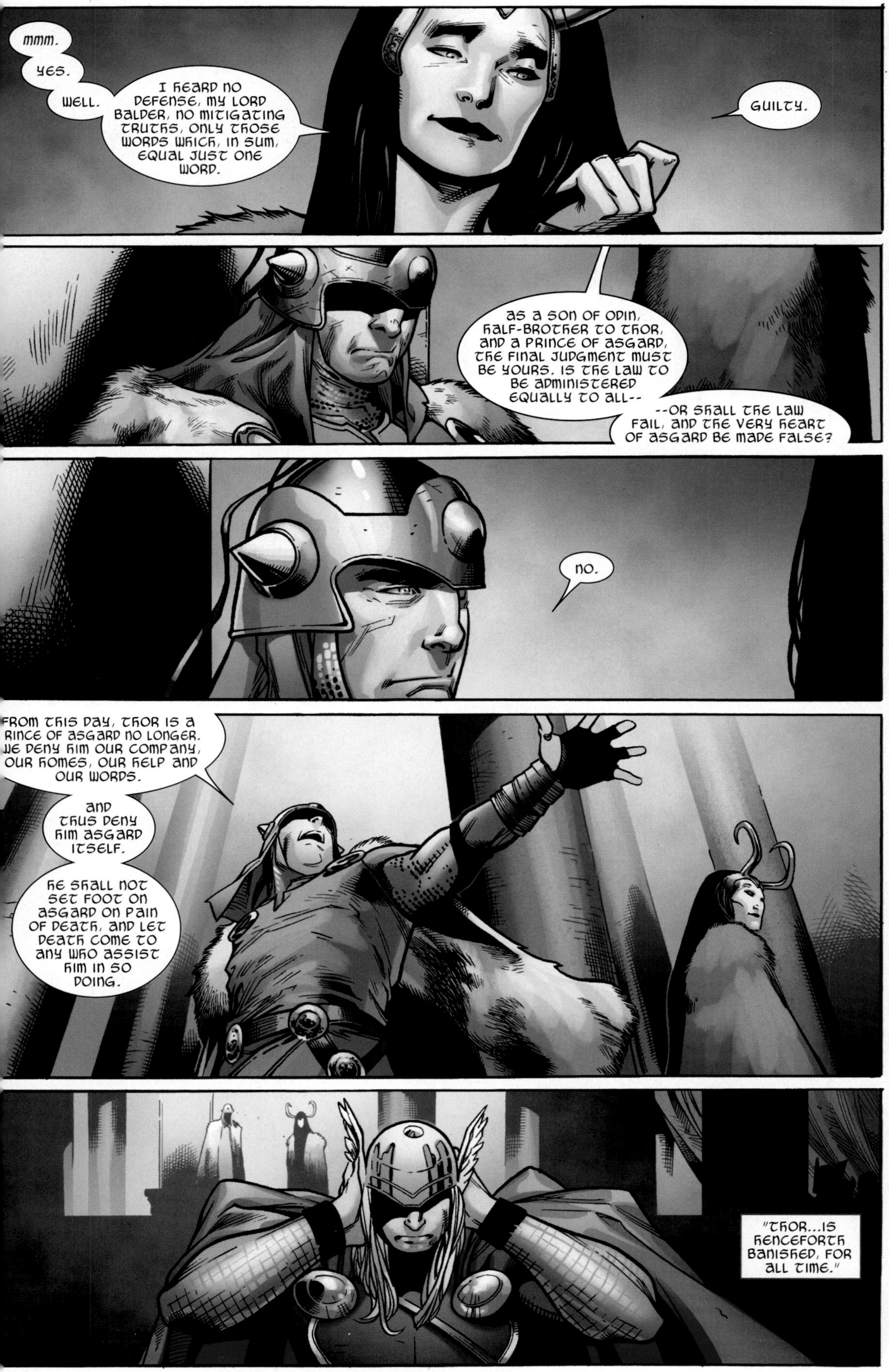
mmm.
yes.
well.
I heard no defense, my lord Balder, no mitigating truths, only those words which, in sum, equal just one word.
guilty.
as a son of odin, half-brother to thor, and a prince of asgard, the final judgment must be yours. is the law to be administered equally to all--
--or shall the law fail, and the very heart of asgard be made false?
no.
from this day, thor is a rince of asgard no longer. e deny him our company, our homes, our help and our words.
and thus deny him asgard itself.
he shall not set foot on asgard on pain of death, and let death come to any who assist him in so doing.
"thor...is henceforth banished, for all time."

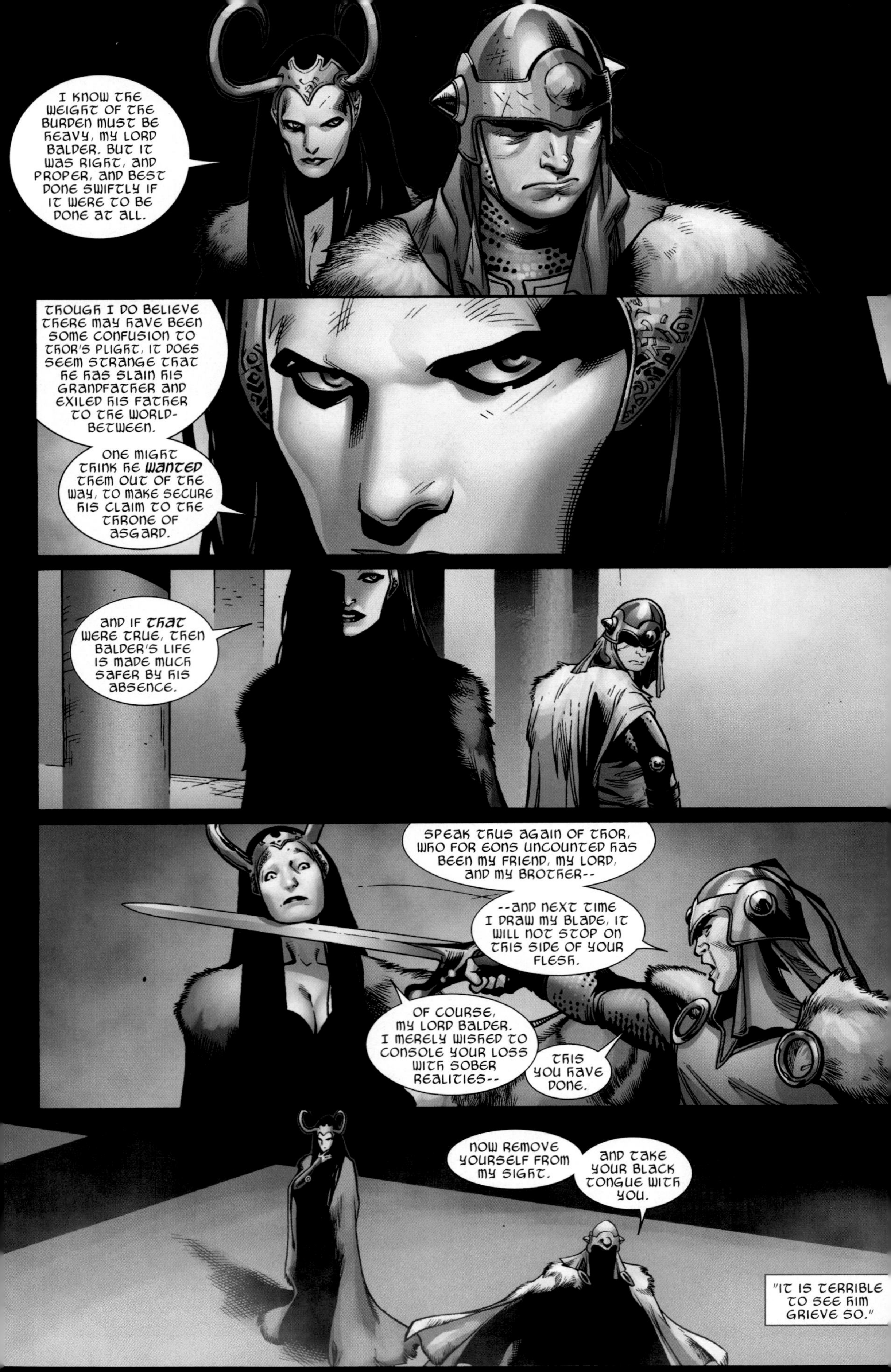
I KNOW THE WEIGHT OF THE BURDEN MUST BE HEAVY, MY LORD BALDER. BUT IT WAS RIGHT, AND PROPER, AND BEST DONE SWIFTLY IF IT WERE TO BE DONE AT ALL.
THOUGH I DO BELIEVE THERE MAY HAVE BEEN SOME CONFUSION TO THOR'S PLIGHT, IT DOES SEEM STRANGE THAT HE HAS SLAIN HIS GRANDFATHER AND EXILED HIS FATHER TO THE WORLD-BETWEEN.
ONE MIGHT THINK HE *WANTED* THEM OUT OF THE WAY, TO MAKE SECURE HIS CLAIM TO THE THRONE OF ASGARD.
AND IF *THAT* WERE TRUE, THEN BALDER'S LIFE IS MADE MUCH SAFER BY HIS ABSENCE.
SPEAK THUS AGAIN OF THOR, WHO FOR EONS UNCOUNTED HAS BEEN MY FRIEND, MY LORD, AND MY BROTHER--
--AND NEXT TIME I DRAW MY BLADE, IT WILL NOT STOP ON THIS SIDE OF YOUR FLESH.
OF COURSE, MY LORD BALDER. I MERELY WISHED TO CONSOLE YOUR LOSS WITH SOBER REALITIES--
THIS YOU HAVE DONE.
NOW REMOVE YOURSELF FROM MY SIGHT.
AND TAKE YOUR BLACK TONGUE WITH YOU.
"IT IS TERRIBLE TO SEE HIM GRIEVE SO."

AS HEAVY AS THE LOSS OF THOR IS THE WEIGHT OF THIS PLACE, THIS LAND, SO UNLIKE OUR OWN. DRY. HOT. BARREN.

FLAT.

HE MIGHT FARE BETTER IN MORE FAMILIAR CLIMES...TO WALK IN SNOW AND COLD, TO HUNT AND CLIMB...TO LET HIS ARM AND HIS ARMOR WIN THE DAY AGAINST WOLF AND--

WHAT'S THE POINT OF WISHING, LOKI? THERE IS NO SUCH PLACE WHERE WE WOULD BE WELCOME.

AH, AND THERE YOU ARE WRONG. I KNOW OF JUST SUCH A LAND, FULL OF SNOW-CAPPED MOUNTAINS AND FAIR GAME, WHERE HE AND WE COULD HUNT AND VENTURE FORTH ON MISSIONS OF GREATNESS... A LAND OF STEEPLED CASTLES AND SMALL VILLAGES.

I HAVE SPOKEN TO THE KING OF THIS LAND, AND HE HAS INVITED ALL OF US--

--ALL OF US--

--TO MOVE FROM THIS DESOLATE PLACE TO HIS COUNTRY. HE WILL MAKE US WELCOME, AND GIVE US ALL WE REQUIRE.

I WOULD MENTION IT MYSELF TO LORD BALDER, BUT IT WOULD, I THINK, BE SERVED BEST IF IT CAME FROM OTHERS.

WE CANNOT MOVE ASGARD ITSELF, FOR ONLY THOR HAD THAT POWER, BUT WITHIN A MONTH WE COULD ALL BE IN THIS NEW LAND, AND THAT WOULD BE OUR NEW HOME, OUR NEW...ASGARD.

AND WHAT LAND IS THIS, LOKI? HOW CAN WE ASK BALDER TO LEAVE HERE AND GO THERE IF WE DO NOT KNOW WHERE *THERE* IS?

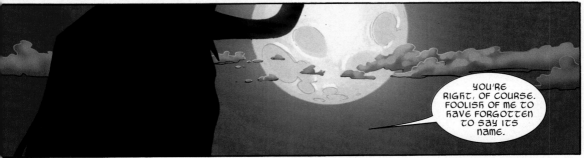

YOU'RE RIGHT, OF COURSE. FOOLISH OF ME TO HAVE FORGOTTEN TO SAY ITS NAME.

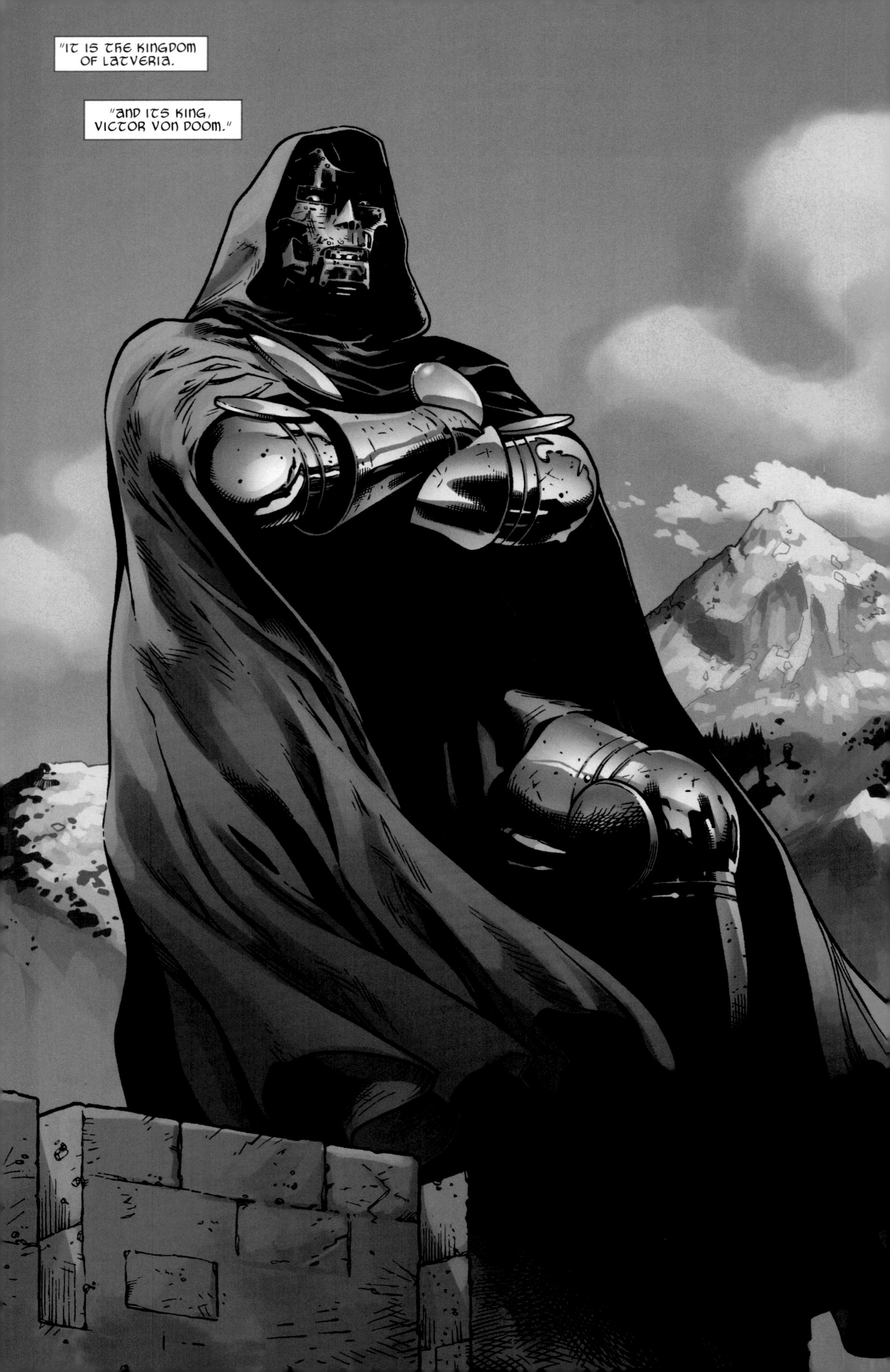
"IT IS THE KINGDOM OF LATVERIA.
"AND ITS KING, VICTOR VON DOOM."

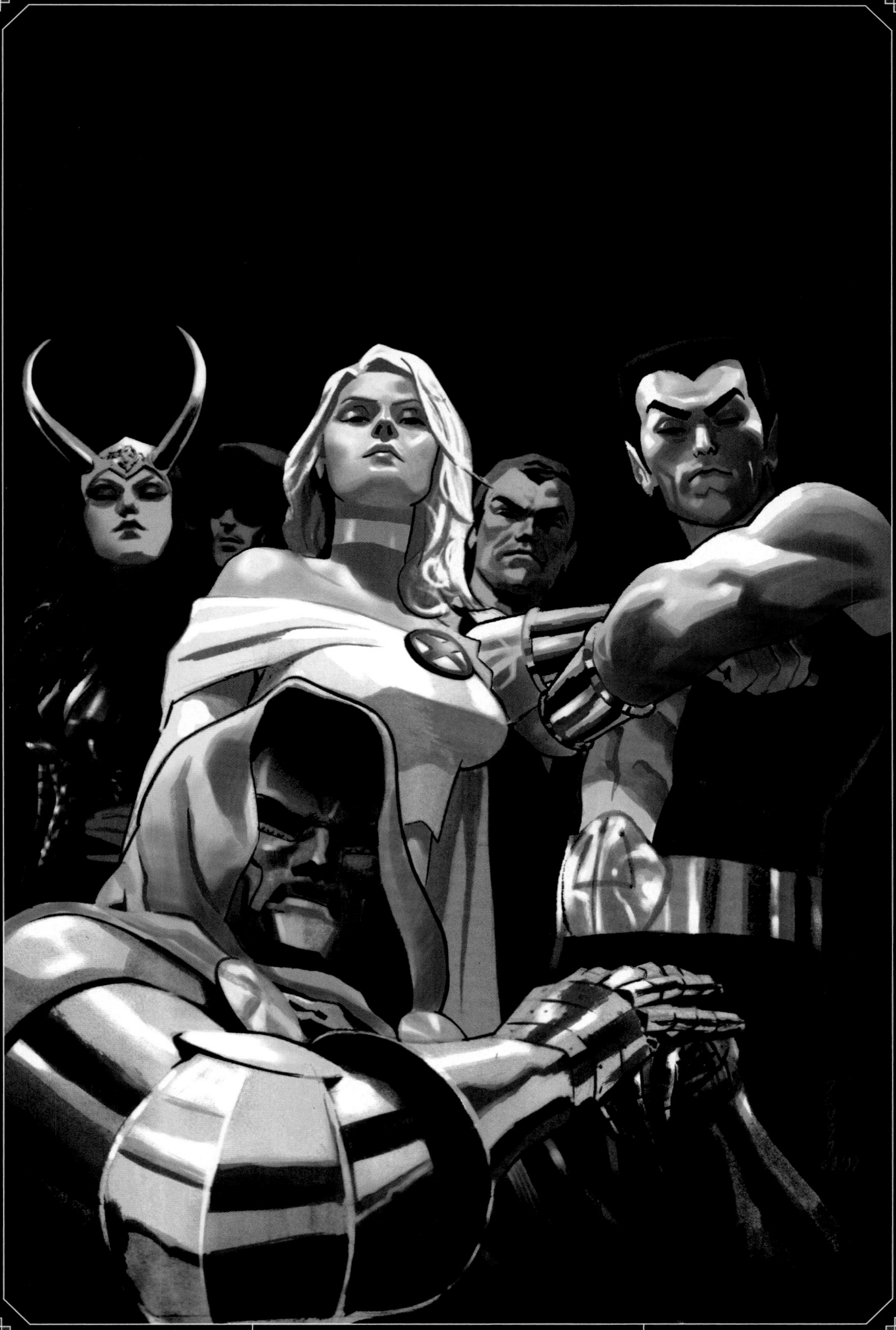

DARK REIGN: THE CABAL

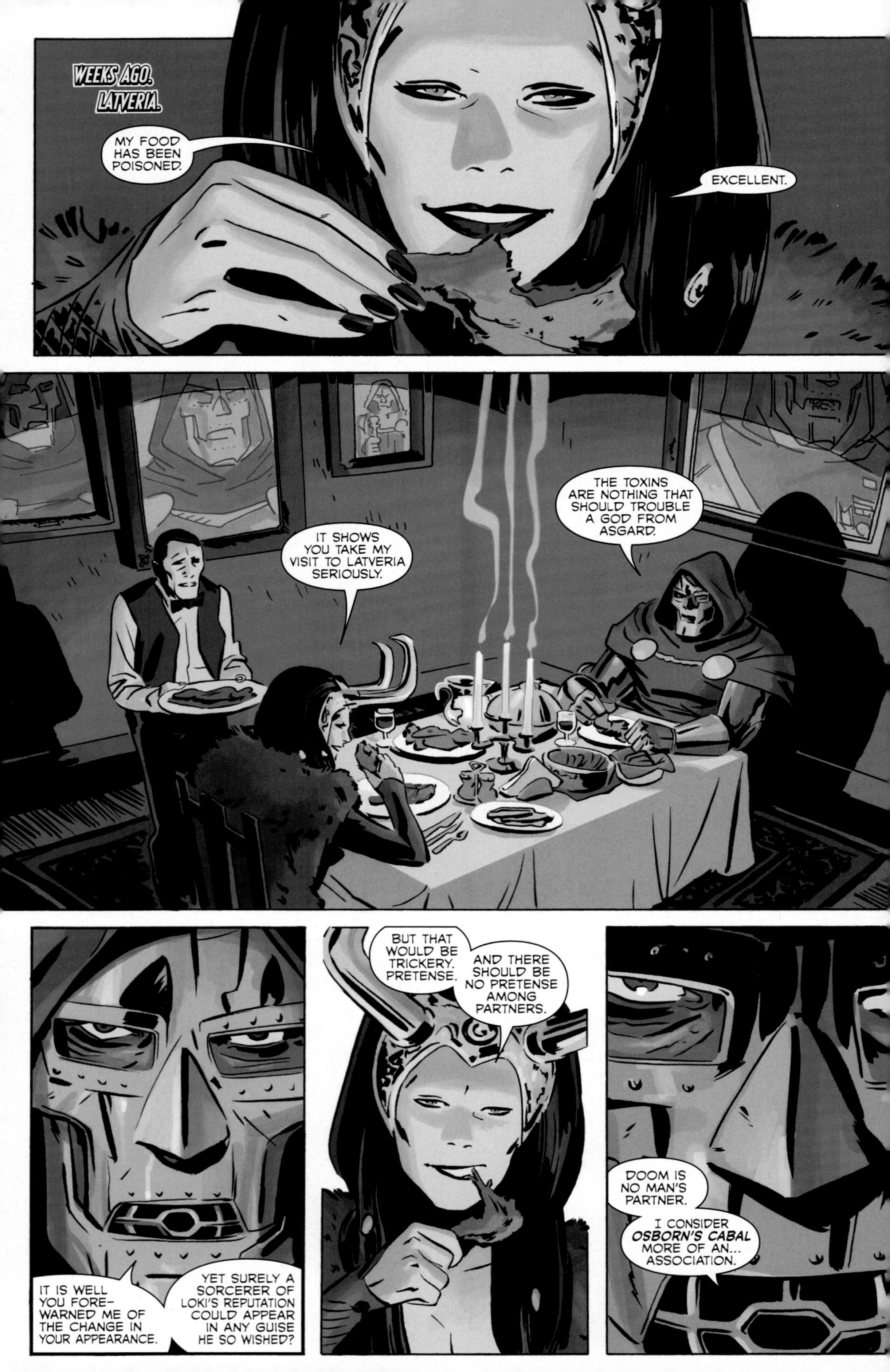

WEEKS AGO. LATVERIA.
MY FOOD HAS BEEN POISONED.
EXCELLENT.
IT SHOWS YOU TAKE MY VISIT TO LATVERIA SERIOUSLY.
THE TOXINS ARE NOTHING THAT SHOULD TROUBLE A GOD FROM ASGARD.
IT IS WELL YOU FORE-WARNED ME OF THE CHANGE IN YOUR APPEARANCE.
YET SURELY A SORCERER OF LOKI'S REPUTATION COULD APPEAR IN ANY GUISE HE SO WISHED?
BUT THAT WOULD BE TRICKERY. PRETENSE.
AND THERE SHOULD BE NO PRETENSE AMONG PARTNERS.
DOOM IS NO MAN'S PARTNER.
I CONSIDER OSBORN'S CABAL MORE OF AN... ASSOCIATION.

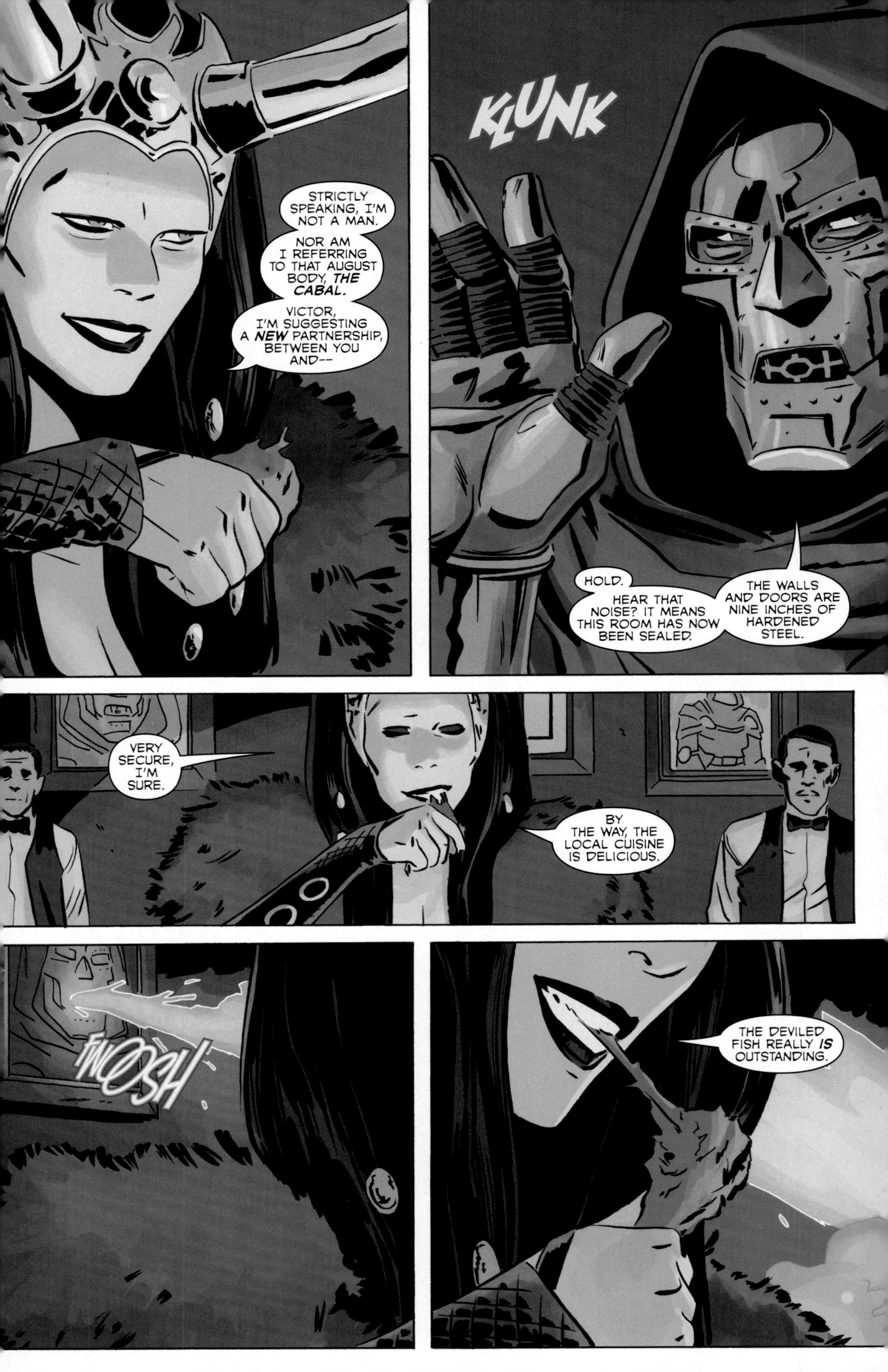
STRICTLY SPEAKING, I'M NOT A MAN.
NOR AM I REFERRING TO THAT AUGUST BODY, *THE CABAL.*
VICTOR, I'M SUGGESTING A *NEW* PARTNERSHIP, BETWEEN YOU AND--
KLUNK
HOLD.
HEAR THAT NOISE? IT MEANS THIS ROOM HAS NOW BEEN SEALED.
THE WALLS AND DOORS ARE NINE INCHES OF HARDENED STEEL.
VERY SECURE, I'M SURE.
BY THE WAY, THE LOCAL CUISINE IS DELICIOUS.
FWOOSH
THE DEVILED FISH REALLY *IS* OUTSTANDING.

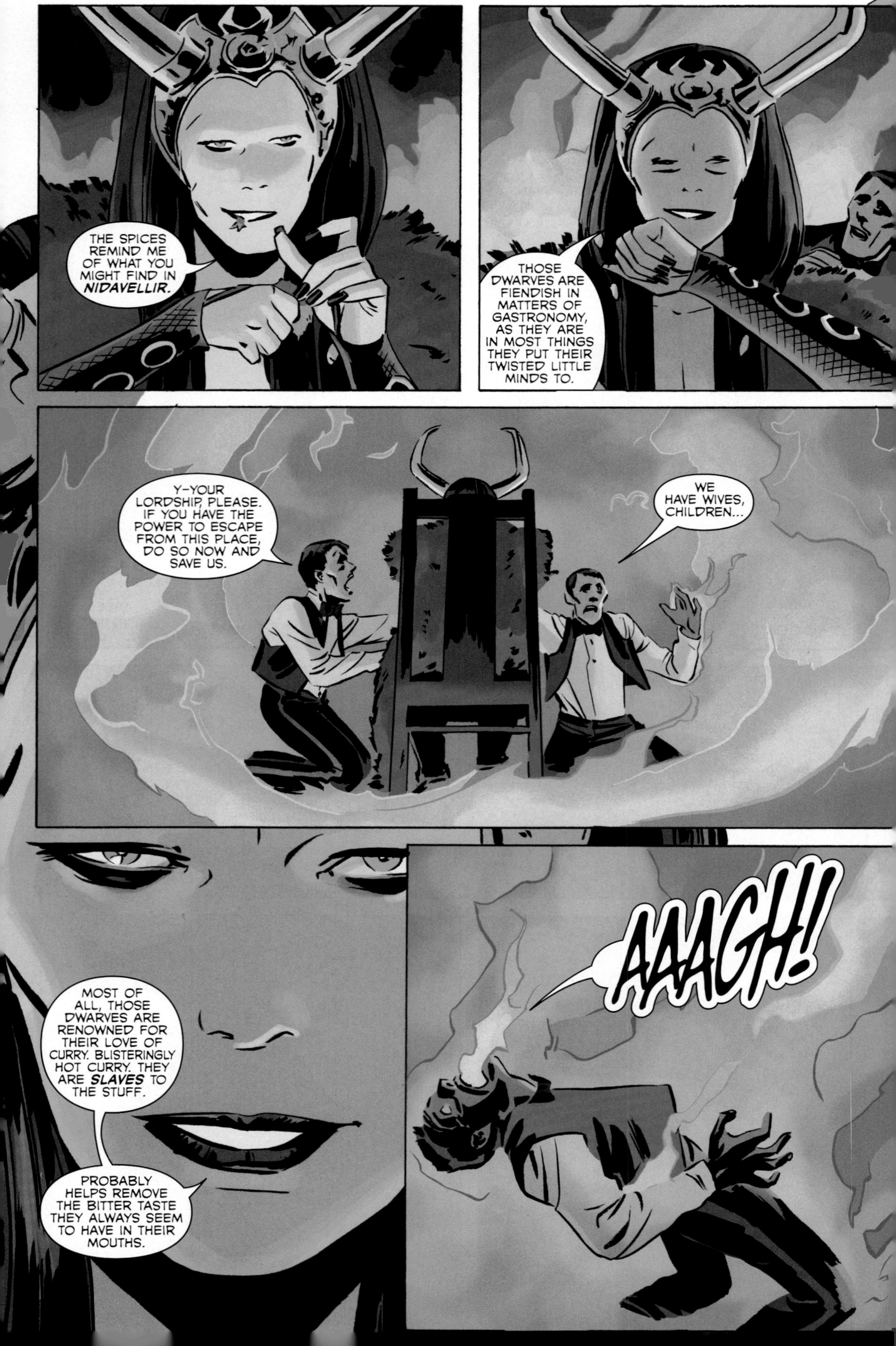
THE SPICES REMIND ME OF WHAT YOU MIGHT FIND IN ***NIDAVELLIR.***
THOSE DWARVES ARE FIENDISH IN MATTERS OF GASTRONOMY, AS THEY ARE IN MOST THINGS THEY PUT THEIR TWISTED LITTLE MINDS TO.
Y-YOUR LORDSHIP, PLEASE. IF YOU HAVE THE POWER TO ESCAPE FROM THIS PLACE, DO SO NOW AND SAVE US.
WE HAVE WIVES, CHILDREN...
MOST OF ALL, THOSE DWARVES ARE RENOWNED FOR THEIR LOVE OF CURRY. BLISTERINGLY HOT CURRY. THEY ARE ***SLAVES*** TO THE STUFF.
PROBABLY HELPS REMOVE THE BITTER TASTE THEY ALWAYS SEEM TO HAVE IN THEIR MOUTHS.
AAAGH!

Hmm.

WELL, DON'T MIND ME.

I'M *USED* TO TALKING TO MYSELF.

I PRESUME YOU'RE WATCHING THIS, DOOM.

ARE YOU *CONVINCED* YET?

AN IMMUNITY TO POISON AND PAIN. A CALLOUS DISREGARD FOR HUMAN LIFE.

I AM WILLING TO CONCEDE THAT YOU ARE LOKI. MAKE YOUR WAY THROUGH THE LOCKED DOOR.

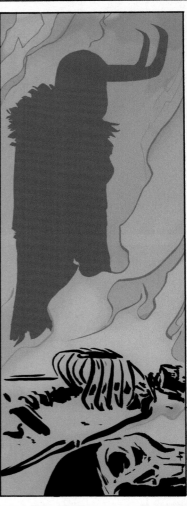

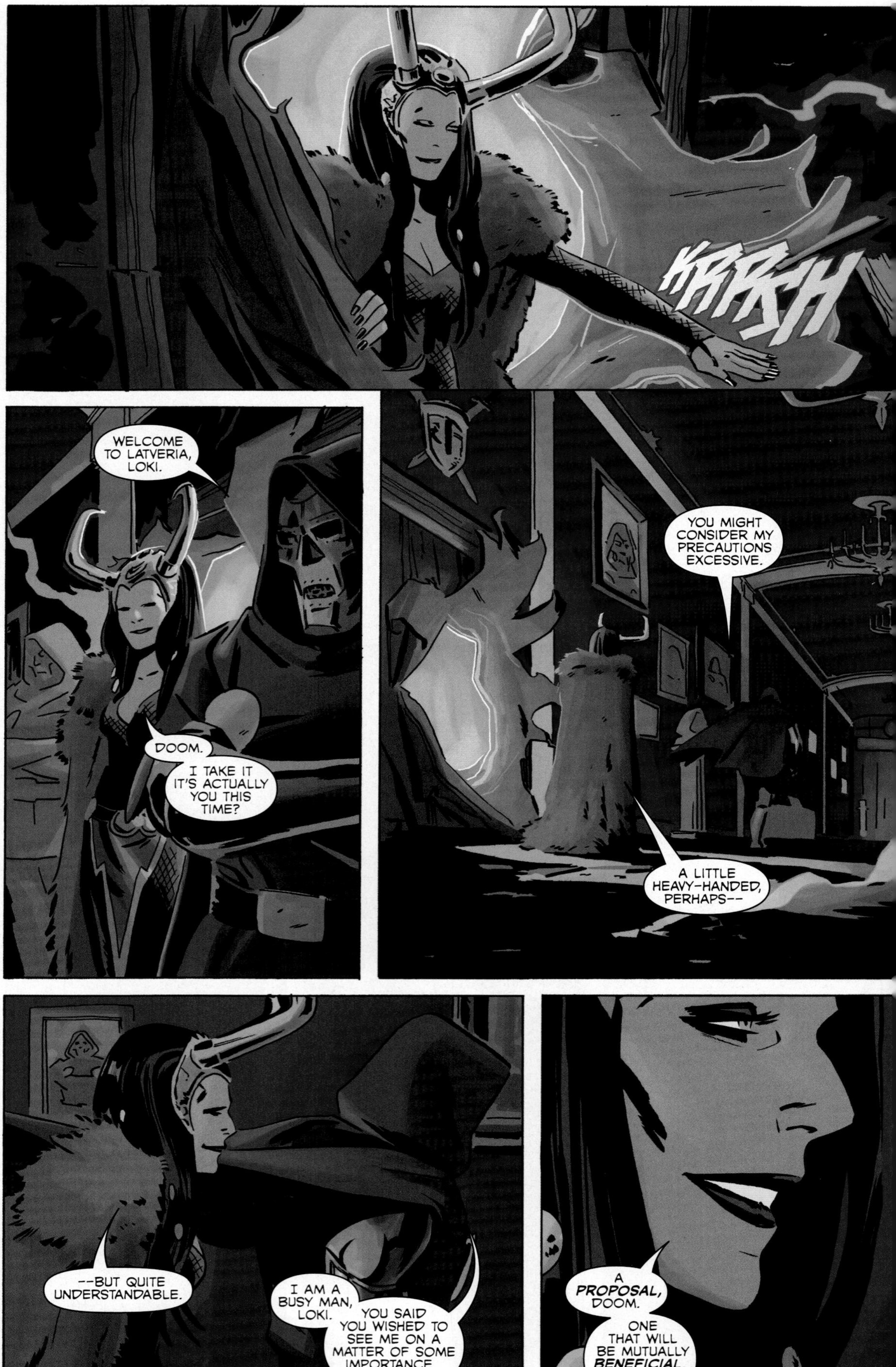
KRRSH
WELCOME TO LATVERIA, LOKI.
DOOM.
I TAKE IT IT'S ACTUALLY YOU THIS TIME?
YOU MIGHT CONSIDER MY PRECAUTIONS EXCESSIVE.
A LITTLE HEAVY-HANDED, PERHAPS--
--BUT QUITE UNDERSTANDABLE.
I AM A BUSY MAN, LOKI.
YOU SAID YOU WISHED TO SEE ME ON A MATTER OF SOME IMPORTANCE.
A PROPOSAL, DOOM.
ONE THAT WILL BE MUTUALLY BENEFICIAL.

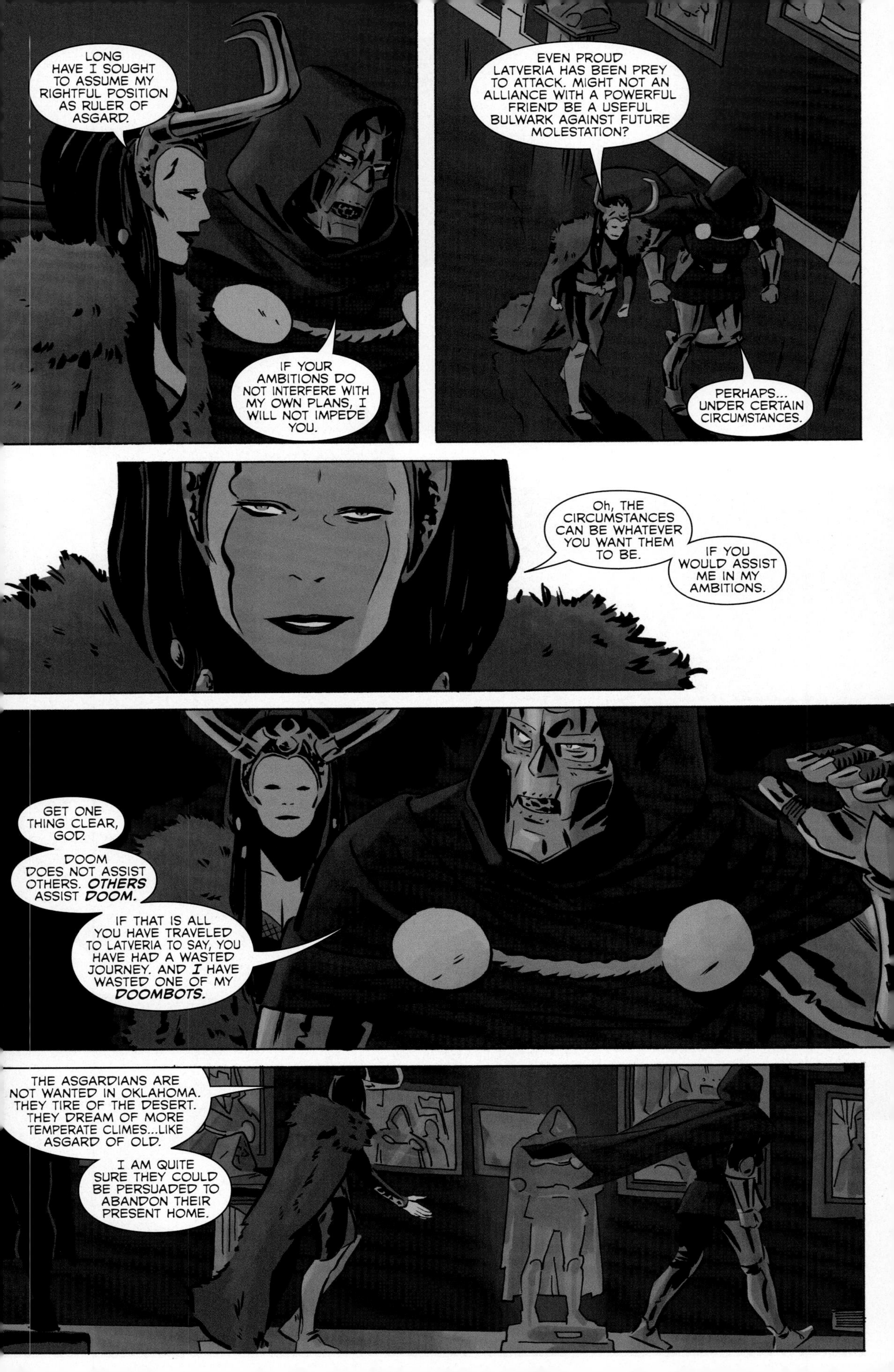
LONG HAVE I SOUGHT TO ASSUME MY RIGHTFUL POSITION AS RULER OF ASGARD.
IF YOUR AMBITIONS DO NOT INTERFERE WITH MY OWN PLANS, I WILL NOT IMPEDE YOU.
EVEN PROUD LATVERIA HAS BEEN PREY TO ATTACK. MIGHT NOT AN ALLIANCE WITH A POWERFUL FRIEND BE A USEFUL BULWARK AGAINST FUTURE MOLESTATION?
PERHAPS... UNDER CERTAIN CIRCUMSTANCES.
Oh, THE CIRCUMSTANCES CAN BE WHATEVER YOU WANT THEM TO BE.
IF YOU WOULD ASSIST ME IN MY AMBITIONS.
GET ONE THING CLEAR, GOD.
DOOM DOES NOT ASSIST OTHERS. ***OTHERS*** ASSIST ***DOOM.***
IF THAT IS ALL YOU HAVE TRAVELED TO LATVERIA TO SAY, YOU HAVE HAD A WASTED JOURNEY. AND ***I*** HAVE WASTED ONE OF MY ***DOOMBOTS.***
THE ASGARDIANS ARE NOT WANTED IN OKLAHOMA. THEY TIRE OF THE DESERT. THEY DREAM OF MORE TEMPERATE CLIMES...LIKE ASGARD OF OLD.
I AM QUITE SURE THEY COULD BE PERSUADED TO ABANDON THEIR PRESENT HOME.

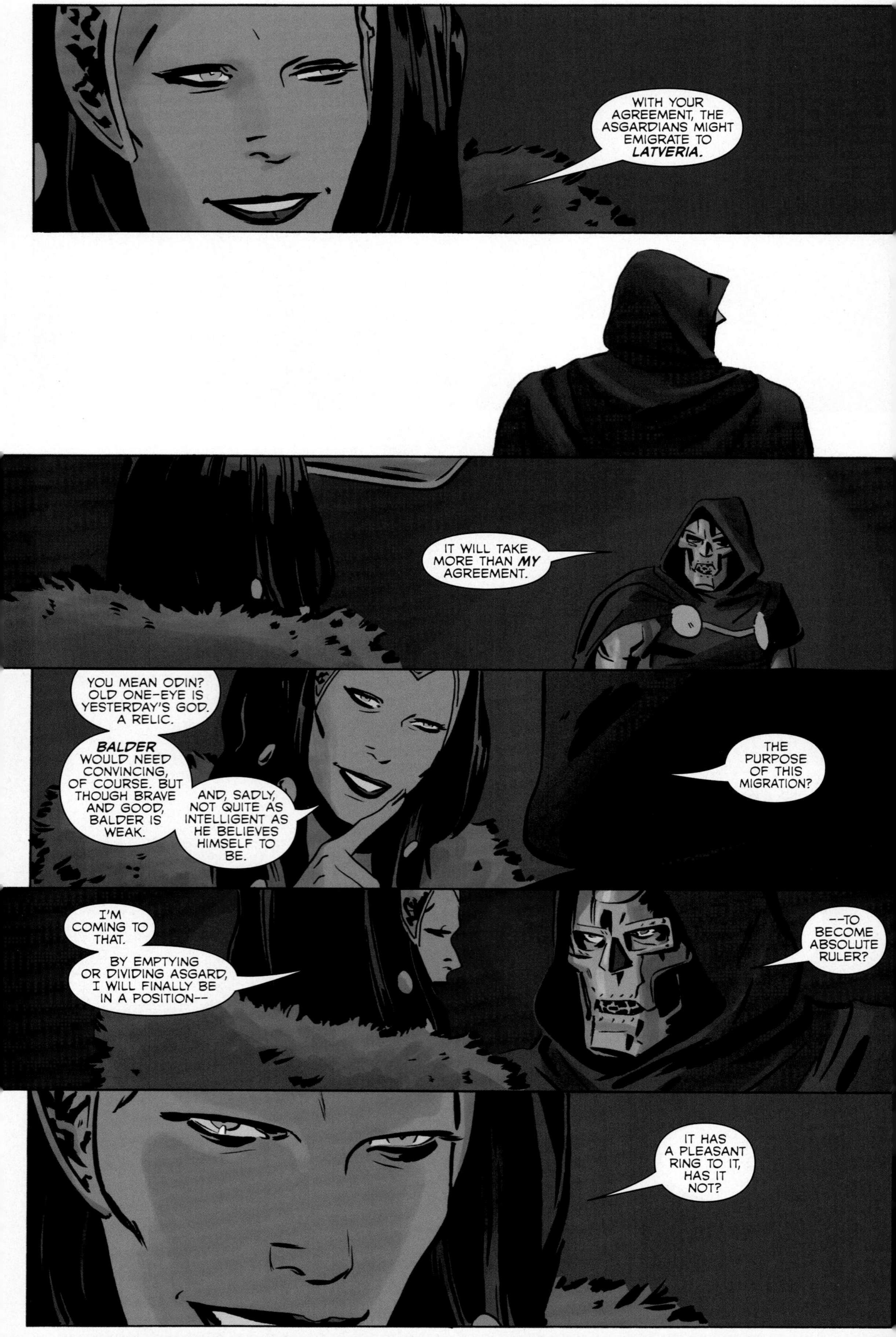
WITH YOUR AGREEMENT, THE ASGARDIANS MIGHT EMIGRATE TO LATVERIA.
IT WILL TAKE MORE THAN MY AGREEMENT.
YOU MEAN ODIN? OLD ONE-EYE IS YESTERDAY'S GOD. A RELIC.
BALDER WOULD NEED CONVINCING, OF COURSE. BUT THOUGH BRAVE AND GOOD, BALDER IS WEAK.
AND, SADLY, NOT QUITE AS INTELLIGENT AS HE BELIEVES HIMSELF TO BE.
THE PURPOSE OF THIS MIGRATION?
I'M COMING TO THAT.
BY EMPTYING OR DIVIDING ASGARD, I WILL FINALLY BE IN A POSITION--
--TO BECOME ABSOLUTE RULER?
IT HAS A PLEASANT RING TO IT, HAS IT NOT?

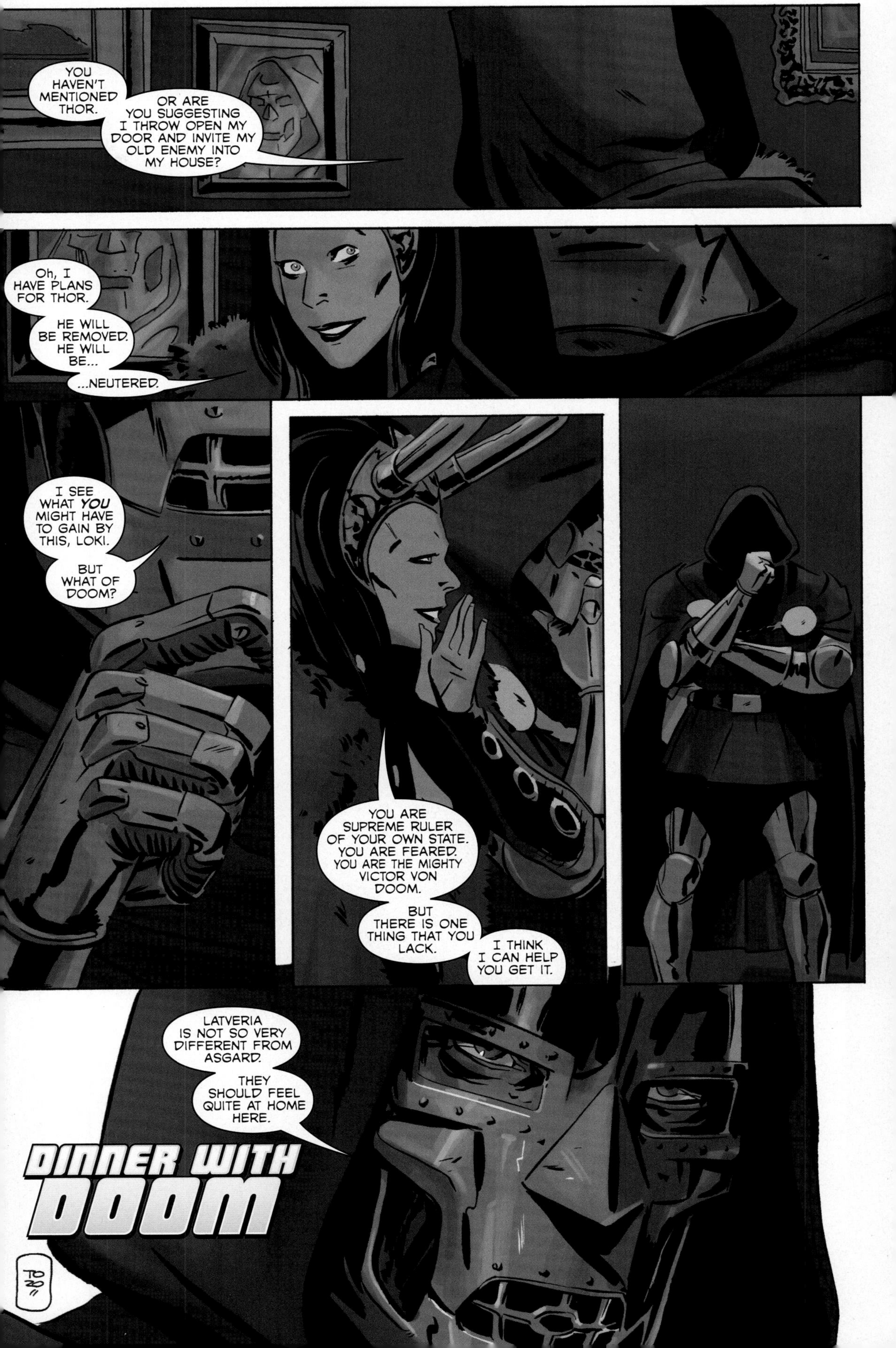
YOU HAVEN'T MENTIONED THOR.
OR ARE YOU SUGGESTING I THROW OPEN MY DOOR AND INVITE MY OLD ENEMY INTO MY HOUSE?
Oh, I HAVE PLANS FOR THOR.
HE WILL BE REMOVED. HE WILL BE...
...NEUTERED.
I SEE WHAT *YOU* MIGHT HAVE TO GAIN BY THIS, LOKI.
BUT WHAT OF DOOM?
YOU ARE SUPREME RULER OF YOUR OWN STATE. YOU ARE FEARED. YOU ARE THE MIGHTY VICTOR VON DOOM.
BUT THERE IS ONE THING THAT YOU LACK.
I THINK I CAN HELP YOU GET IT.
LATVERIA IS NOT SO VERY DIFFERENT FROM ASGARD.
THEY SHOULD FEEL QUITE AT HOME HERE.
DINNER WITH DOOM

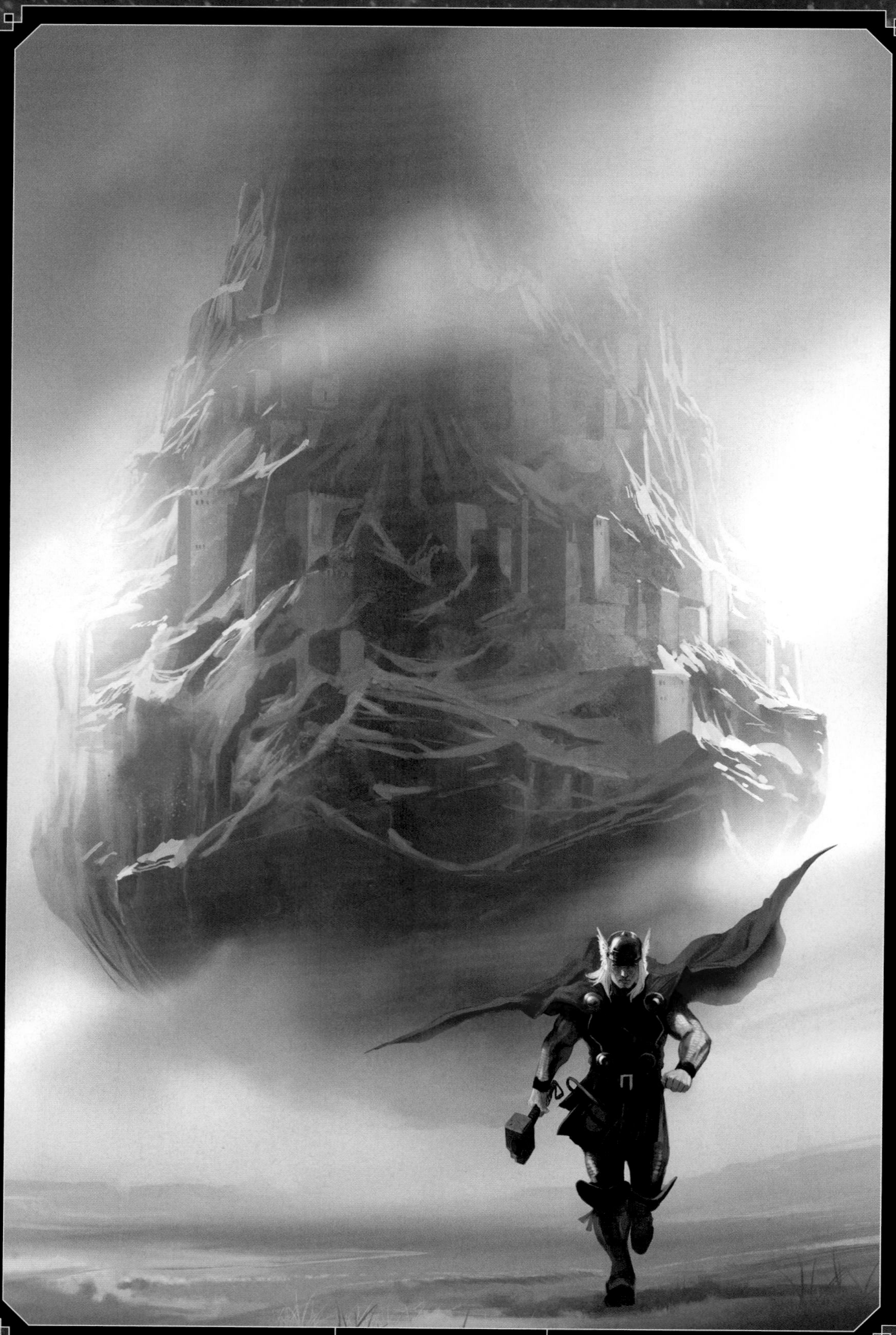

THOR #601

Okay, so just how bad *is* this?

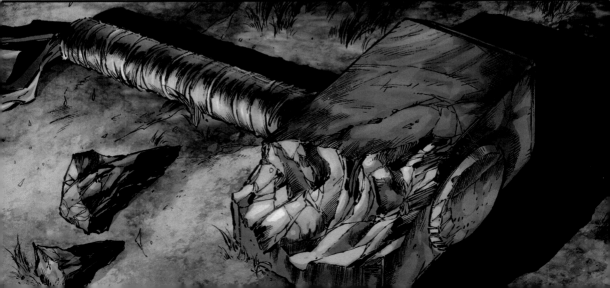

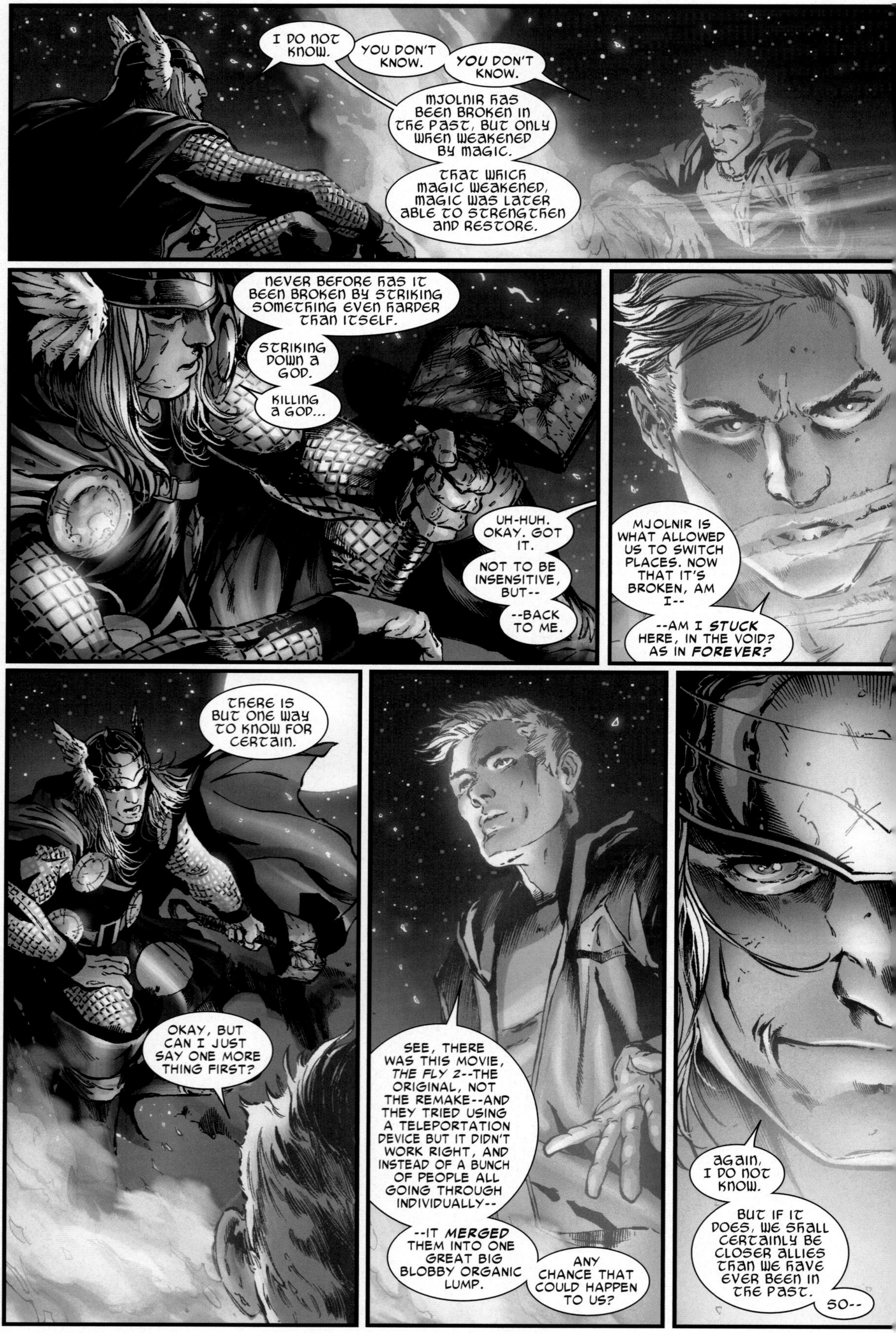
I DO NOT KNOW.
YOU DON'T KNOW.
YOU DON'T KNOW.
MJOLNIR HAS BEEN BROKEN IN THE PAST, BUT ONLY WHEN WEAKENED BY MAGIC.
THAT WHICH MAGIC WEAKENED, MAGIC WAS LATER ABLE TO STRENGTHEN AND RESTORE.
NEVER BEFORE HAS IT BEEN BROKEN BY STRIKING SOMETHING EVEN HARDER THAN ITSELF.
STRIKING DOWN A GOD.
KILLING A GOD...
UH-HUH. OKAY. GOT IT.
NOT TO BE INSENSITIVE, BUT--
--BACK TO ME.
MJOLNIR IS WHAT ALLOWED US TO SWITCH PLACES. NOW THAT IT'S BROKEN, AM I--
--AM I **STUCK** HERE, IN THE VOID? AS IN ***FOREVER?***
THERE IS BUT ONE WAY TO KNOW FOR CERTAIN.
OKAY, BUT CAN I JUST SAY ONE MORE THING FIRST?
SEE, THERE WAS THIS MOVIE, *THE FLY 2*--THE ORIGINAL, NOT THE REMAKE--AND THEY TRIED USING A TELEPORTATION DEVICE BUT IT DIDN'T WORK RIGHT, AND INSTEAD OF A BUNCH OF PEOPLE ALL GOING THROUGH INDIVIDUALLY--
--IT ***MERGED*** THEM INTO ONE GREAT BIG BLOBBY ORGANIC LUMP.
ANY CHANCE THAT COULD HAPPEN TO US?
AGAIN, I DO NOT KNOW.
BUT IF IT DOES, WE SHALL CERTAINLY BE CLOSER ALLIES THAN WE HAVE EVER BEEN IN THE PAST.
SO--

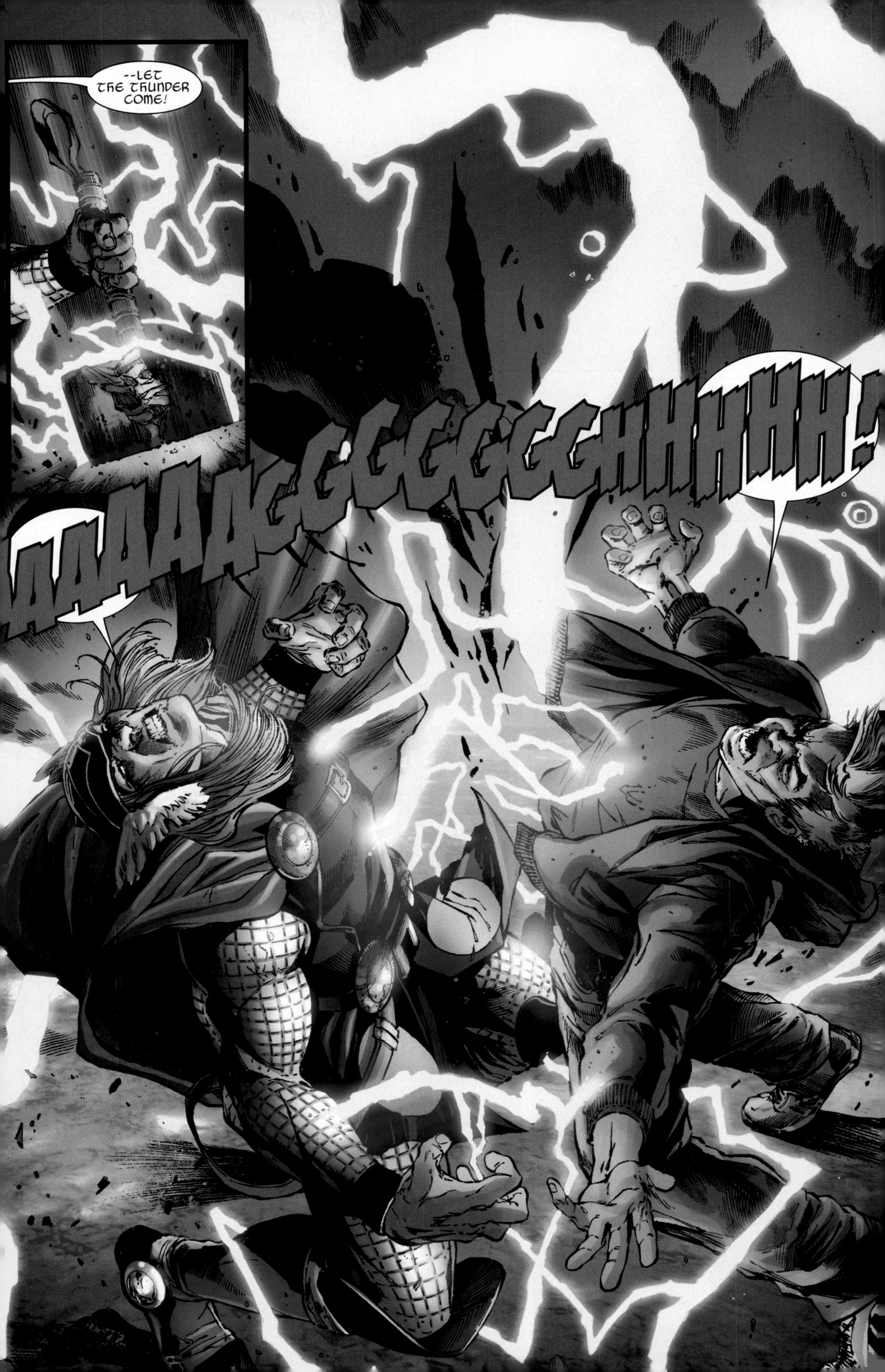
--LET THE THUNDER COME!
AAAAAGGGGGGHHHHH!

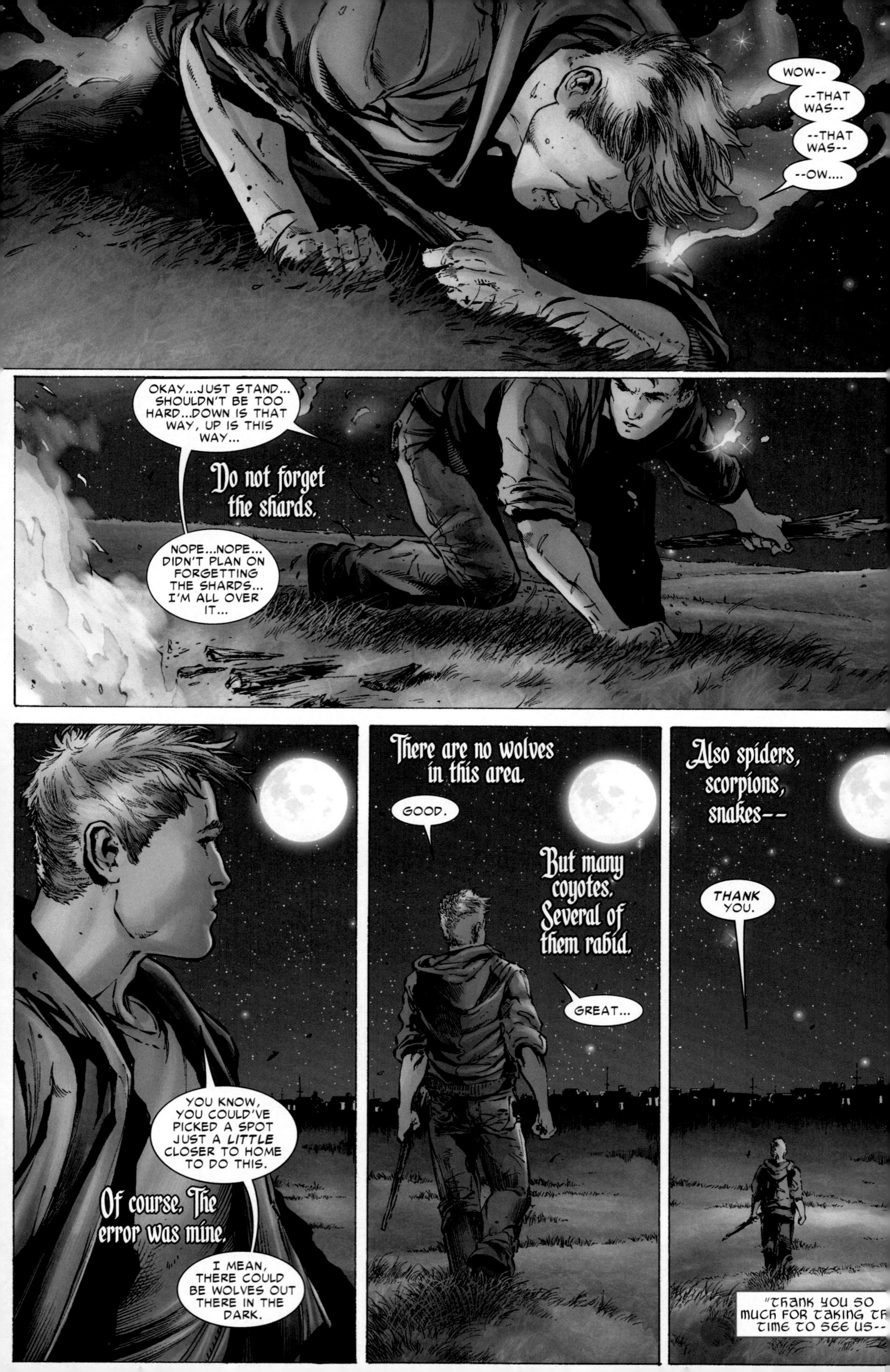
WOW--
--THAT WAS--
--THAT WAS--
--OW....
OKAY...JUST STAND... SHOULDN'T BE TOO HARD...DOWN IS THAT WAY, UP IS THIS WAY...
Do not forget the shards.
NOPE...NOPE... DIDN'T PLAN ON FORGETTING THE SHARDS... I'M ALL OVER IT...
YOU KNOW, YOU COULD'VE PICKED A SPOT JUST A *LITTLE* CLOSER TO HOME TO DO THIS.
Of course. The error was mine.
I MEAN, THERE COULD BE WOLVES OUT THERE IN THE DARK.
There are no wolves in this area.
GOOD.
But many coyotes. Several of them rabid.
GREAT...
Also spiders, scorpions, snakes--
THANK YOU.
"THANK YOU SO MUCH FOR TAKING TH TIME TO SEE US--

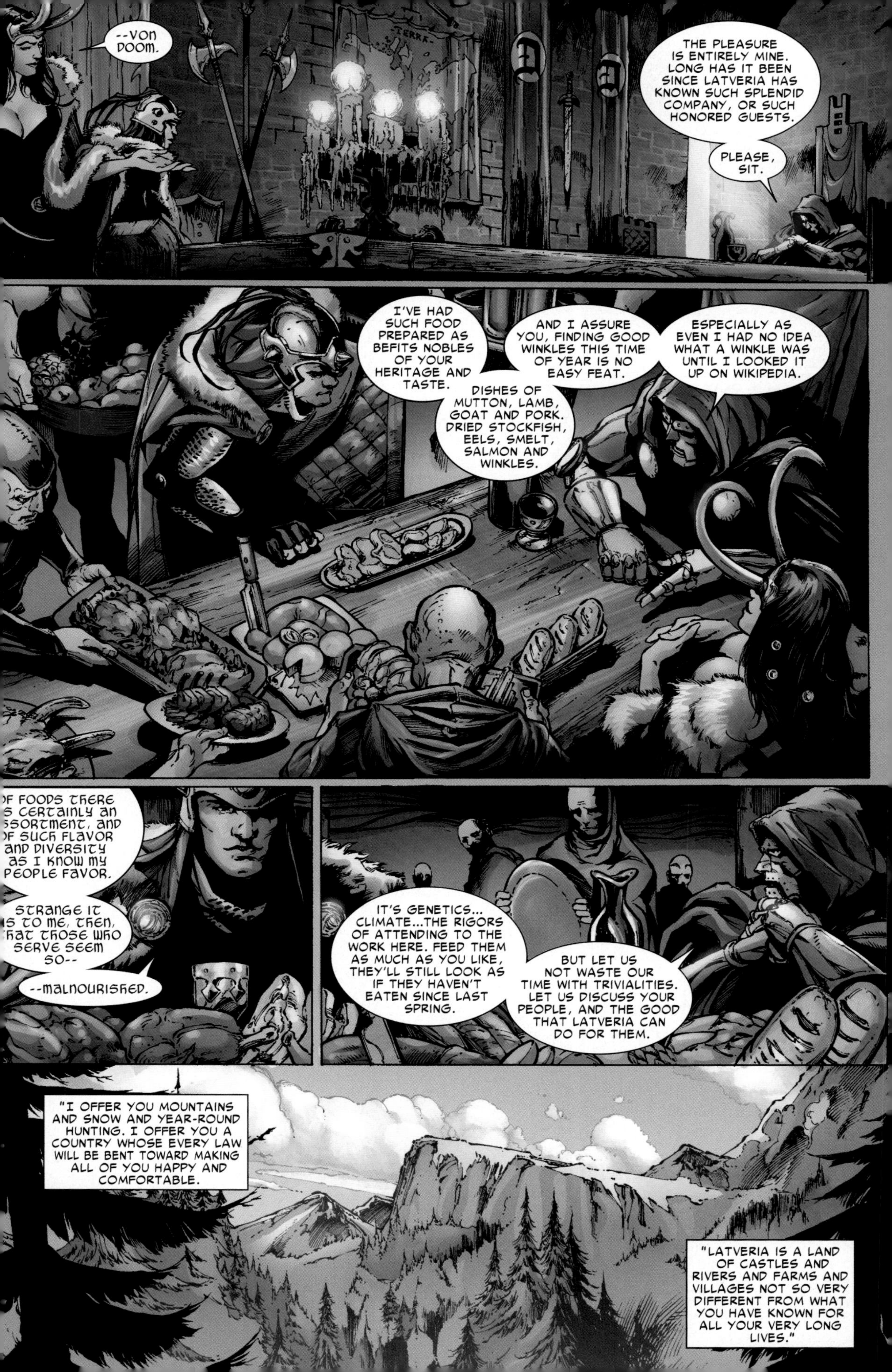
--VON DOOM.
THE PLEASURE IS ENTIRELY MINE. LONG HAS IT BEEN SINCE LATVERIA HAS KNOWN SUCH SPLENDID COMPANY, OR SUCH HONORED GUESTS.
PLEASE, SIT.
I'VE HAD SUCH FOOD PREPARED AS BEFITS NOBLES OF YOUR HERITAGE AND TASTE.
DISHES OF MUTTON, LAMB, GOAT AND PORK. DRIED STOCKFISH, EELS, SMELT, SALMON AND WINKLES.
AND I ASSURE YOU, FINDING GOOD WINKLES THIS TIME OF YEAR IS NO EASY FEAT.
ESPECIALLY AS EVEN I HAD NO IDEA WHAT A WINKLE WAS UNTIL I LOOKED IT UP ON WIKIPEDIA.
SSORTMENT, AND
AND DIVERSITY AS I KNOW MY PEOPLE FAVOR.
SERVE SEEM SO--
--MALNOURISHED.
IT'S GENETICS... CLIMATE...THE RIGORS OF ATTENDING TO THE WORK HERE. FEED THEM AS MUCH AS YOU LIKE, THEY'LL STILL LOOK AS IF THEY HAVEN'T EATEN SINCE LAST SPRING.
BUT LET US NOT WASTE OUR TIME WITH TRIVIALITIES. LET US DISCUSS YOUR PEOPLE, AND THE GOOD THAT LATVERIA CAN DO FOR THEM.
"I OFFER YOU MOUNTAINS AND SNOW AND YEAR-ROUND HUNTING. I OFFER YOU A COUNTRY WHOSE EVERY LAW WILL BE BENT TOWARD MAKING ALL OF YOU HAPPY AND COMFORTABLE.
"LATVERIA IS A LAND OF CASTLES AND RIVERS AND FARMS AND VILLAGES NOT SO VERY DIFFERENT FROM WHAT YOU HAVE KNOWN FOR ALL YOUR VERY LONG LIVES."

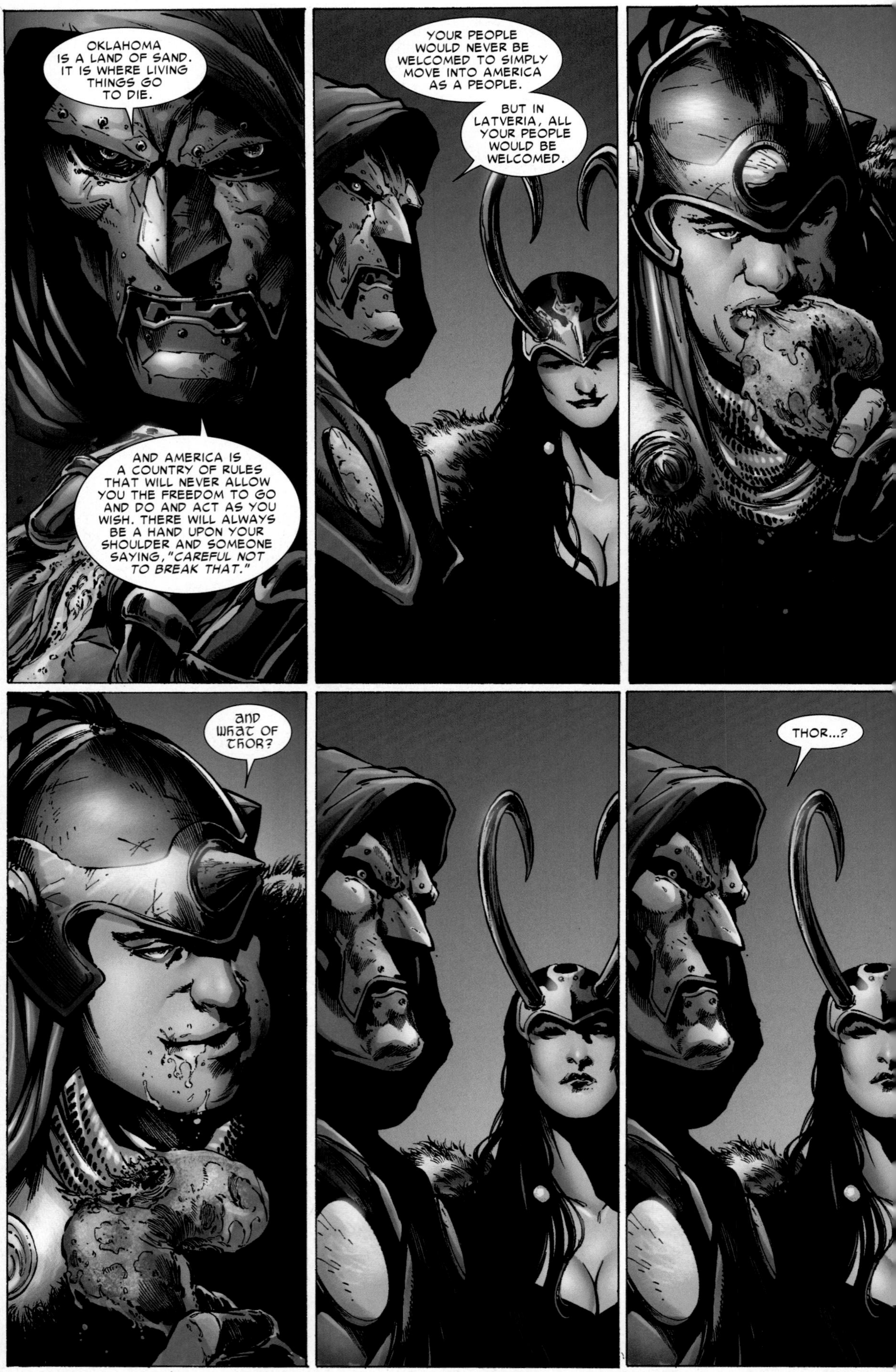
OKLAHOMA IS A LAND OF SAND. IT IS WHERE LIVING THINGS GO TO DIE.
AND AMERICA IS A COUNTRY OF RULES THAT WILL NEVER ALLOW YOU THE FREEDOM TO GO AND DO AND ACT AS YOU WISH. THERE WILL ALWAYS BE A HAND UPON YOUR SHOULDER AND SOMEONE SAYING, "CAREFUL NOT TO BREAK THAT."
YOUR PEOPLE WOULD NEVER BE WELCOMED TO SIMPLY MOVE INTO AMERICA AS A PEOPLE.
BUT IN LATVERIA, ALL YOUR PEOPLE WOULD BE WELCOMED.
AND WHAT OF THOR?
THOR...?

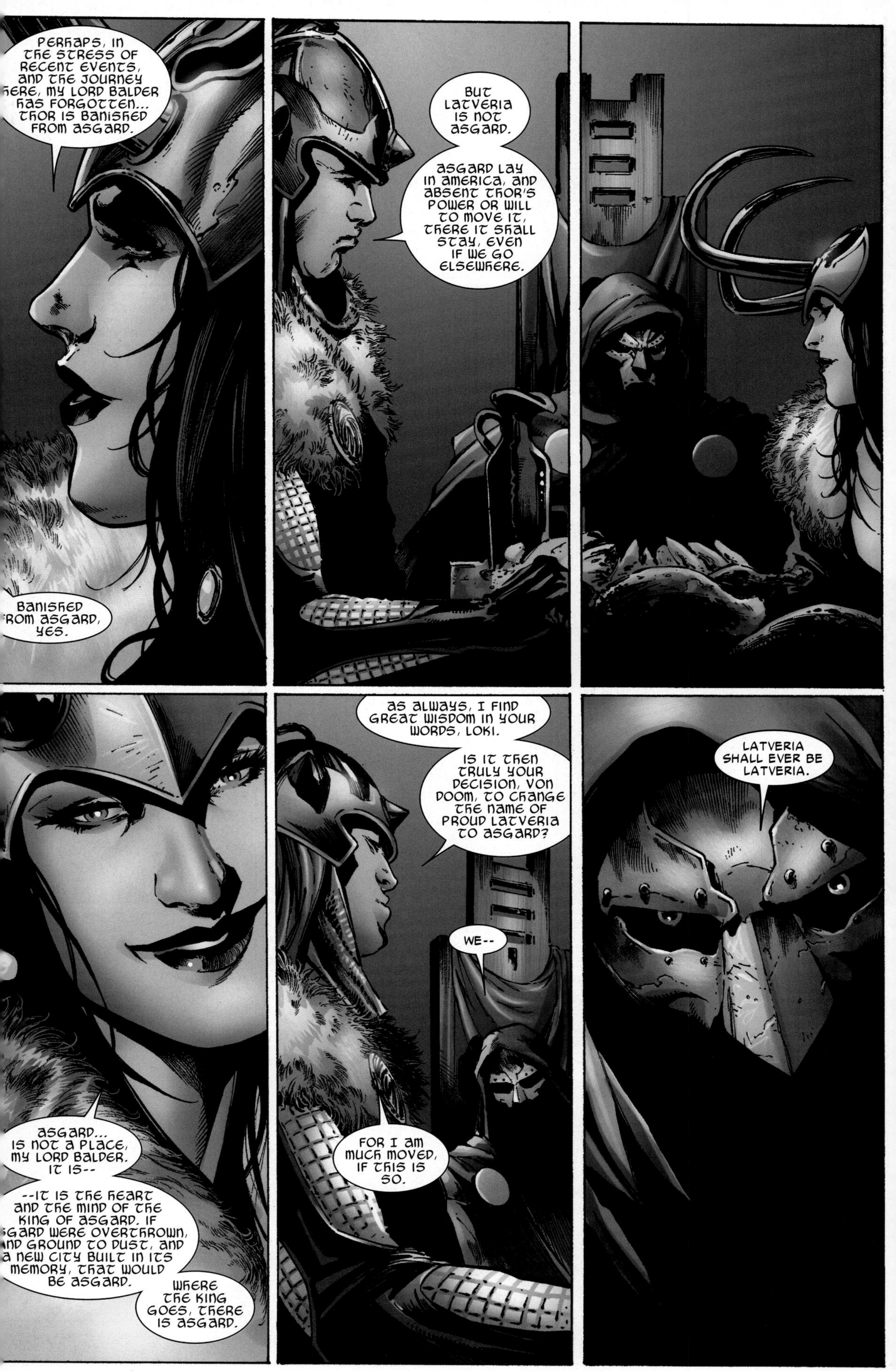
PERHAPS, IN THE STRESS OF RECENT EVENTS, AND THE JOURNEY HERE, MY LORD BALDER HAS FORGOTTEN... THOR IS BANISHED FROM ASGARD.
BANISHED FROM ASGARD, YES.
BUT LATVERIA IS NOT ASGARD.
ASGARD LAY IN AMERICA, AND ABSENT THOR'S POWER OR WILL TO MOVE IT, THERE IT SHALL STAY, EVEN IF WE GO ELSEWHERE.
ASGARD... IS NOT A PLACE, MY LORD BALDER. IT IS--
--IT IS THE HEART AND THE MIND OF THE KING OF ASGARD. IF ASGARD WERE OVERTHROWN, AND GROUND TO DUST, AND A NEW CITY BUILT IN ITS MEMORY, THAT WOULD BE ASGARD.
WHERE THE KING GOES, THERE IS ASGARD.
AS ALWAYS, I FIND GREAT WISDOM IN YOUR WORDS, LOKI.
IS IT THEN TRULY YOUR DECISION, VON DOOM, TO CHANGE THE NAME OF PROUD LATVERIA TO ASGARD?
WE--
FOR I AM MUCH MOVED, IF THIS IS SO.
LATVERIA SHALL EVER BE LATVERIA.

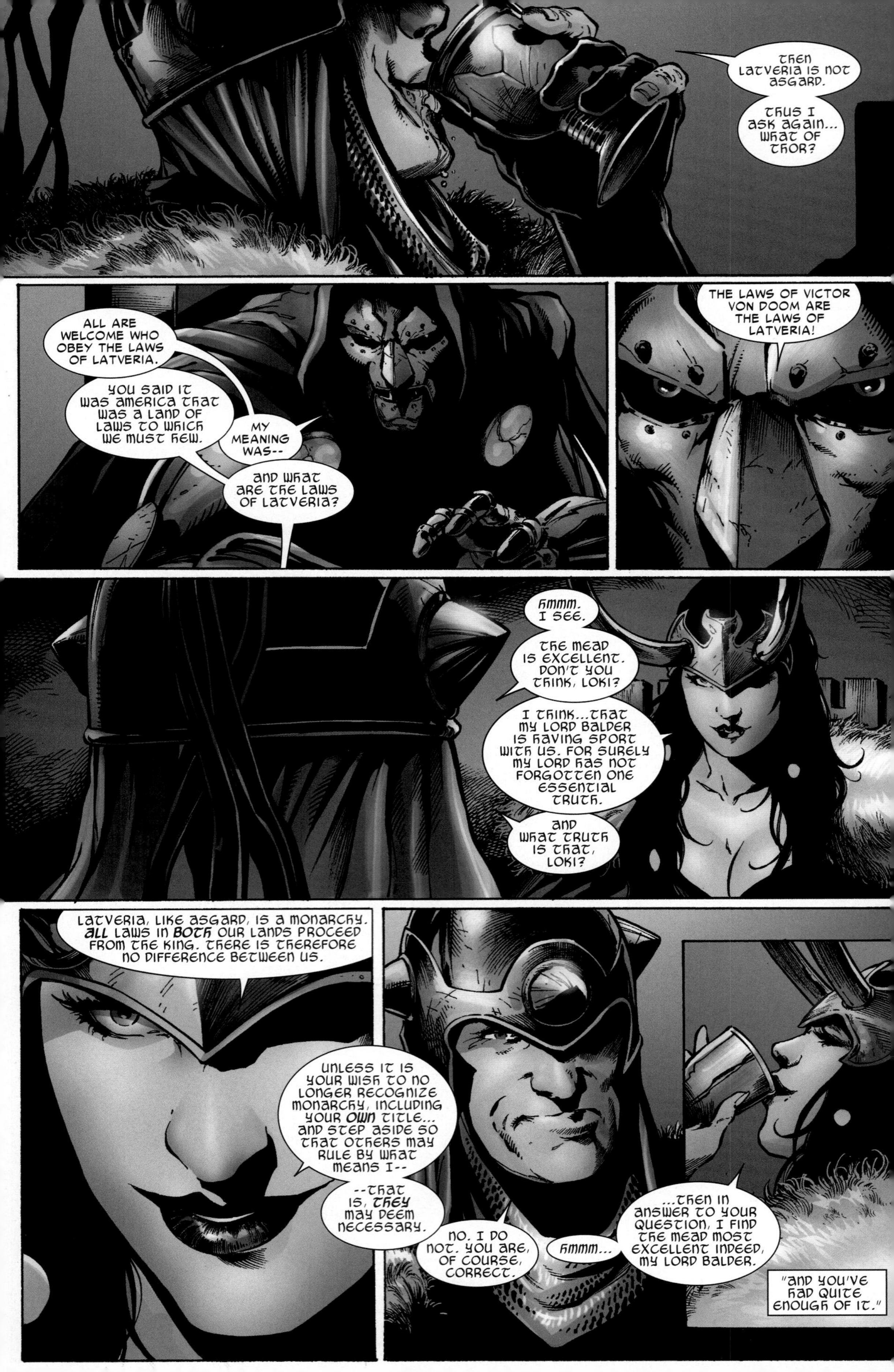
THEN LATVERIA IS NOT ASGARD.
THUS I ASK AGAIN... WHAT OF THOR?
ALL ARE WELCOME WHO OBEY THE LAWS OF LATVERIA.
YOU SAID IT WAS AMERICA THAT WAS A LAND OF LAWS TO WHICH WE MUST HEW.
MY MEANING WAS--
AND WHAT ARE THE LAWS OF LATVERIA?
THE LAWS OF VICTOR VON DOOM ARE THE LAWS OF LATVERIA!
HMMM. I SEE.
THE MEAD IS EXCELLENT. DON'T YOU THINK, LOKI?
I THINK...THAT MY LORD BALDER IS HAVING SPORT WITH US. FOR SURELY MY LORD HAS NOT FORGOTTEN ONE ESSENTIAL TRUTH.
AND WHAT TRUTH IS THAT, LOKI?
LATVERIA, LIKE ASGARD, IS A MONARCHY. ALL LAWS IN BOTH OUR LANDS PROCEED FROM THE KING. THERE IS THEREFORE NO DIFFERENCE BETWEEN US.
UNLESS IT IS YOUR WISH TO NO LONGER RECOGNIZE MONARCHY, INCLUDING YOUR OWN TITLE... AND STEP ASIDE SO THAT OTHERS MAY RULE BY WHAT MEANS I--
--THAT IS, THEY MAY DEEM NECESSARY.
NO. I DO NOT. YOU ARE, OF COURSE, CORRECT.
HMMM...
...THEN IN ANSWER TO YOUR QUESTION, I FIND THE MEAD MOST EXCELLENT INDEED, MY LORD BALDER.
"AND YOU'VE HAD QUITE ENOUGH OF IT."

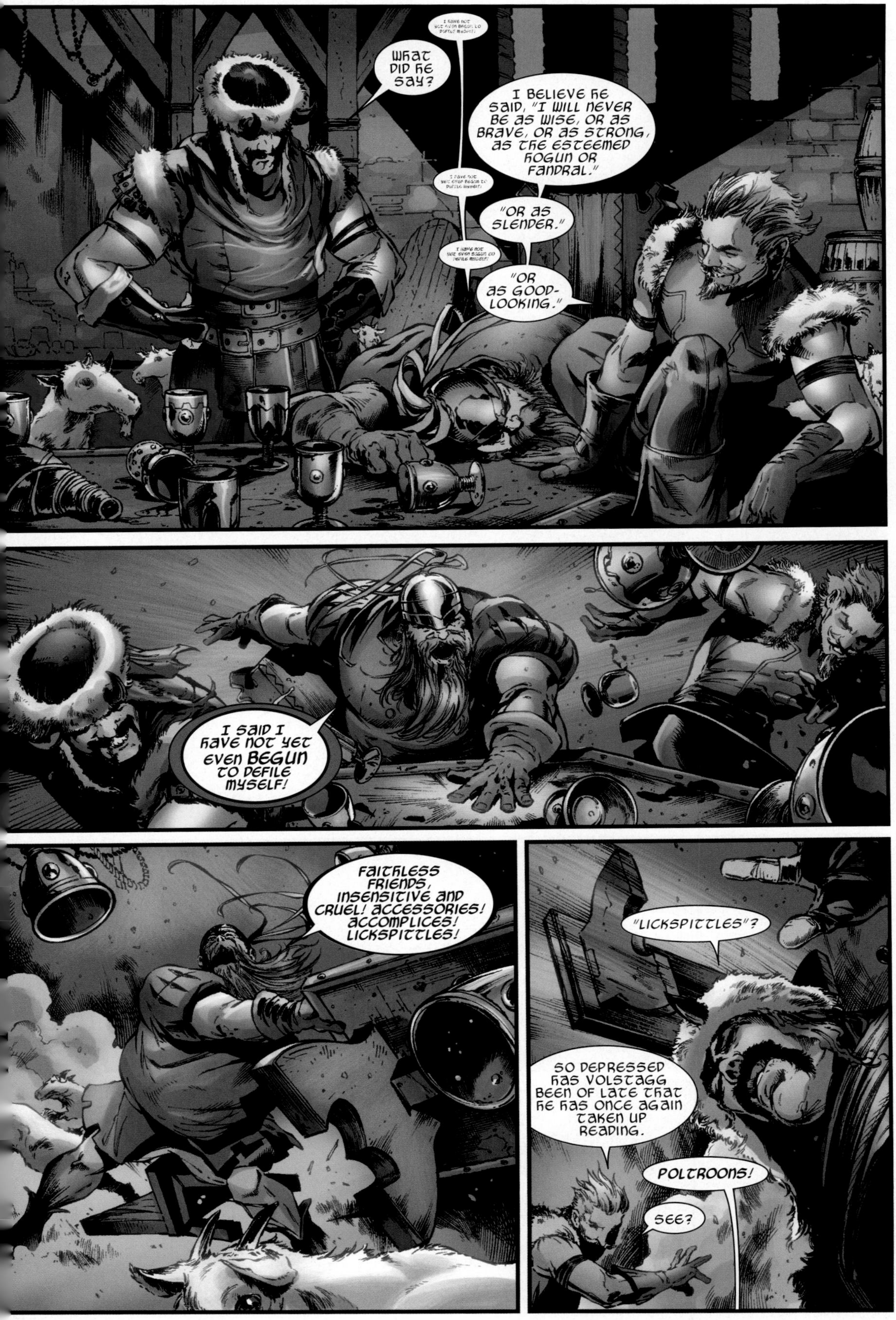
WHAT DID HE SAY?
I BELIEVE HE SAID, "I WILL NEVER BE AS WISE, OR AS BRAVE, OR AS STRONG, AS THE ESTEEMED HOGUN OR FANDRAL."
"OR AS SLENDER."
"OR AS GOOD-LOOKING."
I SAID I HAVE NOT YET EVEN BEGUN TO DEFILE MYSELF!
FAITHLESS FRIENDS, INSENSITIVE AND CRUEL! ACCESSORIES! ACCOMPLICES! LICKSPITTLES!
"LICKSPITTLES"?
SO DEPRESSED HAS VOLSTAGG BEEN OF LATE THAT HE HAS ONCE AGAIN TAKEN UP READING.
POLTROONS!
SEE?

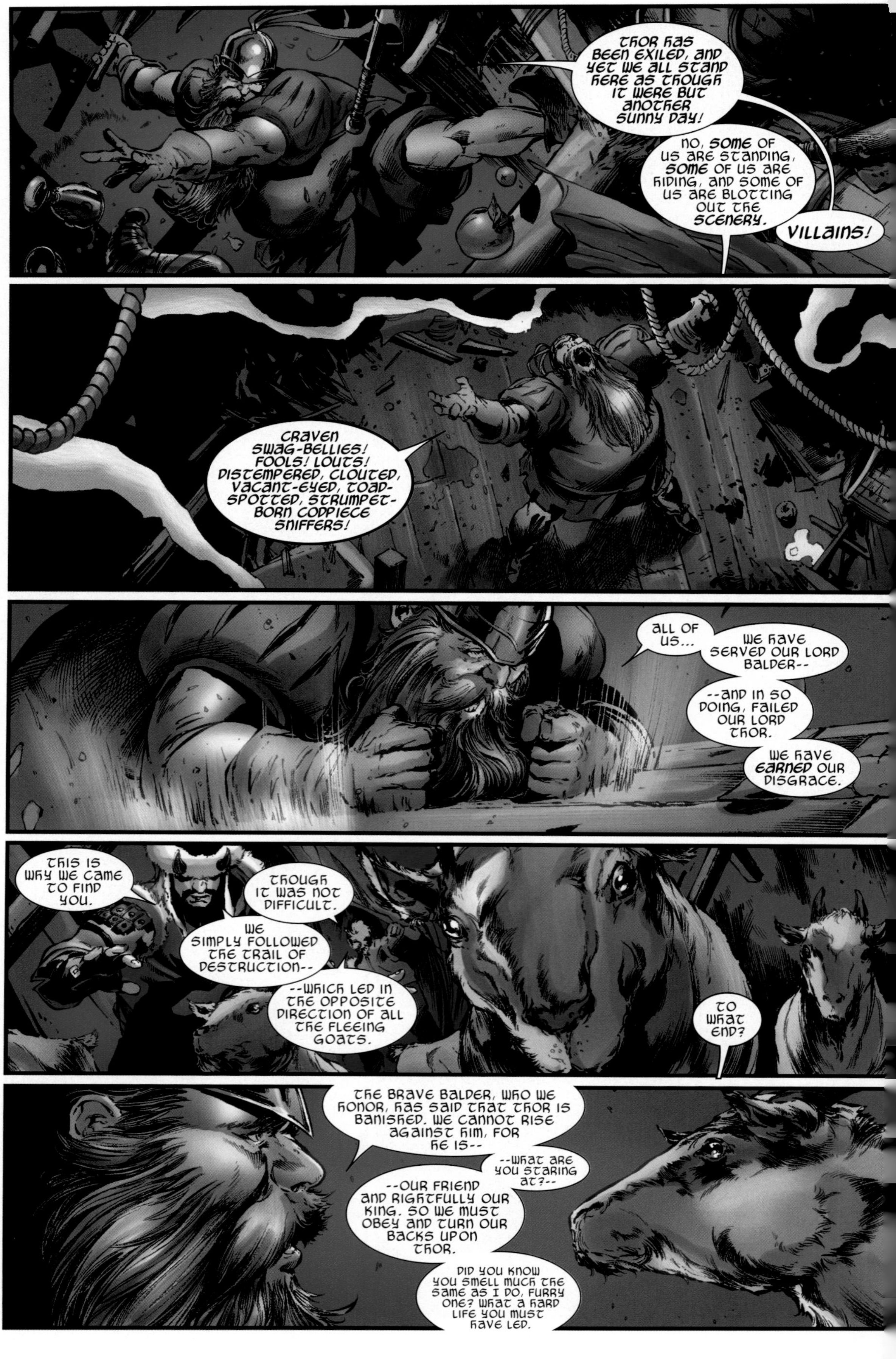
THOR HAS BEEN EXILED, AND YET WE ALL STAND HERE AS THOUGH IT WERE BUT ANOTHER SUNNY DAY!
NO, SOME OF US ARE STANDING, SOME OF US ARE HIDING, AND SOME OF US ARE BLOTTING OUT THE SCENERY.
VILLAINS!
CRAVEN SWAG-BELLIES! FOOLS! LOUTS! DISTEMPERED, CLOUTED, VACANT-EYED, TOAD-SPOTTED, STRUMPET-BORN CODPIECE SNIFFERS!
ALL OF US...
WE HAVE SERVED OUR LORD BALDER--
--AND IN SO DOING, FAILED OUR LORD THOR.
WE HAVE EARNED OUR DISGRACE.
THIS IS WHY WE CAME TO FIND YOU.
THOUGH IT WAS NOT DIFFICULT.
WE SIMPLY FOLLOWED THE TRAIL OF DESTRUCTION--
--WHICH LED IN THE OPPOSITE DIRECTION OF ALL THE FLEEING GOATS.
TO WHAT END?
THE BRAVE BALDER, WHO WE HONOR, HAS SAID THAT THOR IS BANISHED. WE CANNOT RISE AGAINST HIM, FOR HE IS--
--WHAT ARE YOU STARING AT?--
--OUR FRIEND AND RIGHTFULLY OUR KING. SO WE MUST OBEY AND TURN OUR BACKS UPON THOR.
DID YOU KNOW YOU SMELL MUCH THE SAME AS I DO, FURRY ONE? WHAT A HARD LIFE YOU MUST HAVE LED.

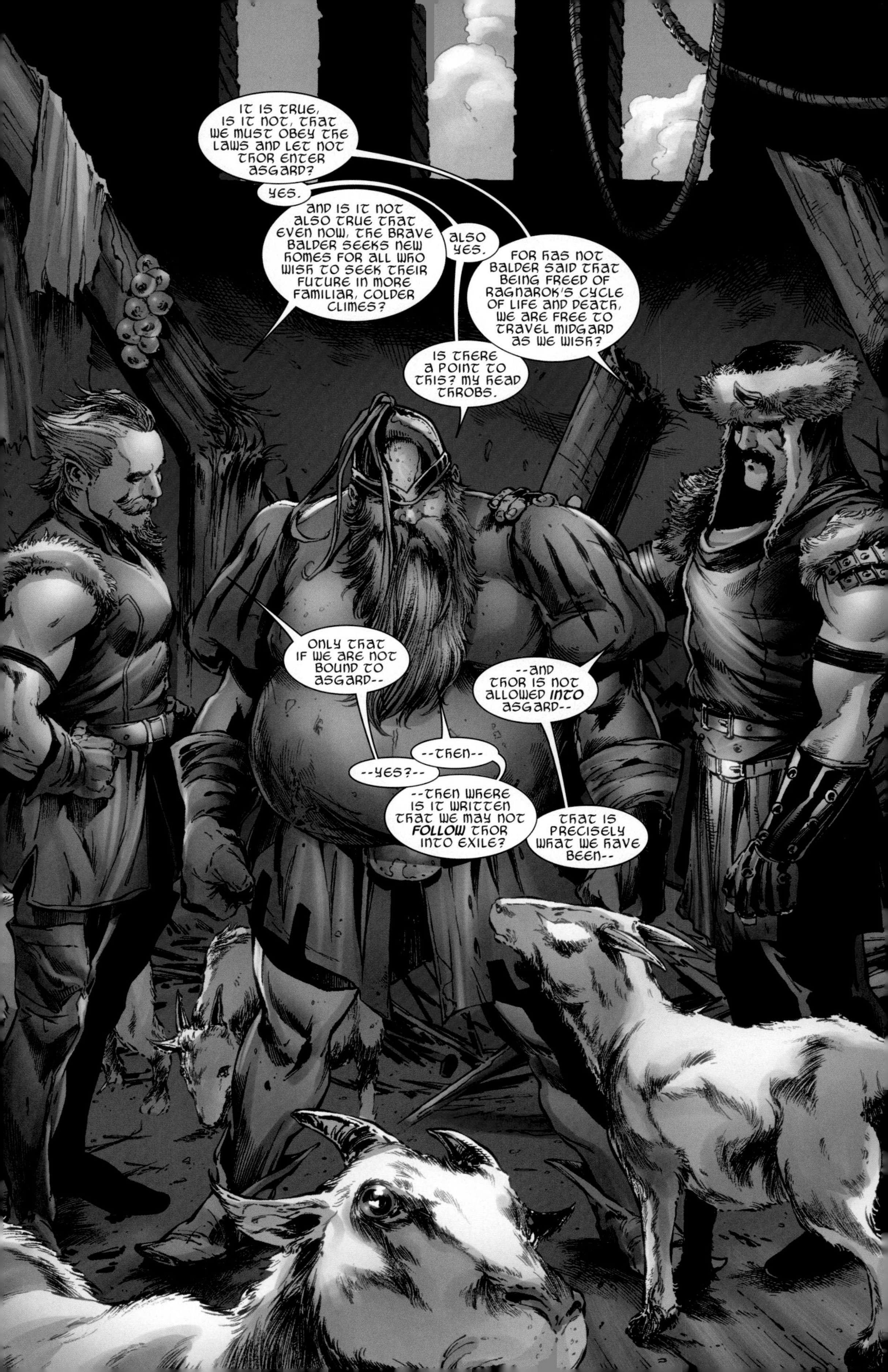
IT IS TRUE, IS IT NOT, THAT WE MUST OBEY THE LAWS AND LET NOT THOR ENTER ASGARD?
YES.
AND IS IT NOT ALSO TRUE THAT EVEN NOW, THE BRAVE BALDER SEEKS NEW HOMES FOR ALL WHO WISH TO SEEK THEIR FUTURE IN MORE FAMILIAR, COLDER CLIMES?
ALSO YES.
FOR HAS NOT BALDER SAID THAT BEING FREED OF RAGNAROK'S CYCLE OF LIFE AND DEATH, WE ARE FREE TO TRAVEL MIDGARD AS WE WISH?
IS THERE A POINT TO THIS? MY HEAD THROBS.
ONLY THAT IF WE ARE NOT BOUND TO ASGARD--
--AND THOR IS NOT ALLOWED *INTO* ASGARD--
--YES?--
--THEN--
--THEN WHERE IS IT WRITTEN THAT WE MAY NOT **FOLLOW** THOR INTO EXILE?
THAT IS PRECISELY WHAT WE HAVE BEEN--

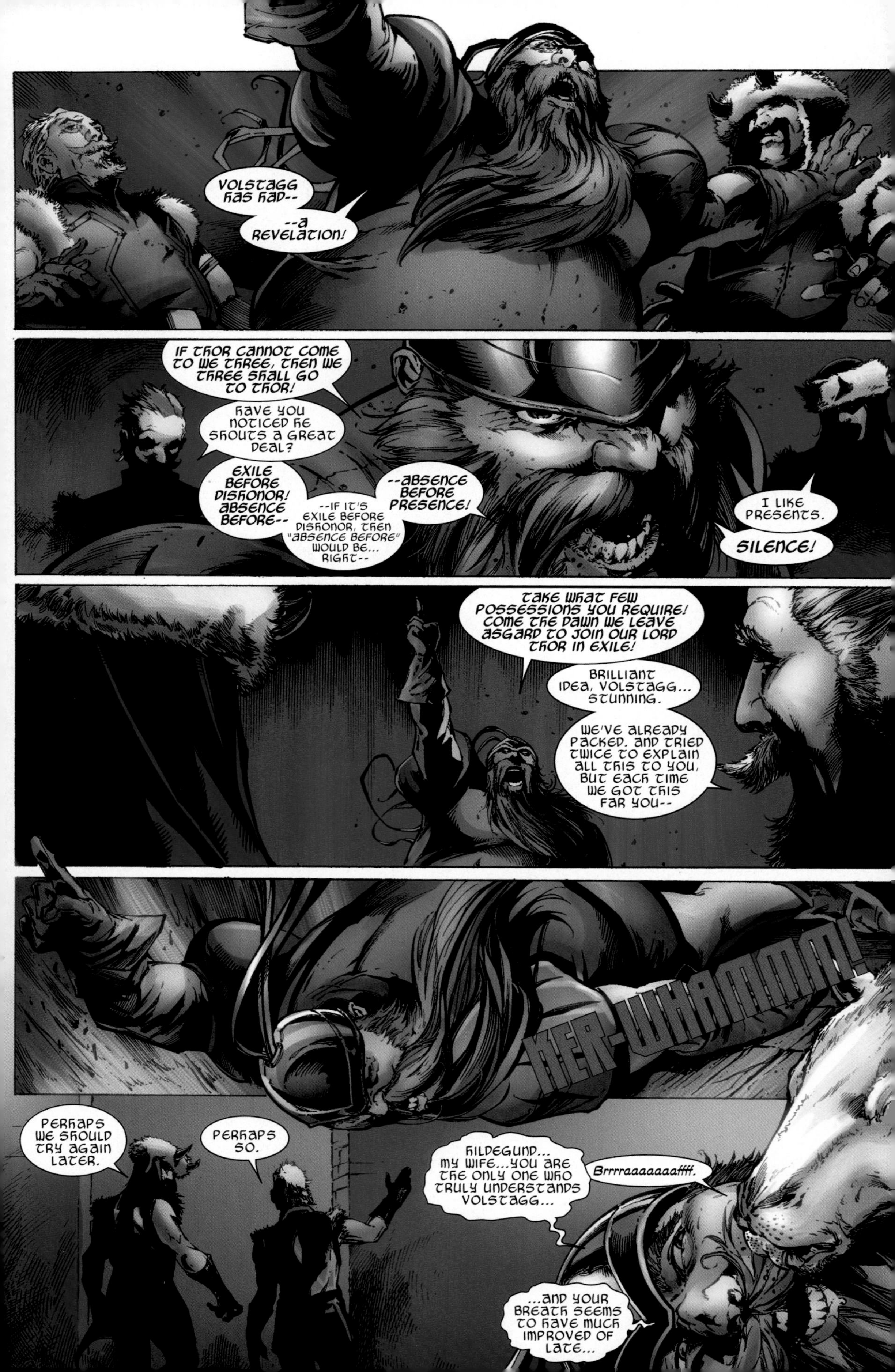
VOLSTAGG HAS HAD--
--A REVELATION!
IF THOR CANNOT COME TO WE THREE, THEN WE THREE SHALL GO TO THOR!
HAVE YOU NOTICED HE SHOUTS A GREAT DEAL?
EXILE BEFORE DISHONOR! ABSENCE BEFORE--
--IF IT'S EXILE BEFORE DISHONOR, THEN "ABSENCE BEFORE" WOULD BE... RIGHT--
--ABSENCE BEFORE PRESENCE!
I LIKE PRESENTS.
SILENCE!
TAKE WHAT FEW POSSESSIONS YOU REQUIRE! COME THE DAWN WE LEAVE ASGARD TO JOIN OUR LORD THOR IN EXILE!
BRILLIANT IDEA, VOLSTAGG... STUNNING.
WE'VE ALREADY PACKED. AND TRIED TWICE TO EXPLAIN ALL THIS TO YOU, BUT EACH TIME WE GOT THIS FAR YOU--
KER-WHAMMM!
PERHAPS WE SHOULD TRY AGAIN LATER.
PERHAPS SO.
HILDEGUND... MY WIFE...YOU ARE THE ONLY ONE WHO TRULY UNDERSTANDS VOLSTAGG...
Brrrraaaaaaaffff.
...AND YOUR BREATH SEEMS TO HAVE MUCH IMPROVED OF LATE...

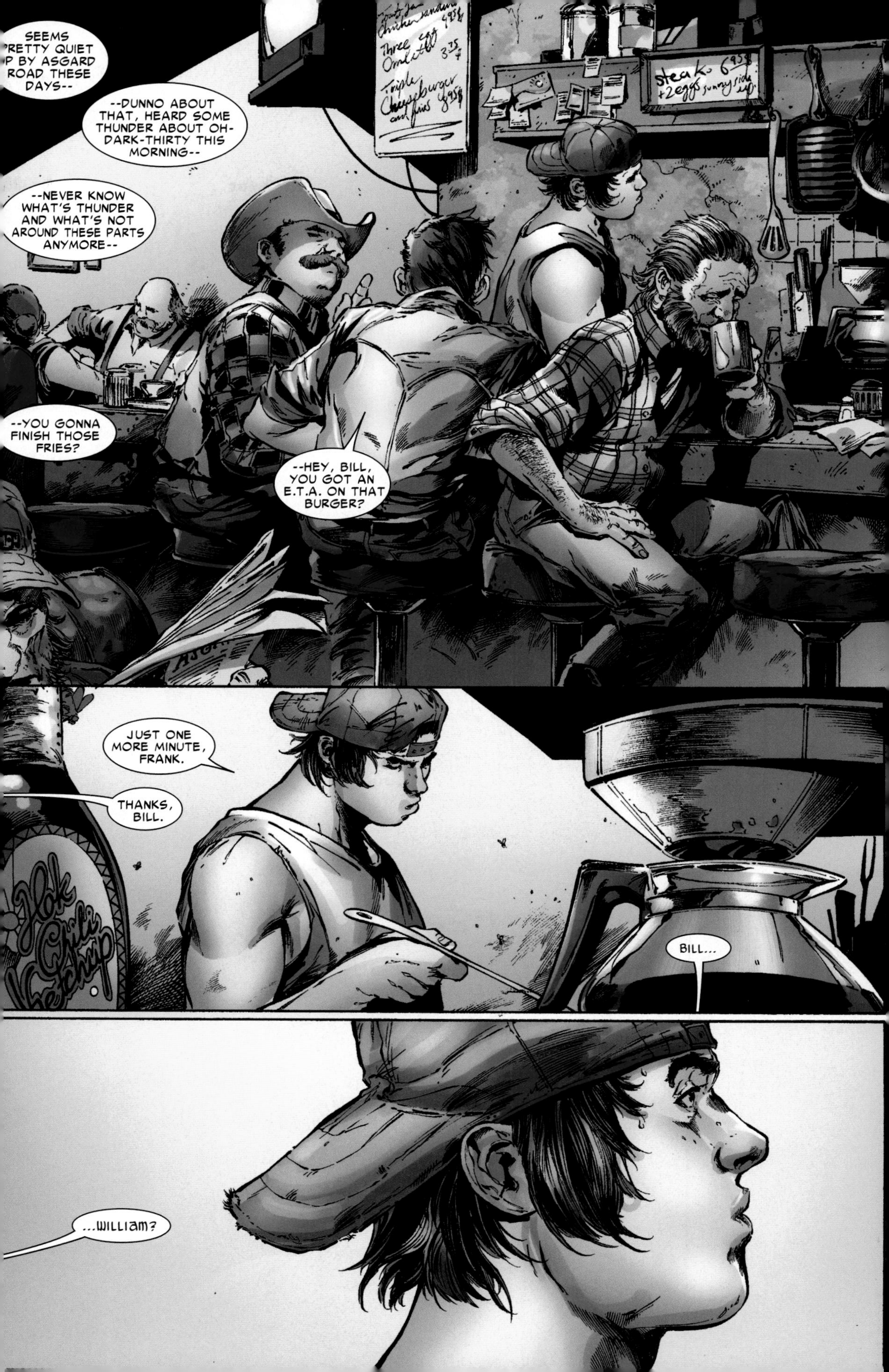
SEEMS PRETTY QUIET P BY ASGARD ROAD THESE DAYS--
--DUNNO ABOUT THAT, HEARD SOME THUNDER ABOUT OH-DARK-THIRTY THIS MORNING--
--NEVER KNOW WHAT'S THUNDER AND WHAT'S NOT AROUND THESE PARTS ANYMORE--
--YOU GONNA FINISH THOSE FRIES?
--HEY, BILL, YOU GOT AN E.T.A. ON THAT BURGER?
JUST ONE MORE MINUTE, FRANK.
THANKS, BILL.
BILL...
...WILLIAM?

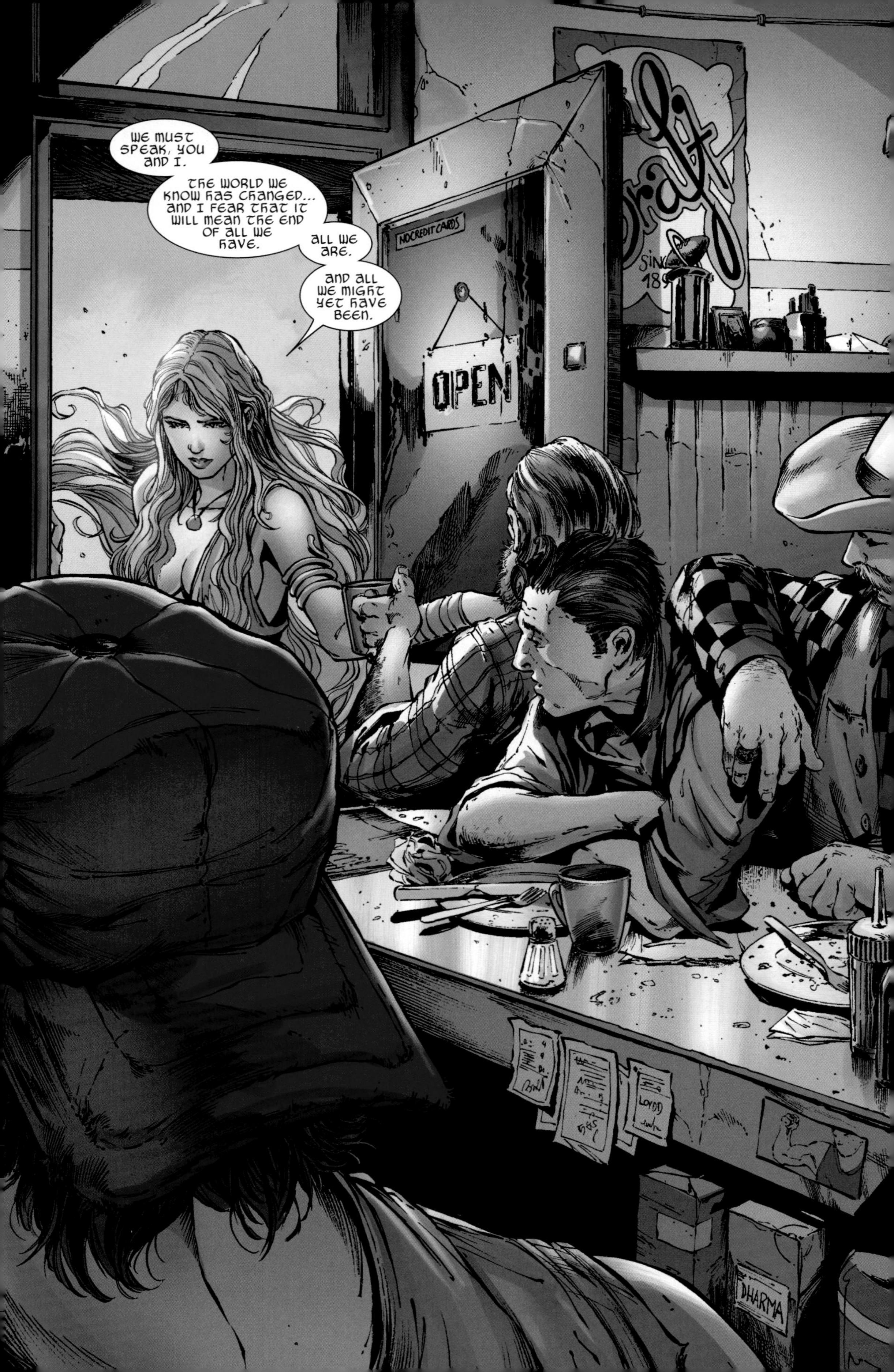
WE MUST SPEAK, YOU AND I.
THE WORLD WE KNOW HAS CHANGED... AND I FEAR THAT IT WILL MEAN THE END OF ALL WE HAVE.
ALL WE ARE.
AND ALL WE MIGHT YET HAVE BEEN.
NO CREDIT CARDS
OPEN
LOYDD
DHARMA

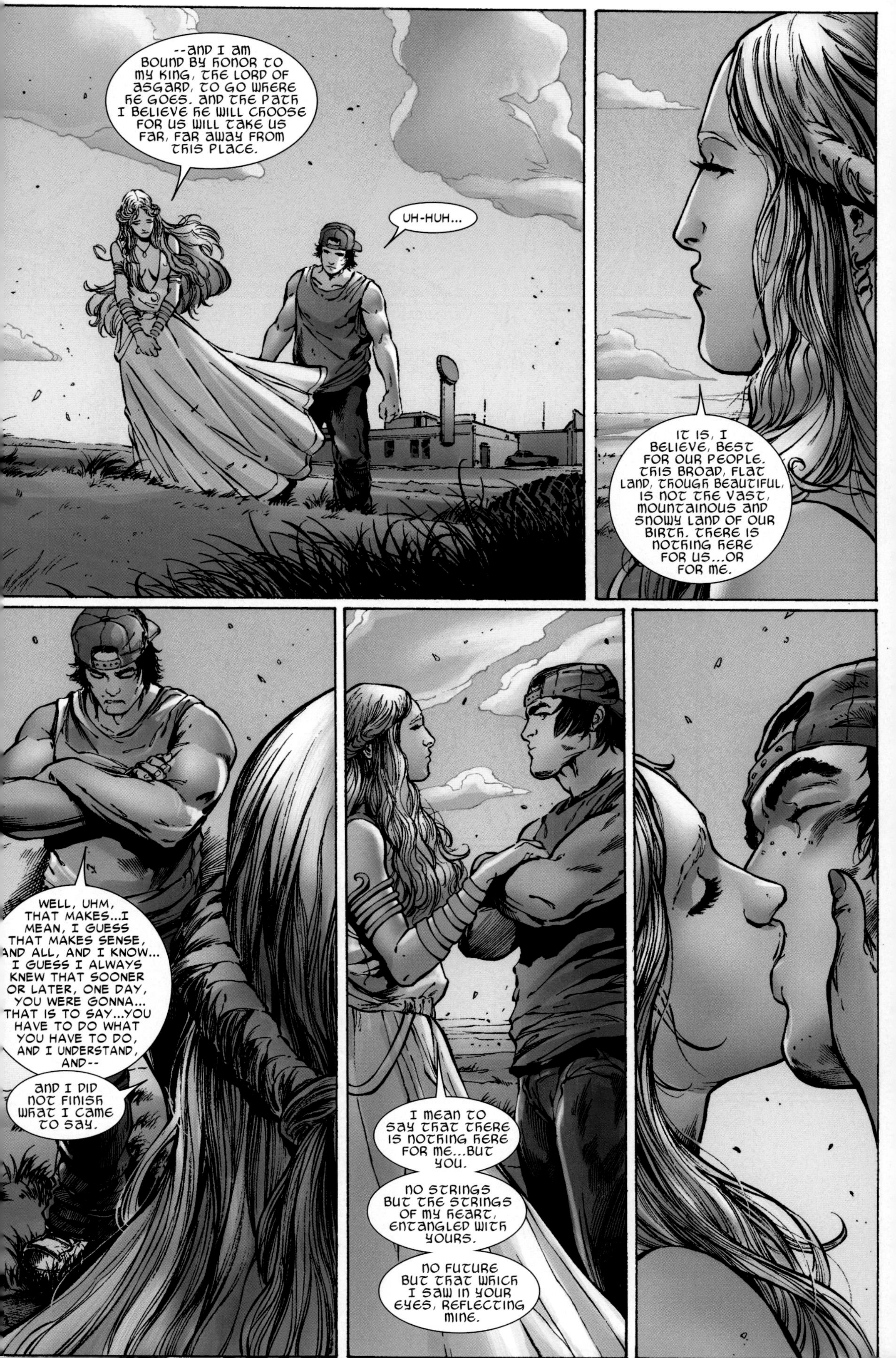
--AND I AM BOUND BY HONOR TO MY KING, THE LORD OF ASGARD, TO GO WHERE HE GOES. AND THE PATH I BELIEVE HE WILL CHOOSE FOR US WILL TAKE US FAR, FAR AWAY FROM THIS PLACE.
UH-HUH...
IT IS, I BELIEVE, BEST FOR OUR PEOPLE. THIS BROAD, FLAT LAND, THOUGH BEAUTIFUL, IS NOT THE VAST, MOUNTAINOUS AND SNOWY LAND OF OUR BIRTH. THERE IS NOTHING HERE FOR US...OR FOR ME.
WELL, UHM, THAT MAKES...I MEAN, I GUESS THAT MAKES SENSE, AND ALL, AND I KNOW... I GUESS I ALWAYS KNEW THAT SOONER OR LATER, ONE DAY, YOU WERE GONNA... THAT IS TO SAY...YOU HAVE TO DO WHAT YOU HAVE TO DO, AND I UNDERSTAND, AND--
AND I DID NOT FINISH WHAT I CAME TO SAY.
I MEAN TO SAY THAT THERE IS NOTHING HERE FOR ME...BUT YOU.
NO STRINGS BUT THE STRINGS OF MY HEART, ENTANGLED WITH YOURS.
NO FUTURE BUT THAT WHICH I SAW IN YOUR EYES, REFLECTING MINE.

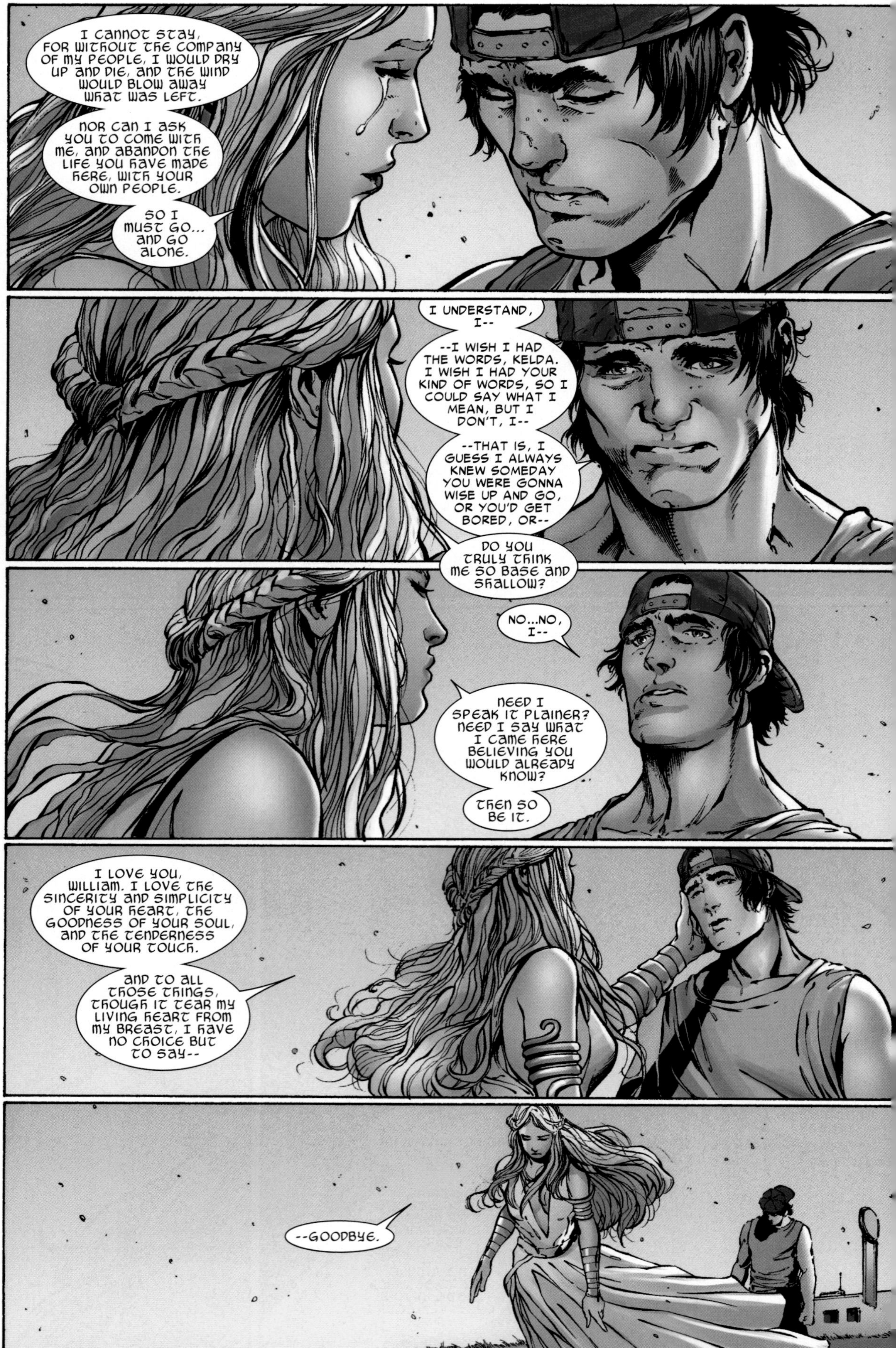

I CANNOT STAY, FOR WITHOUT THE COMPANY OF MY PEOPLE, I WOULD DRY UP AND DIE, AND THE WIND WOULD BLOW AWAY WHAT WAS LEFT.
NOR CAN I ASK YOU TO COME WITH ME, AND ABANDON THE LIFE YOU HAVE MADE HERE, WITH YOUR OWN PEOPLE.
SO I MUST GO... AND GO ALONE.
I UNDERSTAND, I--
--I WISH I HAD THE WORDS, KELDA. I WISH I HAD YOUR KIND OF WORDS, SO I COULD SAY WHAT I MEAN, BUT I DON'T, I--
--THAT IS, I GUESS I ALWAYS KNEW SOMEDAY YOU WERE GONNA WISE UP AND GO, OR YOU'D GET BORED, OR--
DO YOU TRULY THINK ME SO BASE AND SHALLOW?
NO...NO, I--
NEED I SPEAK IT PLAINER? NEED I SAY WHAT I CAME HERE BELIEVING YOU WOULD ALREADY KNOW?
THEN SO BE IT.
I LOVE YOU, WILLIAM. I LOVE THE SINCERITY AND SIMPLICITY OF YOUR HEART, THE GOODNESS OF YOUR SOUL, AND THE TENDERNESS OF YOUR TOUCH.
AND TO ALL THOSE THINGS, THOUGH IT TEAR MY LIVING HEART FROM MY BREAST, I HAVE NO CHOICE BUT TO SAY--
--GOODBYE.

I do not believe this will work.

IT'S WORTH A TRY. IF THE PIECES ARE TAPED BACK TOGETHER THE NEXT TIME I USE IT... ASSUMING I CAN USE IT ON THIS SIDE...MAYBE DURING THE CHANGEOVER MJOLNIR WILL COME BACK FIXED.

I very much doubt it.

YEAH, I KIND OF GOT THAT.

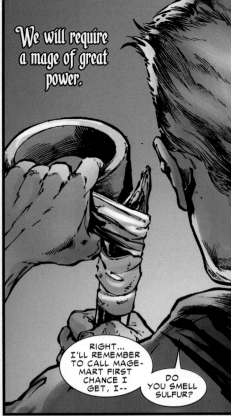

We will require a mage of great power.

RIGHT... I'LL REMEMBER TO CALL MAGE-MART FIRST CHANCE I GET, I--

DO YOU SMELL SULFUR?

LOKI!

FEAR NOT, BLAKE...FOR THIS IS BUT AN IMAGE SENT FROM THE PLACE OF OUR NEW HOME, RATHER THAN MY TRUE FORM. SENT FOR MY PROTECTION.

PROTECTION FROM WHAT?

I HAVE MADE A DARK AND TERRIBLE DISCOVERY, WHICH I BELIEVE WOULD BE OF GREAT INTEREST TO MY HALF-BROTHER THOR, BUT WHICH, IF MISUNDERSTOOD, COULD ALSO ELICIT HIS UNINTENDED RAGE.

FOR WHAT HAPPENED, HAPPENED OF ITS OWN ACCORD, WITHOUT MY KNOWLEDGE UNTIL THIS VERY MOMENT.

RIGHT, AND A DOG ATE YOUR HOMEWORK. SO WHAT IS IT?

I HAVE FOR SOME TIME WONDERED WHY I ASSUMED THIS PARTICULAR FORM IN THE AFTERMATH OF RAGNAROK. GRANTED, I HAD TO ASSUME SOME FORM OTHER THAN MY OWN AFTER BEING SO CASUALLY BEHEADED BY MY DEAR HALF-BROTHER, BUT STILL AND ALL, I WONDERED--

--WHY THIS FORM? WHY THIS BODY?

AND WHY DID IT FEEL SO... FAMILIAR?

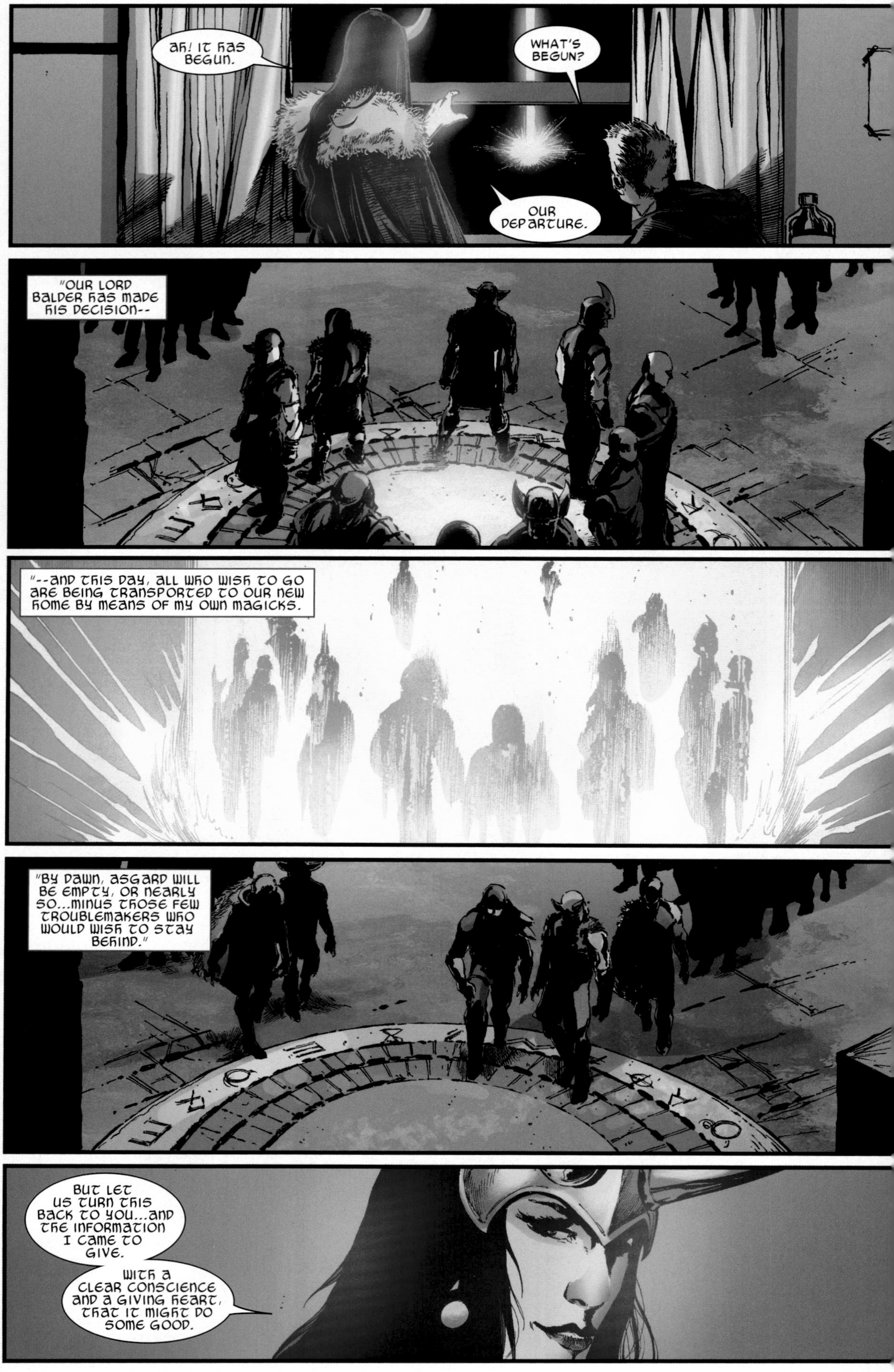

AH! IT HAS BEGUN.
WHAT'S BEGUN?
OUR DEPARTURE.
"OUR LORD BALDER HAS MADE HIS DECISION--
"--AND THIS DAY, ALL WHO WISH TO GO ARE BEING TRANSPORTED TO OUR NEW HOME BY MEANS OF MY OWN MAGICKS.
"BY DAWN, ASGARD WILL BE EMPTY, OR NEARLY SO...MINUS THOSE FEW TROUBLEMAKERS WHO WOULD WISH TO STAY BEHIND."
BUT LET US TURN THIS BACK TO YOU...AND THE INFORMATION I CAME TO GIVE.
WITH A CLEAR CONSCIENCE AND A GIVING HEART, THAT IT MIGHT DO SOME GOOD.

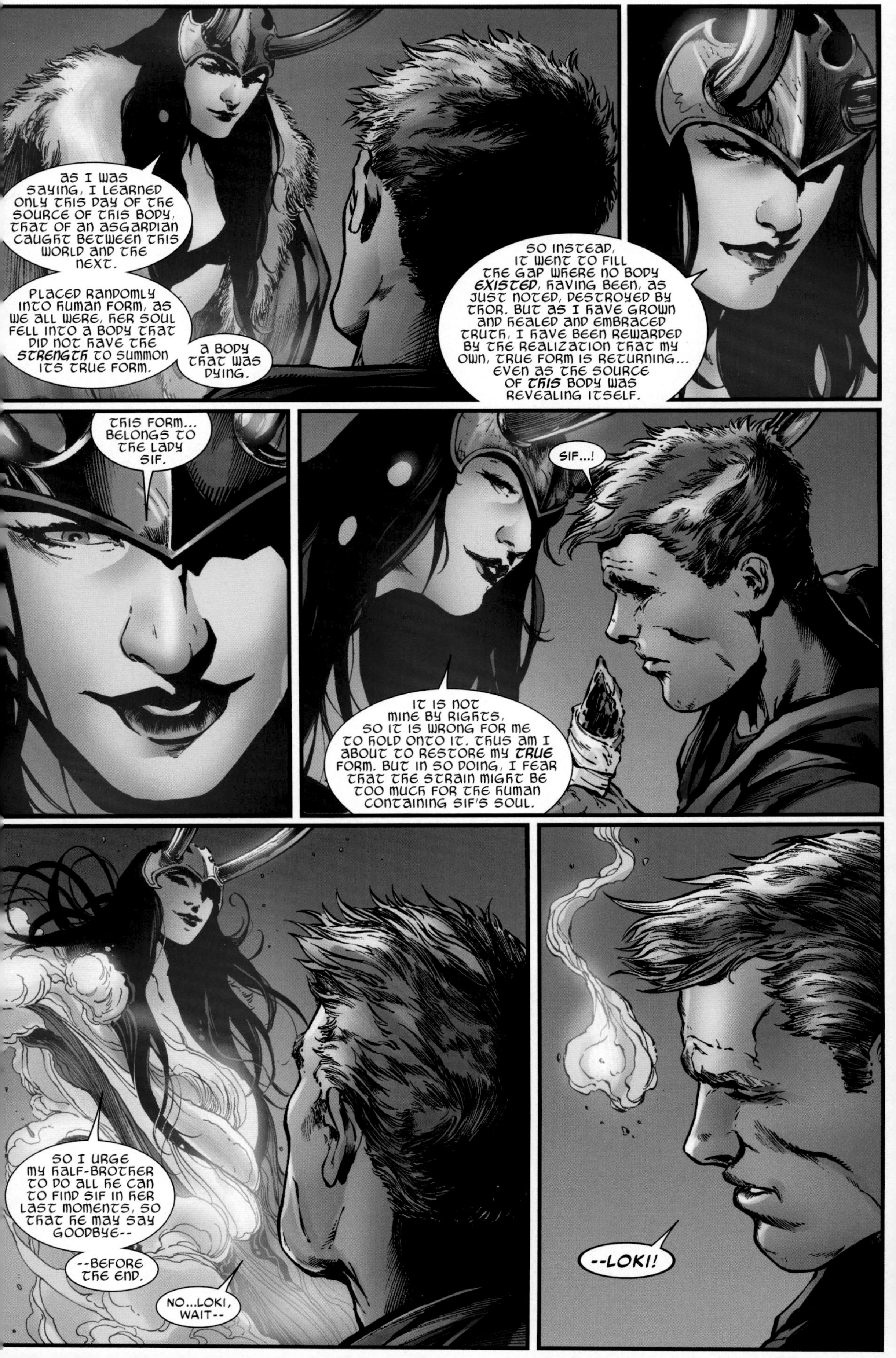
AS I WAS SAYING, I LEARNED ONLY THIS DAY OF THE SOURCE OF THIS BODY, THAT OF AN ASGARDIAN CAUGHT BETWEEN THIS WORLD AND THE NEXT.
PLACED RANDOMLY INTO HUMAN FORM, AS WE ALL WERE, HER SOUL FELL INTO A BODY THAT DID NOT HAVE THE STRENGTH TO SUMMON ITS TRUE FORM.
A BODY THAT WAS DYING.
SO INSTEAD, IT WENT TO FILL THE GAP WHERE NO BODY EXISTED, HAVING BEEN, AS JUST NOTED, DESTROYED BY THOR. BUT AS I HAVE GROWN AND HEALED AND EMBRACED TRUTH, I HAVE BEEN REWARDED BY THE REALIZATION THAT MY OWN, TRUE FORM IS RETURNING... EVEN AS THE SOURCE OF THIS BODY WAS REVEALING ITSELF.
THIS FORM... BELONGS TO THE LADY SIF.
SIF...!
IT IS NOT MINE BY RIGHTS, SO IT IS WRONG FOR ME TO HOLD ONTO IT. THUS AM I ABOUT TO RESTORE MY TRUE FORM. BUT IN SO DOING, I FEAR THAT THE STRAIN MIGHT BE TOO MUCH FOR THE HUMAN CONTAINING SIF'S SOUL.
SO I URGE MY HALF-BROTHER TO DO ALL HE CAN TO FIND SIF IN HER LAST MOMENTS, SO THAT HE MAY SAY GOODBYE--
--BEFORE THE END.
NO...LOKI, WAIT--
--LOKI!

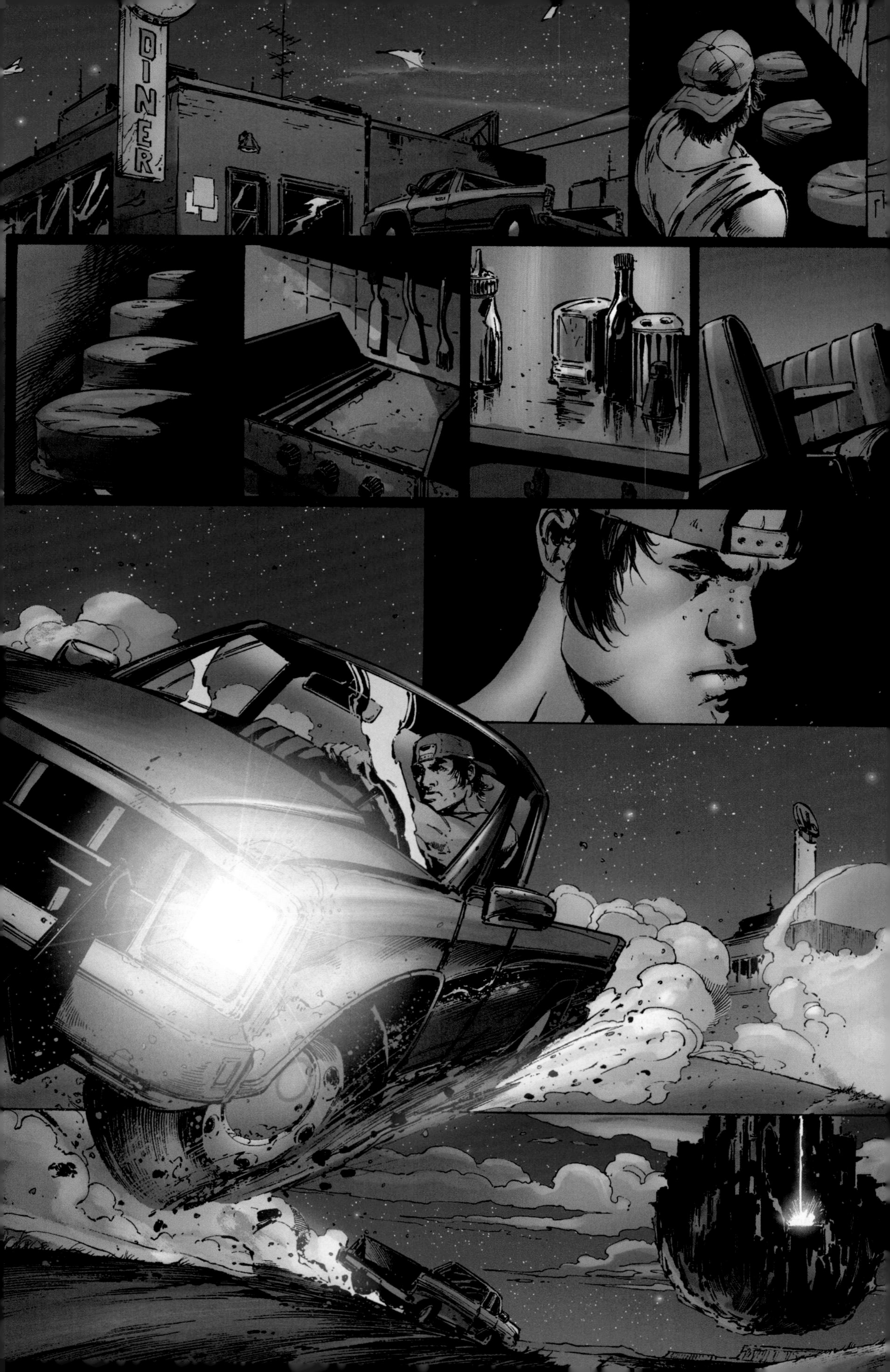
DINER

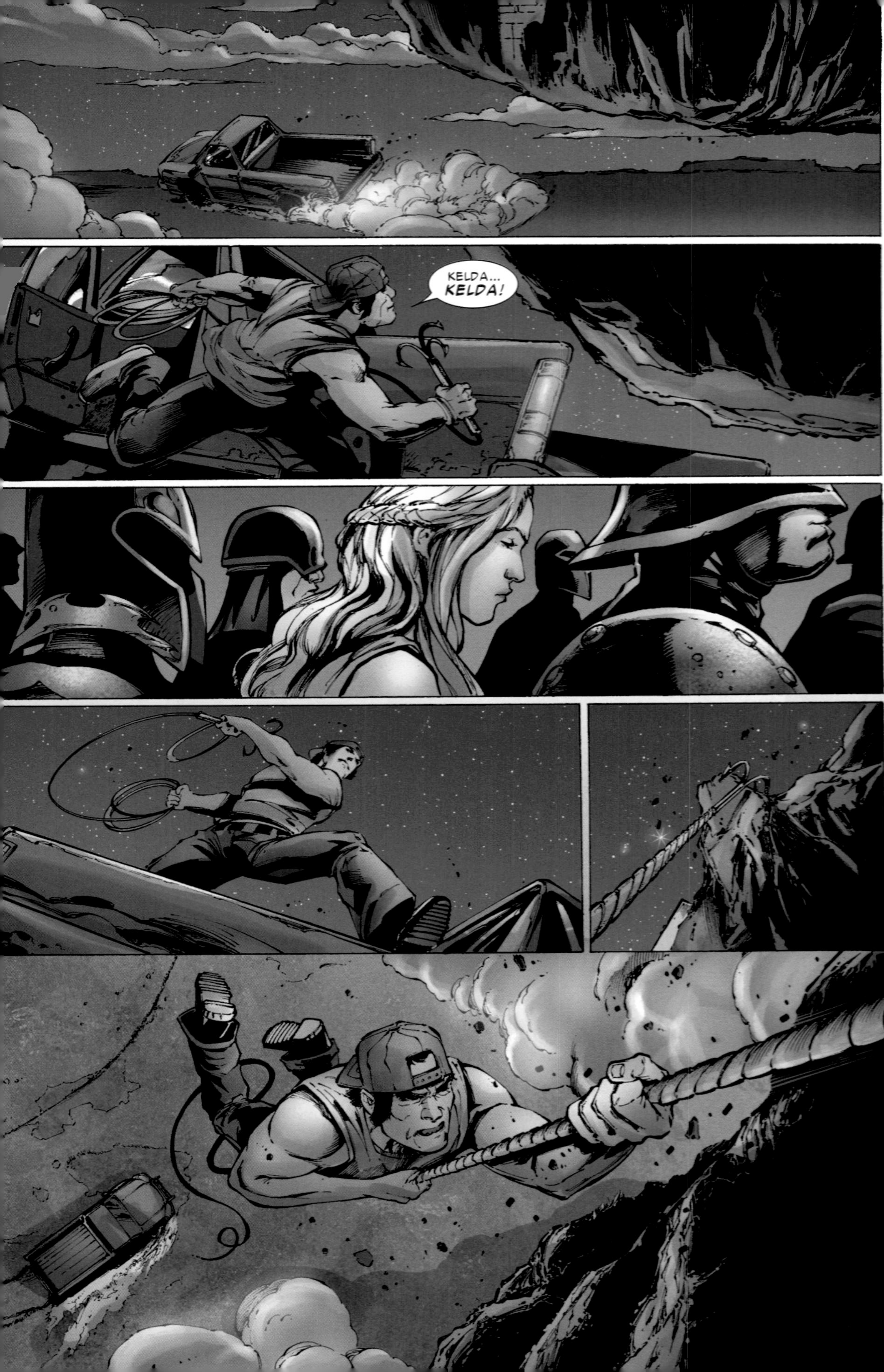
KELDA... KELDA!

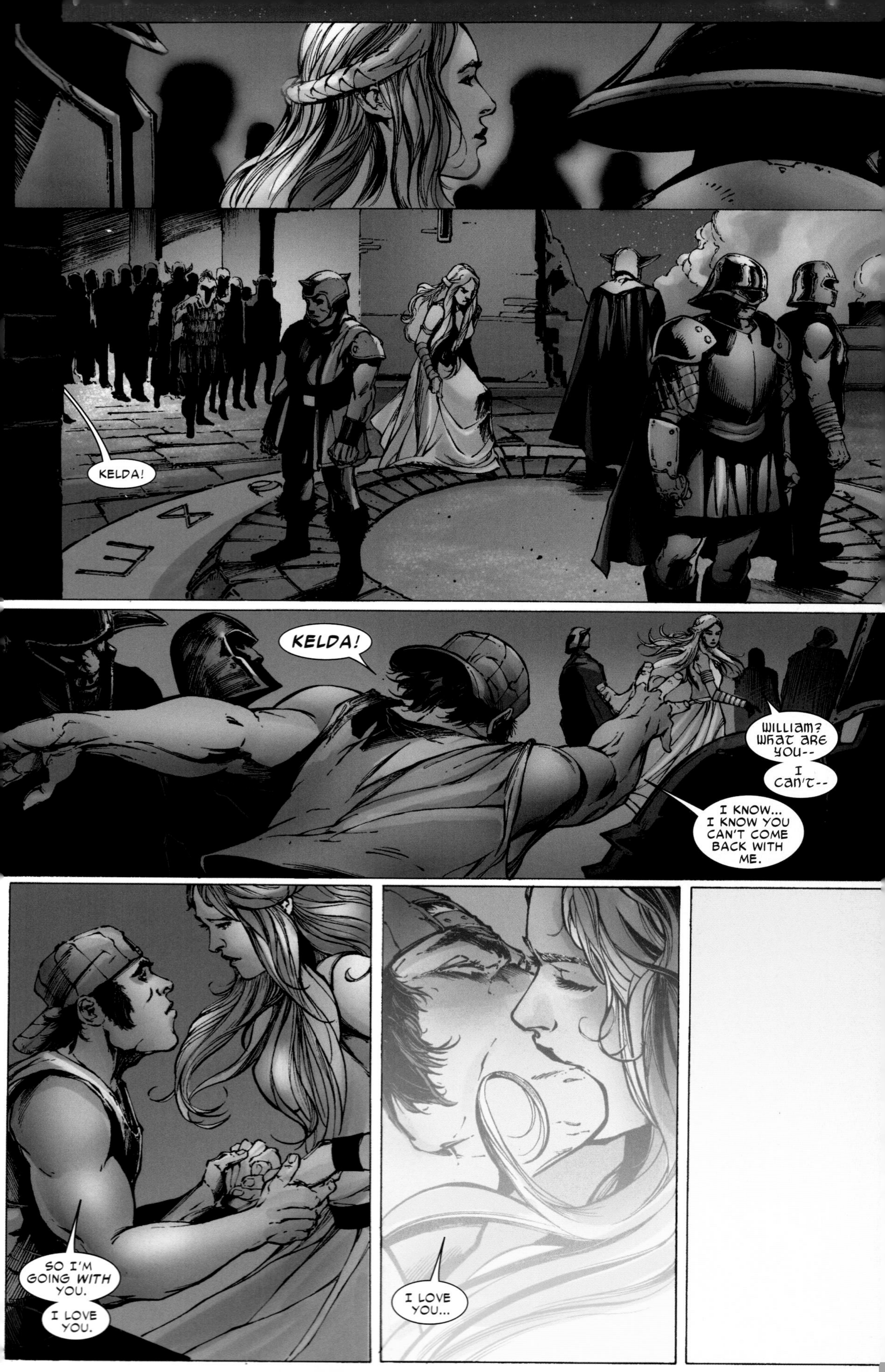
KELDA!
KELDA!
WILLIAM? WHAT ARE YOU--
I CAN'T--
I KNOW... I KNOW YOU CAN'T COME BACK WITH ME.
SO I'M GOING WITH YOU.
I LOVE YOU.
I LOVE YOU...

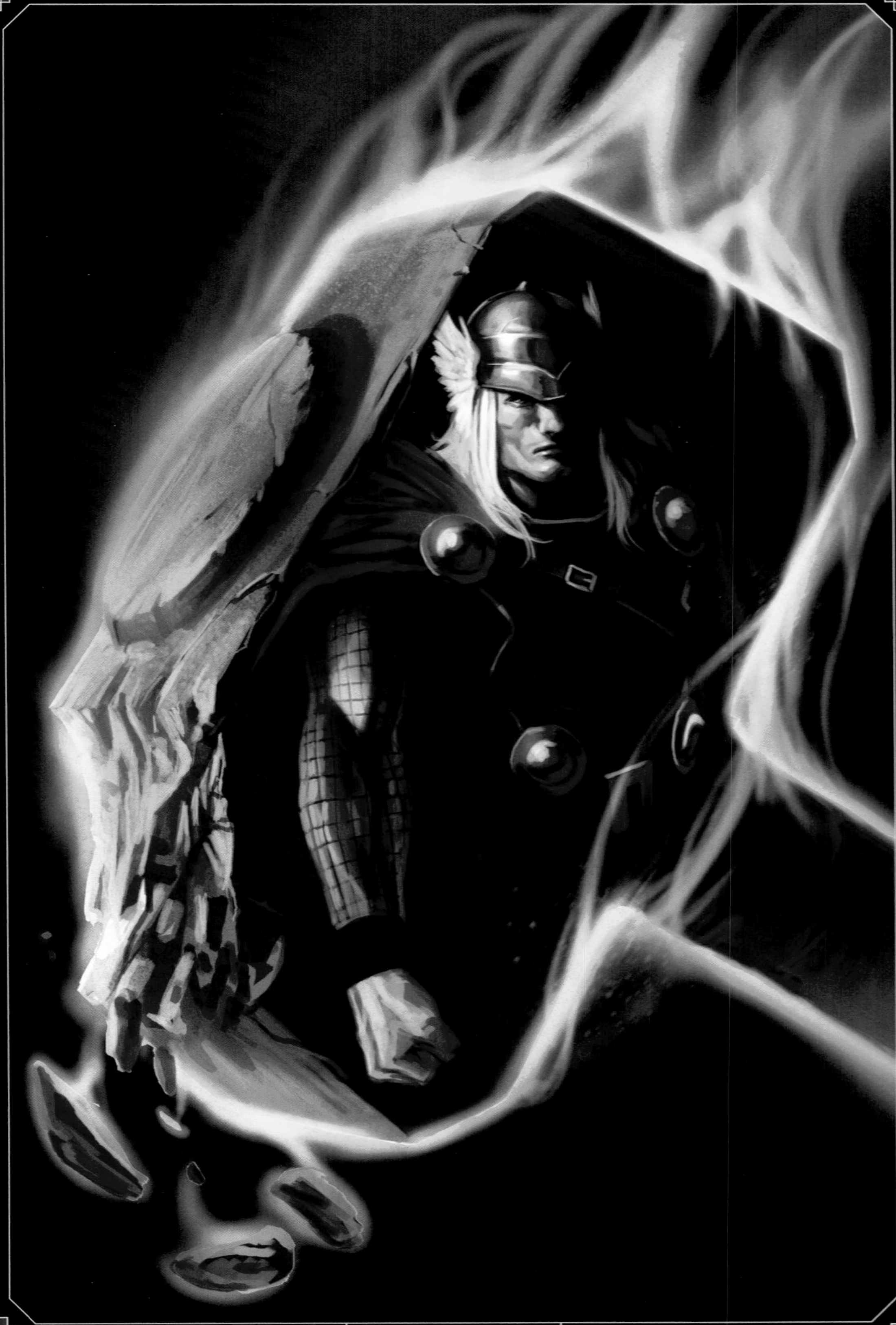

THOR #602

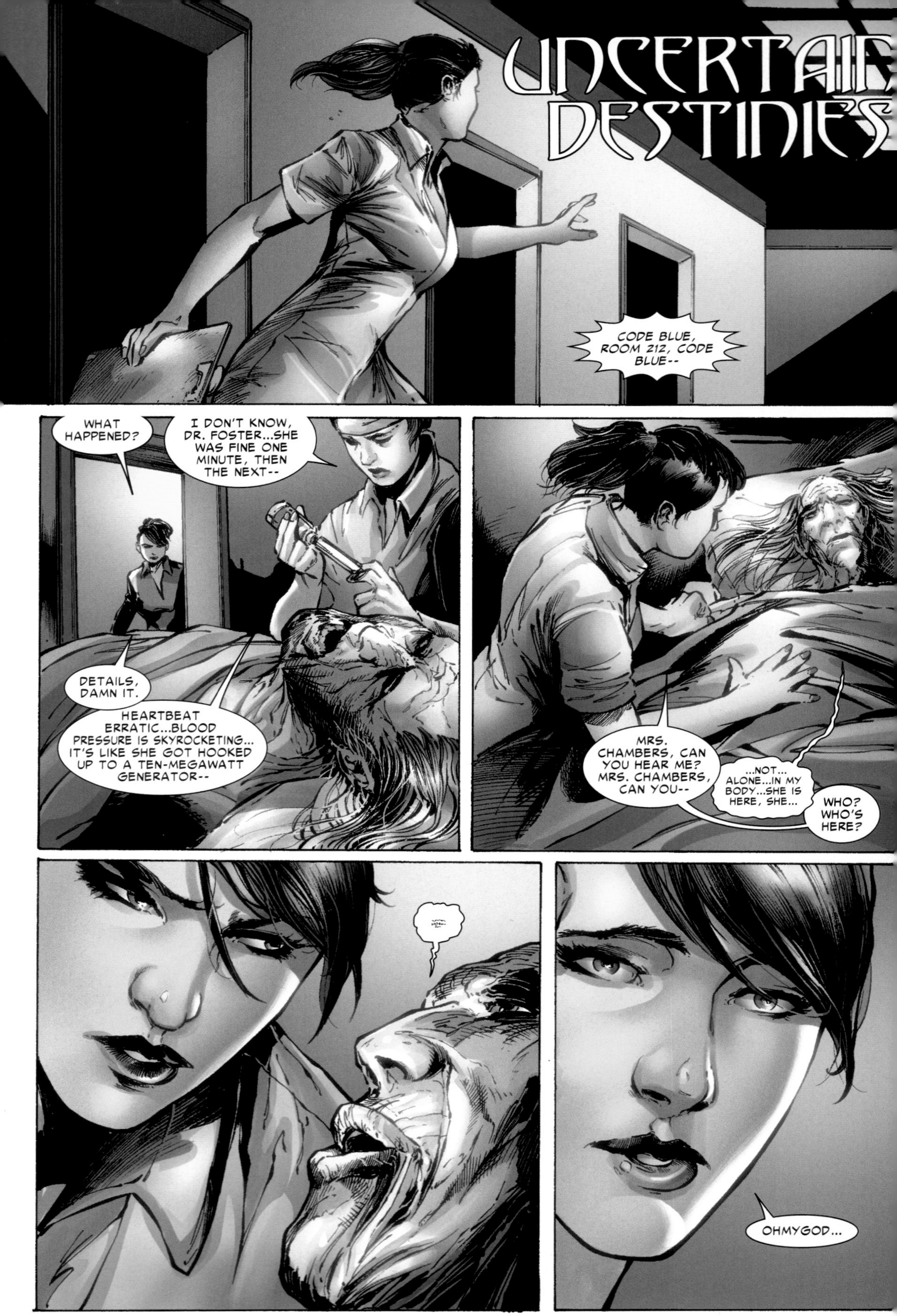
UNCERTAIN DESTINIES
CODE BLUE, ROOM 212, CODE BLUE--
WHAT HAPPENED?
I DON'T KNOW, DR. FOSTER...SHE WAS FINE ONE MINUTE, THEN THE NEXT--
DETAILS, DAMN IT.
HEARTBEAT ERRATIC...BLOOD PRESSURE IS SKYROCKETING... IT'S LIKE SHE GOT HOOKED UP TO A TEN-MEGAWATT GENERATOR--
MRS. CHAMBERS, CAN YOU HEAR ME? MRS. CHAMBERS, CAN YOU--
...NOT... ALONE...IN MY BODY...SHE IS HERE, SHE...
WHO? WHO'S HERE?
OHMYGOD...

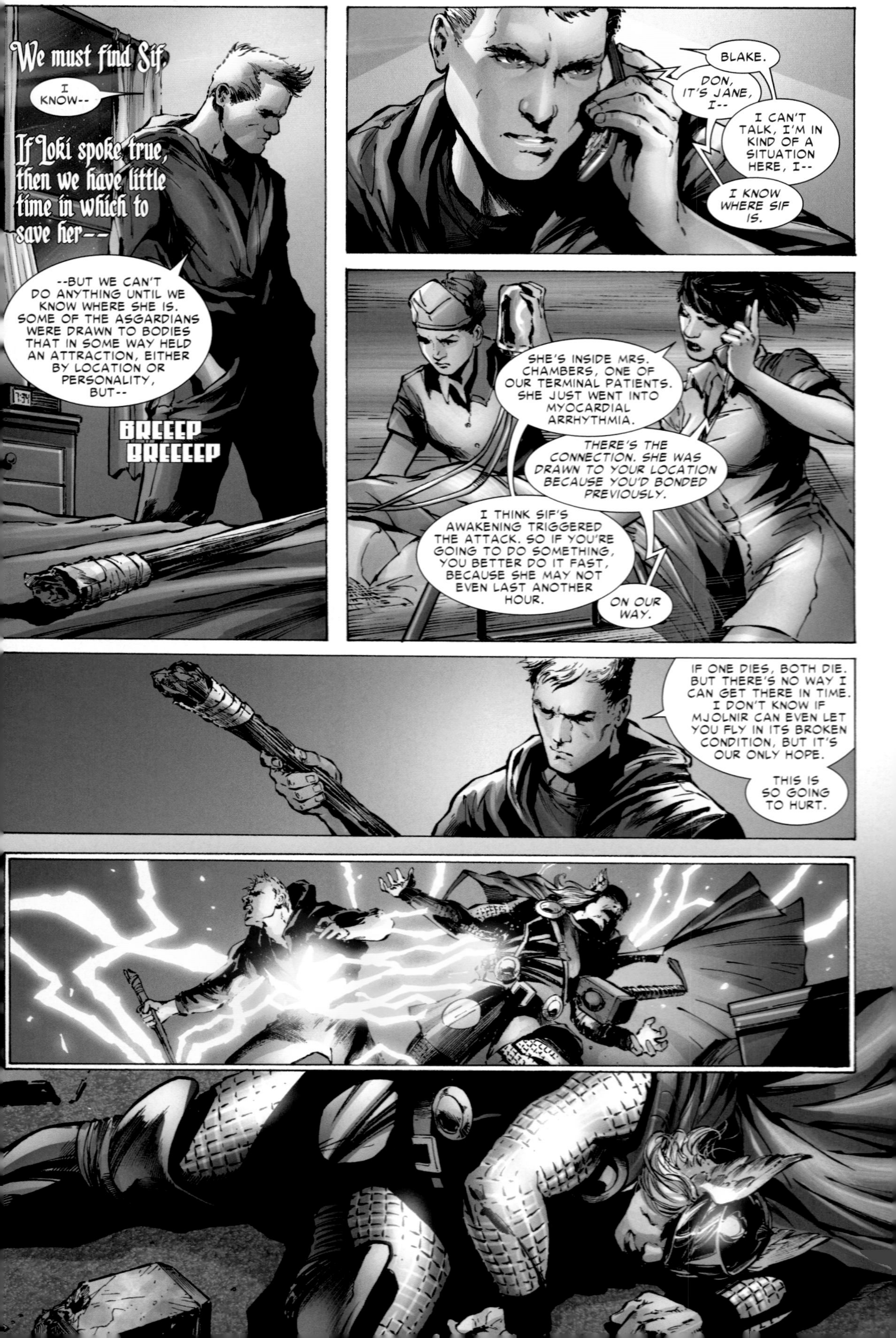
We must find Sif.
I KNOW--
If Loki spoke true, then we have little time in which to save her--
--BUT WE CAN'T DO ANYTHING UNTIL WE KNOW WHERE SHE IS. SOME OF THE ASGARDIANS WERE DRAWN TO BODIES THAT IN SOME WAY HELD AN ATTRACTION, EITHER BY LOCATION OR PERSONALITY, BUT--
BREEEP BREEEEP
BLAKE.
DON, IT'S JANE, I--
I CAN'T TALK, I'M IN KIND OF A SITUATION HERE, I--
I KNOW WHERE SIF IS.
SHE'S INSIDE MRS. CHAMBERS, ONE OF OUR TERMINAL PATIENTS. SHE JUST WENT INTO MYOCARDIAL ARRHYTHMIA.
THERE'S THE CONNECTION. SHE WAS DRAWN TO YOUR LOCATION BECAUSE YOU'D BONDED PREVIOUSLY.
I THINK SIF'S AWAKENING TRIGGERED THE ATTACK. SO IF YOU'RE GOING TO DO SOMETHING, YOU BETTER DO IT FAST, BECAUSE SHE MAY NOT EVEN LAST ANOTHER HOUR.
ON OUR WAY.
IF ONE DIES, BOTH DIE. BUT THERE'S NO WAY I CAN GET THERE IN TIME. I DON'T KNOW IF MJOLNIR CAN EVEN LET YOU FLY IN ITS BROKEN CONDITION, BUT IT'S OUR ONLY HOPE.
THIS IS SO GOING TO HURT.

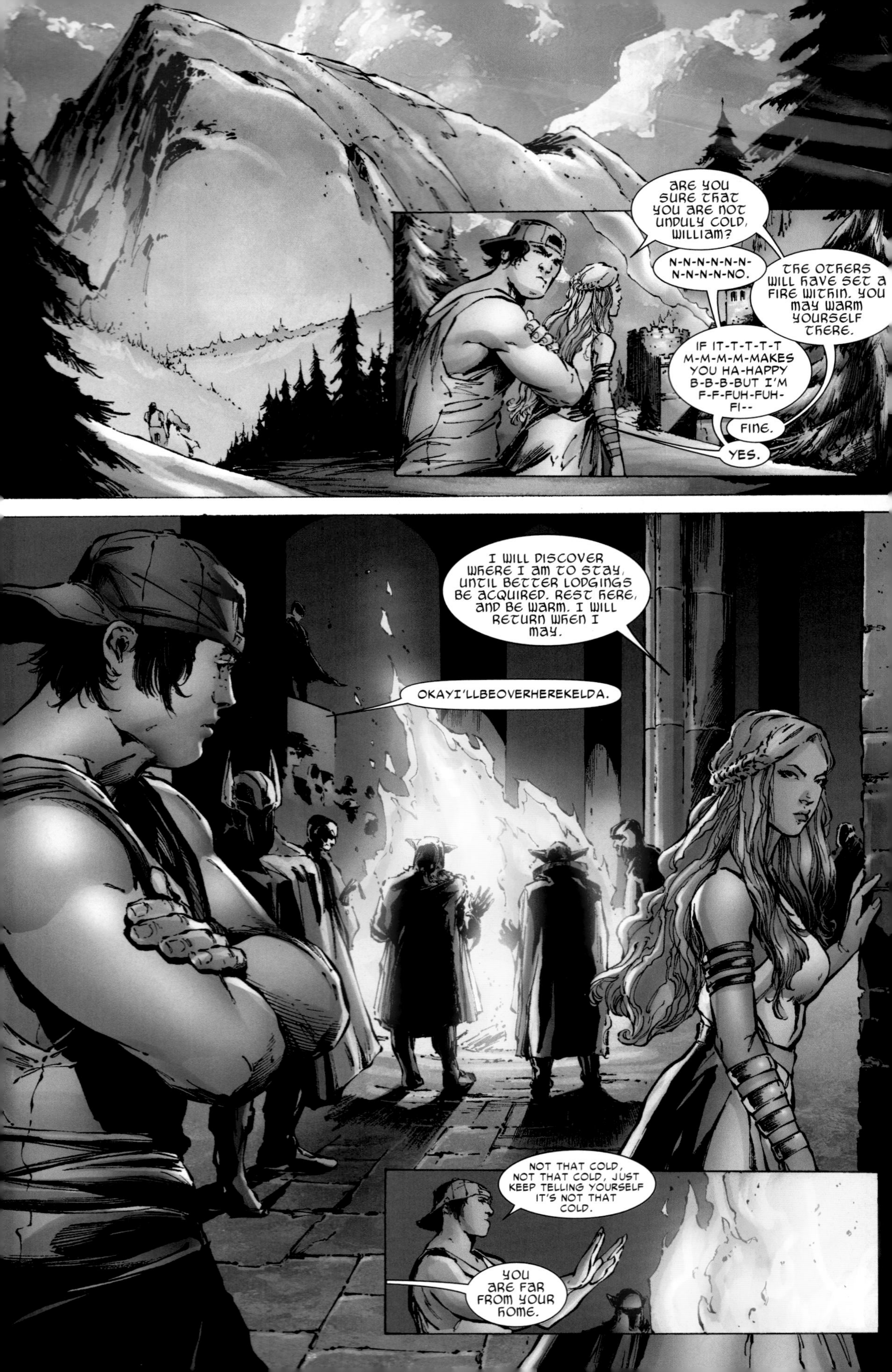
ARE YOU SURE THAT YOU ARE NOT UNDULY COLD, WILLIAM?
N-N-N-N-N-N-N-N-N-N-NO.
THE OTHERS WILL HAVE SET A FIRE WITHIN. YOU MAY WARM YOURSELF THERE.
IF IT-T-T-T-T M-M-M-MAKES YOU HA-HAPPY B-B-B-BUT I'M F-F-FUH-FUH-FI--
FINE.
YES.
I WILL DISCOVER WHERE I AM TO STAY, UNTIL BETTER LODGINGS BE ACQUIRED. REST HERE, AND BE WARM. I WILL RETURN WHEN I MAY.
OKAYI'LLBEOVERHEREKELDA.
NOT THAT COLD, NOT THAT COLD, JUST KEEP TELLING YOURSELF IT'S NOT THAT COLD.
YOU ARE FAR FROM YOUR HOME.

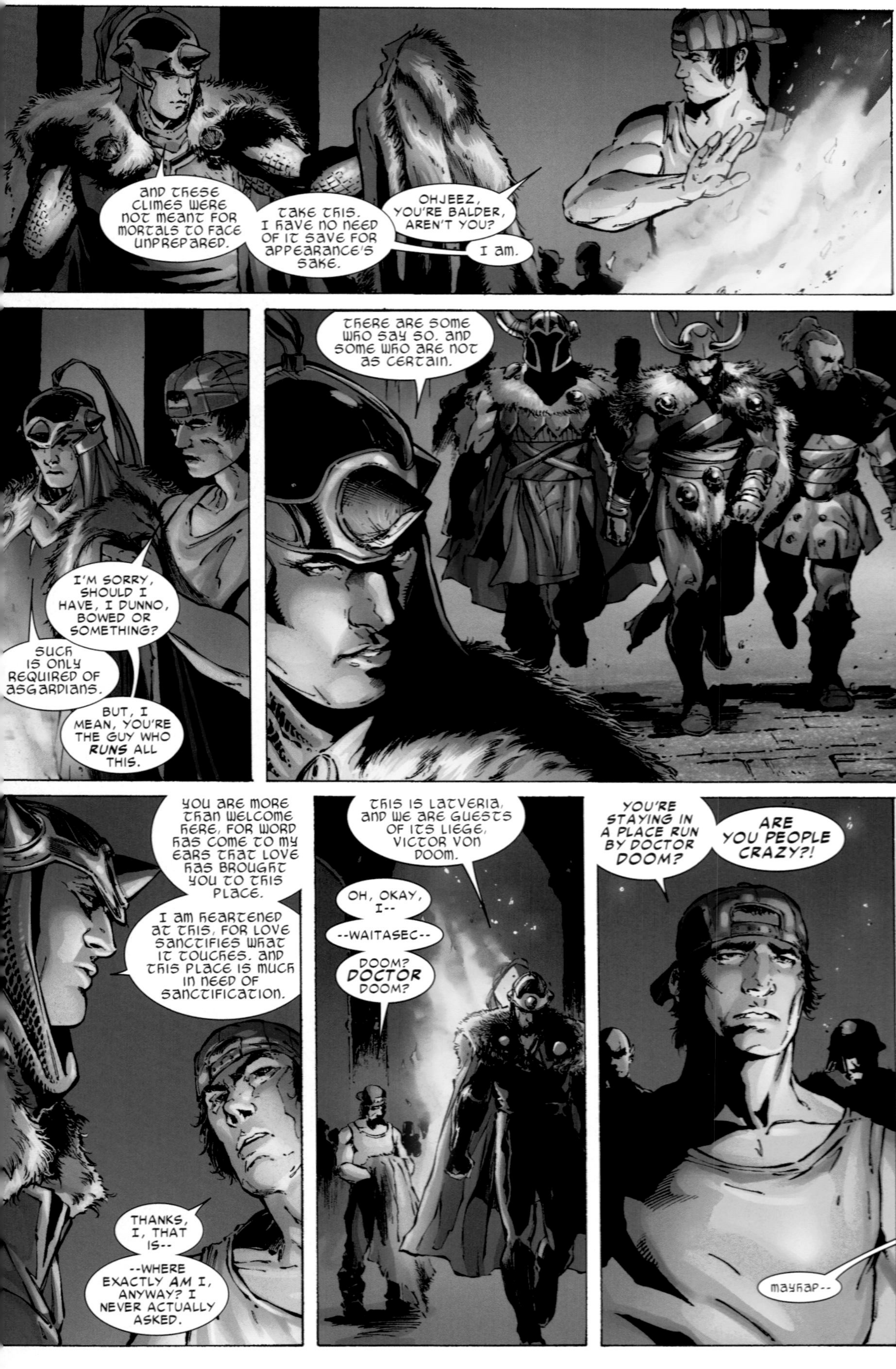

AND THESE CLIMES WERE NOT MEANT FOR MORTALS TO FACE UNPREPARED.
TAKE THIS. I HAVE NO NEED OF IT SAVE FOR APPEARANCE'S SAKE.
OHJEEZ, YOU'RE BALDER, AREN'T YOU?
I AM.
THERE ARE SOME WHO SAY SO. AND SOME WHO ARE NOT AS CERTAIN.
I'M SORRY, SHOULD I HAVE, I DUNNO, BOWED OR SOMETHING?
SUCH IS ONLY REQUIRED OF ASGARDIANS.
BUT, I MEAN, YOU'RE THE GUY WHO RUNS ALL THIS.
YOU ARE MORE THAN WELCOME HERE, FOR WORD HAS COME TO MY EARS THAT LOVE HAS BROUGHT YOU TO THIS PLACE.
I AM HEARTENED AT THIS, FOR LOVE SANCTIFIES WHAT IT TOUCHES. AND THIS PLACE IS MUCH IN NEED OF SANCTIFICATION.
THANKS, I, THAT IS--
--WHERE EXACTLY AM I, ANYWAY? I NEVER ACTUALLY ASKED.
THIS IS LATVERIA, AND WE ARE GUESTS OF ITS LIEGE, VICTOR VON DOOM.
OH, OKAY, I--
--WAITASEC--
DOOM? DOCTOR DOOM?
YOU'RE STAYING IN A PLACE RUN BY DOCTOR DOOM?
ARE YOU PEOPLE CRAZY?!
MAYHAP--

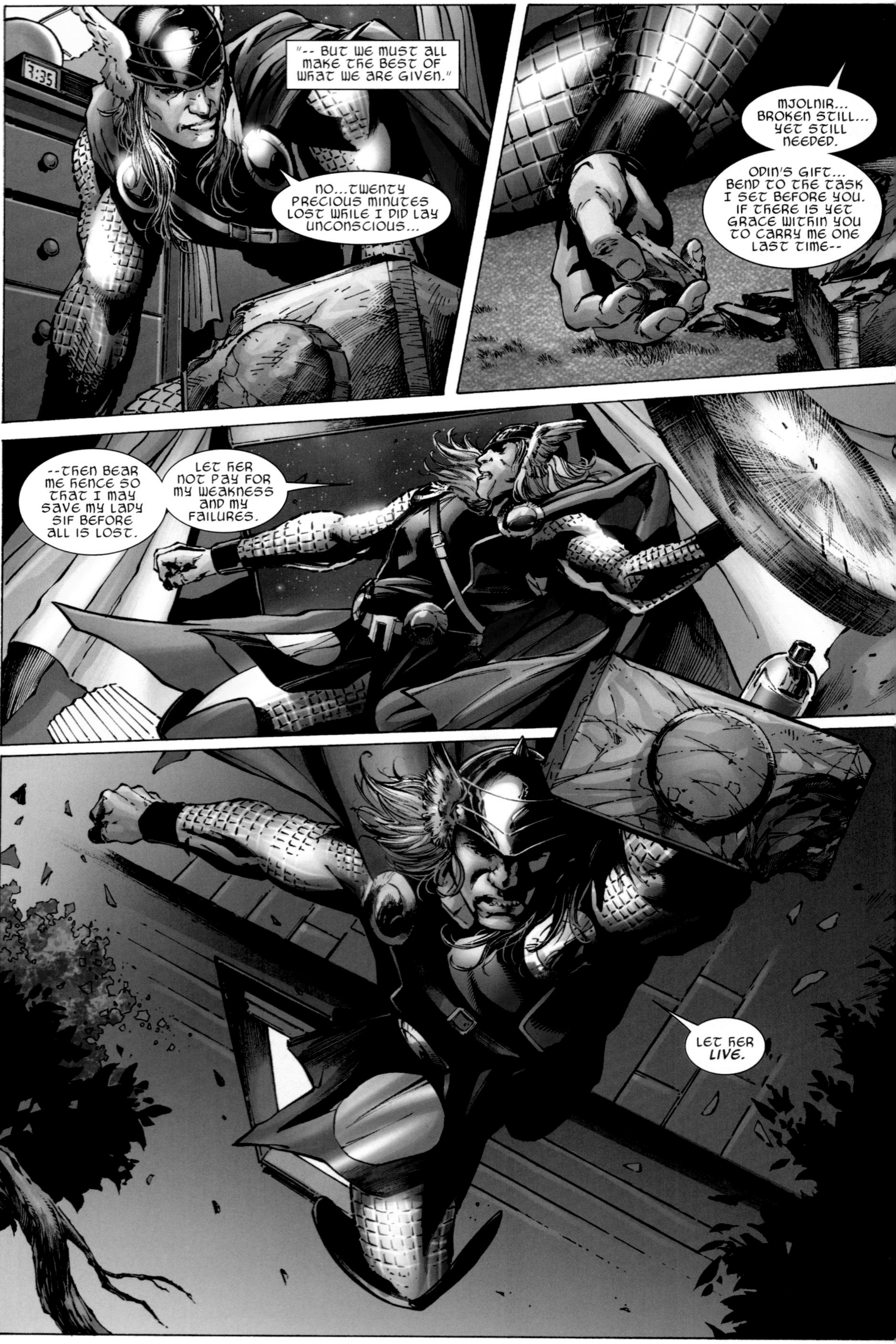
"-- BUT WE MUST ALL MAKE THE BEST OF WHAT WE ARE GIVEN."
NO...TWENTY PRECIOUS MINUTES LOST WHILE I DID LAY UNCONSCIOUS...
MJOLNIR... BROKEN STILL... YET STILL NEEDED.
ODIN'S GIFT... BEND TO THE TASK I SET BEFORE YOU. IF THERE IS YET GRACE WITHIN YOU TO CARRY ME ONE LAST TIME--
--THEN BEAR ME HENCE SO THAT I MAY SAVE MY LADY SIF BEFORE ALL IS LOST.
LET HER NOT PAY FOR MY WEAKNESS AND MY FAILURES.
LET HER *LIVE.*

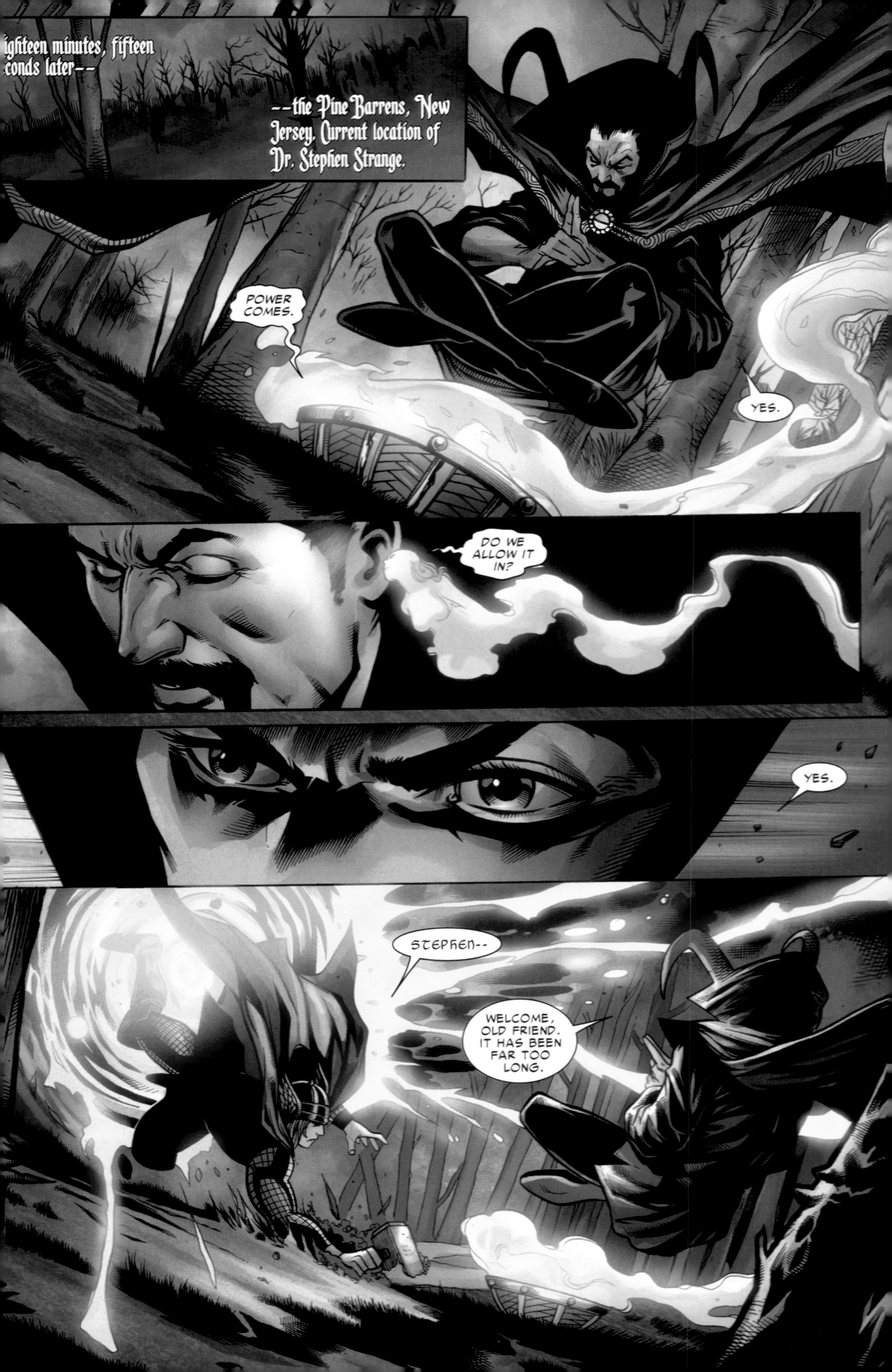
ighteen minutes, fifteen
conds later--
--the Pine Barrens, New Jersey. Current location of Dr. Stephen Strange.
POWER COMES.
YES.
DO WE ALLOW IT IN?
YES.
STEPHEN--
WELCOME, OLD FRIEND. IT HAS BEEN FAR TOO LONG.

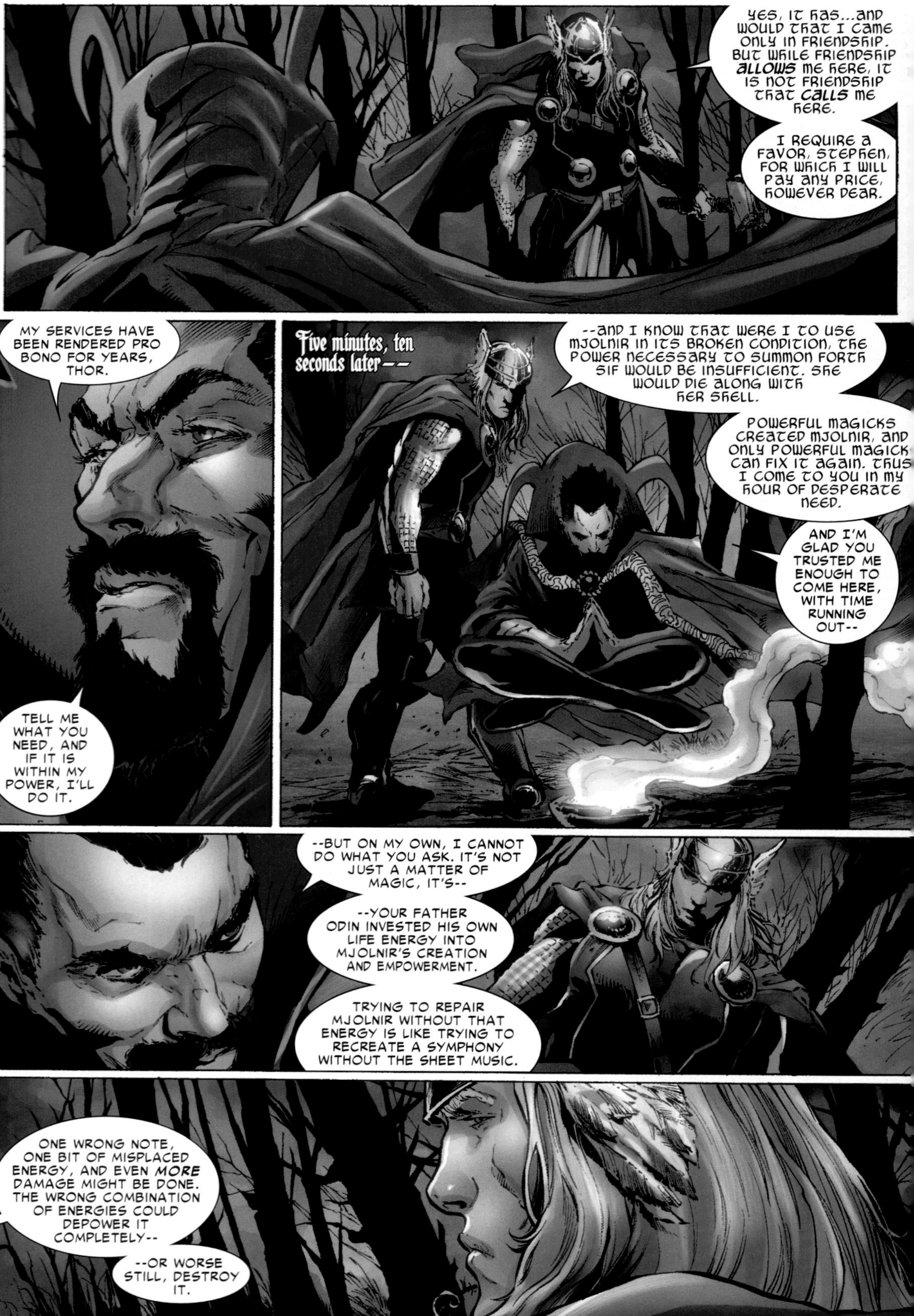
YES, IT HAS...AND WOULD THAT I CAME ONLY IN FRIENDSHIP. BUT WHILE FRIENDSHIP ALLOWS ME HERE, IT IS NOT FRIENDSHIP THAT CALLS ME HERE.
I REQUIRE A FAVOR, STEPHEN, FOR WHICH I WILL PAY ANY PRICE, HOWEVER DEAR.
MY SERVICES HAVE BEEN RENDERED PRO BONO FOR YEARS, THOR.
TELL ME WHAT YOU NEED, AND IF IT IS WITHIN MY POWER, I'LL DO IT.
Five minutes, ten seconds later--
--AND I KNOW THAT WERE I TO USE MJOLNIR IN ITS BROKEN CONDITION, THE POWER NECESSARY TO SUMMON FORTH SIF WOULD BE INSUFFICIENT. SHE WOULD DIE ALONG WITH HER SHELL.
POWERFUL MAGICKS CREATED MJOLNIR, AND ONLY POWERFUL MAGICK CAN FIX IT AGAIN. THUS I COME TO YOU IN MY HOUR OF DESPERATE NEED.
AND I'M GLAD YOU TRUSTED ME ENOUGH TO COME HERE, WITH TIME RUNNING OUT--
--BUT ON MY OWN, I CANNOT DO WHAT YOU ASK. IT'S NOT JUST A MATTER OF MAGIC, IT'S--
--YOUR FATHER ODIN INVESTED HIS OWN LIFE ENERGY INTO MJOLNIR'S CREATION AND EMPOWERMENT.
TRYING TO REPAIR MJOLNIR WITHOUT THAT ENERGY IS LIKE TRYING TO RECREATE A SYMPHONY WITHOUT THE SHEET MUSIC.
ONE WRONG NOTE, ONE BIT OF MISPLACED ENERGY, AND EVEN MORE DAMAGE MIGHT BE DONE. THE WRONG COMBINATION OF ENERGIES COULD DEPOWER IT COMPLETELY--
--OR WORSE STILL, DESTROY IT.

I DO NOT SEE THE PROBLEM. AS I TOLD OU, SOME OF ODIN'S POWER LIVES WITHIN ME STILL--IS THAT SUFFICIENT TO THE CAUSE?

IT IS. BUT--

BUT?

IT WOULD REQUIRE TAKING ALMOST ALL OF THAT POWER FROM YOU, AND INVESTING IT IN MJOLNIR. YOU WOULD BE BACK WHERE YOU WERE BEFORE YOU INHERITED HIS POWER.

I AM WILLING TO--

I KNOW, BUT THERE'S SOMETHING ELSE.

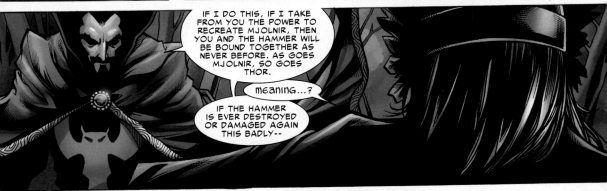

IF I DO THIS, IF I TAKE FROM YOU THE POWER TO RECREATE MJOLNIR, THEN YOU AND THE HAMMER WILL BE BOUND TOGETHER AS NEVER BEFORE. AS GOES MJOLNIR, SO GOES THOR.

MEANING...?

IF THE HAMMER IS EVER DESTROYED OR DAMAGED AGAIN THIS BADLY--

--YOU WILL DIE.

AS A DOCTOR, I HAVE TO HONOR THE WISHES OF MY PATIENTS WHEN GIVEN NEWS LIKE THIS. SO THE DECISION IS YOURS, BUT I WOULD ADVISE AGAINST--

LET IT BE DONE.

THERE ARE SOME TO WHOM I WOULD GIVE FAR, FAR MORE THAN MY LIFE.

DO AS YOU MUST.

VERY WELL.

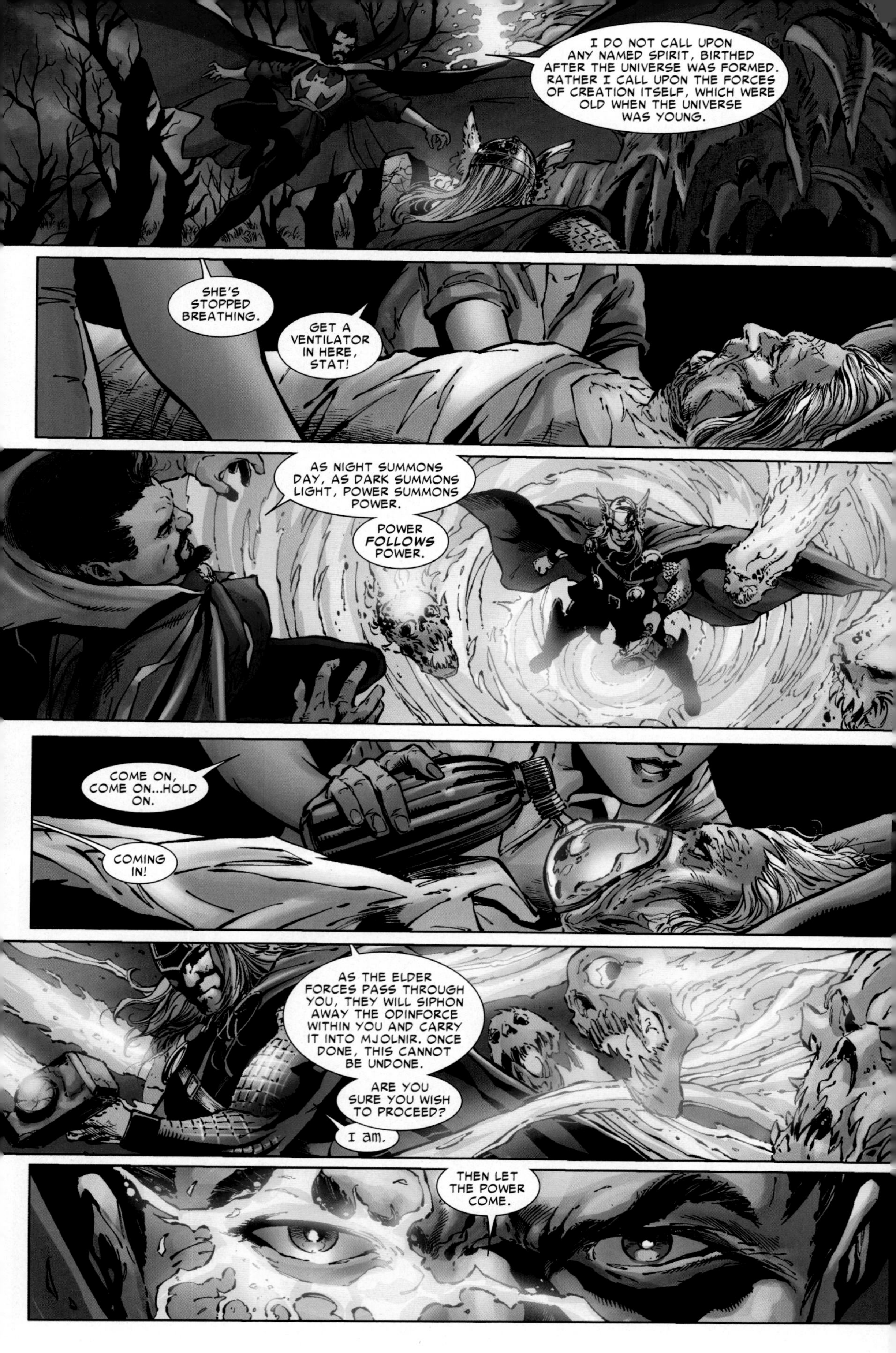
I DO NOT CALL UPON ANY NAMED SPIRIT, BIRTHED AFTER THE UNIVERSE WAS FORMED. RATHER I CALL UPON THE FORCES OF CREATION ITSELF, WHICH WERE OLD WHEN THE UNIVERSE WAS YOUNG.
SHE'S STOPPED BREATHING.
GET A VENTILATOR IN HERE, STAT!
AS NIGHT SUMMONS DAY, AS DARK SUMMONS LIGHT, POWER SUMMONS POWER.
POWER *FOLLOWS* POWER.
COME ON, COME ON...HOLD ON.
COMING IN!
AS THE ELDER FORCES PASS THROUGH YOU, THEY WILL SIPHON AWAY THE ODINFORCE WITHIN YOU AND CARRY IT INTO MJOLNIR. ONCE DONE, THIS CANNOT BE UNDONE.
ARE YOU SURE YOU WISH TO PROCEED?
I am.
THEN LET THE POWER COME.

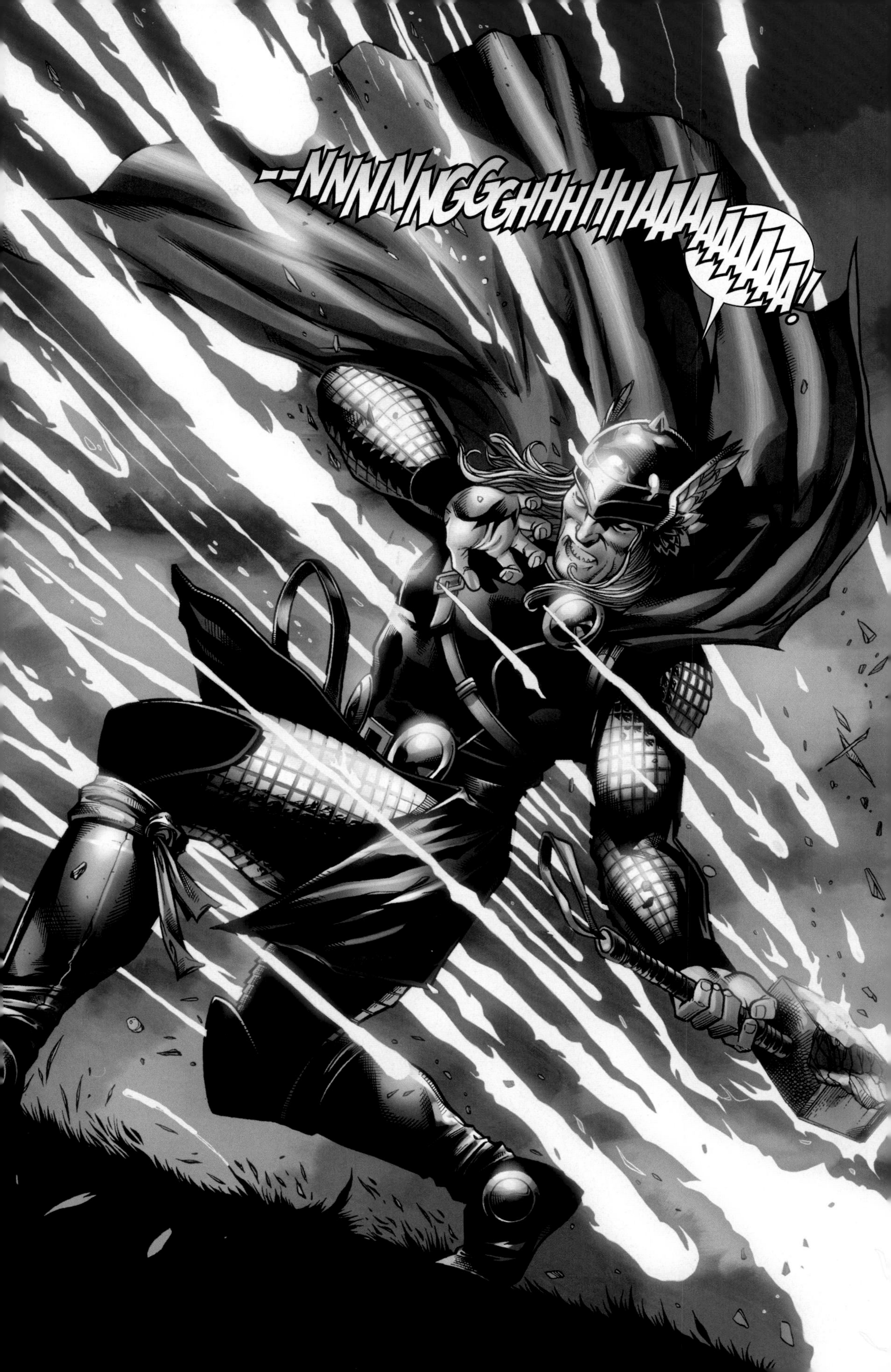
--NNNNNGGGHHHHHAAAAAAAAA!

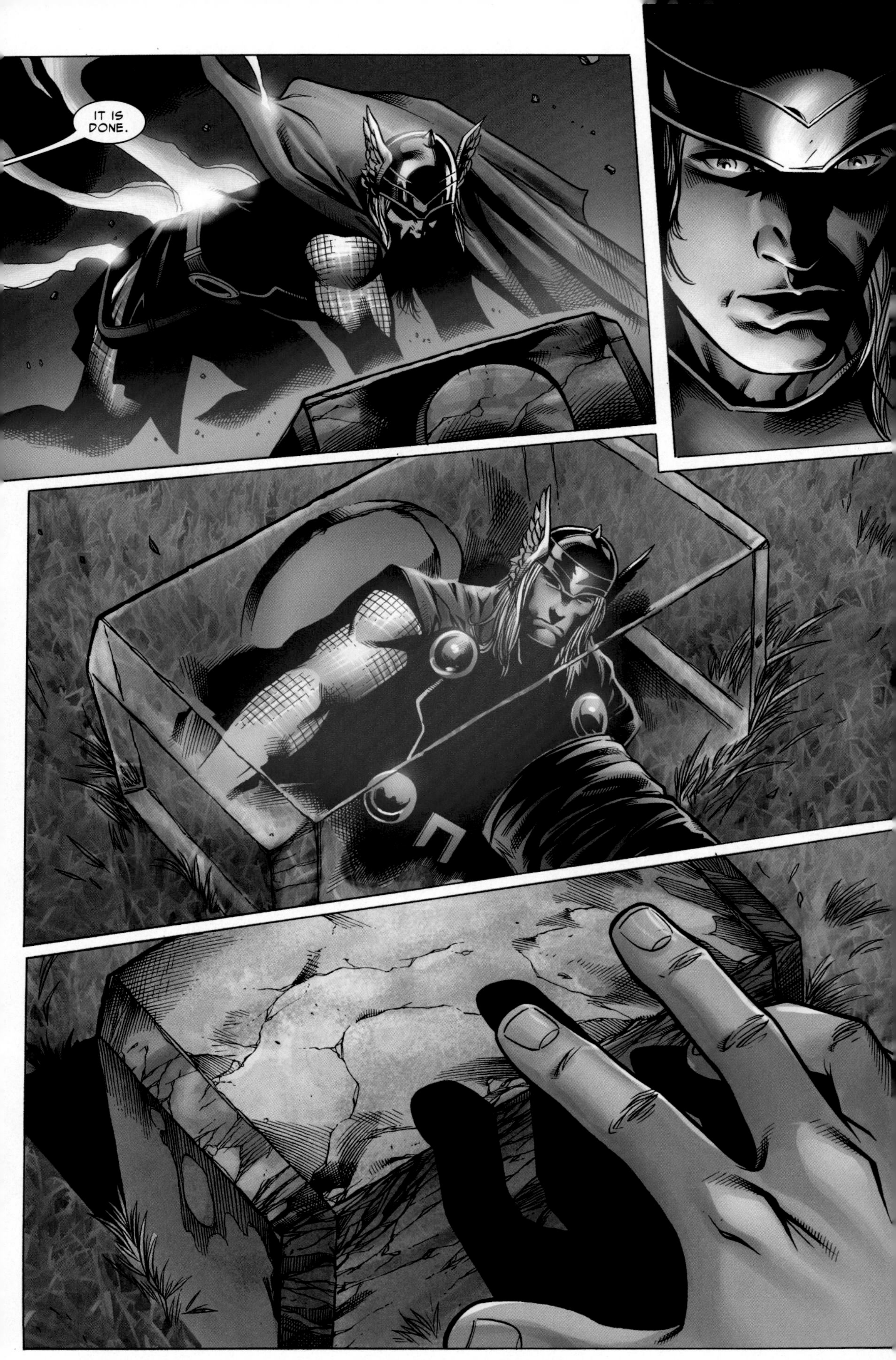
IT IS DONE.

SHE'S GOING INTO CARDIAC ARREST--

NO--

E.K.G. FALLING--

PLEASE--

EEEEEEEEE

--STAND ASIDE.

WHAT THE HELL ARE YOU DOING IN HERE? THIS IS A PRIVATE--

NURSE ROSSI--

--LIKE THE MAN SAID, STAND ASIDE.

EEEEEEEEEEEEEEEEE

SIF...COME FORTH.

EEEEEEEEEEEEEEEEEEEEEEEEEEEEEEEEEEEEE

COME FORTH.

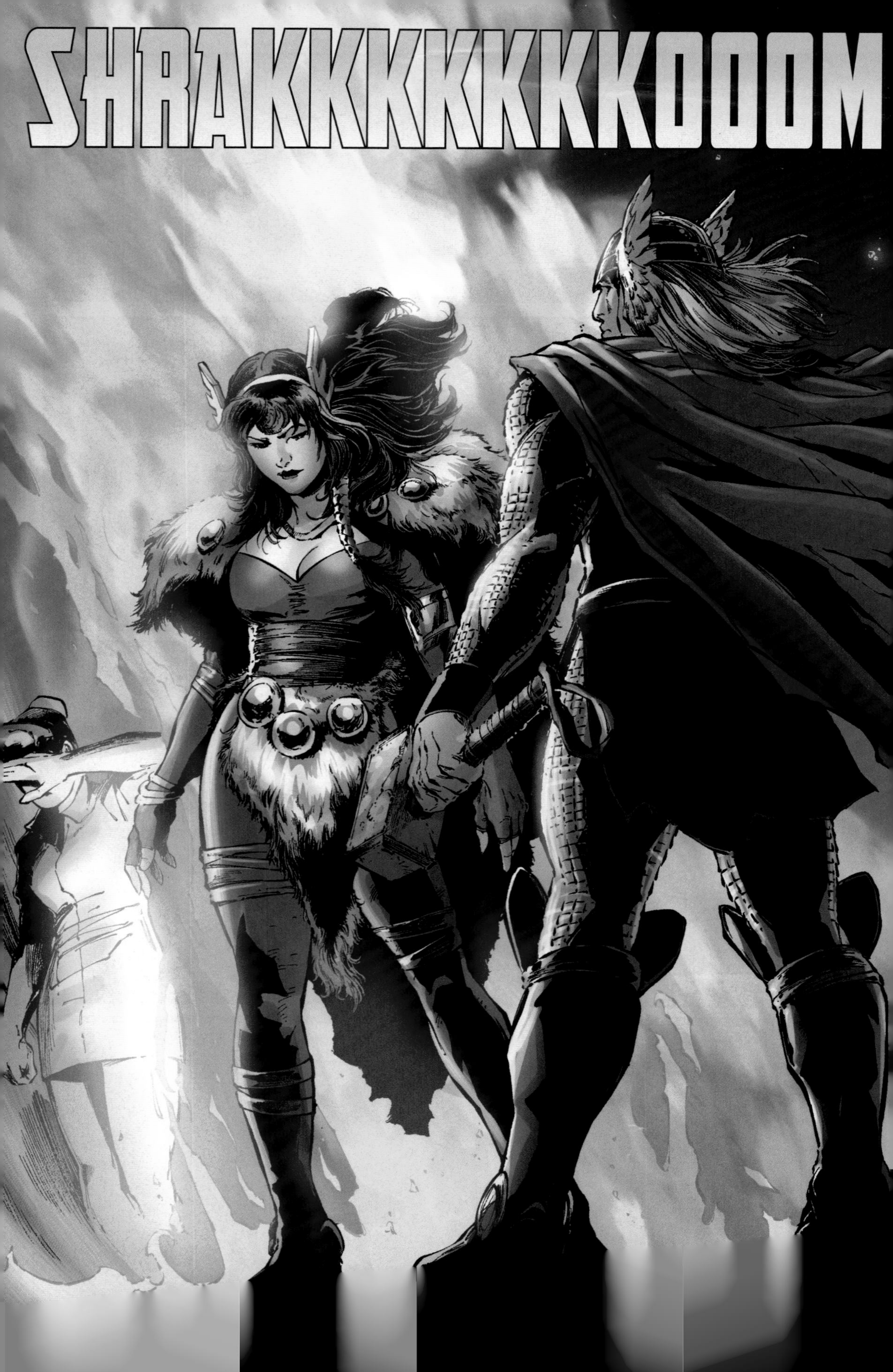
SHRAKKKKKKKKOOOM

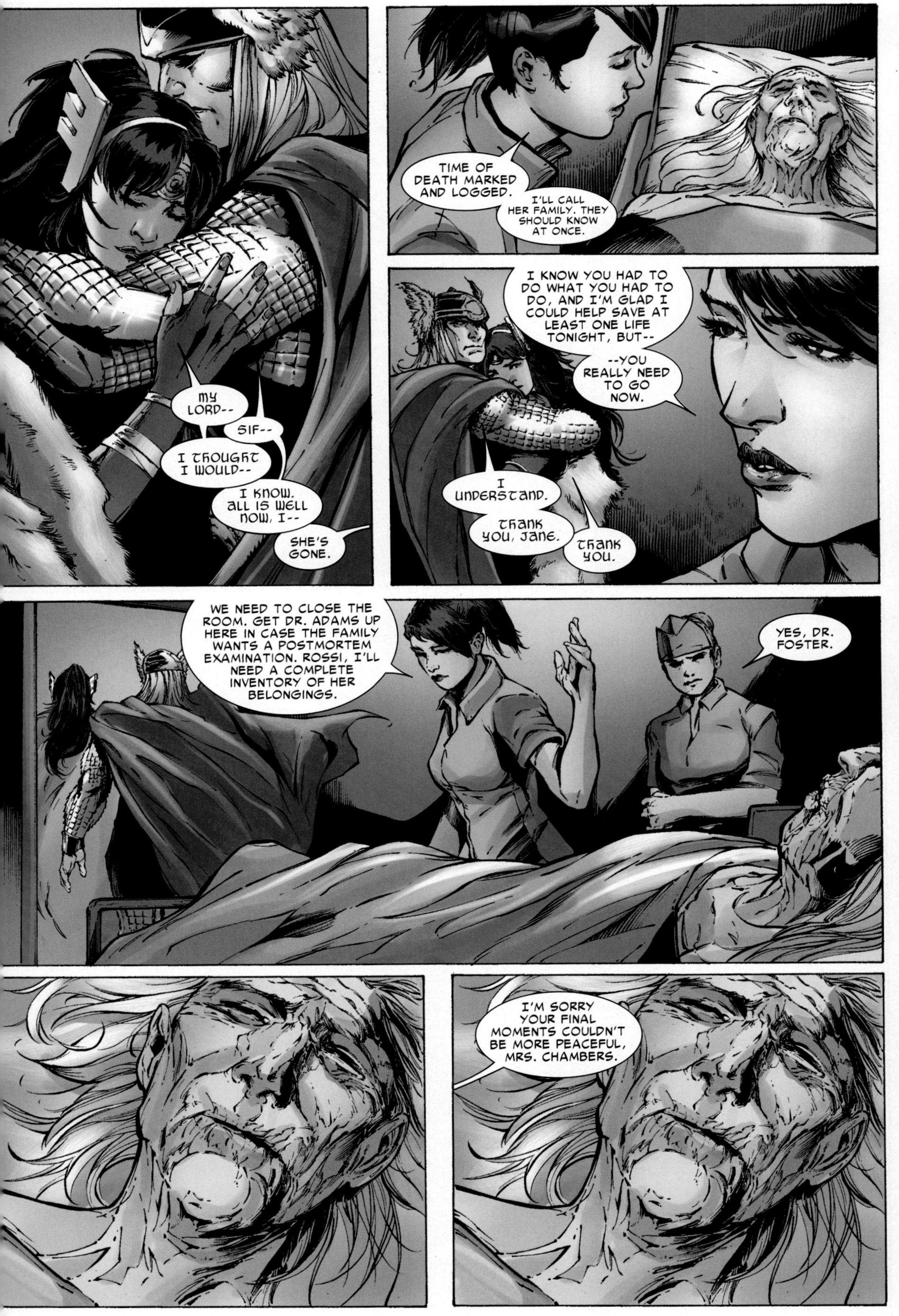
MY LORD--
SIF--
I THOUGHT I WOULD--
I KNOW. ALL IS WELL NOW, I--
SHE'S GONE.
TIME OF DEATH MARKED AND LOGGED.
I'LL CALL HER FAMILY. THEY SHOULD KNOW AT ONCE.
I KNOW YOU HAD TO DO WHAT YOU HAD TO DO, AND I'M GLAD I COULD HELP SAVE AT LEAST ONE LIFE TONIGHT, BUT--
--YOU REALLY NEED TO GO NOW.
I UNDERSTAND.
THANK YOU, JANE.
THANK YOU.
WE NEED TO CLOSE THE ROOM. GET DR. ADAMS UP HERE IN CASE THE FAMILY WANTS A POSTMORTEM EXAMINATION. ROSSI, I'LL NEED A COMPLETE INVENTORY OF HER BELONGINGS.
YES, DR. FOSTER.
I'M SORRY YOUR FINAL MOMENTS COULDN'T BE MORE PEACEFUL, MRS. CHAMBERS.

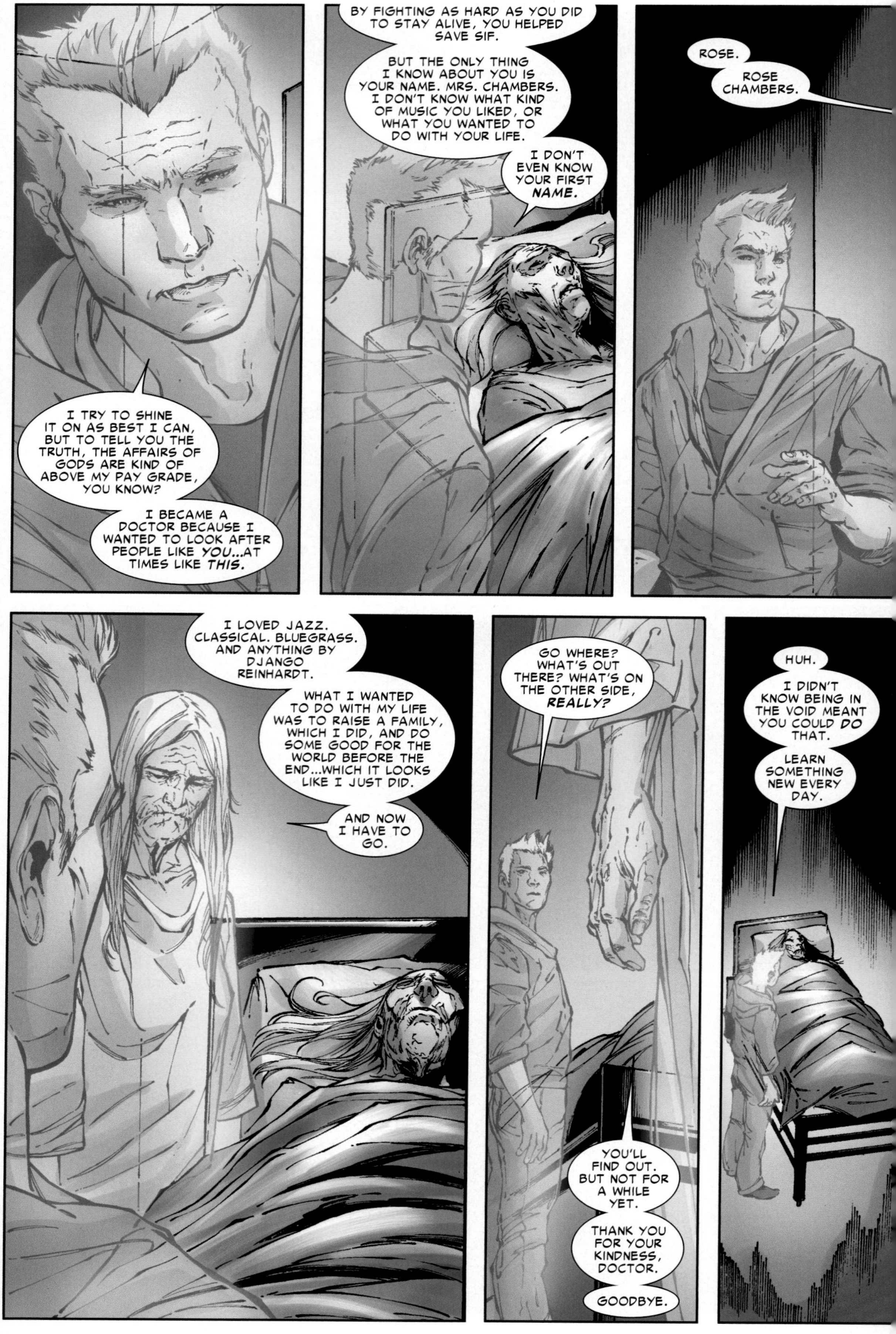
I TRY TO SHINE IT ON AS BEST I CAN, BUT TO TELL YOU THE TRUTH, THE AFFAIRS OF GODS ARE KIND OF ABOVE MY PAY GRADE, YOU KNOW?
I BECAME A DOCTOR BECAUSE I WANTED TO LOOK AFTER PEOPLE LIKE *YOU*...AT TIMES LIKE *THIS*.
BY FIGHTING AS HARD AS YOU DID TO STAY ALIVE, YOU HELPED SAVE SIF.
BUT THE ONLY THING I KNOW ABOUT YOU IS YOUR NAME. MRS. CHAMBERS. I DON'T KNOW WHAT KIND OF MUSIC YOU LIKED, OR WHAT YOU WANTED TO DO WITH YOUR LIFE.
I DON'T EVEN KNOW YOUR FIRST *NAME*.
ROSE.
ROSE CHAMBERS.
I LOVED JAZZ. CLASSICAL. BLUEGRASS. AND ANYTHING BY DJANGO REINHARDT.
WHAT I WANTED TO DO WITH MY LIFE WAS TO RAISE A FAMILY, WHICH I DID, AND DO SOME GOOD FOR THE WORLD BEFORE THE END...WHICH IT LOOKS LIKE I JUST DID.
AND NOW I HAVE TO GO.
GO WHERE? WHAT'S OUT THERE? WHAT'S ON THE OTHER SIDE, *REALLY?*
YOU'LL FIND OUT. BUT NOT FOR A WHILE YET.
THANK YOU FOR YOUR KINDNESS, DOCTOR.
GOODBYE.
HUH.
I DIDN'T KNOW BEING IN THE VOID MEANT YOU COULD *DO* THAT.
LEARN SOMETHING NEW EVERY DAY.

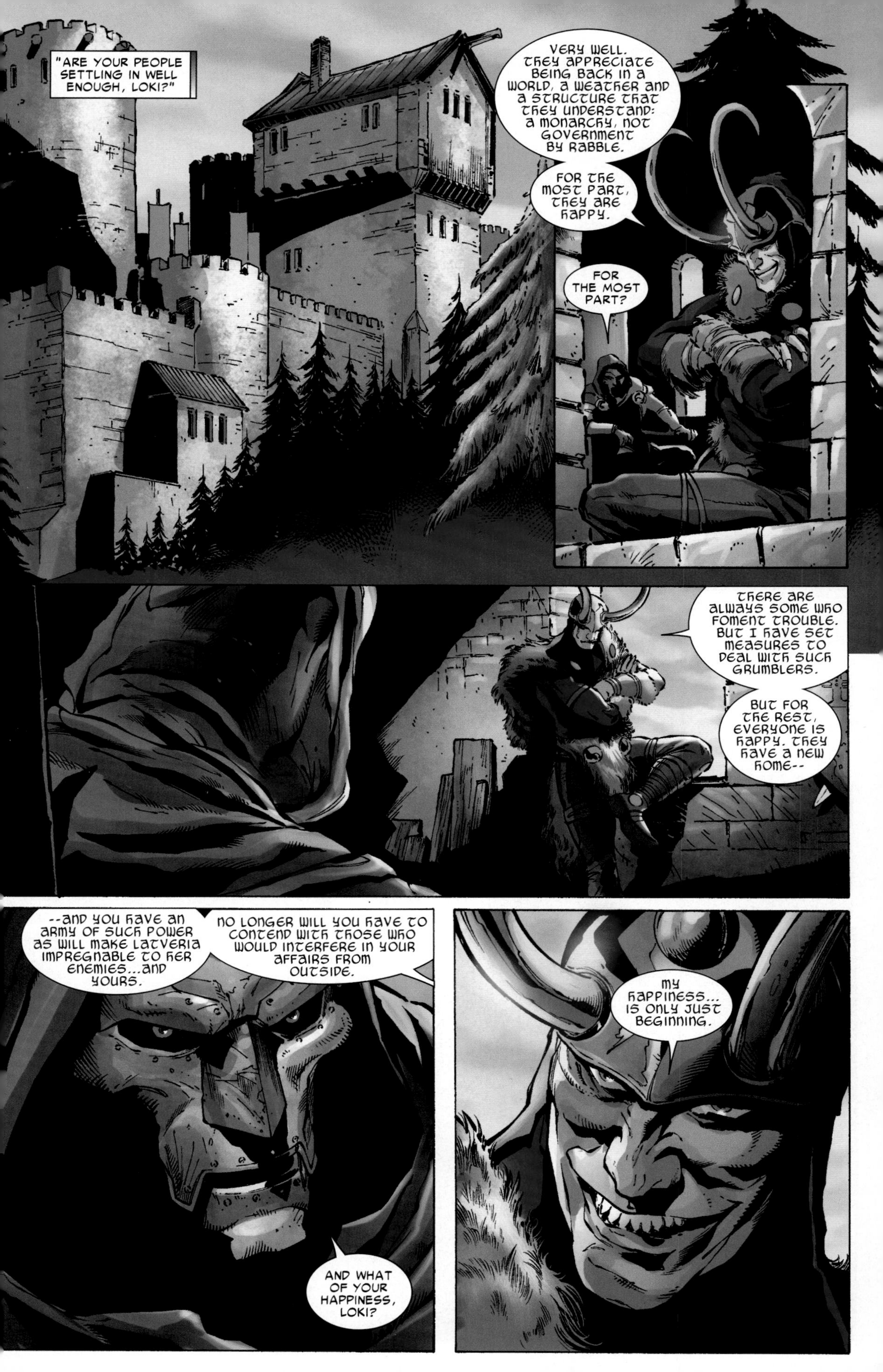
"ARE YOUR PEOPLE SETTLING IN WELL ENOUGH, LOKI?"
VERY WELL. THEY APPRECIATE BEING BACK IN A WORLD, A WEATHER AND A STRUCTURE THAT THEY UNDERSTAND: A MONARCHY, NOT GOVERNMENT BY RABBLE.
FOR THE MOST PART, THEY ARE HAPPY.
FOR THE MOST PART?
THERE ARE ALWAYS SOME WHO FOMENT TROUBLE. BUT I HAVE SET MEASURES TO DEAL WITH SUCH GRUMBLERS.
BUT FOR THE REST, EVERYONE IS HAPPY. THEY HAVE A NEW HOME--
--AND YOU HAVE AN ARMY OF SUCH POWER AS WILL MAKE LATVERIA IMPREGNABLE TO HER ENEMIES...AND YOURS.
NO LONGER WILL YOU HAVE TO CONTEND WITH THOSE WHO WOULD INTERFERE IN YOUR AFFAIRS FROM OUTSIDE.
AND WHAT OF YOUR HAPPINESS, LOKI?
MY HAPPINESS... IS ONLY JUST BEGINNING.

MR. BALDER? I--

--I HATE TO BOTHER YOU DURING DINNER, BUT I'VE BEEN THINKING IT OVER AND--

SIT, WILLIAM, PLEASE. BEING OFF ON ANOTHER OF HIS MANY CURIOUS MISSIONS, LOKI HAS NO NEED OF HIS SEAT.

THANKS, I...IT'S JUST...LOOK, I KNOW YOU PEOPLE ARE NEW IN TOWN AND ALL, AND YOU DON'T READ THE PAPERS OR GET CNN, SO YOU DON'T KNOW HOW BAD THIS DOOM GUY IS.

SO YOU FEEL THAT IN TIME HE WILL BETRAY US.

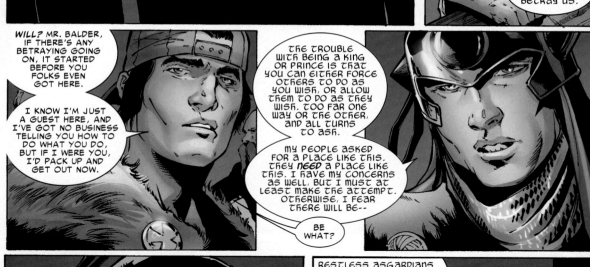

WILL? MR. BALDER, IF THERE'S ANY BETRAYING GOING ON, IT STARTED BEFORE YOU FOLKS EVEN GOT HERE.

I KNOW I'M JUST A GUEST HERE, AND I'VE GOT NO BUSINESS TELLING YOU HOW TO DO WHAT YOU DO, BUT IF I WERE YOU, I'D PACK UP AND GET OUT NOW.

THE TROUBLE WITH BEING A KING OR PRINCE IS THAT YOU CAN EITHER FORCE OTHERS TO DO AS YOU WISH, OR ALLOW THEM TO DO AS THEY WISH. TOO FAR ONE WAY OR THE OTHER, AND ALL TURNS TO ASH.

MY PEOPLE ASKED FOR A PLACE LIKE THIS. THEY *NEED* A PLACE LIKE THIS. I HAVE MY CONCERNS AS WELL, BUT I MUST AT LEAST MAKE THE ATTEMPT. OTHERWISE, I FEAR THERE WILL BE--

BE WHAT?

RESTLESS ASGARDIANS WITHOUT DREAMS TO PURSUE OR ENEMIES TO FIGHT SOON TURN TO SQUABBLING...THEN FIGHTING...THEN GOD TURNS AGAINST GOD.

SO YOU'RE WORRIED ABOUT CIVIL WAR?

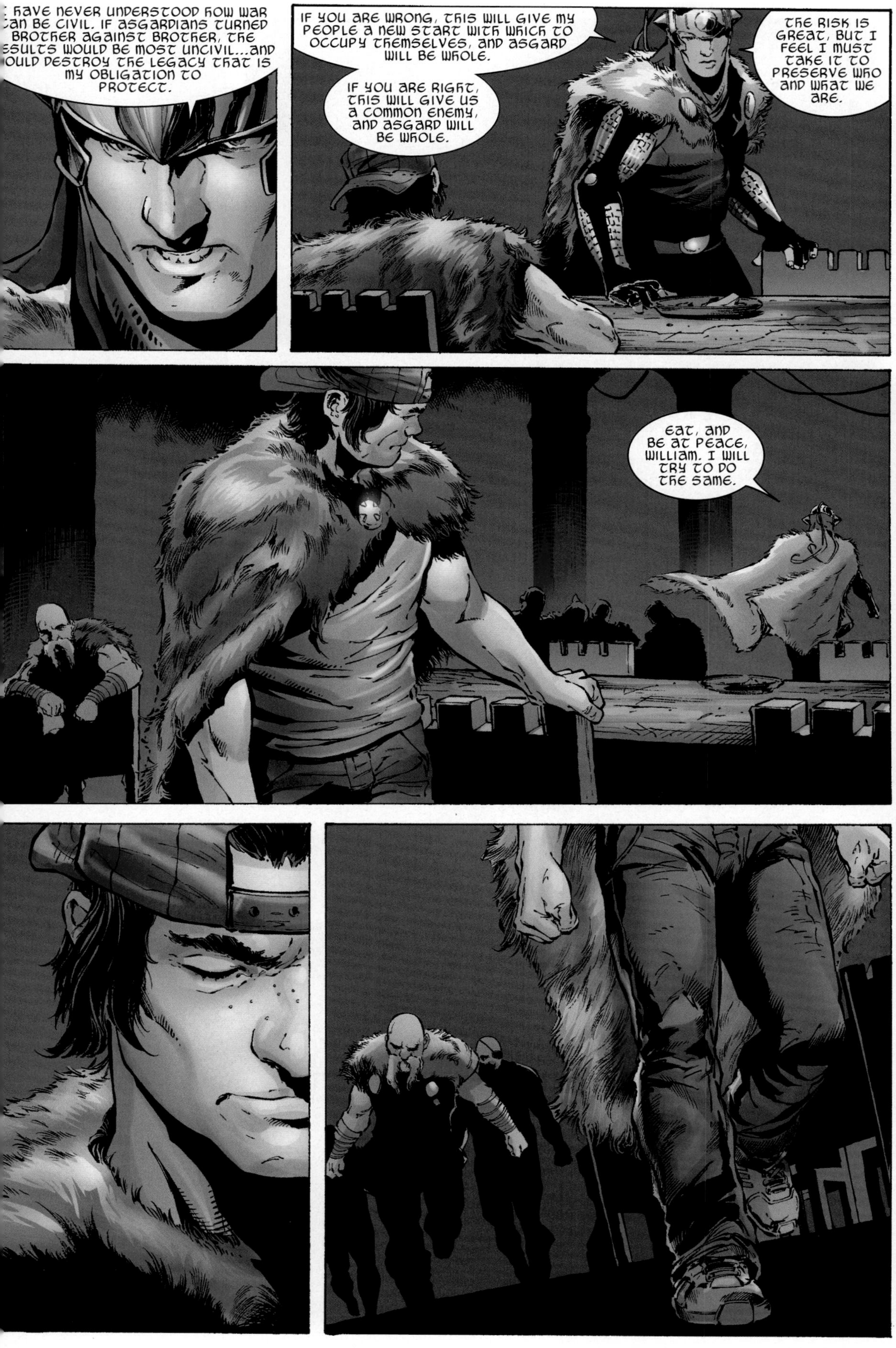
I HAVE NEVER UNDERSTOOD HOW WAR CAN BE CIVIL. IF ASGARDIANS TURNED BROTHER AGAINST BROTHER, THE RESULTS WOULD BE MOST UNCIVIL...AND WOULD DESTROY THE LEGACY THAT IS MY OBLIGATION TO PROTECT.
IF YOU ARE WRONG, THIS WILL GIVE MY PEOPLE A NEW START WITH WHICH TO OCCUPY THEMSELVES, AND ASGARD WILL BE WHOLE.
IF YOU ARE RIGHT, THIS WILL GIVE US A COMMON ENEMY, AND ASGARD WILL BE WHOLE.
THE RISK IS GREAT, BUT I FEEL I MUST TAKE IT TO PRESERVE WHO AND WHAT WE ARE.
EAT, AND BE AT PEACE, WILLIAM. I WILL TRY TO DO THE SAME.

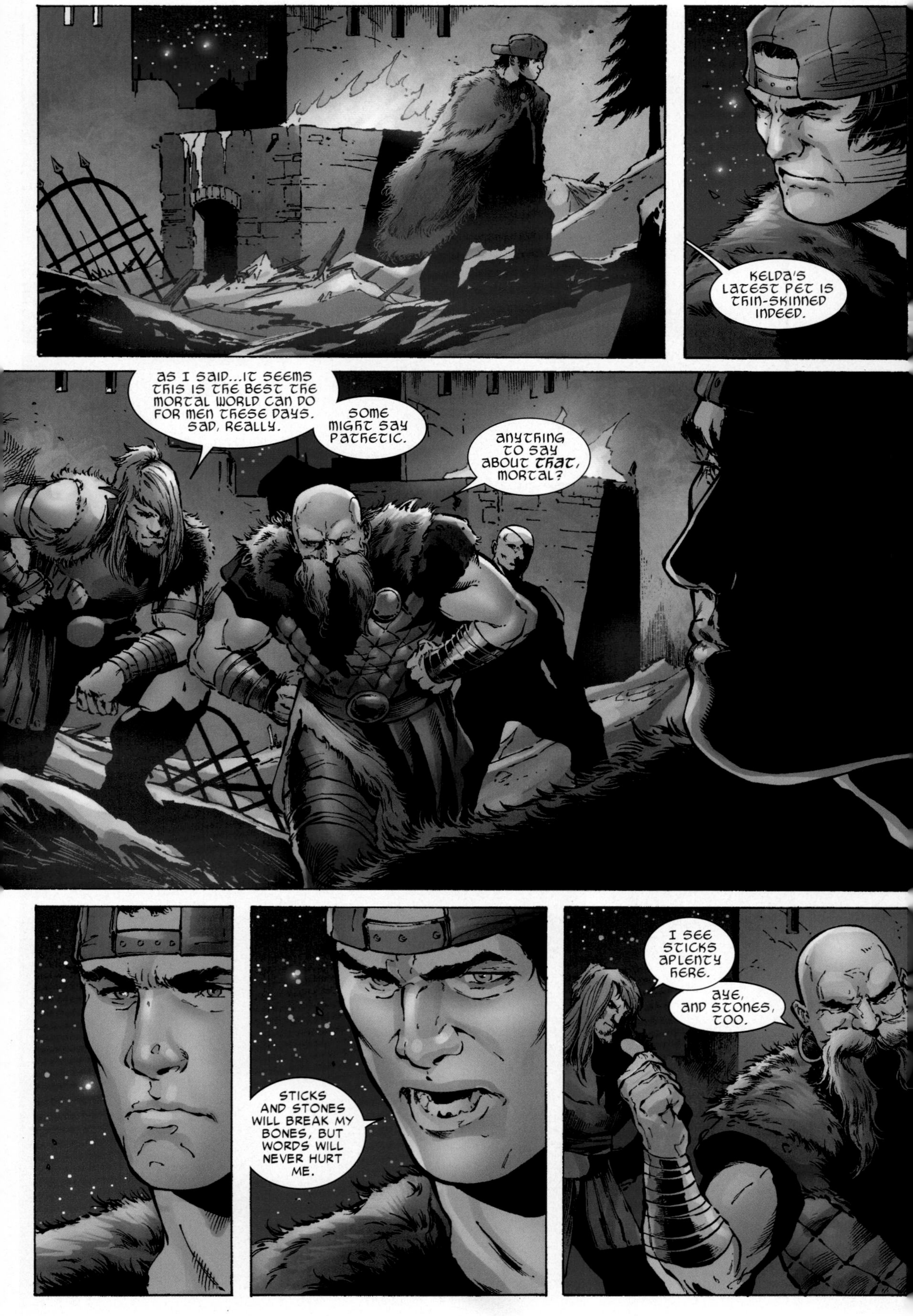
KELDA'S LATEST PET IS THIN-SKINNED INDEED.
AS I SAID...IT SEEMS THIS IS THE BEST THE MORTAL WORLD CAN DO FOR MEN THESE DAYS. SAD, REALLY.
SOME MIGHT SAY PATHETIC.
ANYTHING TO SAY ABOUT THAT, MORTAL?
STICKS AND STONES WILL BREAK MY BONES, BUT WORDS WILL NEVER HURT ME.
I SEE STICKS APLENTY HERE.
AYE, AND STONES, TOO.

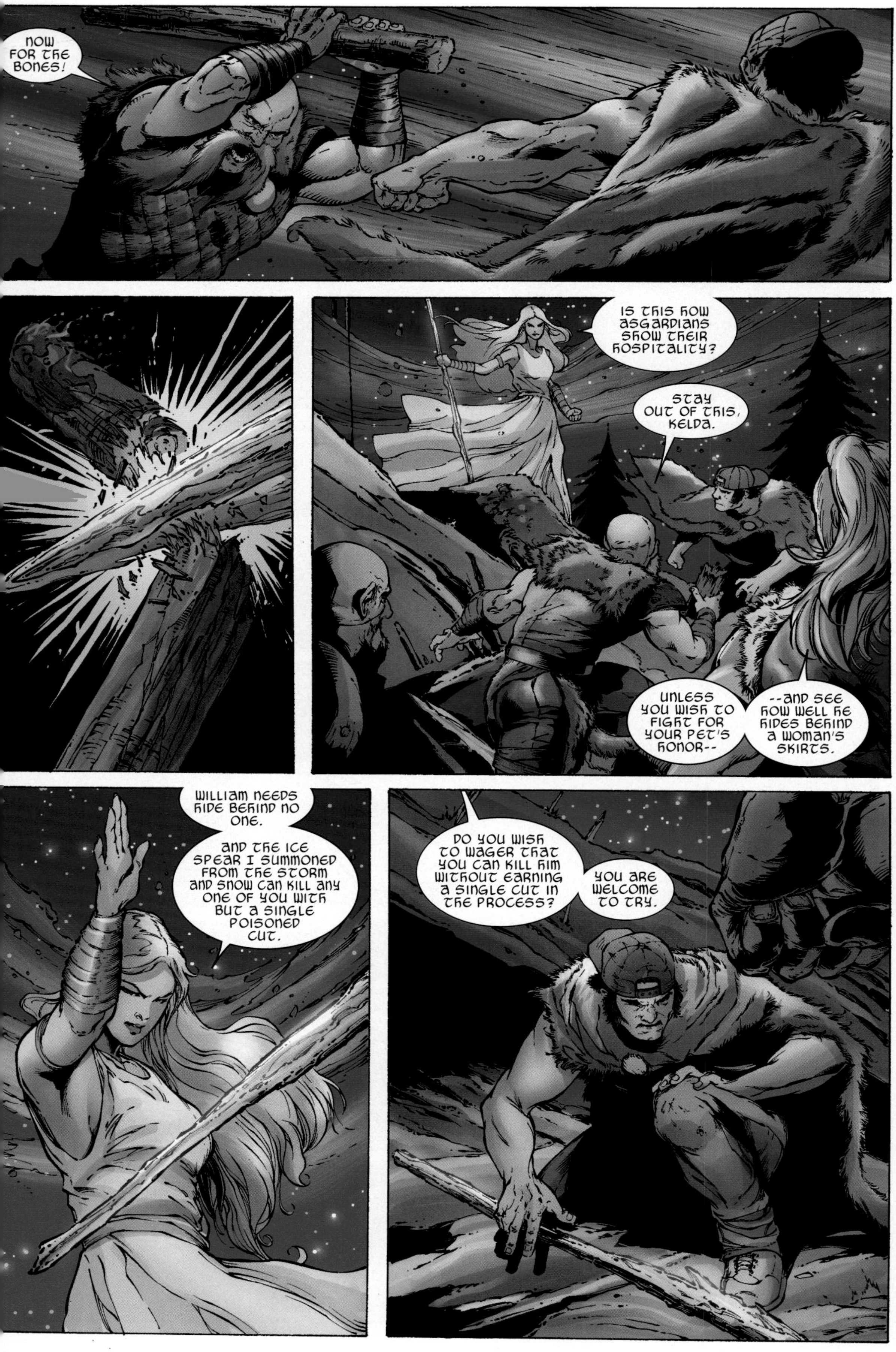
NOW FOR THE BONES!
IS THIS HOW ASGARDIANS SHOW THEIR HOSPITALITY?
STAY OUT OF THIS, KELDA.
UNLESS YOU WISH TO FIGHT FOR YOUR PET'S HONOR--
--AND SEE HOW WELL HE HIDES BEHIND A WOMAN'S SKIRTS.
WILLIAM NEEDS HIDE BEHIND NO ONE.
AND THE ICE SPEAR I SUMMONED FROM THE STORM AND SNOW CAN KILL ANY ONE OF YOU WITH BUT A SINGLE POISONED CUT.
DO YOU WISH TO WAGER THAT YOU CAN KILL HIM WITHOUT EARNING A SINGLE CUT IN THE PROCESS?
YOU ARE WELCOME TO TRY.

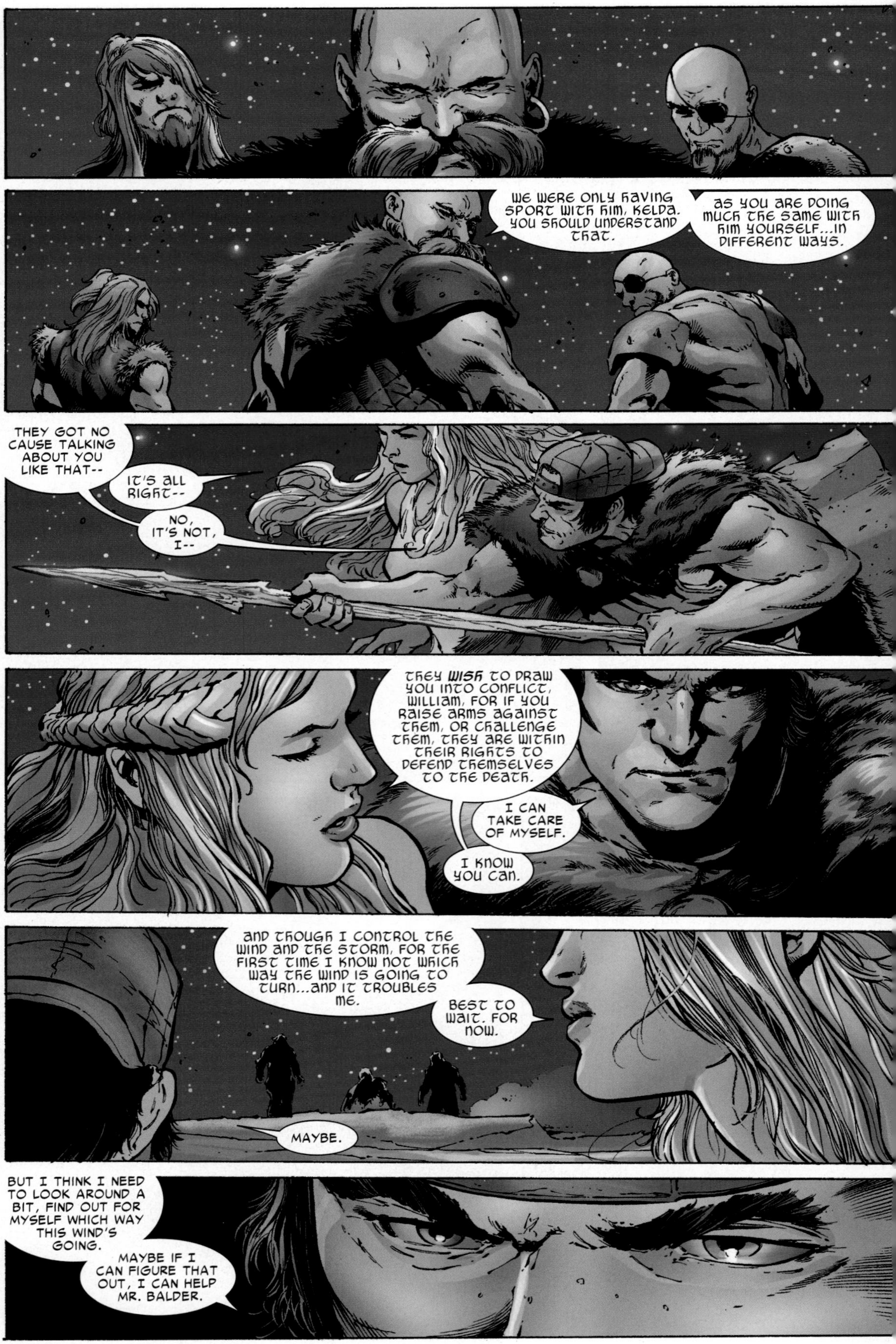
WE WERE ONLY HAVING SPORT WITH HIM, KELDA. YOU SHOULD UNDERSTAND THAT.
AS YOU ARE DOING MUCH THE SAME WITH HIM YOURSELF...IN DIFFERENT WAYS.
THEY GOT NO CAUSE TALKING ABOUT YOU LIKE THAT--
IT'S ALL RIGHT--
NO, IT'S NOT, I--
THEY WISH TO DRAW YOU INTO CONFLICT, WILLIAM, FOR IF YOU RAISE ARMS AGAINST THEM, OR CHALLENGE THEM, THEY ARE WITHIN THEIR RIGHTS TO DEFEND THEMSELVES TO THE DEATH.
I CAN TAKE CARE OF MYSELF.
I KNOW YOU CAN.
AND THOUGH I CONTROL THE WIND AND THE STORM, FOR THE FIRST TIME I KNOW NOT WHICH WAY THE WIND IS GOING TO TURN...AND IT TROUBLES ME.
BEST TO WAIT. FOR NOW.
MAYBE.
BUT I THINK I NEED TO LOOK AROUND A BIT, FIND OUT FOR MYSELF WHICH WAY THIS WIND'S GOING.
MAYBE IF I CAN FIGURE THAT OUT, I CAN HELP MR. BALDER.

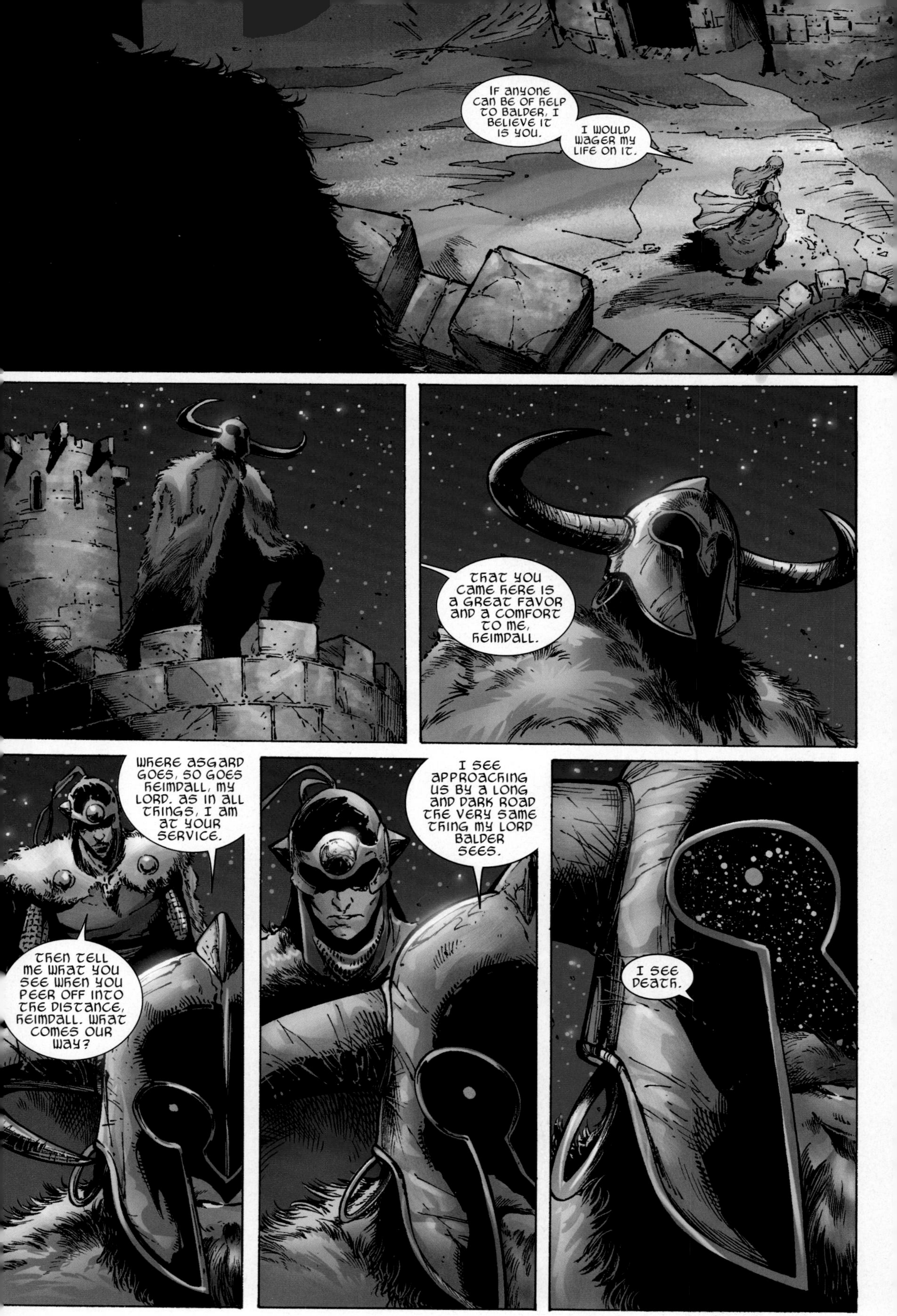
IF ANYONE CAN BE OF HELP TO BALDER, I BELIEVE IT IS YOU.
I WOULD WAGER MY LIFE ON IT.
THAT YOU CAME HERE IS A GREAT FAVOR AND A COMFORT TO ME, HEIMDALL.
WHERE ASGARD GOES, SO GOES HEIMDALL, MY LORD. AS IN ALL THINGS, I AM AT YOUR SERVICE.
THEN TELL ME WHAT YOU SEE WHEN YOU PEER OFF INTO THE DISTANCE, HEIMDALL. WHAT COMES OUR WAY?
I SEE APPROACHING US BY A LONG AND DARK ROAD THE VERY SAME THING MY LORD BALDER SEES.
I SEE DEATH.

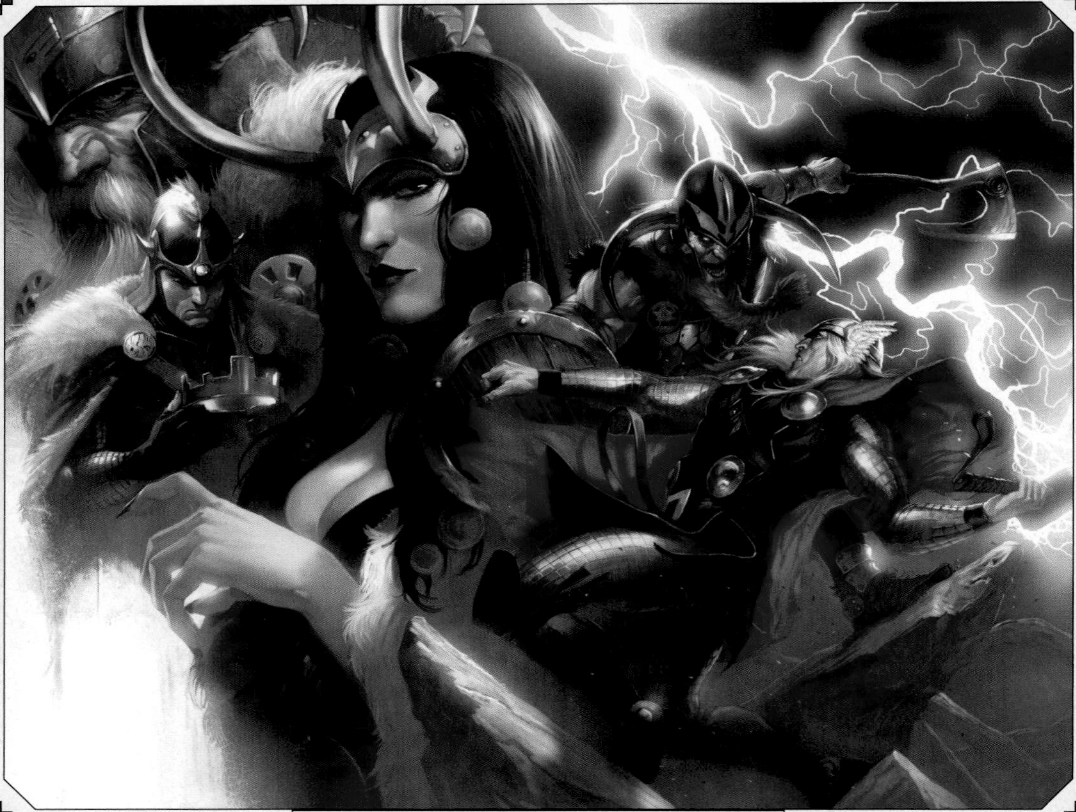

Thor #600 variant by Marko Djurdjević

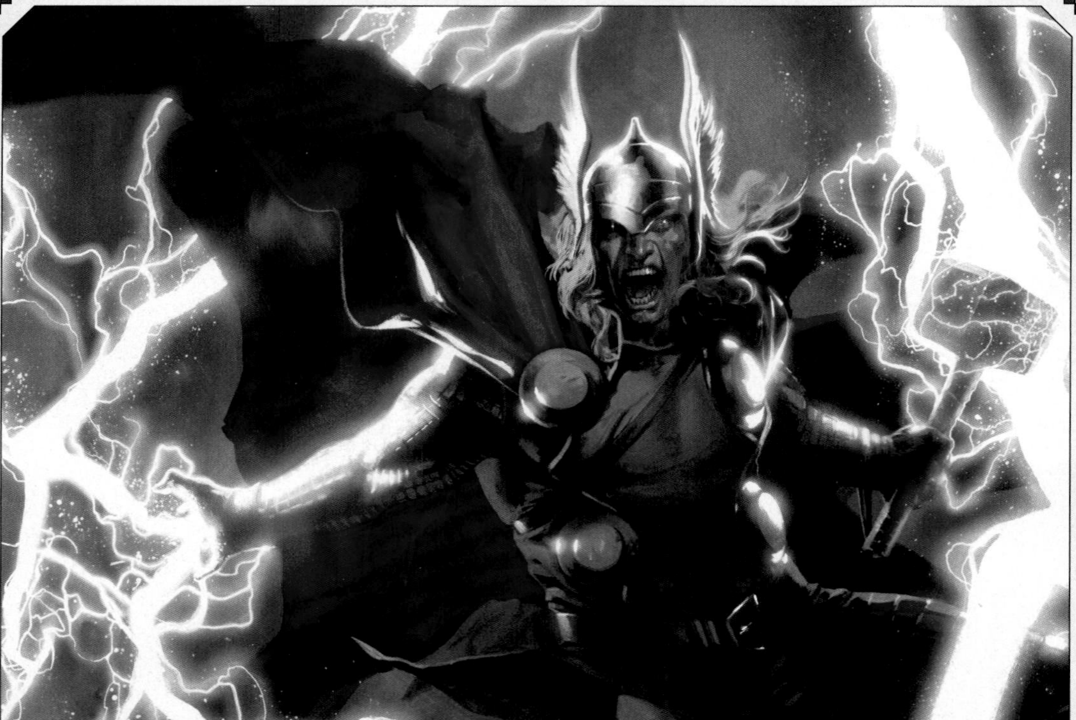

Thor #600 variant by Gabriele Dell'Otto